PASOLD OCCASIONAL PAPERS

General Editor: K. G. PONTING

VOLUME 1

A PRACTICAL TREATISE ON DYING

By William Partridge

Originally published in 1823

This edition edited by K. G. Ponting (1973)

VOLUME 2

EMPLOYER AND EMPLOYED

Ford, Ayrton & Co. Ltd, Silk Spinners

By Elizabeth R. and John H. P. Pafford

VOLUME 3

THE
WEST RIDING WOOL TEXTILE
INDUSTRY

A Catalogue of Business Records
from the Seventeenth to the
Twentieth Century

By Patricia Hudson

VOLUME 4

THE
WEST RIDING WOOL TEXTILE
INDUSTRY 1770–1835

A Study of Fixed Capital Formation

By D. T. Jenkins

The West Riding Wool Textile Industry 1770–1835

A STUDY OF FIXED CAPITAL FORMATION

By D. T. Jenkins

Lecturer in Economic History, University of York

PASOLD RESEARCH FUND LTD

Edington, Wiltshire

1975

ISBN 0 903859 05 X

PRINTED IN ENGLAND BY W. S. MANEY AND SON LTD HUDSON ROAD LEEDS LS9 7DL

FOR

JENNY AND THOMAS

CONTENTS

	ABBREVIATIONS	ix
	ACKNOWLEDGEMENTS	xi
	INTRODUCTION	xiii
1.	FROM THE DOMESTIC TO THE FACTORY SYSTEM	1
	The Yorkshire Wool Textile Industry before 1780	
	Fulling and Finishing Mills	
	The New Mills and Factories	
	The Worsted Trade	
	The Woollen Trade	
	The Location of the Wool Textile Industry in Yorkshire: 1770–1840	
2.	DEVELOPMENTS IN THE SIZE AND DESIGN OF WOOL TEXTILE MILLS	49
	The Early Mill Buildings	
	The Use of Iron	
	Vertical and Horizontal Growth	
	Power and Employees as a Measurement of Size	
3.	THE GENERATION OF POWER	71
	Hand and Horse Mills	
	The Water-wheel	
	The Age of Steam	
	The Capabilities of Power	
4.	MILLWRIGHTS' AND CLOCKMAKERS' WORK	101
	The Transmission of Power	
	The Production Machinery	
	Heating and Lighting	

5. The Valuation of Fixed Capital Stock 139

Measurement Problems

Fixed Capital Values and Formation in the West Riding Wool Textile Industry, 1780–1835

Investment in Power Plant

Investment in Machinery, Buildings and Other Fixed Capital

Investment in Woollen and Worsted Mills

Trends in Fixed Capital Investment

Changes in the Price Level and the Cost of Mill Construction

The Depreciation of Capital

Circulating Capital

6. Sources of Fixed Capital Finance 191

Appendices

I. Yorkshire Woollen and Worsted Mills, 1774–1835 206

II. Yorkshire Woollen and Worsted Mills included in the 1835 Factory Returns 240

III. The Meaning and Reliability of Insurance Valuations of Yorkshire Wool Textile Mills 276

IV. Fixed Capital Calculations 302

Bibliography 316

Index 331

ABBREVIATIONS

Locations:

B.C.L.	City of Bradford Library
B.C.R.L.	Birmingham City Reference Library
B.L.	Brotherton Library, University of Leeds
B.M.	British Museum
B.P.L.	Bolton Public Library
C.L.A.D.	City of Leeds Archives Department
C.L.R.L.	City of Leeds Reference Library
D.P.L.	Dewsbury Public Library
G.L.	Guildhall Library, City of London
H.A.D.	Halifax Archives Department
H.P.L.	Halifax Public Library
Hud. P.L.	Huddersfield Public Library
K.P.L.	Keighley Public Library
W.P.L.	Wakefield Public Library
W.Y.C.R.O.	West Yorkshire County Record Office

Sources:

B.H.	Business History
E.H.R.	Economic History Review
Eng. H.R.	English Historical Review
E.J.	Economic Journal
H.A.S.	Halifax Antiquarian Society Publication
L.I.	Leeds Intelligencer
L.M.	Leeds Mercury
O.S.	Ordnance Survey
T.S.	Thoresby Society Publications
Y.B.E.S.R.	Yorkshire Bulletin of Economic and Social Research
Sun C.R.	Sun Fire Office, Country Registers
Sun O.S.	Sun Fire Office, Old Series Registers
R.E.	Royal Exchange Fire Assurance Company Policy Registers References to fire insurance policies give Volume number, Policy Number and Year; thus Sun C.R. 13/654476/1796.
L. & Y.	Leeds and Yorkshire Fire Office
B. & W.	Boulton and Watt

ACKNOWLEDGEMENTS

The research on which this book is based was initially undertaken with the financial assistance of an Ellis Hunter Studentship at the University of York, financed by an endowment made by Dorman Long and Company in memory of Sir Ellis Hunter. The intermediate stages of the work and the preparation of a doctoral thesis in 1969–70 were generously supported by the Pasold Research Fund. Certain aspects of the more recent research have benefited from a grant from the Social Science Research Council. To all three bodies I would like to express my thanks.

A work of this nature is to a very great extent a co-operative effort. I have been most fortunate in the assistance I have received in the locating of records and in the supplying of references, information and ideas. This help is clearly reflected by the footnotes to the text. The eager co-operation I received from archivists, librarians and their staff in the West Riding, at the University of York and elsewhere deserves, however, special mention. Above all I am most appreciative of the facilities and assistance afforded me at the Guildhall Library in the City of London. Having worked there frequently over a number of years I have a very high regard for the Library.

My interest in the industrialization of the West Riding of Yorkshire can clearly be traced to the concern for the study of it in the Department of Economics and Related Studies at the University of York. I have benefited, in particular, from the enthusiasm and knowledge of Professor E. M. Sigsworth, Mr E. C. Cooney and my other colleagues. This present work is only a small part of a larger project to produce a detailed and comprehensive history of the development and change of the textile industries of the West Riding from the eighteenth century to the present day. Other contributions have already appeared, more are forthcoming.

I have also received helpful advice and comment from Professor Phyllis Deane, Dr R. G. Wilson, and Mr K. G. Ponting. I, however, accept responsibility for any errors and shortcomings in the following pages. I am only too well aware that many of the estimates made regarding mill development and industrial investment are tentative rather than definitive. Both the sources and techniques used have clear limitations. A study of this nature is very much an ongoing process. Clearly new information will come to light to support or amend the evidence used here. Perhaps this book may provide the basis by which this new information may be collected and compared.

Permission to reproduce material in their care was kindly granted by Carter Jonas, agents to the Dartmouth Estate, Huddersfield Public Library, The Brotherton Library, University of Leeds, and Birmingham Central Reference Library.

INTRODUCTION

In recent years much less attention has been paid to the wool textile industry of Yorkshire than to textile manufacture elsewhere during the period of the Industrial Revolution. In particular the rapid growth of the cotton industry from the last quarter of the eighteenth century, the considerable importance of that industry to the British economy in the nineteenth century and the possibility that it might be considered as the 'leading sector' in the development of that economy have all focused much more attention on the Western flanks of the Pennines than on the industrial growth that was taking place in Yorkshire. Recent studies of the Yorkshire wool textile industry have either been in the form of histories of individual firms or detailed examinations of particular features of trade or manufacture. Some of these works do consider broader aspects of the industry but in little detail. For the insight that they give to topics they are, however, invaluable. For a more general and overall history of the industry one still turns to the work of Herbert Heaton, which although first published more than half a century ago remains the standard authority on the Yorkshire industry in the pre-industrial period.

In spite of these contributions our present knowledge of many aspects of the Yorkshire wool textile industry is very limited. One of the major gaps appears to be in the understanding of the transition of the industry from domestic manufacture to factory production. The purpose of this study is to trace this transition by examining the growth in the number and size of mills and factories, the relative importance of steam and water power, the use of new techniques of manufacture and the amount of capital required for the transformation of the industry. The analysis is divided into two parts. In the first the development of mills and factories in woollen and worsted cloth production in the county is examined. Changes in the number, size, position and design of these mills are discussed. New forms of power and methods of lighting and heating are considered and the timing of the introduction of new technology suggested.

The second part of the study attempts to estimate fixed capital stock and formation in the industry during the period. Although in recent years there has been much discussion amongst historians and economists about the role of capital in economic growth, few substantial studies of its importance in different industries have yet appeared. Perhaps the situation was best summed up by a delegate to the Second International Conference of Economic History at Aix en Provence in 1962 who pointed out that the eighteenth and early nineteenth centuries are a prestatistical period as far as capital movements and formation are concerned and any quantitative assessments are rare and of doubtful value. He suggested that the historian is forced to make do with specific examples drawn from the history of particular firms, but even these examples are few and the value of the conclusions they leave us with are uncertain. At the same meeting Professor David Landes pointed out that an increasing interest in economic growth 'has brought capital to the forefront of discussion and compelled economic historians to contemplate it, measure it and assess its significance with an explicitness and precision never required before'. It is hoped that this study will provide a detailed analysis of the growth of fixed capital stock and formation in one of Britain's major industries during its years of fundamental transition from domestic to factory production.

One possible reason why the West Riding wool textile industry has recently been so much neglected by economic historians is the paucity of records of early manufacturers that have survived. Anyone attempting an examination of early factory development in the industry is faced with having to make do with a few incomplete series of records of individual firms, the occasional collection of estate papers, a few surviving local government books, documents and registers and a mass of nineteenth-century topographical literature that often gives conflicting accounts and can only be used with care and reservation. The recent work, by Miss P. Hudson, of producing a very detailed catalogue of what business records are available will be of invaluable assistance to future research. Unfortunately the catalogue shows only too clearly the shortage of valuations and capital accounts that survive amongst the business collections.

For the purposes of this study rather more use has been made of business records not immediately connected with the wool textile industry in Yorkshire. Papers of other industrial companies, for example Boulton and Watt, that had dealings with textile manufacturing concerns through the supply of materials or machinery have proved valuable. The records and registers of the various contemporary fire insurance offices have provided much information on mills and factories, their buildings and machinery and capital values. The use of them, however, presents many difficulties and limitations concerning their meaning and reliability. For this reason a separate discussion of the problem has been incorporated at the end of the volume.

Some reliance has had to be placed on a variety of secondary sources. The use of, for example, contemporary maps or of early topographical accounts is often a hazardous exercise. Whereas one can trust the accuracy of the information in many cases, there are times when considerable doubt arises about the standard of it. Information on maps and plans can be notoriously out of date. A topographer, writing about a particular locality, was not averse to printing hearsay as fact or to making unsubstantiated claims about the success of local heroes. Similar limitations apply to the use of early local directories. A great many were published for the West Riding from the end of the eighteenth century onwards but they show varying degrees of accuracy and comprehensiveness. It was not unknown for the publisher of a directory to pirate the work of his predecessors. The use of early books on the industry, parliamentary reports and newspaper accounts are likewise not without their pitfalls. Particular problems concerning their interpretation will be stressed from time to time.

This study is concerned with the wool textile industry in Yorkshire, which for all intents and purposes means within the textile area of the West Riding. Occasional mention is made of mills further afield, in the dales of North Yorkshire, in Cleveland and at a number of places in the East Riding of Yorkshire. It is doubtful if many of these should be considered as an integral part of the Yorkshire wool textile industry. Their situation was really no different from the other isolated wool textile mills scattered through a number of counties at the time. Their links with the main textile manufacturing areas of the West Riding were probably not well established. They were small in size and few in number. Some may well not have been traced.

Although the work is concerned with the West Riding wool textile industry, references are made, in relation to some points, to the cotton and flax industries. It could be argued that the textile industries of the region should be considered as a whole and not in terms of their different branches. Their mills and factories and, to some extent, their machinery were very similar and there was considerable movement of entrepreneurship, labour and capital between them. It is hoped, in due course, that similar studies of Yorkshire flax and cotton will be prepared.

The work is limited in time to a period of sixty-five years. The reason for its starting date of the 1770s is easily explained. It was in that decade that the first of the new mills came into being, that the first steps to the new factory system were taken. The termination date for the study of the mid 1830s can claim no such clear explanation in terms of the development of the industry. The full emergence of the factory system was not completed. Power combing and weaving had still had little impact. Jenny spinning was still common. Likewise the railways had not yet influenced the locations of mills and their size. The explanation of the date is purely a practical one. It was in that year that the first seemingly accurate survey of mills and factories in the industry was carried out, thereby providing a measuring post for the size of the factory industry by that date. From the late 1830s information on the industry becomes more reliable and more regularly available. The growth of the industry, in terms of mills, power and employment, can be followed rather more closely from contemporary information although a great deal still remains unknown about the experiences of the industry throughout the rest of the century.

For the years 1770 to 1835, this study in no way purports to be a general history of the West Riding wool textile industry. For example little mention is made of the sources of the raw materials required or of the markets for the finished product. The variety of the type of product is only occasionally referred to. Problems of labour, organization, production and competition with the industry elsewhere in Great Britain are only touched upon where they are relevant to the main theme. And that main theme is the physical transition from a domestic system of wool textile manufacture in Yorkshire to the organization of production on a factory basis. It encompasses the growth in the number and size of wool textile mills, the machinery they were using and their fixed capital requirements.

I

FROM THE DOMESTIC TO THE FACTORY SYSTEM

The Yorkshire Wool Textile Industry before 1780

In the years immediately before the first hesitant steps were made to investigate the possibilities of factory production, the manufacturing and merchanting organization of the West Riding wool textile industry was already highly developed and complex. During the almost 100 year period of total transition from the domestic to the factory system this organization became more and more intricate. But in many ways the structure and location of factory production in the West Riding wool textile industry in the decades following the 1780s owed a great deal to the already existing arrangements for domestic manufacture. Some changes were to occur in the location of production of different types of cloth. The new technology in due course allowed a diversification of the types of product. But the basic pre-industrial divisions of the types of manufacture remained and the course of transition to factory production was clearly affected by the system of domestic manufacture from which the transfer was being made. A significant difference was between the woollen branch and the worsted branch of the industry because the organization of domestic manufacture in each was dissimilar, which partly provides an explanation for their different courses of development under the new industrial system, although the growth of, and change in, each was substantially influenced by other factors as well.

It is not necessary here to delve deeply into the experiences of Yorkshire wool textile manufacture before the mid-eighteenth century. The history of the fortunes of the industry is well recorded, compared with the following century or more.[1] For over 500 years Yorkshire had played a major role in Britain's wool textile manufacture but the industry for most of that period was widely distributed throughout the country and Yorkshire's share of total output

[1] See in particular H. Heaton, *The Yorkshire Woollen and Worsted Industries* (Oxford, 1920; second edition 1965); R. G. Wilson, *Gentlemen Merchants* (Manchester, 1971); James Bischoff, *A Comprehensive History of the Woollen and Worsted Manufactures* (1857, new edition 1968), and J. James, *A History of the Worsted Manufacture in England* (1842, new edition 1968).

was not dominant. Along with the West Country and East Anglia the county did however maintain for the whole period a very substantial foothold in the industry. One calculation suggests that in the mid-fifteenth century these three areas accounted for two-thirds of the country's production.[2] Even at the beginning of the eighteenth century wool textile manufacture could be found in every English county although concentration still remained in East Anglia, the West of England and Yorkshire, and indeed these three areas were in a more dominant position nationally.

By the eighteenth century noticeable changes were occurring in the distribution of the industry in the country not only simply through greater concentration in a few areas of production but also in the relative importance of those few areas and the greater emergence of Yorkshire as the main national centre. It has been estimated that the annual value of wool textile output in the early years of the eighteenth century was about five million pounds. Yorkshire's share of that figure was perhaps no more than one fifth or one quarter.[3] The county's worsted industry which was of very minor importance in the sixteenth and seventeenth century was undergoing a revival but in 1700 still formed a very small part of the wool textile output of the county.[4]

The industry nationally experienced very fluctuating fortunes throughout the century. The first three decades appear to have witnessed a slowing down in the rate of growth of the late seventeenth century.[5] Miss Deane has estimated a rate of growth of output of about eight per cent per decade in this period and even this estimate may be too high.[6] Severe competition was being encountered in the home market from linens and cottons. Abroad, rivalry from European producers and a not too healthy state of demand was having its impact.[7] From the early 1730s for twenty years, however, expansion returned. The good harvests at home and the excursions into new markets abroad appear to have benefited Yorkshire rather

[2] Heaton, op. cit., pp. 47–88; G. D. Ramsey, 'The Distribution of the Cloth Industry in 1561–2', *Eng. H.R.*, 57 (1942); H. L. Gray, 'The Production and Consumption of English Woollens in the 14th Century', *Eng. H.R.*, 39 (1924).

[3] P. Deane, 'The Output of the British woollen industry in the eighteenth century', *J.E.H.*, XVII (1957), 207–29.

[4] E. M. Sigsworth, *Black Dyke Mills* (Liverpool, 1958), p. 1.

[5] Wilson, op. cit., pp. 46–7.

[6] Deane, loc. cit., pp. 203–23; Wilson, op. cit., p. 51; R. G. Wilson, 'The Supremacy of the Yorkshire Cloth Industry in the Eighteenth Century', in N. B. Harte and K. G. Ponting (eds), *Textile History and Economic History: Essays in Honour of Miss Julia de Lacy Mann* (Manchester, 1973).

[7] Wilson, *Gentleman Merchants*, op. cit., p. 45.

than the West of England. The Yorkshire clothiers with their low labour costs and, in this period, low wool prices were able to increase the quality of their product without increasing prices. Yorkshire broadcloths became more competitive at the expense of some of the West of England output.[8] Yorkshire's increased excursions into the Southern European market are illustrated by the number of ships leaving Hull for Spain, Portugal, and Italy. In 1717 the number was five. Eleven years later ten set sail and in 1738 they were departing on average at the rate of one a week.[9] Nationally output rose steadily, if not phenomenally; Yorkshire's share of it substantially. This twenty year period saw the Yorkshire industry making major inroads to the East Anglian and West Country trades.

But by the 1750s Yorkshire's proportion of English output was still no more than 30 per cent; its increased share mainly the result of the doubling of its broadcloth production in the previous twenty years.[10] The next fifteen years witnessed hard times. The trough of depression was reached in 1756 for the amount of broadcloth milled in Yorkshire and in 1759 for narrow cloth.[11] Recovery was slow. Yorkshire output did not reattain its 1750 production figures until 1766. There is some indication in this period that the county fared rather worse than the country. National trade was stagnant; Yorkshire's share in it may have slightly fallen.[12]

The late 1760s and early 1770s appear to have been better years. The amount of broadcloth milled doubled between 1765 and 1773; narrow cloth output saw lesser expansion. The figures for cloth milled may however provide a rather too optimistic picture. Increased vigilance by the cloth searchers may account for some of the recorded increase after 1765.[13] Although there are no real signs of a boom in national woollen cloth exports during these years, West Country clothiers were protesting insistently about Yorkshire competition and it would seem that once again Yorkshire's share of the market was on the increase.[14] Recession returned between 1774 and 1782. The disruption of the American market, and, within three years, difficulties in the Mediterranean market brought

[8] Deane, loc. cit., pp. 203–23.
[9] Wilson, *Gentlemen Merchants*, op. cit., p. 47.
[10] Ibid., pp. 46–7.
[11] See the returns of broad and narrow cloth milled in the West Riding of Yorkshire, 1726–1821 in B. R. Mitchell and P. Deane, *Abstract of British Historical Statistics* (Cambridge, 1962), p. 189. See also Figure 14.
[12] Wilson, *Gentlemen Merchants*, op. cit., p. 48.
[13] Ibid., p. 39.
[14] J. de L. Mann, *The Cloth Industry in the West of England from 1640 to 1880* (Oxford, 1971), p. 48.

hardship, and at times bankruptcy, to many Yorkshire manufacturers.[15] The worsted branch of the industry had constructed much of its growth in the previous decades on the North Atlantic trade and the depression in that market created severe consequences for it.[16] The amount of broad cloth milled fell from 120,000 recorded pieces in 1773 to only 87,000 in the following year. A few months of recovery appeared in 1778 but it was not until 1783 that the output returned consistently to above the 1773 figure. Again the returns for narrow cloth milled suggest that this section of the industry was less hard hit. However it was unable to increase its output during the eight year period.

From 1783 trade was clearly much more healthy. Occasional years of depression did occur, for example in 1794 and 1795, but for over twenty years, the years during which the major transition to factory production got under way, the Yorkshire industry prospered. The amount of broad cloth milled doubled between 1783 and 1800. Output of narrow cloth increased by more than 50 per cent during the same period. The worsted branch of the industry saw rather less success. It was still being affected in the 1790s by difficulties in the American market. War on the Continent was also creating problems. In 1800 it was suggested that the value of the output of the Yorkshire worsted industry was £1,400,000, somewhat less than thirty years earlier even without taking into account price rises in the intervening period.[17] Even so Yorkshire output had by now overtaken that of East Anglia in volume and was approaching it in quality.[18]

By the end of the eighteenth century Yorkshire accounted for about 60 per cent of the total English output of woollen cloth.[19] The county's role in national exports may even have been greater for perhaps as much as 90 per cent of Yorkshire broad cloth was going overseas.[20] Yorkshire's competitive position had therefore taken great strides forward by the last decades of the eighteenth century within a system of domestic organization and the emerging factory had a sound economic base on which to construct.

One of the many reasons suggested for the success of the domestic industry in Yorkshire in meeting competition from other areas is to

[15] Wilson, *Gentlemen Merchants*, op. cit., p. 48.
[16] Sigsworth, op. cit., pp. 11–12.
[17] Bischoff, op. cit., p. 329, quoting evidence given to the House of Commons.
[18] Sigsworth, op. cit., p. 11.
[19] Deane, loc. cit., pp. 203–15.
[20] Ibid., Wilson, *Gentlemen Merchants*, op. cit., p. 96.

do with the organization of its production. In the woollen branch of the industry there were distinct differences in organization between Yorkshire and the West of England. The Yorkshire clothier was normally a small, independent man who purchased his raw material himself and with the help of his family, and occasionally other employees, journeymen and apprentices, carried out the various stages of manufacture and then sold the fulled but unfinished cloth to the merchant, perhaps at one of the Cloth Halls. The clothier was therefore self employed, using his own capital and enterprise and aware that the quality and quantity of his work directly affected the financial return from it.[21]

In the West of England the organization of manufacture was in the hands of fewer, rather larger, often wealthy clothiers who put out the work for various processes of production. Most of the cloth produced was sold to a London factor or merchant for resale, either at home or abroad.[22] The clothiers sold some cloth directly to the final customer but normally the West of England clothier did not really do his own merchanting, and his distance from his London merchant contact perhaps meant that he was less directly in touch with market requirements than his Yorkshire counterpart.[23]

The Yorkshire worsted industry was organized rather differently. Relatively fewer manufacturers controlled production on an outwork system often distributing the work for spinning or weaving over a large area. E. M. Sigsworth records how Robert Heaton, a worsted manufacturer of Ponden near Keighley in the mid-eighteenth century, was employing spinners in the Settle area and as far as the Lancashire border.[24] The worsted manufacturer would then sell the woven cloth to the merchant who again would normally deal directly with overseas customers.

There are many other explanations for Yorkshire's success in meeting and beating the competition of other areas. Traditional ideas support the availability of plentiful supplies of soft water and coal.[25] More recent views have stressed that these factors should not be overestimated and that it was in the type of cloth Yorkshire was producing that the answer lies.[26] In general, Yorkshire manufacturers

[21] Heaton, op. cit., p. 92.
[22] Mann, op. cit., pp. 89–119.
[23] Wilson, *Gentlemen Merchants*, op. cit., passim.
[24] Sigsworth, op. cit., p. 13.
[25] P. Mantoux, *The Industrial Revolution in the Eighteenth Century* (new edition, 1961, p. 263).
[26] Mann, op. cit., p. 48.

and merchants concentrated on cheaper cloths of low and medium quality whereas East Anglian and West Country manufacturers were mainly concerned with finer cloths. It has been suggested that the Yorkshire producers were better able to meet the competition of cotton and to vary their output according to changing demand for different types of cloth.[27] Moreover the Yorkshire worsted industry probably benefited from the development of cotton manufacturing through the proximity of new technology and the development of cloths of mixed fibre.[28]

The rather different organization of woollen and worsted cloth manufacture in Yorkshire helps to explain the differences in factory development and size that are noted below. The worsted mills were fewer in number and generally large in size. Many of them were established by the previous domestic organizers. The early woollen mill was more often tiny, perhaps reflecting the small scale domestic manufacturing arrangements and the limited capital available to clothiers wishing to redirect their production to within the factory.

Fulling and Finishing Mills

Under the domestic system of woollen manufacture two stages in the production of woollen cloth were not carried out in the clothiers' homes and workshops. Fulling and the finishing processes had long been the responsibility of others and the use of water power was not new to fulling in the late eighteenth century.

Fulling, the pounding of woven woollen cloth by stocks in water to thicken or felt the cloth to strengthen the cohesion of the fibres, was carried out for the clothier in small water-powered mills. The fulling mill was normally a public mill in that it was not built and owned by the clothiers but was the property of the local lord of the manor or estate owner. The fulling miller would either be employed by the owner or the mill would be let to him and cloth would be accepted for fulling from all clothiers at a pre-determined tariff. The clothiers would either make regular use of a particular fulling mill or would vary their use of mills according to charges and the delay in getting the work done, which in the 1780s and 1790s with the upsurge in output could have been considerable. At that

[27] Wilson, *Gentlemen Merchants*, op. cit., p. 52.
[28] Sigsworth, op. cit., pp. 43–52.

TABLE 1.

WEST RIDING FULLING MILLS – 1780

NARROW CLOTH

Saddleworth area

Kenworthy's*	Andrew's New*	Francis*	
Andrew's*	Delph*	Woodhouse*	Wrigley*
Laughton*	Dobcross*	Mytham*	Denshaw*

Huddersfield

Slaithwaite	Dyson	Hepworth*	Ramsden*
Bradley*	Bankhouse	Paddock Foot*	Banks*
Crosley New*	Mytham Bridge	Two new mills	Steps*
Meltham Old	Meltham New	Crosland Hall	Hobson's
Batty's	Oxspring	Dyer's	Hunshelf
Lockwood*	Dungeon*	Cartworth	Holmfirth
Tong Bridge	Newton	Pudding	Batty Old
Batty New	Holm Bridge	Battye New in Linthwaite*	Holmfirth
Tyas in Foolstone	Tinker New		

Calder Valley area

Brighouse	Dumple Bridge	Shaws' Wife's*	Browbridge
Royston	Holm*	Sowerby Bridge*	James Haigh's
Hollins*	Luddenden Foot*	Mytham Bridge Foot	Meerclough Bottom
Lyley's	Roger's*		Dean*
Elland*	Longbottom*	Bank house	Copley's*

BROAD CLOTH

Wharfe valley

Arthington	Pool	Harewood

Calder valley

Battye	Brighouse Upper	Brighouse Lower	Dewsbury Upper
Dewsbury Lower	Dewsbury New	Horbury	Kirklees
Ledgard	Lenthorp	Mirfield West	Mirfield Lower
Sands	Wakefield Upper	Wakefield Lower	Gomersall

Aire valley

Armley Upper	Armley Lower	Baildon	Calverley
Esholt Lower	Esholt Upper	Hunslet	Idle
Kirkstall Upper	Kirkstall Lower	Knostrop	Nether
Neville's	Ross	Shipley Upper	Beckfoot
Shipley Lower	Thwaites'	Water Bradley	Fall Neck

*Narrow cloth mills where broad cloth was also milled.

Sources: West Riding Quarter Session Books, Pontefract Session, April 1780 and Bradford Session July 1780.

period some clothiers from the south of Leeds were travelling to mills on the Wharfe to have their cloth fulled.[29]

There are records of water-driven fulling mills in the West Riding as early as the twelfth century.[30] Professor E. M. Carus-Wilson lists eleven working in the West Riding in 1327.[31] Government legislation fifty years later which required woollen cloth to be properly fulled before being exported gave a boost to the process and encouraged the building of yet more mills. The clothiers were served by mills at Bradford, Almondbury, Alverthorpe, Castleford, Kirkstall, Rothwell, Wakefield, Burton Constable, and Masham.[32] The fortunes of the mills fluctuated with the prosperity of the industry. By the seventeenth century they were becoming much more numerous and could be found at regular intervals along the banks of the Wharfe, Aire, Calder, and Colne and their main tributaries. In the 1770s, on the eve of the first scribbling mills and woollen factories in the county, over 100 fulling mills were recorded.[33] Not all of these would have been public at this date. Some clothiers, or groups of clothiers, frustrated at the congestion at the mills had by this time built their own private fulling mills to do their own work and, if capacity was available, to take in the work of others. The fulling mills concentrated on broad cloth or narrow cloth according to their location but many milled both types.[34] With few exceptions they were not to survive very long as a separate institution. In many cases they provided the first premises for scribbling machines and by the end of the century the vast majority of them had been converted to scribbling and carding mills. Some of the narrow cloth fulling mills survived longest. Of the mills processing broad cloth in the late 1790s, approximately 60 in number, over 50 can be recognized as also being used for scribbling. Several of the others

[29] B. Wilson, *Our Village* (1860), p. 43; *Minutes of Evidence taken before the Committee appointed to consider the State of the Woollen Manufacture*, 1806 (H.C. 268), III, 30.

[30] R. A. Pelham, *Fulling Mills* (Society for the Protection of Ancient Buildings, Publication no. 5., 1958).

[31] E. M. Carus-Wilson, 'An Industrial Revolution of the Thirteenth Century', *E.H.R.*, XI, 1941.

[32] Ibid., Heaton, op. cit., p. 22.

[33] The fulling mills are listed in the West Riding Quarter Session Books and Rolls of the period. The April Pontefract Session and July Bradford Session for each year names the mills and the cloth searchers appointed to them. The lists for some years seem to be incomplete but, by examining them for a period of several years, a probably comprehensive survey can be obtained. The Books and Rolls are in the care of the West Yorkshire County Record Office. See Table 1.

[34] In 1780 almost one half of the narrow cloth fulling mills were also fulling broad cloth.

served the dual function of corn and fulling mill.[35] A few survived to the second or third decade of the nineteenth century. Most of those that were not converted fell into disuse. The dates of the final demise of many of them can be traced from the Quarter Session records. For example Knostrop Fulling Mill on the Aire milled no more cloth after the third quarter of 1811, Thwaite Fulling Mill nearby ceased working in 1807 as did Drighlington Upper Mill.[36] The first Ordnance Survey maps of the area in the late 1840s do record a few fulling mills, for example Upper Swift Place Mill, near Ripponden, and the Old Mill, Horbury Bridge, but many of these are known to have housed other machinery as well.[37]

The other process that was outside the responsibility of the domestic clothier was the finishing of the cloth. This was normally carried out by the merchant purchaser according to the requirements of his market and the needs of his individual customers. The merchant would either employ his own workers to carry out the various operations in the finishing process or would put out the cloth to a cloth finisher who would process it to the orders of the merchant. Crump suggested that there were often close alliances between merchant and cloth dresser and there appears to be substantial evidence to support this.[38] An advertisement in a Leeds paper in the late 1730s indicates one such type of partnership:

> To be Lett, from May Day. A House in Meadow Lane, Leeds, now occupied by Messieurs Hunter and Tidswell, with very good conveniences for two families, a Merchant and a Cloth Dresser, a good Garden and large Warehouse, two dressing shops, a Garth and three pair of Tenters.[39]

Later in the century merchants' insurance policies often listed buildings and equipment for cloth dressing.[40]

The cloth dressing processes have been well described elsewhere.[41] Gott's mill notebook gives a detailed description for various cloths. The processes were generally carried out by hand, until at least the second decade of the nineteenth century and much later for certain

35 For example, Rouse Mill and Ledgard Mill.

36 See the Quarterly Returns of Broad Cloth Milled. Lupton MSS, 113. B.L.

37 *Ordnance Survey: six inch to one mile survey of Yorkshire, first series.* Surveyed 1845–54. Published 1847–57. British Museum Map Room and C.L.R.L.

38 W. B. Crump (ed.), *The Leeds Woollen Industry, 1780–1820*, Publications of the Thoresby Society, xxxii, for the year 1929 (1931).

39 *Leeds Mercury*, 6 March, 1738–9, reproduced in Crump, op. cit., p. 38.

40 The policy registers of the Sun Fire Office and the Royal Exchange Assurance Company contain many examples of such policies in the late eighteenth century.

41 See J. C. and J. Schofield, *Finishing of Wool Goods* (published by the authors, 1935); and K. G. Ponting, 'Cloth Finishing' in J. G. Jenkins (ed), *The Wool Textile Industry of Great Britain* (1972).

cloths. In the eighteenth century, however, attempts were made to make use of water-powered gigmills and shearing frames. This was simple water-turned equipment used for raising and shearing the cloth. Watson's survey of mills in the parish of Halifax in 1758 recorded four frizing mills and states that there were a great many raising mills.[42] Crump and Ghorbal provided evidence of water power being used to the south of Huddersfield in the late eighteenth century and the evidence to the 1806 Inquiry suggested that the water-powered gigmills and frames were in fairly widespread use in Halifax parish at the same period.[43] Overall however, records of their use are scarce. They were more successfully introduced in the west of England, labour opposition in the West Riding often severely limiting their innovation.[44] In the Leeds area the machines appear to have been almost unknown. Isolated attempts to introduce them quickly incurred the wrath of the workers. Johnson's mill at Holbeck was destroyed in 1799 after a gigmill had been put to work in it and in later years similar destruction occurred.[45] There is no mention of the machines in the inventories of machinery in the mills of the large manufactories around the turn of the century. Only by the 1820s do they come more regularly into favour.

The New Mills and Factories

The use of water power in the fulling process however paved the way for the new scribbling mill. The water-wheels that turned the fulling stocks were often the same wheels that were utilized to turn the new scribbling and carding machinery and, on occasions even the waterframes for worsted spinning. And in due course those same wheels were turned for spinning and weaving woollen cloth.

The gradual transition from the cottage and the cottage workshop to the full scale factory with all the processes of production congregated under one roof, or on one site, gave rise to many intermediate types of production unit. Various processes or combinations of processes were carried out in different premises. In view of the number of types of establishment the use of the terms 'mill' and

[42] J. Watson, *The History and Antiquities of the Parish of Halifax* (London, 1775), pp. 69–70.

[43] W. B. Crump and G. Ghorbal, *History of the Huddersfield Woollen Industry* (Huddersfield, 1935), pp. 94, 100. See also: *Report from the Committee on the Woollen Clothiers Petitions*, 1802–3 (H.C.71), v; *Minutes of Evidence . . . on the State of the Woollen Manufacture*, op. cit., 1806.

[44] Mann, op. cit., p. 141.

[45] *Leeds Mercury*, 25 November 1799.

'factory' often gives rise to much ambiguity. The definitions of a factory vary greatly. Fong discussed what he understood by it and called it a:

> . . . system of industrial organisation under which the manufacturer was the possessor and manager of a whole or a part of the buildings or several buildings where the wage earning workers, with the aid of the manufacturer's machinery or fixed instruments of production, were concentrated under the supervision of the manufacturer or his foreman, to manufacture raw materials of the manufacturer under a closely related series of subdivided processes. Under this definition the essence of a factory consisted in the labour and supervision by the manufacturer and the employment of machinery or other fixed instruments of production.[46]

This is a very rigid description which insists that the manufacturer owned and managed his own factory and only manufactured his own raw materials. A much looser definition is provided by Cooke-Taylor:

> . . . an establishment where several workmen are collected together for the purpose of obtaining greater and cheaper conveniences for labour then they could procure individually at their homes; for producing results by their combined efforts which they could not accomplish separately; and for saving the loss of time which the carrying of an article from place to place during the several processes necessary to complete its manufacture would occasion. The principle of a factory is that each labourer, working separately, is controlled by some associated principle which directs his producing powers to effecting a common result which is the object of all collectively to obtain.[47]

A recent study of the Scottish Woollen Industry understood the term 'factory' to mean:

> . . . a building or group of related buildings, other than dwelling houses, containing power-driven machinery relevant to all the major stages of production, owned or leased by an entrepreneur or body of such, employing labour on a wage basis.[48]

This last definition seems to imply that for a factory to be so-called all the major stages of production had to be carried out therein, whereas, of course, it was well into the nineteenth century before this was the case in the wool textile industry.

The nineteenth century factory inspectors appear to have included under their terms of reference all premises where one or more of the processes of woollen or worsted manufacture were being carried out with the direct assistance of steam or water power.

[46] H. D. Fong, *Triumph of the Factory System in England* (Tientsin, 1930), Chapter II.
[47] W. Cooke-Taylor, *Factories and the Factory System* (1891), p. 1.
[48] C. Gulvin, 'The Scottish Woollen Industry, 1603–1914', Edinburgh University Ph.D. thesis, 1969, p. 235.

They laid down no stipulations about the form of ownership of the premises nor the number of processes that were necessary before an establishment could be called a 'factory'. This did give rise to a certain amount of confusion even in their times. Joshua Robinson of Smithy Place, Honley, was surprised that his mill was classed as a factory for the 1833 Children's Employment Commission. In his answers to the questionnaire that he was sent, he stated:

> I am engaged in scribbling, carding and fulling — it is no factory — neither am I a manufacturer but work the mill for the country domestic manufacturers — there is no spinning or weaving carried on in the mill.[49]

This suggests that contemporary opinion classed a factory as an establishment where a manufacturer, employing wage earning labour and mechanical power, made up only his own raw materials into yarn and later into cloth when weaving had become mechanized. The mill, on the other hand, was where domestic manufacturers could bring their own materials to be taken through the mechanized processes of scribbling, carding and fulling and perhaps through other processes as well. However, this distinction must often have been blurred by either manufacturers taking in some materials of others as well as making up their own or by mill occupiers manufacturing raw materials of their own as well as those of the domestic manufacturers, their customers. The 1833 Committee on the 'Bill to Regulate the Labour of Children in the Mills and Factories of the United Kingdom' did inquire into the difference between mills and factories in the eyes of cloth manufacturers. The evidence of John Allett insisted that there was a considerable difference. He stated that the mill that he worked was not within the factory system but was called a country mill and working hours were shorter. He was then asked about what distinction he made between a factory and a mill and he replied:

> A very great deal: because when one man was at a mill and employs six or seven or nine or ten men to do every department of it, he has some mills that do what we call country work, having forty or sixty different customers who bring their different articles to be manufactured for sale; then the mill is not run as long as the factory; it is when the factory man gets a large order; then he says 'I have got an order and it must be done in

[49] *Supplementary Reports of the Central Board of His Majesty's Commissioners appointed to Collect Information in the Manufacturing Districts, as to the Employment of Children in Factories, and as to the Propriety and Means of Curtailing the Hours of their Labour*, March 1834, Part II, Section C.2. Mill No. 111. (H.C. 167), XIX, 253, XX, 1. Hereafter referred to as *Factories Inquiry Commission, Supplementary Reports Part . . .* 1834.

such a time; you must work so long hours; I must have it done; and they are bound to do it.[50]

When the bill was finally drafted, however, no distinction was actually made between mills and factories:

And be it further enacted that the words 'mill' and 'factory' and 'mills' or 'factories' used in this Act shall be taken and deemed to comprehend and include all buildings and premises used in any manufactures comprehended in the Act.[51]

For the purpose of this study, no distinction has been made between the terms 'factory' and 'mill' according to ownership, or processes carried out. The two words have been taken as synonymous although the word 'factory' has been applied more regularly to the larger establishments. All premises where wool textile manufacture was carried on using steam or water power are included in the study with the exception of fulling mills which, because of their much earlier establishment, should be considered more a part of the traditional scene than of the new system. Buildings that were used solely for the fulling process are, therefore, excluded but where a fulling mill came to be used for other textile manufacturing processes or fulling was just one of the processes in a new mill, then these premises are, of course, included. There is no stipulation otherwise as to what processes had to be carried out using mechanical power before a building could be termed a mill.

The growth in the number of woollen and worsted mills in the county has long been a subject of debate. Estimates based mainly on contemporary accounts and surveys have varied substantially particularly as a result of differing interpretations of the available evidence.. The often quoted figures of the Children's Employment Commission survey of 1833–4 have been shown to be a considerable underestimate of the evolution of mills and factories.[52] The survey was only carried out on a sample basis, did not receive replies from all the millowners who were approached and, through the questions it asked, created confusion about the meaning of the answers. The second question to West Riding millowners asked about their mill, 'What is the date of its erection or application to its present purpose?' There is normally no way of telling from the reply received which part of the question had been answered. Thus the

[50] *Report from the Committee on the Bill to Regulate the Labour of Children in the Mills and Factories of the United Kingdom* 1833 (H.C. 450), xx, 111.

[51] Ibid., p. 263.

[52] D. T. Jenkins, 'The Validity of the Factory Returns, 1833–50', *Textile History*, IV, 1973, 26–8.

date given for Burley Mill, near Leeds, was 1822, the year it was first used for worsted manufacture. There is no mention of it having been employed for woollen manufacture during the previous quarter of a century.[53] The date given by Joseph Isherwood and Sons for their Stonebridge Mill at Farnley was 1832 when they first entered the premises although the mill itself was being used for woollen production as early as 1805.[54] Many millowners or tenants were unable to answer the question. John Ingham and Company, also at Farnley, were not very helpful by entering 'early' in their returns and Thomas and James Brook of Milnesbridge were even less so with their answer of 'time immemorial'.[55]

Only where specific and detailed information is given can one use the 1833 figures to decide when mills were built or converted to woollen or worsted manufacture. Some of the returns were very comprehensive and helpful. For example, the Swaines of Gomersal entered a full history of their premises which, they said, were used as a cloth market from the early 1780s to 1793 when they became a button factory until 1807, the year in which they were first used for woollen manufacture.[56] Barker and Musgrave of Bramley were even more exact when they recorded that their scribbling, carding and fulling mill commenced work on 25 March 1823.[57]

Contemporary reports and estimates, although often useful for the detail they give, cannot be relied upon before 1835 for a comprehensive view of mill development. It is necessary to look elsewhere for information and to build up a picture from a host of sources. In many cases it is very difficult to arrive at an exact date for the building of a mill or the change of use of premises but in almost all cases an approximate date can be calculated.

There is the additional problem of determining when a mill first started working. Often considerable time could elapse between the commencement of the building of a mill and the time when it was first put to use. In some cases the original intention of the builder might change and a mill meant for woollen or worsted use might be finally used for another purpose. Or, say, a building originally

[53] *Factories Inquiry Commission, Supplementary Reports*, Part II, C.2. Mill no. 61.
[54] Ibid., Mill no. 12.
[55] Ibid., Mills nos. 82 and 201.
[56] Ibid., Mill no. 88.
[57] Ibid., Mill no. 55.

TABLE 2

WOOLLEN AND WORSTED MILLS FIRST TRACED ENTERING THE YORKSHIRE INDUSTRY, ANNUALLY 1774–1835

Year	*Woollen*	*Worsted*	*Year*	*Woollen*	*Worsted*
1774	1		1807	5	2
1778	1		1808	8	2
1779	1		1809	5	1
1780	2		1810	1	7
1781	1		1811	—	2
1782	3		1812	4	6
1783	3		1813	5	3
1784	1		1814	1	1
1785	6		1815	7	4
1786	8		1816	14	3
1787	4	1	1817	3	4
1788	5	—	1818	1	7
1789	—	1	1819	6	6
1790	12	2	1820	4	9
1791	5	2	1821	8	7
1792	20	3	1822	24	15
1793	9	4	1823	9	3
1794	14	1	1824	5	5
1795	21	2	1825	15	1
1796	15	2	1826	14	7
1797	43	1	1827	5	5
1798	11	—	1828	10	2
1799	20	1	1829	12	8
1800	26	5	1830	24	11
1801	23	3	1831	4	5
1802	7	—	1832	4	6
1803	9	2	1833	11	7
1804	4	2	1834	4	1
1805	7	1	1835	26	17
1806	8	2			

Source: References given in Appendix I.

intended for cotton, might be employed for worsted manufacture as was the case at Addingham in the 1780s.[58]

Appendix I lists the mills traced as being used for one or more of the processes of woollen or worsted manufacture up to the mid-1830s. The date when each mill is first known to have been in use for wool textile production is recorded. Further details about the list are discussed in the introduction to the Appendix and the statistical results are shown in Tables 2 and 3. It is most unlikely that the list is entirely accurate and complete. It is very much dependent on the sources used. It is probable that relatively more mills have been excluded for the earlier part of the period because of the limitations of the available data. Discrepancies in the identification of mills are possible. It is perhaps realistic to suggest that any mills excluded are likely to have been relatively small and unimportant in view of the lack of information recorded about them. Overall however it is felt that the figures are a realistic reflection of the numerical growth of mills in the industry. Table 2 shows the number of mills traced coming into use year by year from 1774 to 1835. It takes no account of mills being changed to other uses or of premises closing for one reason or another. Thus the cumulative figures for each year do not give an accurate account of the number of mills actually in use in a particular year and must be adjusted to determine the number of premises in use at any one time.

It is often very difficult to be definite about the date when a mill finally closed. In some instances, for example after a severe fire, the destruction of a mill was recorded in the newspapers or mentioned in the insurance records. But when a mill closed through lack of trade the business often gradually ran down, the premises perhaps being partly converted for other purposes and a definite date of discontinuance of wool textile manufacture cannot be determined. Mills were less likely than firms to leave the industry and for most of the period there does not appear to have been a considerable exodus. Premises were occasionally burnt, or, rather more often, converted to other uses, notably cotton. The exception was the first decade of the nineteenth century when it would seem almost as many mills closed as first came into use. Difficulties in tracing the history of some mills perhaps account for some of the recorded closures in this period. Some of the mills may well be listed later

[58] Low Mill, Addingham. The mill was built in 1787 by John Cunliffe and John Cockshott at Smithy Greaves, Addingham; it was originally intended to be a cotton mill but was, in fact, put to work to spin worsted by water power. James, op. cit., pp. 327–8, 355; Factory Returns, 1804, W.Y.C.R.O.

TABLE 3

NUMBER OF WOOLLEN AND WORSTED MILLS IN USE 1774–1835 IN THE WEST RIDING OF YORKSHIRE WITH FACTORY RETURNS FOR 1835, 1845 AND 1850

Year	*Woollen*	*Worsted*	*Year*	*Woollen*	*Worsted*
1774	1		1809	225	32
1778	2		1810	222	38
1779	3		1811	218	40
1780	5		1812	219	46
1781	6		1813	220	49
1782	9		1814	218	50
1783	12		1815	224	54
1784	13		1816	236	57
1785	19		1817	237	61
1786	27		1818	237	68
1787	31	1	1819	243	74
1788	36	1	1820	244	83
1789	36	2	1821	250	90
1790	46	4	1822	268	104
1791	51	6	1823	275	107
1792	71	9	1824	279	112
1793	78	12	1825	293	111
1794	92	13	1826	307	118
1795	111	15	1827	310	123
1796	126	17	1828	318	124
1797	167	17	1829	329	132
1798	178	17	1830	350	143
1799	195	18	1831	354	147
1800	221	22	1832	357	153
1801	243	25	1833	368	160
1802	244	24	1834	372	161
1803	249	26	1835	399	178
1804	240	27			
1805	234	27	1835(a)	406	204
1806	239	29			
1807	238	30	1845(b)	655	438
1808	232	32			
			1850(c)	880	418

(a) *Factory Returns* 1835

(b) *Reports of the Inspectors of Factories* 1845–6

(c) *Factory Returns* 1850

Source: References in Appendix I. See the introduction to Appendix I for further notes.

under different names and with different tenants. Even so it is clear that the period from 1803 to 1811 did see a substantial decline in the rate of growth of the number of mills in use in the industry and, in some years, perhaps an absolute decrease.[59]

Of the 257 mills recorded by 1800 about 14 had ceased operating by that year. In the following decade 100 new mills were traced and about 80 appear to have ceased functioning. During the following twenty-five years however, rarely did more than two or three mills go out of use in one year. In the woollen branch of the industry there were occasional conversions to flax, cotton, corn and wire drawing but more changes of use appear to have been in the opposite direction.

The exodus of mills from the worsted branch of the industry was never very considerable. Except for occasional fire loss and a few mills changing from the manufacture of worsted cloth to cotton or woollen production, worsted mills tended to have a permanent existence. Perhaps the greatest number of changes of use of worsted mills was in the Keighley area, where many mills built for cotton production in the late eighteenth and early nineteenth century were manufacturing worsted yarn by the 1820s. Thus Damens Mill, built in 1789 for cotton was preparing and spinning worsted yarn from 1824.[60] Dowley Gap Mill, however, built about 1818 for worsted later turned to cotton manufacture.[61]

When these changes are taken into accouunt, an annual series of the number of mills actually in use in both branches of the industry is obtained. This series, illustrated in Table 3, shows differing trends for the growth of the number of mills engaged in woollen and worsted manufacture. In the woollen branch of the industry there appear to have been two main periods of growth, the first being from the late 1780s to around the beginning of the first decade of the nineteenth century and the second from the early 1820s to the end of the period which is being considered. There were, however, certain short term fluctuations within the general trends, just as the period from about 1802 to the early 1820s was not altogether one of slow or negative growth.[62]

[59] See Chapter 5.

[60] For this and other examples see J. Hodgson, *Textile Manufacture and Other Industries in Keighley* (Keighley, 1879).

[61] E. E. Dodd, *Bingley: A Yorkshire Town through Nine Centuries* (Bingley, 1958), p. 88.

[62] The extent of and possible reasons for these fluctuations will be considered in Chapter 5, where changes in the rate of fixed capital formation will be compared with other changes in the industry and the economy.

The number of mills in the worsted branch of the industry increased only very slowly from the 1780s to the second decade of the nineteenth century. However, from the end of the Napoleonic war period the growth was much more rapid with an increase from 50 to 200 mills in the following twenty years.

One important result of the survey is the number of mills that have been discovered in operation in the last two decades of the eighteenth century. Fifty have been traced working before 1790 and over 240 at the turn of the century.

There is no clear claimant for the first scribbling mill. The reference to Strawberry Bank Mill, Liversedge in 1774 is unsupported by other evidence.[63] Gill Mill at Baildon was, however, almost certainly scribbling wool by water power in 1778 as was Fenay Mill in Almondbury parish in the following year.[64] Gill Mill was later converted to worsted production in the early 1790s by Halliday and Cockshott who soon after installed a Boulton and Watt steam engine.[65] By the first years of the 1780s many more mills were being used for scribbling in spite of the trade recession. Armley mills near Leeds probably introduced scribbling machinery at this period. An advertisement in the *Leeds Intelligencer* in 1788 referred to them as: 'All those Capital, Ancient and well accustomed Fulling Mills, Scribbling Mills and Corn Mills . . .' thus suggesting that they had been used for scribbling wool for some length of time.[66] In the Huddersfield area other references can be found to scribbling machinery in use by 1780. The earliest newspaper reference to a water-powered scribbling machine appeared in the *Leeds Mercury* in January 1779:

> A complete scribbling machine with new rollers carrying 46 pairs of cards with iron gear in good condition; together with an upright shaft, swimming wheel and nutt (capable of carrying 4 machines) with the tumbling shaft and nutt. Also a smaller machine of seven barrels or rollers with cards in good condition. Likewise a teazing mill on a new construction with the gear thereto belonging to go by water. Particulars may be had by applying to J. Kenworthy of Huddersfield, the owner.[67]

This description suggests that the scribbling engines were not new. The rollers on the first had been replaced. There is also a reference

[63] F. Peel, *Spen Valley — Past and Present* (1893), p. 230.

[64] W. Cudworth, *Round about Bradford* (1876), p. 338; Dartmouth Estate, *Terrier*, 1805, p. 128 at the Dartmouth Estate Office, Slaithwaite.

[65] Boulton and Watt MSS Portfolio 130. Central Reference Library, Birmingham.

[66] *Leeds Intelligencer*, 5 February 1788; also referred to by Crump, op. cit., p. 5.

[67] *Leeds Mercury*, 26 January 1779; also quoted by Crump and Ghorbal, op. cit., p. 68.

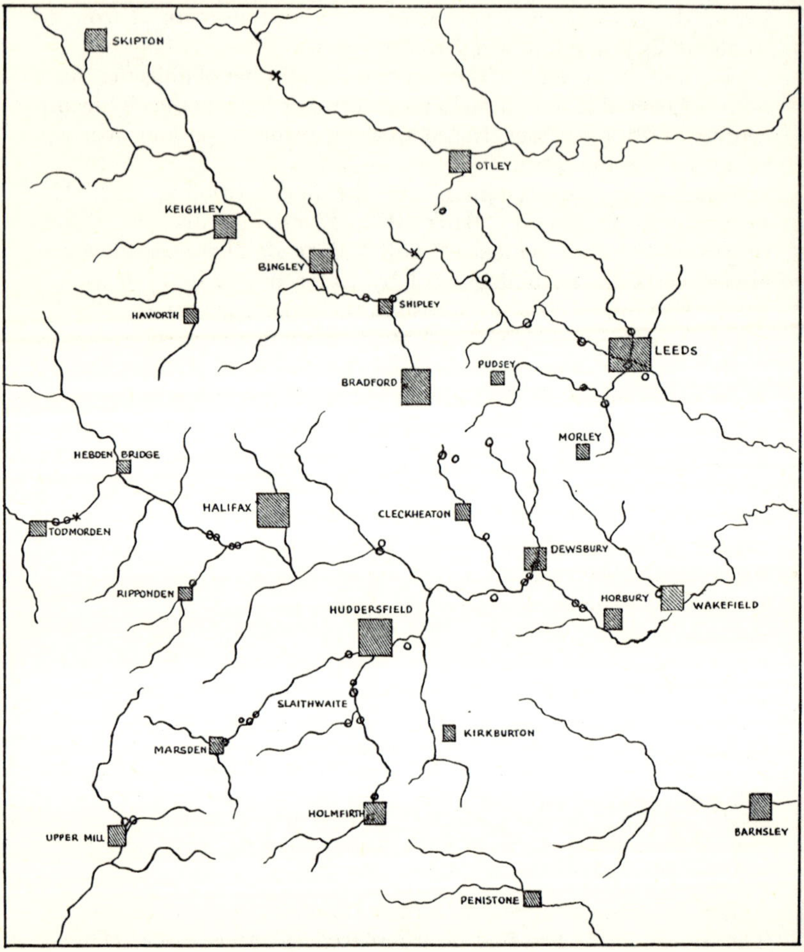

FIG. 1. Location of Woollen and Worsted Mills in the West Riding in 1790
Woollen Mills ○ Worsted Mills ×

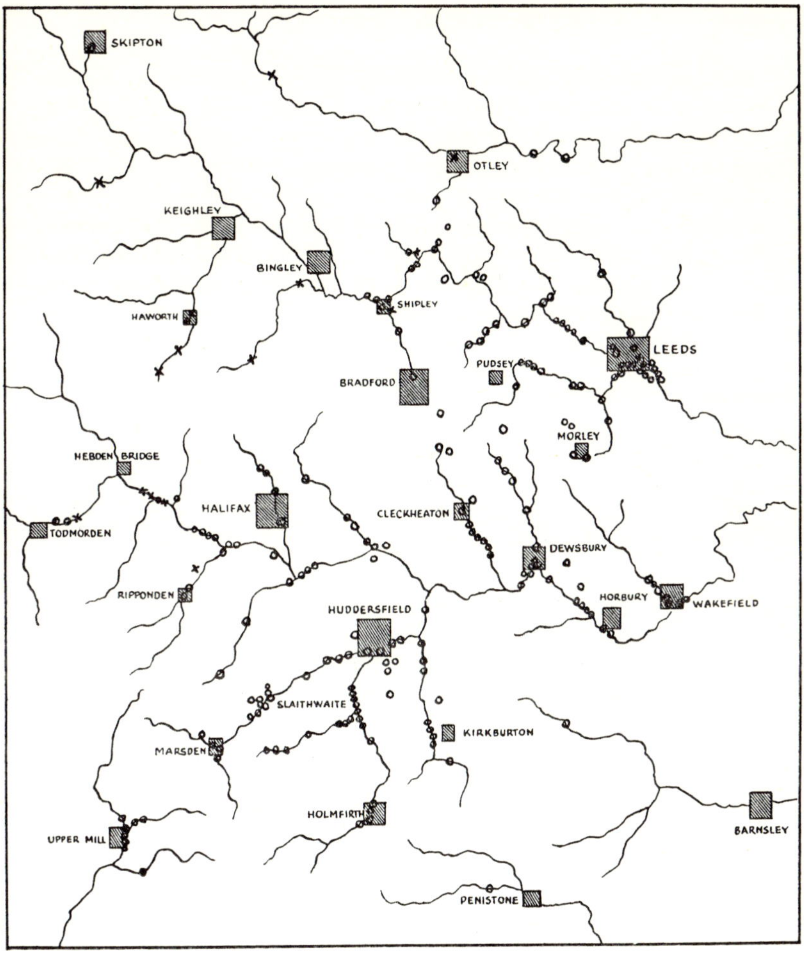

Fig. 2. Location of Woollen and Worsted Mills in the West Riding in 1800
Woollen Mills ○ Worsted Mills ×

to a scribbling engine in the Holmfirth area at about the same period. This was in Ing Nook Mill about 1780 where: 'it appeared in a rude state before the invention of the fly roller and seemed to tumble the wool off the cards like flocks'.[68]

Thus the first rudimentary water-powered scribbling mills probably appeared by the mid-1770s. There is not enough evidence to suggest which was the first but there were certainly several working by 1780 and very many more were constructed, or converted from fulling mills, in the following few years.

Some suggestion has been made in the past that the first movements away from domestic production occurred in the south-west of the region where new techniques in mill building and the construction of machinery first found their way gradually across the Pennine chain from the cotton industry of Lancashire.[69] Certainly mills were being built in the Huddersfield and Halifax areas at an early date but it would seem that within a very short period of time the rest of the region was likewise benefiting from the experience of Lancashire. Scribbling mills were recorded in the eastern part of the textile manufacturing area by the early 1780s.[70] The distribution of steam or water-powered mills engaged in scribbling and worsted spinning by 1790 is shown in Figure 1. There were, it will be seen, several in the Huddersfield area at Honley, Holmfirth, South Crosland, and Slaithwaite but others were working as far east as Ossett, Beeston and Wakefield, and at Baildon and Otley on the northern fringes of the textile area.

In the following decade mill building in Bradford, Leeds, and Wakefield parishes kept abreast of the development in the Almondbury, Halifax, and Huddersfield areas. Figure 2 shows the approximate distribution of all the worsted and woollen mills traced in operation by 1800.

At the beginning of the nineteenth century mill building was widely distributed throughout the textile manufacturing region. With the increased factory development in the worsted sector of the industry from the end of the first decade more rapid growth was taking place in the towns of Bradford, Halifax, and Keighley and their surrounding areas. In the woollen branch of the industry Leeds and Huddersfield parishes saw the most expansion in the same

[68] Crump and Ghorbal, op. cit., p. 68. It was driven by water power.

[69] For example Crump and Ghorbal, op. cit., p. 60.

[70] For example Gill Mill, Baildon; Spring End Mill, Ossett; Guiseley Mills; and Millshaw Mills, Beeston. See Appendix I for references and further examples.

period, partly through the development of more urban steam-powered mills, but from around 1801 to after 1815 was a relatively slack period for the construction of woollen mills. After 1815 expansion was widespread and all the main woollen manufacturing parishes experienced an increase in mill building. There is a comparison in Table 4 of the growth in the number of woollen and worsted mills in the main parishes for each decade from 1790 to 1830.

Figures 1 and 2 and Appendix I do suggest that in the early part of the period, when water power was, for most mill constructors, the prime consideration in the siting of a mill, the most rapid development took place along the banks of the major streams. The water power of the Calder, Colne, and Aire and their major tributaries was being put to substantial use well before 1800. Indeed the need for water power, rather than the proximity to the textile manufacturing areas of Lancashire, might well have been the reason for the early establishment of mills on the higher parts of the Pennines.[71] The presence of water, not just for power, was the dominating factor in the siting of mills throughout the period. The introduction of steam power permitted the use of a wider variety of locations and allowed development in towns such as Batley where water power was scarce or in other towns where riverside positions were at a premium. Steam power allowed more construction to take place in or near the urban centres and created a relative movement from the remoter rural districts, although building of rural mills was continuing in the 1830s with the increase in the price of urban land and the gradual improvements in transport in the area.

Water was not just needed for power. Several of the processes of wool textile manufacture, for example fulling and dyeing, required a supply. Thus most of the steam-powered textile mills were situated close to ponds and streams, which although not necessarily powerful enough to turn a wheel, were still essential to the manufacturer. Many other factors affected location. Prospective mill developers had to take into account the supply of labour, the price of land, the proximity to markets and to a supply of raw materials. The occupiers of steam-powered mills had to be assured of a regular supply of coal without the need to pay high transport costs. But even so there can be little doubt that the availability of water was the most important factor for mill location until well into the nineteenth century.

[71] See Chapter 3 for a discussion of the use and location of water power.

TABLE 4

COMPARISON OF THE GROWTH IN THE NUMBER OF WOOL TEXTILE MILLS IN THE MAIN PARISHES OF THE WEST RIDING TEXTILE AREA 1790–1830

PARISH	*1790* *wool*	*worsted*	*1800* *wool*	*worsted*	*1810* *wool*	*worsted*	*1820* *wool*	*worsted*	*1830* *wool*	*worsted*
Almondbury	7		29		30		35		39	
Bingley				1	1	2	1	8	1	11
Batley			9		8		9		13	
Birstall	4		15	1	12	1	16		23	
Bradford	2		6	5	6	12	4	39	4	60
Calverley			6		10		13	1	21	2
Dewsbury	3		9		9		13		18	
Guiseley	3		5		5		6		8	2
Huddersfield	3		12		14		19		32	
Halifax	9	1	25	9	25	16	27	22	33	42
Kirkburton	3		13		16		17		23	
Keighley		1		1		3		14		24
Kirkheaton	1		5		4		4		5	
Leeds	6		35	1	34	2	43	2	72	5
Otley	1		6	1	5	2	5	3	4	6
Saddleworth	2		6		9		10		13	
Wakefield	1		7	1	10	1	12	3	10	5

Source: Appendix I

Marshall, the Leeds flax spinner, summed up the primary factors influencing the location of mills as being the importance of water both for power and for cleansing but also a cheap and abundant supply of coal, accessibility and commercial facilities. Although he believed steam power brought greater concentration, development still spread along the valley bottoms, the upland villages surviving as domestic weaving centres until the power loom destroyed their prosperity.[72]

The geographical limits of the industry within the West Riding area changed very little over the sixty years. Confined to an area of about 1,000 square miles very few mills were to be found north of the River Wharfe. Skipton appears to have been the limit in the north-west with the exception of isolated mills at Dent, Sedbergh, Gargrave, Aysgarth, Settle, and Linton. In the west the county boundary between Yorkshire and Lancashire defined the limits of the industry, although here again many isolated mills were to be found, at Dolphineholme near Lancaster, in Rossendale, at Colne and Todmorden, and further south on the outskirts of Oldham. In the south-west and south, the townships of Saddleworth, Penistone, and Hoyland formed the boundary, and in the east few were to be found beyond Leeds and Wakefield, although at one time or another there were mills working at Clifford, Selby, Hull, and Driffield. Almost all the woollen and worsted mills were within a radius of fifteen miles from Bradford and the overall centre of the region was within the area bounded by Leeds, Bradford, Halifax, Huddersfield, and Wakefield.

The Worsted Trade

Within the large wool textile manufacturing area there was a considerable amount of specialization, not only between woollen and worsted cloth but in the production of very many types of different cloths. From at least the mid-eighteenth century, Bradford was a centre of worsted manufacture. Mill development, however, was slow in the town itself partly because of the shortage of water power, and thus the earliest worsted mills were scattered around the area at Leeds, Ilkley, Mytholmroyd, Baildon, Addingham, Leeming, Wilsden, and Haworth.

When the Worsted Committee was set up in 1777 six of its 18

[72] PP. 1841. (H.C. 201), VII, 187; quoted and discussed by R. M. Hartwell, *The Yorkshire Woollen and Worsted Industries, 1800–1850*, unpublished Oxford University (Balliol), D.Phil, thesis, 1955, p. 187.

members came from Halifax, four from Bradford, two each from Wakefield and Leeds, and one each from Keighley, Skipton, and Ripon.[73] For the period this membership is probably fairly representative of the relative importance of the industry in these different parishes, although it appears unlikely that Ripon continued as a worsted centre for very long as no record has been found of any mills being constructed in or near the town in spite of the abundance of water power in that area.[74]

The Worsted Committee was established after two Acts of Parliament were passed to try to control or prevent the frauds and embezzlements which were becoming more and more common with the growth of the industry.[75] The Committee was established 'for the purpose of watching over the interests of the trade and bringing to punishment delinquents', and the 'Worsted Acts' as they were known authorized:

> the appointment, at a general meeting of the manufacturers of combing wool, worsted yarn and goods made from Worsted, in the Counties of York, Lancaster and Cheshire, of a Committee of 27 persons; the Yorkshire manufacturers to elect eighteen people from amongst themselves, and the remaining nine to be chosen by the Lancashire and Cheshire manufacturers. This joint Committee to nominate inspectors for the purpose of detecting and prosecuting delinquents. A fund, for effecting the purpose of these Acts, was provided out of the drawback on soap employed in the manufactures from wool.[76]

Seven inspectors were appointed, four of whom were for Yorkshire, the county being divided into the following four districts:

Yorkshire — South District
From Blackstone Edge, the nearest way to Huddersfield thence to Wakefield along the River Calder, till it joins the River Aire and from thence to the Humber including all that part of Yorkshire which is south of that line.

— Middle District
From Ferrybridge to Tadcaster, from thence along the River Wharfe to Otley, through Silsdon and Cross Hills towards Colne, till the road joins Lancashire, and on the edge of Lancashire till it joins that part of Blackstone Edge where the South District begins.

— West District
From that part of the River Wharfe nearest Wetherby to Ripley, Middleham, West Witton, Aisgarth, Askrigg, Hardrow Chapel, Thwaite Bridge to Hell Gill Beck and thence down the borders of Westmorland and Lancashire until it joins the road from Cross Hill to Colne.

[73] James, op. cit., p. 296.
[74] There were cotton mills in the proximity of Ripon. The nearest worsted mill was probably at Masham.
[75] 17 Geo. III ii and 17 Geo. III xvi.
[76] James, op. cit., pp. 292–8.

— North District
From Wetherby by Tadcaster to Ferrybridge, thence towards the sea on the north side of the River Aire and Humber round by the sea until it joins the Bishoprick of Durham thence by the edge of that County and Westmorland to Hell Gill Beck.[77]

This apportioning of the county between the four inspectors suggested that the worsted industry covered a very wide area. In fact, however, worsted manufacture was mainly confined to the territory of the inspector of the 'Middle District' who probably had more to do than all the other three inspectors put together. In the North District, in particular, there could have been very little worsted trade. This is borne out by the drawback on soap, the details of which are given for 1810 and 1830 in Table 5. Although there were difficulties in the collection of the drawback, John James considered that 'By perseverance and good management all these obstacles were surmounted and eventually, the whole machinery of the Committee and its officers worked effectively and well'.[78] Thus one might accept the returns of the drawback on soap as being fairly representative of the scale of worsted manufacture in different areas. For the main centres a comparison is made in Figure 3 between the drawback collected in 1810 and 1830.[79]

TABLE 5

DRAWBACK ON SOAP FROM WORSTED MANUFACTURERS IN YORKSHIRE IN 1810 and 1830

	1810 £	*1830* £		*1810* £	*1830* £
Addingham	157	131	Bradford	851	5259
Allerton	—	50	Bramhope	2	5
Ardsley	10	—	Brighouse	—	82
Almondbury	19	155	Burley	—	13
Alverthorpe	1	—	Burton	12	—
Barkisland	1	6	Carthorpe	1	—
Baildon	24	816	Catterick	3	—
Bedale	1	—	Clayton	—	231
Beeston	1	—	Clayton West	—	89
Bierley	20	19	Cleckheaton	—	102
Bingley	159	622	Cottingley	—	—
Birkenshaw	13	55	Cumberworth	6	26
Bolton	—	5	Cullingworth	23	441
Bowling	62	79	Dalton	10	411

77 Ibid., p. 298.
78 Ibid.
79 The drawback on soap was the rebate that manufacturers could claim from the general tax on soap at the period.

TABLE 5 continued

	1810 £	1830 £		1810 £	1830 £
Denby Dale	—	10	Ossett	—	47
Dewsbury	3	14	Otley	4	242
Eastburn	—	28	Ovenden	118	272
Eccleshill	14	94	Pontefract	4	—
Elland	41	30	Raistrick	6	225
Emley	1	—	Rawden	6	4
Erringdon	—	4	Ripon	5	—
Esholt	—	52	Rothwell	9	—
Farnley Tyas	—	88	Silsden	4	21
Farsley	—	2	Shelf	2	27
Flockton	1	—	Shipley	18	278
Gomersal	14	231	Shepley	1	—
Greetland	—	13	Selby	10	—
Halifax	257	1905	Skelmanthorpe	5	37
Hawes	6	—	Skipton	119	352
Haworth	382	288	Skircoat	12	1
Heaton	33	—	Southowram	25	57
Heckmondwike	23	—	Sowerby	5	102
Heptonstall	48	13	Soyland	5	36
Hipperholme	77	153	Spotland	—	14
Honley	11	4	Snaith	13	—
Horbury	1	184	Snape	13	—
Horton	7	145	Stainland	201	116
Huddersfield	1	188	Stanningley	—	437
Hunslet	5	—	Stansfield	69	313
Idle	10	98	Steeton	—	66
Keighley	199	1866	Sutton	3	83
Kirkburton	4	62	Thornton	43	189
Kirkheaton	20	11	Thornes	8	—
Kildwick	69	—	Tong	153	42
Knaresborough	3	—	Todmorden	—	26
Leeds	354	277	Tadcaster	2	—
Lepton	51	81	Wakefield	112	725
Lothersdale	9	—	Wadsworth	243	268
Liversedge	—	17	Warley	101	276
Lower Booths	—	150	Well	12	—
Manningham	5	22	Wilsden	70	170
Marsden	21	36	Woodhouse	1	193
Masham	89	—	Wrenthorpe	5	—
Marston	—	4	Yeadon	4	16
Midgley	3	114	York	18	—
Morton	—	8			
Morley	4	—	Dent	—	2
Norland	8	—	Sedbergh	—	5
Northowram	41	133	Thwaitehead	—	1

Source: This table is based on James, op. cit., p. 369, and Appendix, p. 13. Figures given are to the nearest £1.00.

By 1810, according to the figures for the drawback on soap, Bradford had become the most important worsted manufacturing centre with Haworth taking second place. Leeds, however, had a greater return than either Halifax or Keighley. Other centres were Addingham where there were two large mills, Bingley, Ovenden, Skipton, and Stainland. The village of Masham, over forty miles from the other textile towns had a surprisingly large drawback, accounted for by one big mill near the village.

In 1830 Masham does not appear in the returns; worsted manufacture in that area presumably having died out. In the intervening twenty year period Bradford, Halifax, Keighley,

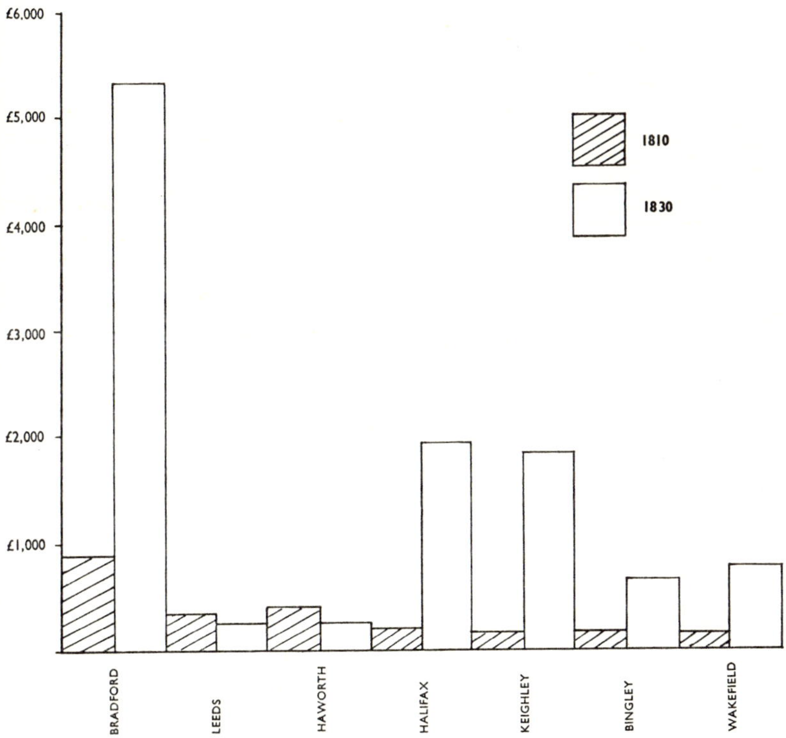

FIG. 3. Comparison of drawback of soap from worsted manufacturers in the main centres, 1810 and 1830

Bingley, and Wakefield all grew in both absolute and relative importance. On the other hand, Leeds and Haworth had declined. Whereas the former five towns accounted for over 50 per cent the drawback in 1830, less than 30 per cent of the total was collected from them in 1810. Thus there would appear to have been a greater growth of the worsted trade in the main towns and an overall greater concentration of the industry around Keighley, Bradford, and Halifax; such outlying places as Masham, Ripon, Hawes, Kildwick, Selby, and York all apparently ceasing their worsted manufacture. Because of the changes in the various rates of drawback and the amount of soap used, a direct comparison between the totals in 1810 and 1830, in order to show the growth of the industry and its output, is not possible.

In 1830 there were still centres of worsted manufacture at various places some distance from the main manufacturing area. Manufacturers at Otley and Skipton, for example, were paid drawbacks of £242 and £352 respectively and manufacturers at Almondbury, in the heart of the woollen manufacturing area, were paid over £150, although no worsted mills were recorded in the latter parish by the Factory Inspectors five years later.

The growth in the town of Bradford increased rapidly in the first two or three decades of the nineteenth century by which time it had gained a really predominant position as a worsted manufacturing centre. In 1851 it was written:

> No single portion of the English provinces can boast of a greater prosperity, during especially the last half century, than Bradford which from a comparatively insignificant market town, has during the period referred to risen by the energy of its inhabitants, the material resources for manufacturing purposes it possesses and its geographical position to be — beyond all challenge — the Capital of the worsted trade.

After describing the position of the town at 'a very convenient central point between . . . the whole of the towns and villages in the West Riding, where the manufacture of worsted, in any of its multifarious branches, is carried on to any extent', the account continues with an explanation of the reasons for the importance and prosperity of the town:

> Bradford owes its commercial prosperity not so much to the fact of its being seated in the very heart of the manufacturing district of the West Riding of Yorkshire, as it does to its coalmines; its ironworks which are very extensive, and from which the cannon-ball as well as the ponderous steam boiler, is fabricated; its vast quarries yielding an abundance of stone of the most durable character; its canal and railway accommodation; and the

three brooks in addition to the numberous small streamlets which impart a plentiful supply of water, both for domestic, manufacturing and dyeing purposes.[80]

It is not made clear from this description, however, that the brooks and 'streamlets' mentioned were hardly powerful and regular enough to supply the power to turn machinery. Thus with few exceptions, the early Bradford mills were steam-powered and came at a slightly later date than mills elsewhere in the county. Indeed one wonders whether the other factors were a sufficient reason for the establishment of the factory industry in the town. Other localities might have had greater advantages including water power. One might doubt, for example, the value of the Bradford water for cleansing purposes. James Smith in his Report on the Condition of the Town of Bradford gave the following description:

The main sewerage of the town has been very defective . . . The chief sewerage, if sewerage it can be called, of the inferior streets and of the courts, is in open channels, and from the rough and unequal surface of the streets the flow is tardy and the whole soil is saturated with sewage water. The main sewers are discharged either into the brook or into the terminus or basin of a canal which runs into the lower part of the town. The water of this basin is often so charged with decaying matter that in hot weather bubbles of sulphuretted hydrogen are continually rising to the surface; and so much is the atmosphere loaded with that gas, that watchcases and other materials of silver become black in the pockets of the workmen employed near the canal. The stench is sometimes very strong and fevers prevail much all around. Taking the general condition of Bradford, I am obliged to pronounce it to be the most filthy town I visited.[81]

It was not, however, just the difficulties of obtaining water that delayed mill building in Bradford. The hostility of the local inhabitants prevented the erection of a mill by Mr Buckley in 1793 and it was seven years later that Messrs Ramsbotham, Swaine and Murgatroyd braved the wrath of some of the inhabitants to build Holme Mill, powered by a 15 horse power engine.[82] James records the opposition the partners encountered even though many mills had been erected elsewhere:

A man had commenced conveying stones for the building of the mill when a large number of the inhabitants assembled to prevent his preceding to

[80] Collinson, Burton and Company, *West Riding Worsted Directory*, 1852, Chapter I. Historic Sketch of the Town of Bradford, pp. 97–8.

[81] *Second Report on the Commission for Inquiring into the State of Large Towns and Populous Districts*; Vol. II, 1845, XVII (H.C. 299), 150.

[82] James, op. cit., pp. 605–6; W. Cudworth, *Worstedopolis* (1888), p. 35; *Factories Inquiry Commission, Supplementary Reports*, Part II, C.2. Mill no. 47. Mr Buckley's mill was to have been a cotton mill.

the site of it and laid hold of the horse's head. One of the partners (Mr. Murgatroyd) being a man of considerable prowess stripped his coat and literally boxed the way clear, and the persons who had assembled to stop the work, seeing his determination and probably remembering the unlawfulness of their conduct, allowed the horse and cart to proceed. Under such discouraging circumstances was the first of those structures, which have raised Bradford to its present importance among the towns of England, built.[83]

Other mills soon followed in and around the town using Arkwright's water frame or throstle. Four mills started working in the town in the first decade of the nineteenth century, one of which, Laister Dyke Mill, was converted from woollen manufacture and the other three purpose built.[84] In the following decade a more rapid growth was apparent, nine mills being built with another seven entering the industry in the 1820s. The growth of the number of mills in Bradford, and its associated townships, is shown in detail in Table 6. By 1830 both Keighley and Halifax recovered a similar amount of drawback on soap although twenty years earlier Halifax appears to have been the more important worsted manufacturing centre. Keighley developed from a cotton to a worsted producing town although in the middle of the eighteenth century the woollen trade was the towns' staple industry and cotton remained of importance as the worsted trade developed. A number of cotton mills were erected in the town before 1800, but long before that date Keighley was also producing worsteds, and from the middle of the eighteenth century silk. The first mill in the town, besides fulling mills, was built for cotton and commenced working in June 1780. A local historian claimed that it was the first cotton mill erected in the county and that the proprietors obtained machinery and children to work the mill from Arkwright's works at Cromford.[85]

Within the next thirty years at least another twenty cotton mills were built in the parish.[86] There is, however, some doubt as to which was the first mill in Keighley to be used for worsted manufacture. Nearby, at Hewenden, Leeming, and Haworth, worsted mills were built in the 1790s. The first mill possibly constructed specifically for worsted production was Aireworth Mill in 1880.[87]

[83] James, op. cit., p. 592.

[84] West Brook Factory, Laister Dyke Mill, and Union St Mill in Bradford township and Horton Lane Mill in Little Horton township. See Appendix I for references.

[85] R. Holmes, *Keighley, Past and Present* (1858), pp. 107–8. It is by no means certain that this was the first cotton mill erected in Yorkshire.

[86] Ibid., and Hodgson, op. cit.

[87] Holmes, op. cit., p. 110.

Table 6

THE GROWTH IN THE NUMBER OF MILLS IN THE TOWNSHIPS OF THE PARISH OF BRADFORD — 1800–35

Townships	*Mills in 1800*		*1810*		*1820*		*1835**	
	Woollen	*Worsted*	*Woollen*	*Worsted*	*Woollen*	*Worsted*	*Woollen*	*Worsted*
Bowling						1		2
Bradford	2	1	2	5		14		25
Great Horton						4		6
Little Horton				1		4		8
Eccleshill					2	1	2	1
Haworth		2		2		4		10
Oxness		2		3		4		7
Manningham	1		1			2		1
Shipley	3	1	3	1	2	5	2	4
Thornton								5
Totals	6	6	6	12	4	39	4	69

*According to the 1835 Factory Returns
Source: Appendix I and *Factory Returns* 1835.

4

But it is almost certain that some of the cotton mills were also spinning worsted before that date. At Ingrow Mill and Higher Providence Mill cotton and stuff pieces were being made early in the century.[88] Many worsted mills were erected in the second decade of the century and more in the 1820s, whilst several of the cotton mills were converted wholly to worsted manufacture.

By 1835 there were 22 worsted mills working in the parish powered by nine steam engines and 15 water-wheels, employing an average of fifty workers each. The Keighley mills were, generally, smaller than those of Bradford. This is, no doubt, explained by the availability of water power. The two streams through the town, both suitable for use for power, permitted early mill growth but in later years limited the amount of power available and were the cause of the slower adoption of the steam engine.

The other major centre of worsted production by 1830 was the town of Halifax, where at one time or another, many branches of woollen and worsted manufacture were carried on. In the 1790s a contemporary observer recorded that: '. . . the woollen manufacture has flourished here for centuries: the principal fabrics are tammies, callimancoes, russets, broad and narrow cloths.'[89] However, by the time that this was written the town had been converted mainly to worsted. In 1795 Aiken found that the town was of most importance as a worsted centre although woollen manufacture was continuing on a large scale.[90] In 1835 the Factory Inspectors recorded 43 worsted mills in the parish of which 14 were actually in the town. At the same period there were 38 woollen mills in the parish of which only four were in the town. The average power at the worsted mills was 21 horse power provided by 34 steam engines and 25 water-wheels, and the mills employed an average of eighty-four workers. The mills were thus slightly smaller than those in Bradford parish, again, presumably because of the limitations of water power on size. The woollen mills had a slightly higher average power of 23 horse power, in spite of the predominance of water power but their average employment was sixty-five workers.

In worsteds the factory system came even slower to the township of Halifax than to Bradford, thus impeding the town's development and leaving it always behind Bradford in importance in the factory

[88] Hodgson, op. cit., p. 48.
[89] F. M. Eden, *The State of the Poor* (London, 1797), Vol. III, 821.
[90] J. Aiken, *A Description of the Country from 30 to 40 Miles around Manchester* (London, 1795), pp. 563–4.

trade. There were few mills in the town itself before 1820. James's explanation for this was:

One of the main causes which contributed to give Bradford the start of Halifax in the race of competition, and finally altogether to distance the latter arose from the early adoption in the town of Bradford of the factory system and to full and free development there. Besides in the parish of Halifax the woollen and cotton businesses were carried on extensively, so that the energies of the inhabitants were directed to many branches . . . until the early portion of the present century Halifax stood at the head of the worsted manufacturing seats in the North of England.

But when the factory system began to be introduced into the worsted business, Halifax betrayed the same apathy to it, as Norwich did in more recent times, and thus lost the vantage ground it had formerly by great enterprise and labour obtained.[91]

Elsewhere in Halifax parish mills were built or converted for woollen and worsted manufacture at an early date nine woollen mills and one worsted mill were at work by 1790 and twenty-five woollen and nine worsted by 1800.

The importance of the worsted trade in Leeds declined during the period. The earliest steam-powered worsted mill traced was at the Bank in Leeds where Markland, Cookson and Fawcett installed a 30 horse power Boulton and Watt engine in 1792 and started spinning both cotton and worsted.[92] But although nine other mills were spinning worsted yarn at one time or another in the following forty years, the overall output of the industry, judged by the drawback on soap, declined in the town.

Besides these main centres of worsted manufacture there were a number of worsted mills in quite isolated parts of the West Riding. Joseph Smith was producing worsted yarn at his mill at Gargrave by the early 1830s and the Birkbeck's at Linton sent details of their large worsted mill to the Factory Inspector in 1803.[93] Elsewhere worsted mills were recorded in 1835 as far apart as Dent and High Hoyland.[94]

[91] James, op. cit., p. 617.

[92] Normally recorded as a cotton mill, this mill was being used mainly for worsted soon after it opened. Sun C.R. 8/636966/1795; 13/653223/1796; 17/666225/1797; 22/674510/1798; 24/681849/1798; 27/693428/1799; 32/701514/1800; 45/731575/1802; Boulton and Watt MSS Portfolio 91 and List of Leeds Engines. See also Table 13.

[93] Factory Returns, 1804, W.Y.C.R.O.; Sun C.R. 85/835754/1809; Papers of Thos Brown, 'Agent in Account with the Royal Exchange Assurance Co.,' Skipton, now in the care of Messrs Charlesworth, Wood and Brown, Solicitors, Skipton, who kindly allowed me to examine them.

[94] *A Return of the number of Persons Employed . . . in Factories in the United Kingdom, 1835* (H.C. 138), 1836, XIV; hereafter referred to as *Factory Returns, 1835*. See Appendix I for these and other examples of isolated worsted mills.

The types of worsted cloth varied from one town to another within the region. One cannot generalize where a large number of kinds of cloth were being produced and, indeed, this subject merits a separate study. Some idea can, however, be given of the types of production and specialities of the different areas based on contemporary accounts and descriptions.

Bradford's fame stemmed from the variety of cloth its inhabitants manufactured rather than from their specialization. However, the town was particularly celebrated for its orleans and coburgs.[95] A Bradford manufacturer was quoted as saying:

Every variety of ladies' dress goods, checked in coloured worsted and mohair, or cotton and silk can be ordered or purchased from the Bradford manufacturers at most moderate prices, while for its staple articles of orleans and coburgs this town has undoubtedly, and deservedly, the highest reputation of any in the world. In the variety and general excellence of its productions this district certainly rivals any other manufacturing town with which we are acquainted.[96]

According to James the Bradford trade was mainly in mixed fabrics 'where the warps are altogether of cotton and silk'.[97] But Collinson in his *History of the Worsted Trade* stated:

The pure worsted fabrics (i.e. fabrics not mixed with cotton or silk) are mainly produced in Bradford, Halifax, Keighley and contiguous districts in the West Riding of Yorkshire . . .[98]

A very wide variety of cloths were produced by the worsted manufacturers. Collinson listed casting, crapes, serge, orleans, cassinetts, twills, dobbies, french figures, figures and embroidered alpacas, parisiens, damasks, camlets, merinos, challis, mousseline-de-laines, coburgs, paramaters, shalloons, durays, taminets, khybereens, poplins, calimancoes, bombazeens, figured rateens, cubicos, mohairs, fancy waistcoatings and others, all of which were manufactured in Yorkshire.[99]

Baines provided an even more comprehensive list which also showed the very many additions to the types of worsted cloth manufactured, that were made in the early years of factory production.[100] With such a wide variety one cannot easily divide the

[95] James, op. cit., p. 602.
[96] Ibid.
[97] Ibid., p. 604.
[98] Collinson, Burton and Company, op. cit., p. 82.
[99] Ibid., pp. 80–1. 'Paramaters' were normally called 'parammattas'.
[100] E. Baines, *The Woollen Manufacture of England: with special reference to the Leeds Clothing District* in T. Baines, *Yorkshire Past and Present* (1871), pp. 667, 673. The section has been reprinted as *Baines's Account of the Woollen Manufacture of England,* with a new introduction by K. G. Ponting (Newton Abbot, 1970).

types of woven fabric into district areas of production. Various contemporary advertisements and reports do, however, suggest that there was some specialization geographically. One, dated 1840, recorded that:

. . . the principal kinds of stuffs made in the villages around Bradford are 6/4 shalloons, or double twills, called in the shops when finished, french merinos; 6/4 plainbacks, or common merinos, which are twilled on one side only; 6/4 wildbores or plain stuffs; 3/4 wildbores, figures stuffs, moreens.[101]

and at about the same time a note in a Bradford newspaper described the increased use of cotton in the industry.[102] The early introduction of cotton warp probably first occurred in the Keighley area but soon became common in Bradford where there was a declared policy of providing a cloth that 'the masses' could buy; but at the same time greater specialization was occurring.

Thus while Bradford concentrated more and more on the mixed cloths Halifax became better known as a centre for pure worsted fabrics. John James obtained from James Akroyd and Son details of the goods manufactured by their firm at different times. This list gives a useful insight into the manufactures of one of Halifax's most important firms:

1798	Calimancoes, plain and ribbed; lastings; prunelles
1803	Serges de Berri, shalloons, Russets, wildbores
1811	Moreens, says, duroys
1813	Three-fourth bombazetts, or plain backs
1819	Bombazines and Norwich crepes
1829	Camlets, Taborines, fancy Russells, dobbies
1824	Damasks
1826–7	French merinos and full twills
1834	French figures
1836	Alpaca figures
1836–40	Figured orleans[103]

The Woollen Trade

The capital of the woollen industry throughout the period was Leeds, the largest town in the West Riding, and an important manufacturing and merchanting centre for the whole county. Situated on the eastern fringe of the textile district its communications

[101] *Reports of the Assistant Commissioners for Handloom Weavers*, 1839–40, Part III on the West Riding of Yorkshire, by H. C. Chapman (H.C. 4311), PP. 1840, XXIV, 557, quoted by Sigsworth, op. cit., pp. 43–4.
[102] *Bradford Observer*, 6 September 1838, quoted by Sigsworth, op. cit., pp. 44–5.
[103] James, op. cit., p. 618.

with the coast by means of the Aire and the Aire and Calder Navigation gave it a distinct advantage over other towns, with the possible exception of Wakefield. The opening of the Leeds and Liverpool Canal provided a useful link to other parts of the textile manufacturing area and to the industrial and commercial facilities of Lancashire.[104] Aiken described Leeds's importance in the 1790s:

Though the woollen trade in Yorkshire has properly no common centre, yet the town of Leeds has latterly been always reckoned, in opulence and population, the principal place of the West Riding and it bears a high rank among our manufacturing towns.[105]

As early as 1714 eight mills were recorded on Sheepscar Beck alone, probably fulling and corn mills, and there were many others along the Aire and the various other streams.[106] The first scribbling mills were established in or near the town at a fairly early date. In the 1780s, Millshaw Mill at Beeston, Armley Mill, Low Mill, and Ross Mill, all within a few miles of the town were working before the end of the decade. Nearer the town Copley's Mill in Hunslet Lane and Scothall Mills were also scribbling in the same period. By the turn of the century thirty-five mills had commenced manufacturing. For the next fifteen years there was little expansion in the number of mills but after 1815 the construction of new buildings was considerable both in the parish and the township.

As the town grew many vivid descriptions were recorded of it. In 1835 it left quite an impression on Sir George Head:

There is no manufacturing town in England, I should imagine, where more coal is consumed in proportion to its extent than Leeds. The sun himself is obscured by smoke as by a natural mist and no sooner does he descend below the horizons than streams of brilliant gas burst forth from thousands of illuminated windows.[107]

And the Commissioners examining the State of Large Towns in 1845 found a very sorry state of affairs and much evidence that the

[104] The Leeds and Liverpool canal was initially planned in the 1760s. Building started in the 1770s with the section between Leeds and Shipley being completed in 1777, joining up with the section between Bingley and Skipton which had been finished three years earlier. Leeds was not joined to Liverpool until the canal was completed in 1816.

[105] Aiken, op. cit., p. 570.

[106] T. Baines, op. cit., Vol. II, 129.

[107] Sir George Head, *A Tour of the Manufacturing District of Great Britain* (1835), p. 140.

town had rapidly developed with little or no thought or effort being given to design, sanitation or other services.[108]

A few mills were constructed close to the centre of the town but the majority throughout the period sprung up on the edges in Sheepscar, Woodhouse, Hunslet, and Holbeck, and along the Kirkstall Road, the development of the urban area following and encroaching them in time. By 1835 77 woollen mills and 10 worsted mills were working in the parish, of which 42 woollen mills and seven worsted mills were in the township itself. The mills were mainly powered by steam, eighty-seven steam engines being recorded compared with only nine water-wheels.[109]

Close by, the villages of Hunslet and Holbeck and the others in the parish all had mills at an early date. The factory inspectors recorded ten in Bramley alone by 1835. These small villages were particularly active in the woollen trade but whereas some acquired the traditional characteristics of manufacturing centres others have managed to retain their rural environment to this day in spite of factory growth.

Parsons provided particularly lurid descriptions of Hunslet and Holbeck:

> . . . no place in the whole district has experienced such a total change in external appearance . . . Hunslet Lane still contains a number of good houses connected generally with extensive mercantile establishments but the whole village, or rather, suburb of Leeds, is irregularly and frequently meanly built consisting of narrow dirty lanes, branching out from the great thoroughfare to Wakefield and from the principal street passing by the Chapel. The general aspect of the place is strangely uncouth, and perhaps a more dismal scene cannot be presented than the tract of mud and mush called Hunslet Moor on a rainy day.

Holbeck was likewise described as: 'one of the most crowded, one of the most filthy, one of the most unpleasant and one of the most unhealthy villages in the County of York'.[110]

The majority of the villages in the parish of Leeds specialized in mixed cloth manufacturing rather than in fancy cloths, for which the Huddersfield area was noted. Gott produced many types of cloth at various times but was perhaps best known for his good plain cloth. Crump records that:

[108] *Second Report of the Commissioners on the State of Large Towns and Populous Districts, 1845* (H.C. 299), XVII, 1845, Vol. II, 146, Report on the Condition of the Town of Leeds by James Smith of Deanston.

[109] *Factory Returns, 1835.*

[110] E. Parsons, *The Civil, Ecclesiastical, Literary, Commercial and Miscellaneous History of Leeds, Halifax, Huddersfield, Bradford, Wakefield, Dewsbury, Otley, and the Manufacturing Districts of Yorkshire* (London and Leeds, 1834), p. 202.

The older Leeds broadcloth, whether common or superfine, was a plain-woven cloth, dyed black or a uniform colour, and the dressing of it was all important. When the first gentleman in Europe visited Leeds in 1806 and declared that he would wear with pride the beautiful specimens of cloth manufactured at Bean Ing that he had accepted from the firm, and when as George IV he bought at five pounds a yard a whole piece of superfine cloth that William Hirst had made from specially selected wool as a challenge to the world, these samples of Leeds manufacture would be plain, smoothfaced cloths, made from the choicest wools of Saxony or Spain, dyed from fashionable colour and finished with all the skill that Gott and Hirst could command.[111]

Gott also produced army cloths and blankets and the Leeds Directories for the early nineteenth century record that some fancy cloths, such as swansdowns, toilinets and kerseymeres, were also being manufactured locally. The main product of the Leeds manufacturers was, however, plain cloths ranging from coarse and cheap lengths to very high quality pieces fetching exceptional prices.

The woollen manufacturing area stretched much further south and south-west than the parish of Leeds alone. Wakefield was a great market centre for the textile area because of its advantageous position for communications. Its Cloth Hall was a thriving market in the eighteenth century but declined in importance and early in the nineteenth century was being used as a worsted mill.[112] In 1795 the town was described as:

> one of the most opulent of the clothing towns . . . possessing a considerable share of the business . . . the goods principally brought to this market are tammies and camlets, and also some white cloths.[113]

There were a number of fulling mills on the Calder close to the town in the 1780s and several scribbling mills are recorded near the town before 1790. By 1800 several more had opened on the western side of the town, and within a few years the first worsted mill was built.

In 1835 there was an equal number of woollen and worsted mills in the township, the five worsted mills being considerably larger than those manufacturing woollens. Elsewhere in the parish two woollen mills and one worsted mill were at work in Alverthorpe with four woollen mills in Horbury. In spite of the River Calder and Balme Beck, however, only one mill was still using water power by that date.

[111] Crump, op. cit., p. 32.
[112] J. W. Walker, *Wakefield: Its History and People* (1939), p. 400.
[113] Aiken, op. cit., p. 579.

In spite of its natural advantages Wakefield never developed into a serious rival to Leeds, Dewsbury, and Huddersfield. There appears to have been considerable opposition at times to the building of mills.

> . . . the aristocracy of Wakefield who had already made their fortunes (by commerce in the eighteenth century) refused to permit mills and factories to be established there . . .[114]

One of the entrepreneurs who met with opposition was Titus Salt, who later became world famous for his massive industrial complex and model village at Saltaire. He attempted to erect a mill at Wakefield in the 1820s but encountered much resistance and had to move from his native town to Bradford and then finally built his mill at Shipley in 1851.[115] It is difficult to gauge how successful this campaign of opposition was. Mills were built close to the centre of the town. It is not apparent how some managed to establish mills and others did not.

To the west of Wakefield the towns of Dewsbury and Batley with the surrounding villages had established a number of woollen mills by the mid 1790s although Aiken makes little mention of them in 1795. The population of Dewsbury almost doubled between 1801 and 1831 as the blanket industry and the shoddy trade were expanded.[116] Shoddy was first used in Dewsbury in the second decade of the nineteenth century but it was not until the 1830s that its use became widespread.[117]

Three mills were being used for scribbling in Dewsbury by 1790 and another six came into use in the following decade. With the exception of the River Calder, the water supply to Dewsbury, Batley and the neighbouring villages was poor and hardly sufficient to turn wheels. The small stream that flows from Birstall down through Batley, Batley Carr, and Dewsbury was very weak and provided only unreliable power. The only other reasonably strong stream in the area was the Spen flowing through Heckmondwike to the Calder, several miles to the west of Dewsbury and Batley. The lack of water power did not prevent, however, the building of mills away from the banks of the main river. There is much evidence of the early introduction of the steam engine in the area. At Morley,

114 C. Camidge, *A History of Wakefield* (1866), p. 8.
115 J. Walker, *Fortunes Made in Business* (1884), Vol. 1, 294–5.
116 *Census 1831: Abstract of Answers and Returns*, P.P. 1833 (149), XXXVI.
117 Parsons, op. cit., p. 241.

another town poorly endowed with water, a mill powered by a steam engine was built in 1790 and a few years later others were at work.[118]

As the scale of industry increased Dewsbury tended to concentrate more on stout coarse woollens such as blankets and army cloths and Batley became the centre of the shoddy and mungo trades. Heckmondwike was manufacturing carpets, rugs, and blankets and Mirfield was engaged in similar business. By 1835 there were 17 woollen mills in Batley parish, all worked by steam power. In Dewsbury, Soothill, and Ossett, 29 woollen mills were recorded most of which, again, were steam powered with the notable exceptions of Dewsbury and Sands Mills.[119]

To the south of the Calder in the area of Penistone, Thurlestone, and Denby Dale a number of small woollen mills were being operated, with the occasional worsted mill such as the one recorded at High Hoyland in 1835. There was no large scale growth in this area but ideal locations for harnessing water power were made use of and a variety of cloths produced.

Further west, however, the woollen sector of the industry had more intensively developed, Huddersfield growing as a factory town in its own right and as the commercial centre of a flourishing woollen cloth producing area. The banks of the various tributaries of the River Colne and of the river itself provided sites for a large number of woollen mills. No worsted mills were recorded in either Huddersfield or Almondbury parishes in 1835.

The town itself was rather slow to develop, but Aiken in 1795 saw it as having been 'raised from an inconsiderable place to a great degree of prosperity and population . . .'[120] Several mills were working close to the town in the 1780s, and during the first two decades of the nineteenth century the banks of the Colne supported the erection of a host of large factories including Starkey's at Longroyde Bridge, Bradley Mills and others amongst the largest in the West Riding.

[118] Crank Mill, Morley was built in about 1790 and started working in about 1792. It was constructed by Lord Dartmouth for James and Joseph Webster and was described as 'a large scribbling mill chiefly worked by steam'. Dartmouth Estate, *Terrier*, 1805, p. 239; W. Smith, *History and Antiquities of Morley* (London, 1876), p. 212; W. Smith jun., *Rambles About Morley, with Descriptive and Historical Sketches also an Account of the Rise and Progress of the Woollen Manufacture in This Place* (London, 1866), p. 87.

[119] *Factory Returns, 1835*.

[120] Aiken, op. cit., p. 552.

By the mid 1830s, 45 woollen mills were working in Huddersfield parish and another 42 in the adjoining parish of Almondbury. Water power continued to play an important role but overall more power was being generated by steam than by water at this date.

The town came to the attention of the commissioners examining the state of large towns in 1845 and their observations were very similar to those made on Bradford and Leeds:

> There are in Huddersfield many unpaved streets, many without sewers, and a considerable extent of damp and filth in the streets, courts and alleys; and in such localities, fevers and a low tone of general health prevail.[121]

In other directions, however, the town's reputation was high. It was celebrated for the manufacture of fine cloths of various types. Aiken was full of praise:

> The trade of Huddersfield comprises a large share of the clothing trade of Yorkshire, particularly the finer articles of it. These consist of broad and narrow cloths; fancy cloths, as elastics, beaverettes, etc., also honleys and kerseymeres. The qualities run from 10d. to 8s. per yard, narrows; and broads as high as the superfines of the West of England . . .[122]

Similar production was recorded in 1822, registering very little change in the types of cloth manufactured, but the town's reputation for the production of fancy cloths was increasing, particularly after the vogue of lighter more colourful materials which started in the 1820s and for which the Huddersfield manufacturers adapted their production.[123] The introduction of the jacquard loom into the area in 1830 or 1831 extended the production of fancy cloths. The popularity of waistcoatings with intricate designs increased and as it did so the designers became more and more skilful with their patterns.

Thus throughout the period from 1780 to the mid 1830s, Huddersfield concentrated on the production of high quality fancy cloths both for the home and overseas market. But some of the finest cloths appear to have been made by the small manufacturers in the villages of Saddleworth parish. Even when the industry in the area was entirely domestically based, Saddleworth's fame was spreading. Aiken stated categorically 'The finest broads in Yorkshire are made at Saddleworth' and 'Many of the superfine broads made here vie with those of the West of England'.[124] Saddleworth parish could boast no large town nor indeed any settlement larger

[121] *Second Report on the State of Large Towns*, op. cit., p. 144.
[122] Aiken, op. cit., p. 554.
[123] T. Langdale, *Topographical Dictionary of Yorkshire* (1822), p. 322.
[124] Aiken, op. cit., pp. 554, 558.

than a village. It marketed its cloths through Huddersfield, twelve miles away over Dean Head and Foul Moss and used the power of innumerable little streams flowing down from the moors to turn the machinery in its mills. The latter were invariably small. The 52 recorded by the Factory Inspector in 1835 showed a predominant dependance on water power, only nine steam engines being in use at that date. The overall average power in use per mill was under 10 horse power and the normal mill employed less than thirty persons. When one deducts from these figures the two or three large mills including Wrigley's at Dob Cross and Taylor and Gibson's at Spring Head with a total power between them of 54 horse power and employing 687 workers then one realizes that most of the other mills must have been very small indeed.[125]

TABLE 7

WOOLLEN MILLS IN THE PARISH OF SADDLEWORTH AS RECORDED BY THE FACTORY INSPECTOR IN 1835

Distribution of Power in 52 Woollen Mills

Steam Engines

	39/30 hp.	29/20 hp.	19/10 hp.	Under 10 hp.	Total
No. of Engines	1	2	4	2	9
Power	30	46	42	12	130

Water-Wheels

	Over 50 hp.	29/20 hp.	19/10 hp.	Under 10 hp.	Total
No. of Wheels	1	1	19	30	51
Power	50	20	233	149½	452½

Total Power	582½ hp		
Actual Power Used	518½ hp.	Average Power Used	10 hp.
Total Hands Employed	1536	Average No. of Workers employed	30

Source: *Factory Returns* 1835

Very little information survives about the early mills in the parish. A mill at Quick was probably scribbling wool in 1782 and another commenced at Upper Mill in the following year.[126] G. and J. Knight were scribbling wool at Stonebreakes in 1794.[127] The limited and

[125] *Factory Returns, 1835*; *Factories Inquiry Commission, Supplementary Reports*, Part II, C.2. Mills nos. 249 and 237.
[126] Ibid., Mills nos. 233 and 237.
[127] Sun C.R. 3/627881/1794.

incomplete information contained in the Report of the 1833 Commission on the Employment of Children suggests many mills were erected in the second and third decades of the nineteenth century. On the other hand one might have expected that many of the fulling mills recorded in the eighteenth century had taken up scribbling by that time.[128]

Elsewhere in the West Riding woollen mills were to be found in almost all localities, and indeed elsewhere in Yorkshire. The other major centre, however, was Halifax of which some mention has been made in connexion with the production of woollen cloth, when worsted manufacture there was being discussed. Aiken records that the town and neighbouring villages were a centre for the:

> ... manufacturing of kerseys, and half-thicks, also of Bockings, and baize, principally in the hands of merchants of property in the neighbourhood of Sowerby and made in the valley from Sowerby Bridge up to Ripponden and higher. The whole of the British Navy is clothed from this source. Large quantities are also, in times of peace, sent to Holland, and some to America. But the most promising branch of manufacturing is that of cloth and coatings which has been introduced within these four years by a few persons of enterprise who have, at vast expense, erected mills on the Calder and other smaller streams, the falls of water in this uneven country being very favourable for that purpose. The success of these factories has been such as to excite the jealousy of the Leeds merchants, who are accustomed to buy the same article from the lower manufacturers at their cloth hall.[129]

Although, as has been shown, worsted mills outnumbered woollen mills in the town itself in 1835, woollen mills predominated in some parts of the parish. Ten were recorded in Rastrick, six in Elland, four in Hipperholme and fourteen elsewhere. Some of these mills were quite large. They had an average of over 23 horse power, two having 40 horse power water-wheels. Water power was of prime importance for the woollen mills but steam provided most of the power for worsted manufacture. Woollen mills employed an average of sixty-two workers.

The factory inspectors also visited woollen mills in almost all the villages in the area bounded by Huddersfield, Halifax, Leeds, and Wakefield and between the former two towns and the Lancashire and Derbyshire borders. Forty-nine mills were traced in Almondbury parish and twenty-eight in the parish of Kirkburton and the inspectors had to travel much further afield to visit isolated mills.

[128] See Table 1. Eleven Fulling Mills were recorded in the Saddleworth area in 1780.

[129] Aiken, op. cit., p. 559.

Although one cannot stipulate, too strictly, the different localities for different types of cloth one can generalize, without too much danger, about the specialities of various areas, and show that in some parts production was concentrated on certain types of cloth. Aiken divided the manufacture between mixed cloths and white cloth:

The mixed cloth manufacturers reside partly in the villages belonging to the parish of Leeds; but chiefly at Morley, Guildersome, Adwalton, Driglington, Pudsey, Farsley, Calverley, Eccleshal, Idle, Baildon, Yeadon, Guiseley, Rawden and Horsforth, in or bordering upon the vale of Aire, chiefly west of Leeds; and at Batley, Dewsbury, Ossett, Horbury and Kirkburton west of Wakefield, in or near the vale of Calder. Not a single manufacturer is to be found more than one mile east, or two north of Leeds; nor are there many in the town of Leeds and those only in the outskirts.

The white cloth is manufactured chiefly at Alverthorpe, Birstal, Hopton, Mirfield, Orchet, Cleckheaton, Littletown, Bowling and Shipley; a tract of country forming an oblique belt across the hills that separate the vale of Calder from the vale of Aire, beginning about a mile west of Wakefield leaving Huddersfield and Bradford a little to the left, terminating at Shipley on the Aire, and not coming within less than about six miles of Leeds on the right. The districts of the white and coloured cloth manufacturing are generally distinct, but are a little intermixed at the south east and north west extremities.[130]

This description applies to the broad cloth manufacture. The narrow cloths, the chief of which was kersey, were more the concern of the manufacturers in and to the west and south west of Huddersfield. Production in this area concentrated more on fancy cloths of all qualities but including some of very high class. Saddleworth was, however, also noted for its fine broad cloths.[131]

The Location of the Wool Textile Industry in Yorkshire: 1770–1840

An overall view of the seventy years from 1770 to 1840 suggests two main trends in the location of woollen and worsted mills within the county. One appears to have been a movement towards a greater concentration of mills within a somewhat smaller geographical area, in other words an increased delineation of the wool textile area within the West Riding and accompanying that, a more noticeable division between woollen cloth and worsted cloth producing areas. Many of the mills that at one time existed on the outer fringes of the textile areas had been converted to other uses by 1835. Those that remained by that date were almost without

[130] Ibid., pp. 573–4.
[131] Crump and Ghorbal, op. cit., pp. 128–32.

exception very small, still reliant on water power and often, when their location is examined, their development restricted by their sites. Some of them appear to have survived through specialization on a certain type of production, some through their links with other establishments or their ability to tap a local trained labour supply. They were often disadvantaged by their distance from market centres and the new transport routes. There is some evidence to suggest that these were amongst the mills that were most affected by trade depression. Several of them appear to have gone out of use at times, only to restart production when trade was prospering.

The other trend was towards a greater concentration of mills close to the major towns and along the main lines of communication. The mills of the eighteenth century were very widely spread throughout the area with really little noticeable increase in numbers close to the established towns. The availability of water power was initially paramount and the best sites rarely coincided with the major towns. Leeds, Bradford, Halifax, and Huddersfield, and to a lesser extent Wakefield, do not appear to have attracted a large number of mills close to them at this early date. The use of coal, the demand for larger labour forces and the need for closer proximity to markets and transport facilities were clearly however having their effects by the 1820s when in Leeds and Bradford, in particular, but also in Halifax and Keighley potential mill builders were competing for sites on the fringes of the early development. A good example of this was the steady development through the 1820s and 1830s between the River Aire and the Kirkstall Road in Leeds upstream from Park Mills. Sites with sufficient water available for the various processes that required it were certainly in short supply close to the main market towns by the 1830s. It is less clear however, that there was at any time a desperate shortage of sites where water power could be harnessed, a problem which appears to have occurred in the West Country.[132] Some streams, for example the Colne and Upper Holme, were heavily utilized, others were capable of much more use, particularly in the worsted manufacturing area but also along many of the tributaries of the middle stretches of the main rivers. Certainly the best sites, particularly those where the water power could be utilized without major damming and leating works were mostly used. Those that required somewhat more investment and enterprise in harnessing the water were often

[132] Mann, op. cit., pp. 133, 155.

disregarded and there appear to have been a few big water channelling schemes for West Riding mills.

The industry by the 1830s had established a geographical pattern both within the county and between the rural and urban areas that was not to be fundamentally altered in the following 100 years except in so far as urban development encroached upon the urban fringe mills and in many cases the originally completely rural ones.

2

DEVELOPMENTS IN THE SIZE AND DESIGN OF WOOL TEXTILE MILLS

The Early Mill Buildings

The mills of the 1780s were far removed in size and design from those being constructed towards the middle of the following century. The small building of the earlier period bore little resemblance to the large complexes of buildings that had developed on many sites by the 1830s. Few of the very early mills remain today in their original state. New wings, extra storeys, the ravages of fire and flood and extensive programmes of rebuilding in the second half of the nineteenth century, have more often than not altered original buildings beyond recognition. In the West Riding of Yorkshire there are, however, a few mill buildings still standing that date back to the 1780s and contemporary sketches and plans provide more information. These show rectangular structures of a width seldom more than 30 ft. with perhaps two to four storeys along with cellar and garret rooms.

The main features of such buildings were their gable ends, their low and narrow rooms, walls wider at the base than at the top, often comparatively few and small windows and a total reliance on the traditional building materials of stone and timber, with occasionally some brick. These features were caused partly by the requirements of the machinery that the buildings housed and by the limitations posed by the materials and methods of the builders. The foundations would have been solid to stand up to possible undermining by the millstream and the weight of the storeys that they supported; the walls would have been thicker at their base for similar reasons. The cellar was often used as a store for raw materials and finished goods and perhaps as a stable. The width of the building at this early period was restricted by the need for adequate light to work the machinery. The length of the mill was limited by the power of the wheel or steam engine. The further away from the source of power that machinery was positioned, the more power was lost in the gearing and transmitting machinery. Mill rooms tended to be low. W. D. Shepherd has suggested that in most of the earlier textile mills the height from floor to floor was over 10 ft.[1] In the West Riding the more common height was 8 or 9 ft. The size of the early machinery did not require any greater height than this and because of the limitations on the size of the buildings there was no desire to waste space. Moreover, lower rooms wasted less heat and could be kept warmer. Even in the later larger factories ceiling heights appear rarely to have exceeded nine feet until after the 1840s.

Few of the early buildings were architect designed. The larger millowners like Benjamin Gott and John Marshall called on the assistance of architects and engineers to design and calculate the load bearing strength of their main buildings.[2] Most textile entrepreneurs learned from each other's experience. The designs of the smaller mills rarely differed radically from each other and any smaller innovatory practices in construction were carefully watched by neighbours. Joseph Rogerson kept a close eye on new ideas in his neighbourhood.[3] The mill owner would also often supervise and assist in the building of the mill, employing craftsmen directly and overseeing their work. It was perhaps unusual for the smaller entrepreneur to put the construction of his building entirely in the hands of others.

The floors, doors, beams and window frames were all made of wood as was the roof frame. The small size of the windows, in spite of the requirements for light in the mill, was partly the consequence of the traditional window size in other buildings and possibly the result of the unwillingness of the builders to do anything that might weaken the structure of the building. Occasionally an early mill was built with wider windows in the upper storey, after the style of the weavers' cottages and workshops where long horizontally linked windows were characteristic.

The first of the West Riding woollen mills were small, sturdy, functional buildings of a plain and simple design, often the only

[1] W. D. Shepherd, A.R.I.B.A., Unpublished thesis for the Institute entitled *Early Industrial Buildings, 1700–1850*, Chapter 1, p. 6. My thanks are due to the author for loaning me his personal copy.

[2] Both Gott and Marshall consulted William Fairbairn. See Sir William Fairbairn, *On the Application of Cast and Wrought Iron to Building Purposes* (4th ed., London, 1870); W. Fairbairn, *Treatise on Mills and Millwork* (London, 1861–3), W. G. Rimmer, *Marshalls' of Leeds: Flax Spinners 1788–1886* (Cambridge, 1960). Hives and Atkinson's flax mill and John Wilkinson's cotton mill, both at Leeds, were designed by John Clark: J. Tann, *The Development of the Factory* (London, 1970), p. 169.

[3] E. Hargrave and W. B. Crump, 'The Diary of Joseph Rogerson, Scribbling Miller of Bramley, 1808–1814', in W. B. Crump (ed.), *The Leeds Woollen Industry*, op. cit. The manuscript diary is in the care of the Thoresby Society, Leeds.

variety in their styles caused by the restrictions and requirements of their sites and occasionally by the addition of small extra sheds and other buildings attached to the mill. The low garret or attic rooms were used for storage and hand processes, the attached or adjacent small buildings as offices, warehouses and stabling. There were often a separate drying house and cottages and workshops in the mill yard.

The early mill normally had an external water-wheel either on one end of the building or, less often, adjoining the side. Internal water-wheels appear to have become more common by the 1820s. The Dartmouth Estate owned several mills with internal wheels. Blackmoor Holme Mill and Bankgate Mill on the Holm Brook near Slaithwaite are examples. The former was a building of traditional size and shape 85 ft. long by 34 ft. wide, with three storeys and a loft and built of stone with a slate roof. There was a 28 ft. fall of water for the wheel which had wooden axles and arms and buckets with iron shields and was capable of generating about eight horsepower for the nine months of the year when there was sufficient water. Bankgate Mill was a rather larger group of buildings of varying dates, the first erected in about 1797. It had a large wood and iron internal wheel 4 ft. wide and turned by a fall of water of 36 ft. It too was restricted to working for only nine months each year but power was supplemented by a steam engine.[4]

One of the best preserved of the early mills is Hartlington Mill near Burnsall, which, although originally used for cotton manufacture was later adapted for worsted spinning. Its building is possibly fairly typical of the early mills. It is rectangular in shape, had two storeys and an attic and was powered by a small water-wheel fed from a dam and reservoir a few yards up the valley. Adjacent to the mill were a house and a number of smaller buildings.[5]

Sands Mill near Dewsbury is another example. The building still stands in a semi derelict state, following several recent fires, and a stone in the wall at the west end is carved with the date 1751.[6] It was a water-powered mill and, although the wheel has long since disappeared, the silted up mill stream is still evident, as is the former position of the wheel and its transmitting axle. The building is rectangular and of two storeys with a basement half above and

[4] See Dartmouth Estate, *Slaithwaite Terrier*, 1828 and Figure 4.
[5] At map reference O.S. SE042609.
[6] Sands Mill had a variety of uses between 1751 and 1835. In 1794 it was being employed as a 'fulling, rasping, chipping and friezing mill'. Scribbling machines were installed in the following year. In 1797 one building was being used as an oil mill. Sun C.R. 4/623600/1794; 12/648173/1795; 19/671207/1797.

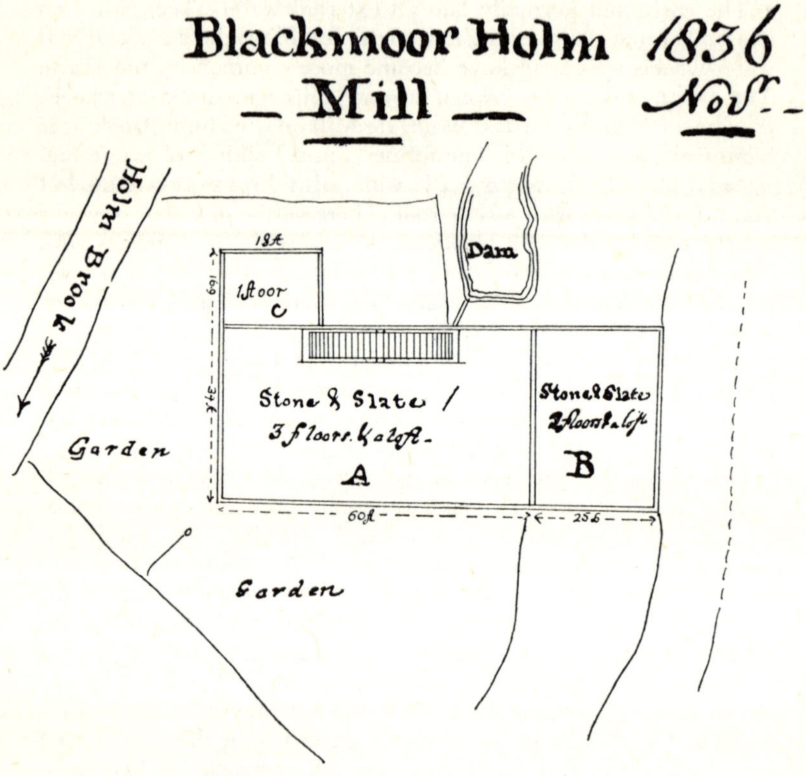

FIG. 4a. Blackmoor Holm Mill, Slaithwaite

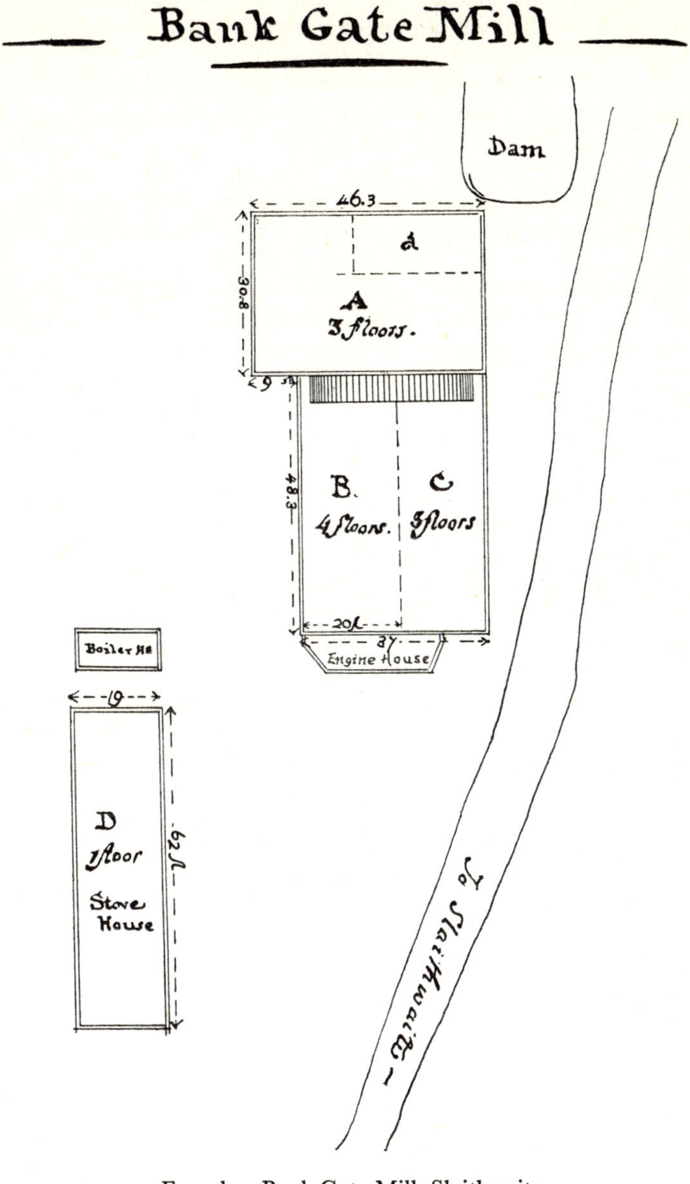

FIG. 4b. Bank Gate Mill, Slaithwaite

half below ground level. It is approximately 35 ft. high from ground level to roof peak and is about 100 ft. long by 30 ft. wide. The wheel was enclosed in a wheelhouse on the south side of the building. The mill was built of stone and timber and had a particularly solid base perhaps because of the flooding which is not infrequent along this stretch of the River Calder.

In the Huddersfield area, Shaw Carr Wood Mill at Slaithwaite provides another example of this type of simple rectangular mill building. The mill was constructed in 1787. Other small buildings were later erected nearby. The main mill building was 37 ft. wide by 81 ft. long and had three storeys and an attic. A sketch plan of it survives in the Dartmouth Estate *Terrier* and is reproduced[7] (Fig. 5).

Some of the later mills of, for example, the second and third decades of the nineteenth century, maintained the simple proportions but displayed rather more exterior ornateness. Arkwright's Masson Mill at Cromford, built in 1783, in a way set this example. Its exterior was a strange version of Georgian architecture, a notable feature being the shape of the windows which suggested that there should have been more than just a factory behind them.[8]

This desire for an ornate exterior façade was, however, less common at this period in Yorkshire than elsewhere; the Yorkshire entrepreneur being perhaps less worried about appearances and more concerned about the function and the layout of the building. The first change to be noted in the West Riding was one of scale. The small rectangular stone scribbling mills, very similar in design to the earlier fulling mills, played little part in the development of an industrial landscape. By the early 1790s, however, consideration was being given to much larger buildings that were to change the face of the West Riding and the scale of manufacture.

One of the first to be constructed was Park Mill in Leeds. On a pleasant meadow by the River Aire called Bean Ing, Benjamin Gott and Henry Wormald erected a factory in 1792. Crump described the edifice thus:

> Park Mill, as the factory was called, is a red brick structure surrounding three courtyards; the first, or northern one, wide but of little depth; the second to the south east of great size; and a third smaller one to the south west. The scale of the whole is impressive at the present day, and to the relatively small Leeds community of 1800 it must have represented an enterprise of unprecedented magnitude.[9]

[7] See Figure 5 and Dartmouth Estate, *Slaithwaite Terrier*, 1828.
[8] J. Tann, *The Development of the Factory*, op. cit., p. 156.
[9] Crump, op. cit., p. 173.

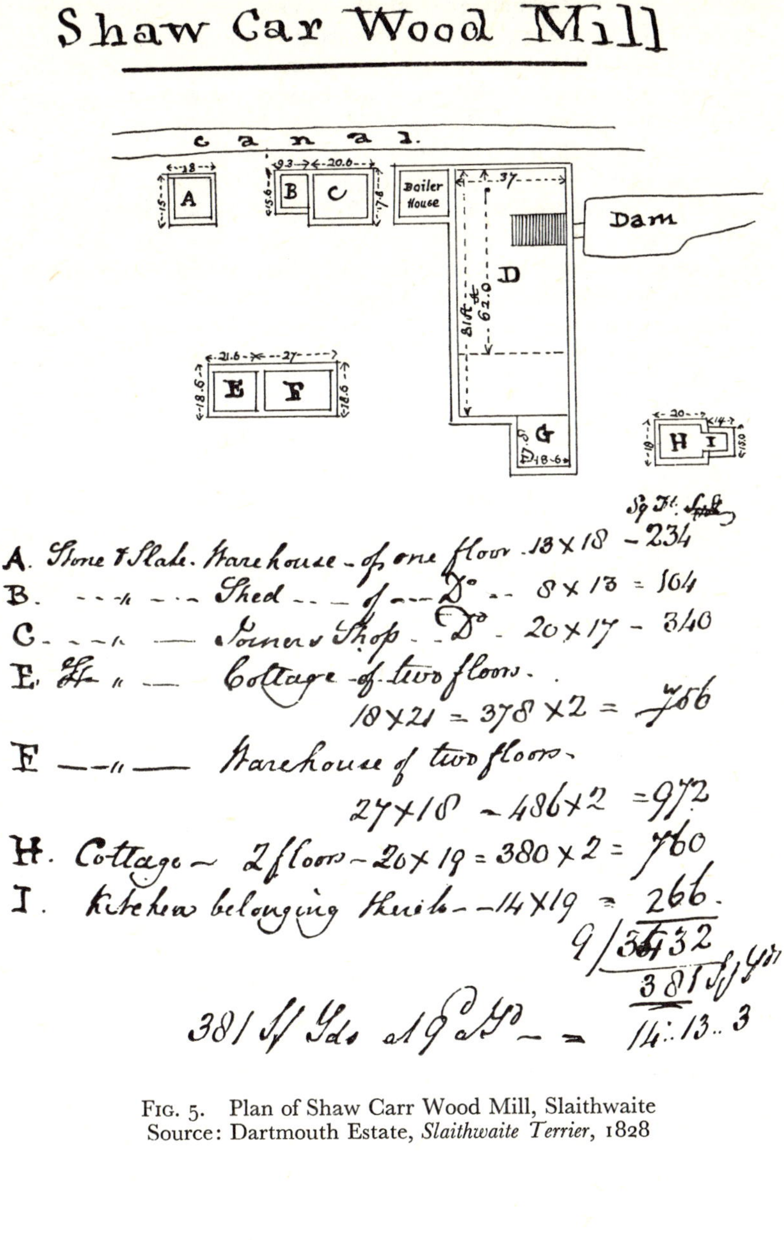

FIG. 5. Plan of Shaw Carr Wood Mill, Slaithwaite
Source: Dartmouth Estate, *Slaithwaite Terrier*, 1828

The Bean Ing estate was added to and altered a great deal during the nineteenth century and in the 1960s the buildings were demolished. However, from various sketch plans and comments amongst the Gott papers one can reconstruct a picture of the original mill building of 1792.[10] As Crump pointed out, it was planned on a huge scale for the period, springing out of nothing. Although the mill was destroyed by fire in August 1799 one can gauge its size from the fact that it was insured for £5,400 in 1794, and for £6,000 three years later.[11] The building had four storeys and was L-shaped. In spite of the length of the building, its width was still restricted to less than 40 ft. and even this width would have required at least two rows of columns.

During the remaining years of the 1790s other buildings were erected on the site. New hand-weaving shops were incorporated and warehouses and workshops were constructed on the east side of the yard, stables and sheds to the north. Seven cottages and a new mill for grinding dyeing wares and a woollen drying stovehouse, with a drying chamber over it, were built on the west side of the yard.

After the disastrous fire of 1799, the main building had to be reconstructed and the rebuilding was to much the same design as the previous mill[12] A manuscript plan of April 1806 shows a four-storey building, 200 ft. long, 34 ft. wide, with a wing, giving the building an L-shape again, used as spinning rooms. Other development took place in 1802 so that by 1806 a large industrial complex for the period had come into being, far removed from the little scribbling mills described earlier. The manuscript plan of 1806 and sections of the buildings show both the scale of the building and of the development that had taken place within the span of a few years. A few similar but smaller factories soon followed in Leeds and elsewhere but remained the exception rather than the rule until the 1820s. The first major change in construction technique was the substitution of iron for wood.

The Use of Iron

Iron was first used in textile mill construction in 1792 at Derby where William Strutt built a six storey calico mill. There, cast-iron columns supported brick arches with wrought iron tie rods. Within

[10] A number of early plans of the mill survive in the Boulton and Watt MSS and the Gott MSS. One, drawn for fire insurance purposes, is reproduced in Fig. 6.
[11] Sun C.R. 4/627124/1794; 19/667675/1797.
[12] See Gott MSS, no. 232.

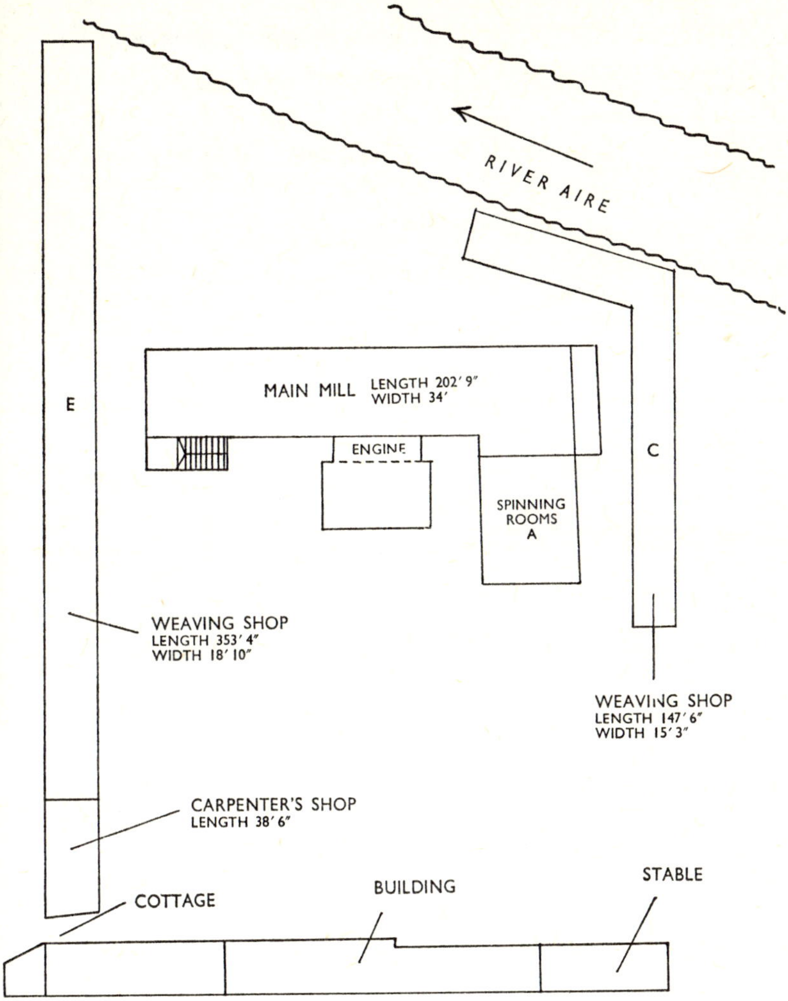

Fig. 6. Plan of Park Mills, Leeds, in April 1806

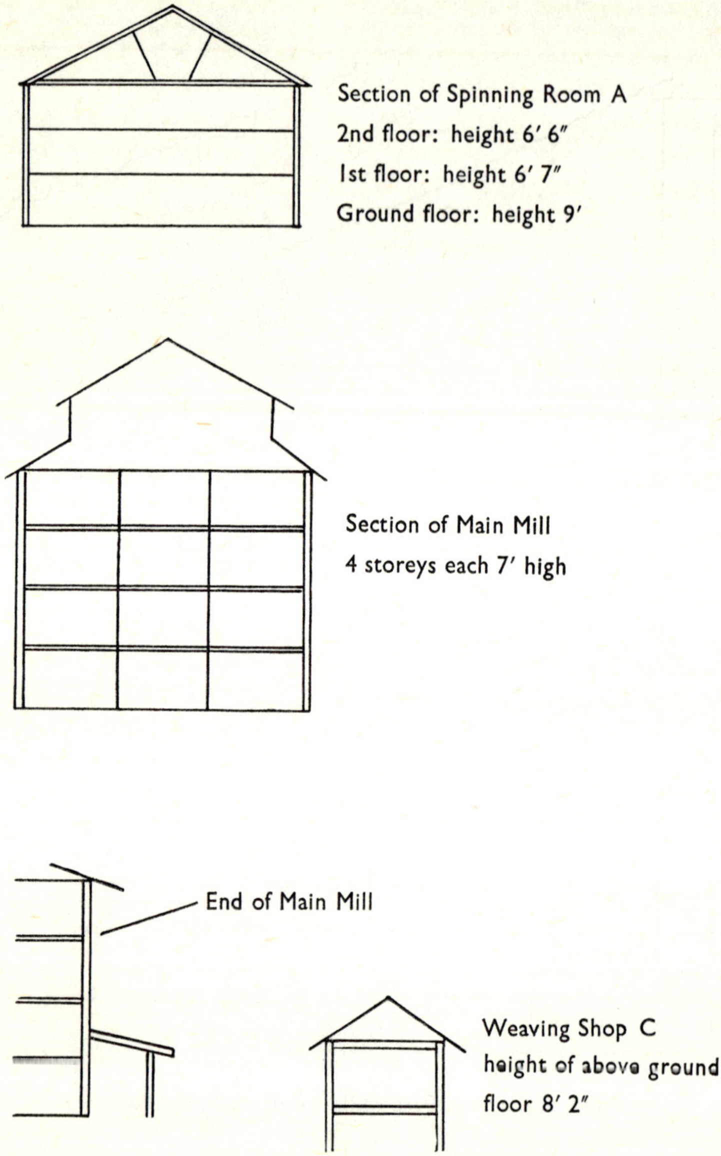

FIG. 7. Sections of the main mill buildings at Park Mills, Bean Ing, Leeds, in April 1806

a year he commenced buildings of similar construction nearby at Milford and Belper and with these three edifices pioneered a more widespread use of iron and other fireproofing methods in industrial building.[13] Cast-iron window and door frames and the use of iron for roof trusses were soon to follow. The first mill building with both beams and columns of iron was at Shrewsbury where Charles Bage constructed a flax mill in 1797.[14] Five years later Messrs Phillips and Lee used similar building methods for their Salford cotton spinning factory.[15] William Fairbairn, who thought it was the first iron-framed factory, described it thus:

The mill is a large building of about 140 feet long, 42 feet wide and seven stories high. It contains about 648 square yards on each floor; and the iron beams which extend across the building, from wall to wall at regular distances of nine feet are divided to three lengths. . . . Altogether the experiment, considering the construction of such buildings at that time, was eminently successful and became the pioneer of that system of fireproof structure which now distinguishes the manufacturing districts of this country.

From 1801 until 1824 little or no variation took place in the form of beams and for a quarter of a century Messrs. Philips and Lees' mill offered the model for similar buildings.[16]

When Phillip Bewicke, a director of the Sun Fire Office, visited the mill in October 1806 he was very impressed and recorded that the mill was 'deemed incombustible' and was therefore not insured.[17]

Other developments followed, including the introduction of iron roof frames, and the use of iron in construction became more common but by no means frequent. In the West Riding Messrs Benyon and Bage built a flax mill in 1803, which was described as 'completely fire proof, no timber whatever being used in the building'.[18] Fireproofing took various forms in different mills and the use of the term 'fireproof' did not necessarily mean that the mill had an iron frame. Thus some attempt was made to lessen fire risk at Gott's main mill by 1816 by covering the floor with sheet iron.[19]

[13] J. M. Richards, *The Functional Tradition in Early Industrial Buildings* (London, 1958), p. 76. See also T. Bannister, 'The First Iron-Framed Buildings', *Architectural Review*, 107, 1950; A. W. Skempton and H. R. Johnson, 'The First Iron Frames', *Architectural Review*, 131, 1962; J. Tann, op. cit., pp. 135–47.

[14] W. G. Rimmer, 'The Castle Foregate Flax Mill', *Transactions of the Shropshire Archaeological Society*, LVI, 1959.

[15] W. Fairbairn, *On the Application of . . . Iron . . .*, op. cit., pp. 2–4; Tann, op. cit., p. 143.

[16] W. Fairbairn, *On the Application of . . . Iron . . .* , op. cit., p. 4.

[17] Sun Fire Office, *Special Report Book*, MS 11,935A, Vol. 1., p. 27.

[18] Tann, op. cit., pp. 137, 139.

[19] Sun C. R. 114/916916/1816.

But a new mill building constructed at Bean Ing in 1824 had cast-iron pillars and beams and iron roof trusses.[20] This was probably the gig, brushing, shearing and spinning mill with an iron roof recorded in 1827. In the same year some of the pressing and weaving shops had iron roofs and a wool warehouse had iron doors and an iron frame.[21]

Fairbairn recorded that he had had the contract for:

> . . . The construction of several extensive fireproof buildings, one for Messrs. Gott of Leeds, and another for Mr. Wood of Bradford; and entertaining doubts as to the security of the cast iron beams, a series of experiments was made on a large scale in order to give confidence in the safety of the construction.[22]

Gott had apparently expressed concern about the strength of the 18ft. beam span.

Boulton and Watt were responsible for the installation of a gas plant at John Wood's mill at Bradford. Cross-sections of the buildings and a plan of the mill were drawn for the installation and show the iron beams and columns.[23]

In the early 1820s, Abraham Rhodes built a large fireproof mill at Woodhouse Carr near Leeds which he used for both woollen and worsted manufacture. This was a five storey building of considerable size. It was continually referred to in its insurance as a fireproof mill to after 1840. Other fireproof buildings were constructed on the premises during the 1820s and 1830s, Rhodes presumably being quite certain that the extra cost involved was worthwhile.[24]

Messrs Titley, Tatham and Walker's flax mill in Water Lane, Leeds, constructed in 1808, although not mentioned as being fireproof at the time, was later so called in insurance policies.[25] John Greenwood, Lister Ellis and Jonas Whitaker had a cotton mill at Burley near Otley that was fireproof in 1812 according to the insurance details of it.[26] Marshall and Company's third mill built on the south side of Water Lane, Leeds in 1815 and 1816 was a six storey rectangular building with iron beams and columns,

[20] Sun C.R. 158/1055369/1827; Tann, op. cit., p. 145.
[21] Sun C.R. 158/1055369/1827.
[22] W. Fairbairn, *On the Application of Iron* . . ., op. cit., p. 5. There was correspondence between Fairbairn and Gott about the problems. See Gott MSS no. 152. Letter from Fairbairn and Lilly to B. Gott and Sons, 21 October 1824.
[23] See Fig. 12 and Boulton and Watt MSS, Portfolio 508.
[24] Sun C.R. 150/1032216/1825; 167/1077705/1828; 187/1120142/1831; 189/1135138/1832; 237/1248002/1837; 249/1280878/1838.
[25] Sun C.R. 176/1093261/1829; Rimmer, op. cit., p. 124.
[26] Sun C.R. 100/868473/1812.

approximately 150 ft. long by 40 ft. wide and in 1813 Thomas Micklethwaite was using an 'iron warehouse' in Simpsons Fold nearby.[27]

A number of other examples can be cited in and after the second decade of the nineteenth century but they were by far the exception rather than the rule throughout the first half of the century. The high building costs involved may have been prohibitive for many mill builders and although the saving on insurance premiums were substantial they could not hope to outweigh the extra building costs. Insurance valuations suggest that the use of iron could increase building costs by perhaps 100 per cent. A three storey fireproof mill at Meltham in 1828, for example, was insured for 30 shillings per square yard of floor area compared with a typical figure for a similar sized mill of the same period of between 15 and 20 shillings.[28]

And fireproof mills were certainly not immune from fire destruction. In December 1824, Airedale Mill at Leeds, which was described as a fireproof building of 'all stone and iron', suffered a major fire caused by the ignition of oil-saturated waste.[29]

Vertical and Horizontal Growth

Mill design retained, on the whole, its rectangular shape throughout the period in spite of the increase in the size of buildings. The mills expanded upwards to five or six or occasionally more storeys and outwards to a length of over 100 yds in some cases. A mill in Mill Street, off Canal Road, in Bradford had a frontage of about 370 ft. in the 1840s and Dean Clough Mills in Halifax were about the same length. Both were no more than 40 ft. wide. The second mill building at Dean Clough was, however, 450 ft. long and 150 ft. wide.[30] When in 1851 Titus Salt constructed his mill at Shipley the buildings took on an even greater scale.

There were, however, exceptions to the general rule. A number of single storey mill buildings were constructed, in the early years of the nineteenth century, with skylight roofs which provided better

[27] Rimmer, op. cit., p. 135; Sun C.R. 214/1195192/1835; 107/888285/1813.

[28] The fireproof mill at Meltham was used for cotton spinning. It had three stories and a floor area of 800 sq. yds. It was insured for £1,200. At about the same period the insurance on the various mills on Lord Dartmouth's estate varied from 14 shillings to 18 shilling per square yard of floor area.

[29] *Norwich Union Minute Book No. 2*. Entries for 6 and 20 December 1824; Leeds and Yorkshire Fire Office, *Secretary's Book, No. 1*. Entry for 28 July 1825. See bibliography for locations.

[30] Ordnance Survey, *5' Town Plans of Bradford and Halifax*, 1851–2, British Museum Map Room.

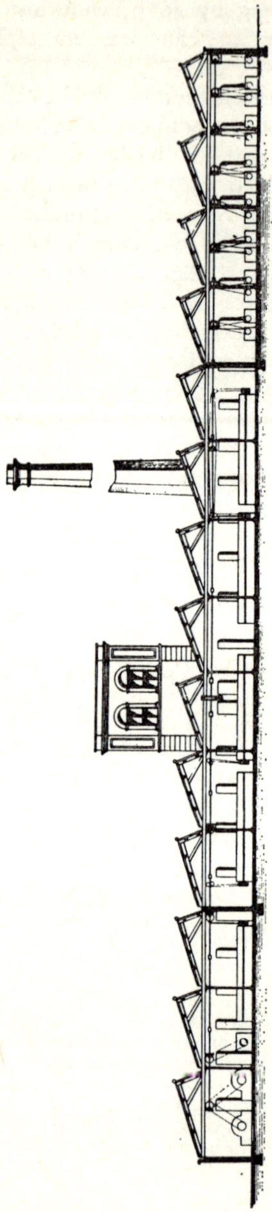

Fig. 8. Section of a single-storey mill and weaving shed

lighting than that obtainable in the traditional design and which allowed a much greater amount of open floor space to be used. One such place was Wellington Mills on the Kirkstall Road in Leeds close to Gott's Park Mills. Here the original building had a single storey measuring 140 ft. square, although other two and three storey constructions were erected adjoining. The building still survives although not as a textile mill. Marshall's Temple Mill in Leeds built in 1841 was a single storey building of exceptional design. It had a flat roof and a system of round skylights. Considerable thought and research took place before the decision was made to construct the mill. William Fairbairn and David Roberts provided two designs for Marshall; Fairbairn's was for a seven storey warehouse and a six storey mill and Robert's was for a single storey building.[31] Marshall estimated the cost of the competing buildings and discovered that a single storey building of the same floor area as the six storey mill worked out at six shillings per square yard cheaper. He concluded that:

> . . . in no case could the one storey be more expensive than the six storey. We have a model one third the full size and six feet high by 24 feet each way put up on boards on Mill C yard by which we can compare accurately the light given on the two plans of the mill. Light by the skylights (of the one storey mill) though only half the area of the other windows is clearly and decidedly better and more uniform and there is no difficulty from shadows from it being too vertical; the height of the room, number of skylights and reflected light from floor prevent this . . . The concentration of the one storey plan I still think a great advantage for arrangement of work, overlooking etc. . .[32]

Single storey buildings were not however common in the Yorkshire wool textile industry before the introduction of power loom weaving. Then the single storey weaving shed became a frequent addition to mill premises and many examples are still being used to this day.

Another major change in mill development between the 1780s and the 1830s was the construction alongside the main mill of other buildings for various uses. Although in the late eighteenth century there were occasionally other small buildings on the mill site most of the early scribbling premises seem to have consisted of single buildings housing all the processes being carried out and being used for the warehousing of raw materials and finished products, as well as including under their roofs counting houses, offices, stabling,

[31] Rimmer, op. cit., pp. 202–3.
[32] Ibid., p. 203.

workshops and even living accommodation. For example a mill at Farnley near Leeds included a scribbling mill, cottage, barn, joiner's shop and counting house 'all under one roof' in 1785.[33]

By the early years of the nineteenth century quite large complexes of buildings had been developed at some mills. Gott's premises at Bean Ing in 1794 consisted only of:

. . . A stable and shed adjoining . . .
. . . Workshops and warehouses adjoining . . .
. . . 7 cottages . . .
. . . Engine house and boiler house in one building . . .
. . . Large buildings including dyehouse, warehouse, counting houses, press shops and roving shops all under one roof . . .

In 1827 the same firm insured on the same site:

. . . Fulling, Scribbling, Carding and Cloth Pressing Mill (by machinery only) all communicating . . .
. . . Wool warehouse, hand spinning and burling rooms all under one roof . . . communicating with the mill . . .
. . . Cloth friezing and steaming shops all under one roof adjoining the mill . . .
. . . building used as warehouses with small room therein used for drying teazles . . .
. . . Warehouse, teazle rooms, dressing and weaving shops all communicating and with a cloth dryhouse . . .
. . . Dyehouse and gas house and glossing shop . . .
. . . Counting house and offices . . .
. . . Stables . . .
. . . Weaving shops . . .
. . . Two tenements in the tenure of servants . . .
. . . Weaving shops and lasting rooms . . .
. . . Scouring house with hand spinning rooms over . . .
. . . Steam dyehouse adjoining the last above mentioned . . .
. . . Building used as mechanics workshop, oil and dye warerooms and weaving shops . . .[34]

He also had other buildings used as warehouses and counting houses elsewhere in Leeds, and other insurance policies for about the same period suggest there were other cottages and dyehouses at Bean Ing.

Gott at Bean Ing and John Brooke, near Huddersfield, were possibly the two largest manufacturers of woollen cloth in the County. Brooke employed over 1,000 persons at his mill in the

[33] Sun C.R. 8/636964/1795.
[34] Sun C.R. 5/627124/1794; 158/1055369/1827.

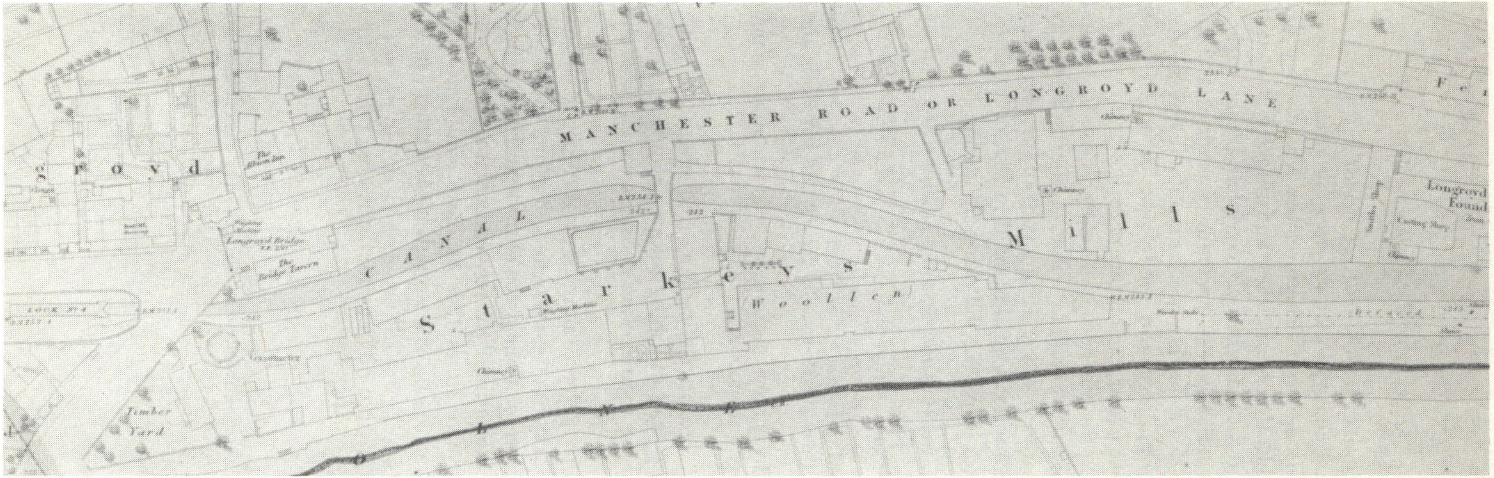

FIG. 9. Starkey's Mills, Huddersfield

Reproduced from the Ordnance Survey 5 ft. town plan of Huddersfield published in 1851

early 1830s and Benjamin Gott had 1,120 workers at Park Mills in 1830.[35] One of the largest factory sites by area, however, was Starkey's Mill at Longroyde Bridge on the Manchester Road just outside Huddersfield. Messrs Starkey and Buckley started building this mill in 1819 and it was virtually complete by the early 1830s.[36] In 1834 the firm had three 28 horsepower engines and employed 521 workers.[37] At this date they were manufacturing in three large rectangular mill buildings and using over a dozen other small buildings for various processes and purposes. Their mill site stretched about 350 yds along the northern bank of the River Colne and either side of the Huddersfield Canal.[38] One of the mill buildings (the East Factory) was 100 yds long. The layout of the premises showing their extent and complexity is illustrated in Fig. 9. Their insurance policies in the 1830s listed the following buildings:

Two Wool spinning, weaving and finishing buildings of five storeys and an attic.
The Cross Factory of four storeys and an attic used for spinning
Press Shops
Boiler and Wool Drying House
The Old Factory of three stories used for fulling and scribbling and housing a steam engine.
The East Factory of five storeys and an attic used for scribbling, spinning and finishing and housing a steam engine Boiler House.[39]

Other mills had separate drying houses, dyehouses, engine rooms, workshops, burling and finishing shops, counting houses, hand spinning and weaving rooms, often cottages, sometimes schools and chapels.

There was clearly therefore not just an increase in the number of mills in the period between the 1780s and 1835 but also in the physical size of mills. The average floor space of mills and ancillary buildings in the earlier decade probably rarely exceeded 1,000 sq. yds. At the later date four or five times that amount would not have been unusual. In the late 1840s, when rough measurement from maps is possible, the average ground floor area of the mills and ancillary buildings in the township of Dewsbury was about 1,750 sq. yds and

[35] Crump, op. cit., p. 58.
[36] *Factories Inquiry Commission, Supplementary Reports, 1834*, Part II, C.2., Mill no. 134.
[37] The mill was described as being used for all processes of woollen manufacture.
[38] Ordnance Survey, *5' Town Plan of Huddersfield*, 1851–2. Hud. P.L.
[39] Sun C.R. 184/1114570/1830; 190/1131936/1831; 214/1197383/1835; 225/1216363/1836; 244/1268084/1838;

the average for the total area was probably three times this figure or more.[40]

Rate surveys give more detailed evidence. The one for Warley township in Halifax parish in 1829 shows that the rural mills were rather smaller. Many did remain unaltered for a long period after they were built. Longbottom Mill was perhaps typical of many. It consisted of a four storey mill building with a floor area of 1,660 sq. yds and three warehouses, two drying houses and a weaving shop, all single storey buildings with floor areas totalling a little over 1,000 sq. yds.[41] By comparison a mill in King's Cross Road, Halifax twenty-two years later powered by an average size 24 horsepower steam engine consisted of the following sized buildings:

	Number of Storeys	*Total Floor Area (Sq. Yds)*
Engine House	2	110
Mill	3 (+ attic and cellar)	1890
Additional Cellar	1	137
Card Shop	4 (+ attic)	1548
Boiler House	2	206
Shed	1	54
Shed	1	62
Stoving Room	1	15
Wash Place	1	24
Office, Spinning Room and Cellar	1½	100
Wool Comb Shop	1	76
Weighing House	1	28
Stable and Carriage House	2	170
Total Floor Area:		4,420 sq. yds[42]

At that time Halifax mills ranged very widely in size. Other premises recorded in the survey varied from about 1,500 sq. yds to over 5,000. Any assessment of the increase in average size of Yorkshire

[40] Rough estimates based on the Ordnance Survey, *5′ Town Plan of Dewsbury*, 1851–2. A similar calculation for mills within the town boundary of Huddersfield produced a figure of 2,300 square yards for average ground floor area of wool textile mill buildings. D.P.L. and Hud. P.L.

[41] Archives Department, Halifax Public Library: *Survey and Valuation of the Township of Warley, 1829.*

[42] Archives Department, Halifax Public Library: *Survey and Valuation of the Township of Halifax, 1852.*

mills during the forty or fifty years can be no more than a very rough estimate. A three-fold increase in floor space is perhaps a realistic figure.

Power and Employees as a Measurement of Size

The size of mill buildings can also be assessed from the number of persons employed or the amount of power used. Power: employment: capital ratios will be used in later calculations. It is reasonable to expect a fairly constant correlation between physical size and the number of employees and amount of power. The correlation will not be exact because of some variation in processes carried out from one mill to another and because of underused capacity and differences in warehousing facilities for example.

The analysis cannot be carried out for before the early 1830s because of an absence of information. Even the statistics in the sample survey of the 1834 Supplementary Report of the Commission for the Employment of Children in Mills and Factories give a rather false impression because of the preponderance of larger mills.[43] However, the number of employees per mill has been tabulated (Table 8) and some idea of these can be obtained of the mean size of employment in mills. In spite of the probably optimistic bias, there were many more mills with less than 75 employees than mills with more than that number. In fact the average number of employees, as suggested by the Report, was about 88 for all the wool textile mills included in the survey but more than half the mills employed less than 50 workers, the average being considerably increased by the seven mills that were exceptionally large, with over 400 employees. When on considers that the average number of workers in 1835 was 68 according to the comprehensive Factory Inspectors' survey, an even greater preponderance of small mills is suggested.

The 1834 Report recorded five mills with between 500 and 600 employees and one with more than 600. It did not, however, include Gott's mill at Leeds, nor Henry Brooke's. The Report, however, also listed over 40 mills with less than 25 employees, the smallest being Thomas Hinchcliffe's Mill at Thirsting near Honley, first used in 1790 and being employed for scribbling, carding and slubbing wool in 1833. It had both a small wheel and an engine but the wheel

[43] See D. T. Jenkins, 'The Validity of the Factory Returns', op. cit., for a discussion of the representativeness of mills recorded in the 1834 Supplementary Reports.

TABLE 8

NUMBER OF EMPLOYEES IN WOOLLEN AND WORSTED MILLS RECORDED BY CHILDRENS EMPLOYMENT COMMISSIONERS IN 1833

Employees	*Woollen Mills*	*Worsted Mills*
Under 25	28	13
25–49	46	24
50–74	31	10
75–99	10	8
100–49	10	9
150–99	8	6
200–99	5	6
300–99	—	4
Over 400	4	3

Source: *Factories Inquiry Commission, Supplementary Reports*, Parts II and III, 1834.

could only be used for about three months of the year when it was fed by nearby springs. Neither the engine nor the wheel could generate more than 3 horsepower. In 1833 the mill was in poor condition and only irregularly occupied. At the time of the inquiry, two male adults, five boys and one girl were employed.[44] Thomas Varley's mill at Sunlainbottom, Lingards on Bradley Brook, powered by a four horsepower wheel and used for carding and slubbing was probably no bigger. It employed only three adults and four children.[45] There are many other mills recorded with less than 15 workers.

Thus in spite of the industrial complexes which sprang up in the first three decades of the nineteenth century and which tend to be better documented and recorded, some surviving to the present day, these figures for employment show that, at least numerically, the small mill predominated in the industry.

Similar calculations may be carried out based on the amount of power being generated. These are examined in detail in the next chapter but, for the present, the size of engines and wheels can be seen from Tables 9 and 12. No distinction is drawn between large mills using several small engines and wheels, and those using one large wheel or engine, but even so they show that over one half of the wheels

[44] *Factories Inquiry Commission, Supplementary Reports, 1834*, Part II, C.2. Mill no. 102.

[45] Ibid.,'Mill no. 193.

were under 10 horsepower and one half of the engines were under 20 horsepower. They suggest that the small mills were often powered by water but even so there were a considerable number of tiny steam-powered premises. Few mills had wheels that could produce more than 20 horsepower but some had engines that could provide over 50. Of the 610 mills working in 1835 less than 50 had power units of more than 40 horsepower.

3

THE GENERATION OF POWER

Hand and Horse Mills

With the availability of new machinery for the scribbling and spinning processes in woollen production and for spinning in worsted manufacture in the 1770s and 1780s attempts were made to use various types of power to operate the machinery.[1] Hand and horse-power, water and steam were all the subject of investigation by wool manufacturers within the space of a few years. And whilst water power was to predominate in the industry for several decades the importance of the use of these other power sources should not be underestimated.

Heaton considered that the main economic advantage of the factory in the West Riding resulted from: 'the use of machinery, capable of performing work quickly, and the use of power which can make the machinery go at high speed.'[2] He believed that until the elements of speed were available there was no great advantage of the factory system over cottage industry. However, there is evidence of considerable transference from the domestic scene to specially constructed or converted buildings before the application of mechanical power. In spite of the outlay involved, many manufacturers saw advantages in having their workpeople and their machinery collected under one roof where the work could be supervised to maintain a constant standard; where perhaps a greater division of labour could be organized, the working hours of the labour force controlled and the time normally wasted in the carriage of raw materials and finished products under the domestic system eliminated.

With the gradual change from the system of domestic manufacture to the mechanized factory there were a great many types of premises housing different branches of wool textile manufacture. Clothiers and merchants wishing to make use of the new machinery but perhaps unable to raise sufficient finance for large buildings and

[1] See Chapter Four for a discussion of the development of scribbling and spinning machinery.

[2] Heaton, op. cit., p. 352.

costly forms of water or steam power, or unwilling initially to take large risks with relatively untried new methods, experimented with the machines in converted sheds and workshops, barns, warehouses and other buildings using hand and horse power, and some manufacturers continued in this way for many years.

Earlier in the eighteenth century textile 'manufactories' had been recorded in Yorkshire. In the 1750s Sir George Strickland built a 'woollen manufactory' at Boynton near Bridlington which was visited by Arthur Young on his Northern Tour and described as:

> . . . a building large enough to contain on one side a row of looms of different sorts, and on the other a large space for women and children to spin. The undertaking was once carried so far as to employ 150 hands but the decay of the woollen exportation reduced them so much that those now employed are, I believe, under a dozen.[3]

A few years later there was a 'carpet manufactory' at Ripon presumably worked by hand, and before the end of the seventeenth century there was, at Malton, 'An establishment by mine Lord Ewer's coheiress' who used the rooms of outbuildings and the gatehouse of an old mansion 'for weaving and linning cloth having set up a manufactory for linners which does employ many people'.[4]

At the end of the eighteenth century the records of hand-powered mills amongst insurance policies include one for Joseph and John Wainwright, clothiers of Armley, who insured cottages and a 'hand scribbling mill' with the Sun Fire Office for £100.[5] Some of these hand establishments later started to use horses, and in more than one instance introduced steam engines.

Thus the first source of power for new machinery in buildings used specifically for wool and worsted cloth production was the human hand. It would be wrong to think that these mills were widespread in the West Riding of Yorkshire but the few that have been traced are sufficient in number to suggest that there was the beginnings of a movement from the cottage industry to production in special buildings before the application of water or steam power.

Besides these hand operated premises, there appears to have been a number of purpose-built or converted buildings using horses to power their machinery. Again references can be found in insurance policies to horse mills. John Bateson of Farnley near Leeds, a

[3] Arthur Young, *A Six Month's Tour through the North of England* (1771), Vol. II, 7; quoted by Heaton, op. cit., p. 355.

[4] Heaton, op. cit., pp. 285, 354, quoting Celia Fiennes, *Through England on a Side Saddle*, p. 74.

[5] Sun C.R. 8/638509/1795.

clothier and miller, insured his horse spinning mill for £60 in 1795. The gearing was also insured for £20 and the working machinery for £180. A few years later this mill was, almost certainly, powered by a steam engine.[6] In 1797 Benjamin Grimshaw of Rawden, a 'manufacturer of wool' was working 'a horse woollen scribbling, slubbing and spinning mill' and in the same year George Cromack had a horse scribbling mill, attached to his 'new dwelling house' at Armley.[7] Also at Armley, James Ellis, a young master clothier, was trained to use horses for power. In evidence to the 1806 Inquiry he said:

> I learnt to slub upon the billy; the master I was apprenticed to had a billy, he had a carding mill which went by horse and slubbing mill too; it was in the house, but not in the living or sleeping rooms; the carding was by horse, the slubbing and spinning by hand.[8]

A lot in the sale of the estate of Mr Robert Myers of Bramley in November 1797 consisted of: 'All that spacious new building used as a carding mill with the carding machines, horsewheel, and slubbing billy therein . . .'[9] In January of the previous year Myers and Samuel Hague, another clothier, had insured a horse spinning mill for £30 and carding and breaking engines for £120.[10]

These horse-powered mills, although normally very small, were not necessarily so. An advertisement in the *Leeds Intelligencer* in 1799 read as follows:

> To be Sold: a Horse Mill or Ginn, with shafts and gearing for Four horses and connecting wheels and Drum for working six machines. The whole esteemed to be constructed upon the best arrangement and in excellent repair.[11]

It is possible that some time before the application of water power to scribbling and spinning considerable thought was given to powering machinery by horses. Arkwright's spinning frame, developed and patented in the 1760s, was originally intended to be driven by a horse gin before it was adapted to water power and became known as the 'water-frame'.[12] Dolphineholme Mill, possibly

[6] Sun C.R. 11/649652/1795.
[7] Sun C.R. 17/666458/1797; 19/671057/1797.
[8] *Report of the Select Committee on the State of the Woollen Manufacture of England*, 1806, p. 63.
[9] *Leeds Mercury*, 25 November 1797.
[10] Sun C.R. 13/653068/1796.
[11] *Leeds Intelligencer*, 17 June 1799.
[12] Crump, op. cit., p. 8.

the earliest worsted spinning mill, built in 1784, probably originally used horses as well as water power.[13] James draws our attention to a James Taylor of Ashton under Lyne obtaining a patent in 1754 for: 'an Engine, to be worked either by men or horses, wind or water, for spinning cotton wool into yarn, which will spin more and better cotton yarn,'[14] and he also mentions that Wyatt's roller spinning machine, when first tried out in Birmingham in 1741, was turned by a gin worked by a couple of asses, and attended by ten girls.[15]

That much consideration should have been given to the powering of machinery by horses is not surprising. For centuries horse corn mills had existed; three were working at Shrewsbury in 1267 and *De Re Metallica*, published in 1556, shows a picture of a horse wheel being used in mining.[16] However, it was soon realized by textile manufacturers in the second half of the eighteenth century that water could provide a much greater amount of power for the new machinery than the poor horse could ever generate. Even so, horse mills were still to be found in the Leeds area as late as the second decade of the nineteenth century. In 1809, Israel Smithies was operating Rachael Dade's horse-scribbling mill at Woodhouse Carr and in 1810 John Beckett of Meanwood owned a horse scribbling mill at North Hall.[17]

In one way the mill horse heralded the introduction of the steam engine. 'By calculations based on the load raised over a pulley by a mill horse going at a certain pace, Watt was able to establish a standard measure of power for his engine and the customer was asked to pay on that basis.'[18] However, any foothold that the horse might have gained was not prevented so much by the introduction of steam power, but primarily by the harnessing of water to turn the mill wheel and power the new machinery.

[13] James, op. cit., pp. 338–9; P. Hall, 'Dolphineholme: A History of the Dolphineholme Worsted Mill, 1784 to 1867', *Transactions of the Fylde Historical Society*, 3, 1969.

[14] James, op. cit., p. 339.

[15] Ibid.

[16] *Transactions of the Shropshire Archaeological Society*, 1894, p. 341; *De Re Metallica*, Agricola, 1556; illustration reproduced in T. K. Derry and T. I. Williams, *A Short History of Technology* (Oxford, 1960), Vol. IV, 130.

[17] Sun C.R. 85/829564/1809; 90/842789/1810.

[18] Sir Eric Roll, *An Early Experiment in Industrial Organisation* (London, 1930), p. 116.

The Water-wheel

Water power was, of course, well known and well tried in Yorkshire by the eighteenth century. It was in widespread use for corn milling, lead smelting, iron working and, particularly, for fulling. All the 100 Yorkshire fulling mills of the 1770s were reliant on water power and the technical expertise existed to build, operate and repair water-wheels and gearing.

As a separate unit, however, the fulling mill did not have a long existence after the end of the century. By 1800 many of them were also being used for other purposes. After the middle of the eighteenth century another process in woollen cloth manufacture was being mechanized and having water power rapidly applied to it. Scribbling and carding engines and the slubbing 'engine' or 'billy' found their way into the area probably some time in the mid-1770s and by 1800 there were about 220 mills in operation scribbling and carding wool by water power. Some of them were quite large and housed many machines. Often the machines were installed in the earlier fulling mills but, in many cases, new buildings were erected specifically for the purpose.

The next step forward was the application of water power to spinning. This came about first in the silk and cotton industries and was linked with the various technical developments in spinning machinery. Many instances can be quoted of attempts to apply water power to spinning in the first half of the eighteenth century. In the woollen branch of the industry in Yorkshire the hand-powered 'jennies' invented by James Hargreaves were the only means of spinning until the 1820s when Crompton's mule was adapted to spin wool. In the worsted branch of the industry Arkwright's water-frame was first introduced into specially built worsted mills in 1787 and twenty-two mills were turning them by water before the end of the century. There is some suggestion that attempts were made to spin wool by frames in the 1790s but contemporary records are confusing about the use of different types and makes of machinery and rarely give much indication about the success of the operation. The 'jenny' was at times referred to as a 'spinning frame'.[19]

The mule played only a minor role in the development of the industry before the mid-1830s. Spinning by water power was

[19] See Chapter Four.

confined mainly to the use of Arkwright's frame in worsted manufacture. The first factory survey is not detailed enough to calculate how many mills were spinning by water power in 1835.

The application of water power to weaving in wool textile manufacture had hardly come about by the early 1830s, although there had been numerous attempts at various times to introduce power to this process. Cartwright's power loom was patented in 1785 but several decades went by before its use in the Yorkshire wool textile trade. The sample survey carried out by the inspectors in 1833 found only three manufacturers weaving by water power, however. They were Thomas Atkinson of Kirkheaton, who had a wheel at his woollen mill on the River Colne, Stansfield and Briggs at Burley Mill, and Robert Whettam of Turvin Woollen Mill, Sowerby, who had a small wheel fed from a reservoir.[20] Although this survey was incomplete, and full information was not always given for every mill included, one can only conclude that, by this date, very little weaving by water power was being carried on. Two years later the Report of the number of power looms being used in factories recorded 48 mills weaving by power, of which no more than 12 employed water power. At least five of these 12 had not been weaving by power two years earlier, thus suggesting that it was not until the mid-1830s that mechanized weaving developed. Moreover, the figures show that power weaving was more widespread in steam-powered mills.

With the publication of the first Factory Returns in 1835, a comprehensive although not necessarily entirely accurate survey of the amount of water power in use at the time is available. The inspectors recorded 343 water-wheels in operation, providing a total horsepower of 3,545½ to wool textile manufactures, an average of about 10 horsepower per wheel. Two hundred and forty-one of the wheels were in woollen mills and the other 102 in worsted mills. Table 9 shows the comparative power of the wheels turning woollen and worsted machinery.

Statistics are next available for the 12 months ending 30 June 1838 when the factory inspector and his assistants for the West Riding of Yorkshire traced 243 wheels in woollen mills and a further 95 in worsted mills.[21] The figures suggest that the expansion in the use of water power in the wool textile mills was coming to a close. Twelve

[20] *Factories Inquiry Commission, Supplementary Reports, 1834*, Part II, C.2., Mills nos. 30, 61, and 268.

[21] *Factory Returns*, 1838. See D. T. Jenkins, 'The Validity of the Factory Returns, 1833–50', op. cit., for a discussion of the Factory Inspectors' Returns for 1838.

TABLE 9

POWER GENERATED BY WATER-WHEELS IN THE WEST RIDING WOOL TEXTILE INDUSTRY IN 1835

Woollen Branch

Power of Wheel (hp.)	*Total Power*	*No. of Wheels*
50+	210	4
49–40	160	4
39–30	125	4
29–20	306	14
19–10	1242	101
Under 10	629	114
TOTALS	2,672	241

Average power of wheels in woollen mills was therefore just over 11 horsepower.

Worsted Branch

Power of Wheel (hp.)	*Total Power*	*No. of Wheels*
39–30	60	2
29–20	84	4
19–10	400	32
Under 10	329½	64
TOTALS	873½	102

Average power of wheels in worsted mills was therefore about 8½ horsepower.

* These totals, as calculated by the inspectors themselves, do not tally with the actual tabulated information as detailed township by township but the difference is not so considerable as to affect the general picture of the extent of the use of water power.

Source: *Factory Returns 1835*.

years later, in spite of the number of mills having more than doubled compared with 1835 there had been almost no increase in the overall amounts of water power being harnessed.[22] Many mills still continued their manufacture with a sole reliance on water power; particularly those on the large rivers where an adequate supply of water was more reliable. Thus, the large enterprise of Dewsbury Mills, which installed a huge new iron water-wheel in

[22] *Factory Returns*, 1850.

1827–8 at a total cost of £2,899, was still worked entirely by water power from the River Calder two decades later.[23] On the River Aire, Calverley Mills had no steam engine before 1840 and, on the River Wharfe, mills at Linton and Otley were still only using power from the river at the same period.[24] Elsewhere, however, manufacturers were often changing to the use of steam because of the uncertainties caused by flood and drought. Although, for example, in 1825 'the owners of the mills driven by the Mixenden and Wheatley streams were so content with water power that they decided to make a reservoir at Ogden . . .' they changed their minds in the following year when a drought curtailed the supply water and they installed steam engines.[25]

With the exception of the building of one or two very large water-wheels in the 1820s, there was really very little change in the method of using water power during the period. The wheels were normally very small; the 60 horsepower wheel at Almondbury, the largest known to have been working in 1840, was quite exceptional. Only another thirteen were recorded as being able to produce more than 30 horsepower by that date.[26] This excludes the massive wheel at Lothersdale, 45 ft. in diameter, which was one of the largest internal water-wheels in Great Britain but was not used for wool textile production until later in the century; and then only after a steam engine had also been installed.[27]

Considerable thought was given in the second half of the eighteenth century to the construction of water-wheels and technical improvements were still being introduced in the middle of the nineteenth century. One important change in their construction was the introduction of iron parts in place of wood. This afforded greater durability and enabled a more efficient design to be used. Although a few overshot wheels were constructed for woollen mills in the West Riding, they were often only suitable for the higher reaches of streams where a sufficient fall of water could be arranged. They were, however, also used where auxiliary steam power was available to supply water.

The more usual type of wheel was the breast wheel where the

[23] F. J. Glover, *Dewsbury Mills: A History of Messrs. Wormalds and Walker Limited, Blanket Manufacturers, of Dewsbury: with an Economic Survey of the Yorkshire Woollen Cloth Industry in the Nineteenth Century*, unpublished P.hD. thesis, University of Leeds, 1959, p. 397.
[24] Sun C.R. 256/1314077/1839 and *Factory Returns*, 1838.
[25] T. W. Hanson, *The Story of Old Halifax* (1920), p. 239.
[26] *Factory Returns*, 1838.
[27] *The Dalesman*, December 1967, p. 716.

fall of water did not have to be so high or so constant in pressure. Although the same volume of water provided less power with a breast wheel the machinery was less susceptible to fluctuations in water supply. Fairbairn points out that another advantage of the breast wheel:

> ... is the ease with which it overcomes the obstruction of backwater. The breast wheel is not only less injured by floods but the retarding force is overcome with greater ease, and the wheel works in a greater depth of back water.[28]

The undershot wheel was also, however, frequently used particularly in the middle and lower reaches of the rivers where only the natural speed of the water was available, and where it was not always possible to construct weirs and dams to build up sufficient water for breast and overshot wheels.

All types of wheel were susceptible, to some extent, to a lack or surfeit of water. On many streams periods of drought often caused considerable concern and some mills became resigned to a lack of power for a part of the year. Thomas Cook of Dewsbury Mills recorded in his evidence to the commissioners in 1833 that his mill, powered entirely by water-wheels, using between 160 and 200 horsepower, had excess of water for 15 or 20 days of the year, and an 'occasional want of water'.[29] He estimated that his fulling mill lost a sixth of the year through flood and want of water. In the same report the occupiers of Burley Mill complained of frequent dearth or excess of water; the Priestleys of Sowerby were worried about irregular water supply and John Pollard at St Helen's Mill, Bramley recorded that there was often insufficient water for his large 40 horsepower wheel on the Aire.[30]

Mills on Lord Dartmouth's estates suffered likewise and the extent to which his Lordship was aware of the problems is shown by the measures he took to improve the conservation and fall of water:

[28] Fairbairn, *Treatise on Mills* . . ., op. cit., Part I, 114–16. Fairbairn describes the types of vertical wheel as follows: 'Vertical waterwheels, the plane of rotation being vertical and the water received and afterwards discharged at the same orifice on the external periphery. These may be subdivided into: (a) Overshot wheels, where the water is applied over the crest, or near the upper extremity of the vertical diameter. (b) Breast wheels, where the water is applied below the crest at the side of the wheel. (c) Undershot wheels, where the water is applied near the bottom of the wheel and acts, (i) By gravitation, as in the improved undershot wheel or (ii) By impulse, as in the ordinary undershot and pencelet wheel.'

[29] *Factories Inquiry Commission, Supplementary Reports, 1834,* Part II, C.2. Mill no. 61.

[30] Ibid., Mills nos. 266 and 185.

At the head of this last stream (Holt stream) a large reservoir has been made on Lingarth's Moor which, it is imagined, will be of great service in keeping a regular supply of water to the foregoing mills.[31]

One of the mills where Dartmouth did have considerable trouble was Rowley Mill at Honley, a scribbling and slubbing mill in the tenure of Ibbetson and Company. Here there was a 26 ft. diameter water-wheel producing about 6 horsepower but:

The stream, however, is poor and weak and at the best time can only work six months in the year and what is to be particularly observed the water is taken from its course two or three hundred yards although Lord Dartmouth has, with but one exception, land on one side of the stream. If any lease is ever granted this must be attended to, that we may not guarantee a water power where in reality we possess none.[32]

The problems of water supply were the cause of many disputes. The erection of mill dams, the diversion of the course of streams and the construction of canals all, at one time or another, gave rise to legal actions, or in some cases, even fights between mill owners or tenants. Many complaints are recorded in contemporary newspapers, legal reports and company records. At Dewsbury Mills there was a dispute lasting several years with the Calder and Hebble Navigation. A law suit came before York Assizes in 1791 after considerable correspondence but the problem was not resolved until 1796.[33] Mill interests on the Hebble and Calder rivers petitioned Parliament in 1792 for protection against the activities of canal builders.[34]

Attempts were always being made to improve water supply. Weirs and dams were constructed across rivers to hold back water; reservoirs were built to store water for periods of drought, or even overnight in some cases, so that water would not be wasted. Some of these schemes were very successful and served the intended purpose but, often, they also created problems. Disputes arose between mill tenants on the same stream as to when water should be released from the reservoirs. The construction of weirs and dams, or other interference with the natural flow of rivers, could cause silting and starve some mills completely of water.

[31] Dartmouth Estate, *Terrier*, 1805, p. 50. The mills that benefited from this reservoir were Upper Holt Mill, Lower Holt Mill, and Lingarth's Mill.

[32] Dartmouth Estate, *Honley Terrier*, 1828, p. 90. The purchase of water rights could be a substantial expense for mill owners.

[33] Glover, thesis, op. cit., p. 358.

[34] B. R. Law, 'The Calder Millowners and the Rochdale Canal', *H.A.S.*, January 1954.

However, during the period there appears to have been also a more general problem concerning the provision of water power. Fairbairn described it in detail:

At the commencement of the present century, when the land was imperfectly drained, the soil and surrounding marshes, having no outlet, retained and stored up the rainfall and became the great holders or reservoirs by which the waters were impounded and the flow of our rivers regulated with greater uniformity than at present. Since the introduction of an extended system of drainage the whole character of our rivers has been changed and now discharge their contents with much greater rapidity and in larger volumes than they were accustomed to before these improvements were introduced. The result of this has been favourable to the land but injurious to the mills, both as regards uniformity and the loss of power, as nearly one half the supply is carried off by floods and cannot be retained for the use of the mills. In all districts of the country where drainage and an improved system of tillage have come into operation the effect has been a serious loss to the owners of water mills, and has driven most of them to the use of steam, either as an auxilliary or in some instances exclusively as a substitute for water.[35]

The Age of Steam

The many difficulties and disadvantages of water power induced the discussion of an experimentation for another more reliable means of powering mill machinery. The use of steam power permitted the development of the industry away from the often inaccessible sites on the banks of streams and in the depths of steep sided valleys. A more compact plant could be used and there was more scope for the improvement of transmission machinery and mill construction.

The history of the steam engine is well documented. There is no need in this study to trace the course of its development from the late seventeenth century to the improvements made by Watt, and from the beginning of the nineteenth century, its widespread manufacture throughout the land. The early introduction of steam power to the West Riding wool textile industry has, however, received little attention and those who have attempted to trace it appear to have considerably underestimated its importance in the closing years of the eighteenth century.[36]

Pessimistic views of the introduction of steam power at that time appear to stem from the reports of the malfunctioning of engines at

[35] Fairbairn, Treatise . . . op. cit., Part I, Section III, Chapter I, p. 70.

[36] There has been very little discussion of the introduction of steam power in the Yorkshire wool textile industry. There is some mention in Crump, op. cit., pp. 187–92; See also A. E. Musson and E. Robinson, 'The Early Growth of Steam Power', *E.H.R.*, XI, 1959, 418–39; J. R. Harris, 'The Employment of Steam Power in the Eighteenth Century', *History*, LII, 1967, 133–48.

the period, the strength of Boulton and Watt's patent until 1800 together with their acknowledged dislike of supplying textile concerns in the early 1780s. In consequence of an order from a Burton-on-Trent firm in 1782, Watt wrote to Boulton:

From their letter and the man they have sent here, I have no great opinion of their abilities . . . If you come home by way of Manchester, please not to seek for orders for cotton mill engines, because I hear that there are so many mills erecting on powerful streams in the North of England that the trade must soon be overdone and consequently our labour may be lost.[37]

By the late 1780s, however, the partners had seen the possibilities of applying steam power to textile machinery. Even so, in the West Riding of Yorkshire, only a few Boulton and Watt engines were working in textile mills by the end of the century. As Table 10 shows, the firm's business in Yorkshire textiles was never very important.

TABLE 10

BOULTON AND WATT ENGINES IN YORKSHIRE WOOL TEXTILE MILLS, 1792–1835

Sun and Planet Engines:

A 40 h.p. engine ordered in August 1792 by Messrs. Wormald, Fountain and Gott for Park Mills, Leeds. B. & W. MSS, Portf. 93

A 30 h.p. engine ordered in August 1792 by Messrs. Markland, Cookson and Fawcett for their cotton and worsted mill at Leeds. B. & W. MSS, Portf. 91

A 20 h.p. engine ordered in September 1793 by John and James Walker for their woollen mill at Wortley. B. & W. MSS, Portf. 105

A 20 h.p. engine ordered in October 1795 by Joshua Foster for his woollen mill at Horbury. B. & W. MSS, Portf. 125

A 20 h.p. engine ordered in November 1795 by Gowland, Clark and Co. for their cotton mill at Leeds. The mill was later a worsted mill. B. & W. MSS, Portf. 126

A 12 h.p. engine ordered in January 1796 by Thos. Halliday and John Cockshott for their worsted mill near Baildon. B. & W. MSS, Portf. 130

A 16 h.p. engine ordered in May 1796 by Messrs. Nevins and Gatliff for Larchfield woollen mill, Hunslet. B. & W. MSS, Portf. 134

A 20 h.p. engine ordered in July 1796 by Messrs. Nussey and Co. for their woollen mill at Birstall. B. & W. MSS, Portf. 138

A 20 h.p. engine ordered in December 1796 by Messrs. M. and J. Bateson for their cotton mill at Wortley. The mill soon changed to manufacturing wool. B. & W. MSS, Portf. 143

[37] P. Mantoux, *The Industrial Revolution in the Eighteenth Century* (new edition, 1964), pp. 333–4 quoting a letter from Watt to Boulton, December 1782.

A 10 h.p. engine ordered in February 1793 by Messrs. Holland and Bridge of Manchester and erected in their mill there. This engine was later sold to Thomas Smith of Old Lane Mill, possibly at Halifax.
Engine Book pp. 8–9 and B. & W. MSS, Portf. 98

Beam (Crank Type) Engines:

A 14 h.p. engine ordered in April 1804 by Joshua Foster for his worsted mill at Horbury. B. & W. MSS, Portf. 348 and Engine Book 20/6/1804
A 40 h.p. engine ordered in May 1824 by Messrs. York, Sheepshanks and Co. for their woollen mill at Leeds. B. & W. MSS, Portf. 490
A 80 h.p. engine ordered in August 1824 by Benjamin Gott for Park Mill, Leeds. B. & W. MSS, Portf. 491
A 80 h.p. engine ordered in April 1825 by John Wood, Jnr., for his mill at Bradford and a similar engine ordered in January 1833 also by Wood. The mill is described as being used for cotton in the Boulton and Watt records but was, almost certainly, a worsted mill
See James, op. cit., p. 605. B. & W. MSS, Portfs. 496 and 500

Side Lever Type Engines:

A 6 h.p. engine purchased by Mr. A. Dean for Thomas Halliday and Co. of Baildon, presumably also for his worsted mill. B. & W. MSS, Portf. 736

Side Lever (Boat) Type Engines:

A 30 h.p. engine purchased by Messrs. Townend Bros, of Cullingworth and erected in their worsted mill in 1824. B. & W. MSS, Portf. 103
A 80 h.p. engine ordered in 1829 by Messrs. Benjamin Gott and Sons, as their third engine at Park Mills, Leeds. B. & W. MSS, Portf. 1069½

Source: Birmingham Reference Library, Boulton and Watt MSS.

* T. & H. Lodge of Halifax purchased a second hand Sun and Planet Engine from Messrs Howard and Houghton's paper mill at Hull in August 1802.

It can, however, be shown that many other engines were at work in Yorkshire. It would seem that about a third of all woollen and worsted mills in the county were employing steam power by 1800. Table 11 list 81 steam engines known to have been in operation by the turn of the century. It is not suggested that the list is complete but the number traced shows the extent to which steam power had been introduced to the local wool textile industry by that early date.

Unfortunately, except for the Boulton and Watt engines, it has not been possible to trace the type or makes of the engines, nor can the earliest engine in use be definitely shown. The list, however, illustrates that by 1800 the introduction of steam power to Yorkshire wool textile manufacture had gained faster ground than has hitherto been realized.

TABLE 11

STEAM POWER IN YORKSHIRE WOOL TEXTILE MILLS BEFORE 1800

Mill	*Steam Power by*	*Mill*	*Steam Power by*
Strawberry Bank Mill, Liversedge	(?)1780	Philadelphia Mill, Gildersome	1798
Gill Mill, Baildon	1795	Troughton Mill, Drighlington	1796
Spring End Mill, Ossett	1796	Garnet's Mill, Hunslet	1796
Hopton Mill, Mirfield	1792	At Danehouse Lane, Honley	1796
Millshaw Mills, Beeston	1796	Upper Mill, Wortley	1797
Croft Mill, Dewsbury	1797	Batley Subscription Mill, Batley	1797
Copley's Mill, Hunslet	1791	Rosemary Mill, Rastrick	1797
Low Mill, Wortley	1793	Dogley Mill, Kirkburton	1797
At Holbeck (Browne)	1790	At Heckmondwike (Dex & Kighley)	1797
Aldams Mill, Dewsbury	1795	At Heckmondwike (Barker)	1797
Spring End Mill, Horbury	1798	At Gildersome (Murgatroyd)	1797
Foster's Old Mill, Horbury	1795	Smithies Mill, Birstall	1797
Meltham Mills, Meltham	1793	Rods Mill, Morley	1797
Park Mills, Leeds	1792	At Liversedge (Wormald)	*1797
At Hunslet Lane, Leeds (Brookes)	*c.* 1792	At Gomersal (Carr)	1797
At Birkenshaw, Gomersal	1790	Oddy's Mill, Hunslet	1797
Farnley Mill, Farnley Tyas	*c.* 1792	Dean House Mill, Almondbury	1797
Crank Mill, Morley	1792	Larchfield Mill, Hunslet	1797
At Heckmondwike (Carr)	1792	At Milnesbridge, Birstall	1797
At Cleckheaton (Birkley & Waite)	1792	Hough Mill, Bramley	1797
Brookroyd Mill, Birstall	1792	Union Bridge Mill, Pudsey	1798
At Hunslet (Hodgson, Rainforth & Hinchcliffe)	1793	At Holbeck (Glover, Lister & Roper)	1798
Browbridge Mill, Elland	1796	At Bramley (Strickland)	1798
Holbeck Mills, Holbeck	1793	Low Mill, Stanningley	1798
At Bank, Leeds (Markland, Cookson & Fawcett)	1793	At Colne Bridge, Kirkheaton	1798
At Shelly Woodhouse, Huddersfield	1797	At Stanningley (Jarrat, Dawson & Hardy)	1798
Company Mill, Stanningley	1794	At Hunslet (Tuton, Waring & Wilks)	1799
Rowley Mill, Kirkburton	*c.* 1794	Holme Mill, Bradford	1800
Pildacre Mill, Ossett	1794	At Linfit Lane, Kirkburton (Cocker)	1800
Turton's Mill, Gildersome	1795	Marshall Hall Mill, Elland	1800
At Hunslet (Wilkinson)	1795	Peg Mill, Cleckheaton	1800
At Mill Green, Holbeck	1795	At Holbeck (Sykes & Kindle)	1800
Heckmondwike Mill	1795	Holbeck Lane Mill, Holbeck	1800
At Lockwood (Bentley)	1797	Broom Mill, Farsley	1800
Burnley's Mill, Farnley, Leeds	1795	Bowling Dyke Mill, Northowram	1800
Chickenley Mill, Dewsbury	1795	At Heckmondwike (Brook & Popplewell)	1800
At Dewsbury (Chaster, Wilson & Rhodes)	*1795	At Park Lane, Leeds (Knubley & Wainwright)	1800
At Flanshaw, Wakefield (Wood & Cook)	1796	Kilncroft Mill, Dewsbury	1800
Thornes Lane Mill, Wakefield	1796	Carr Mill, Batley	1800
Westgate Common Mill, Alverthorpe	1796		

*2 Engines

Sources: The references for the existence of these steam engines are, in general, the same as the ones given against the mills concerned in Appendix I.

The majority of the engines were, no doubt, pumping engines of the Savery and Newcomen designs. From the contemporary reports, records and insurance data from which the list has been compiled, it is evident that most engines were used in conjunction with water; not always, however, to pump water to turn a wheel but sometimes to augment the power in times of water shortage.

In the woollen branch of the industry there are many instances of mills using steam engines by the 1790s. An advertisement in a Leeds paper in 1793 offered:

> To be Sold by Private Contract. Situate near Balme Beck in Hunslet in the Parish of Leeds. All that scribbling mill consisting of five machines and a willey turned by a fire engine, also a scribbling machine and a carding machine turned by a Beck or Rivulet, called Balm Beck, together with two Billeys.[38]

At this mill the engine was separately powering machinery although water power was also being used. This was probably also the case at Chaster, Wilson and Rhodes's mill at Dewsbury where in 1796 two steam engines were employed for scribbling.[39] At Wetherill's Mill at Morley, although referred to in an insurance policy as a water scribbling mill, there would appear to have been a small steam engine by 1796.[40]

On the Dartmouth Estate both Rowley and Farnley Mills were using steam engines in the 1790s to compensate for the poor supply of water as were Dogley Mill and Morley Mill by the turn of the century.[41]

The Troughtons of Drighlington were using a steam engine to pump water back above the wheel at their mill at Cockersdale.[42] This was clearly also the case at a mill at Farnley for which two shares were advertised in 1799.

> To be sold by Private Contract two undivided quarter shares of and in all that newly erected Water Fulling and Scribbling Mill, situate upon Farnley Beck, within the township of Farnley, with a steam engine for throwing back the water upon the wheel when necessary.[43]

A number of mills were also established in the 1790s, however, to use only steam power. In 1794 a mill at Gomersall was advertised as: 'A large new erected scribbling and corn mill wrought by a

[38] *Leeds Intelligencer*, 28 October 1793.
[39] Sun C.R. 13/656219/1796.
[40] Sun C.R. 13/653405/1796.
[41] Dartmouth Estate, *Terrier*, 1805, pp. 129, 171, 239.
[42] Sun C.R. 13/653861/1796.
[43] *Leeds Intelligencer*, 4 April 1799.

steam engine. Situate at Castle Hill in Gomersall. The scribbling mill contains eight engines for scribbling and carding wool'.[44]

Likewise, the Heckmondwike Mill Company, one of the first of the Company mills, were scribbling, carding and spinning wool by steam power in 1795, with no mention of any water power.[45] At the same period Grimshaw's mill at Mill Green, Holbeck, and Murgatroyd's mill at Gildersome, amongst many others, appear to have been using steam power alone to turn their machinery.[46]

None of the above mentioned engines, were supplied by the firm of Boulton and Watt. The insurance valuations and other miscellaneous information that is available for these early engines suggest that they were very small. Many were insured for under £100. Garnet, who had a tiny scribbling mill at Hunslet, valued his at only £15.[47] On the other hand, certain of the engines were presumably quite large. The one at the Old Mill at Dewsbury was insured for £600 and the same firm had another valued at £400 in their new mill.[48] The Brookes at Honley valued theirs at £650 in 1799. These larger engines were, however, the exception rather than the rule.[49]

No definite idea can be given at present as to which woollen mill was the first to install steam power. The first might well have been before 1780. There were certainly engines in use in other industries in Yorkshire well before that date. Frank Peel suggested on the basis of local tradition:

> It was about this period that the steam engine was being brought into use, and one of the first which was applied in this locality (the Spen Valley) to manufacturing purposes was erected at this mill (Strawberry Bank Mill) by Peter Lawford. Up to about 1780 this steam engine had no crank or Governor and was simply, indeed, a pumping engine and, therefore, in order to get the circular motion it was applied in the way of pumping water which was poured on to the waterwheel.[50]

It was not until the 1790s, and later, that the steam engine really became efficient and reliable enough to start seriously competing with water power. The introduction of Watt's engine into the cotton industry in the late 1780s, and then, in the 1790s, into a few woollen and worsted mills in the West Riding heralded the more widespread

[44] *Leeds Intelligencer*, 4 August 1794.
[45] Sun C.R. 12/648362/1795.
[46] Sun C.R. 12/648553/1795; 49/737385/1802; 22/674145/1798.
[47] Sun C.R. 13/656410/1796.
[48] Sun C.R. 13/656219/1796.
[49] Sun C.R. 30/696784/1799; Dartmouth Estate, *Terrier*, 1805, p. 133.
[50] Peel, *Spen Valley* . . . op. cit., p. 230.

and effective use of steam power. Watt, by introducing a rotary motion to drive machinery as opposed to the crank motion, which was really only suitable for pumping, permitted woollen textile manufacturers to drive their machinery directly from the steam engine, although, in fact, Boulton and Watt engines were still introduced in some cotton mills to pump water back above the wheel.[51]

Attempts had been made to bring Boulton and Watt engines to the Yorkshire wool textile industry before 1790. One enterprising gentleman, Mr Robert Spence of Leeds, was advertising in 1785 for:

> Any person inclined to advance the sum of 1,500 or 2,000 pounds in erecting a set of mills near Leeds to be worked by one of Boulton and Cos. patent engines are requested to leave their proposals . . .[52]

This was in the same year that the first Boulton and Watt engine was erected in a cotton mill — at Robinson's mill at Papplewick.[53]

One of their engines was already at work in Yorkshire, in an oil mill at Sculcoates near Hull, where it generated seven horsepower, and within the next three years two more were at work at corn and paper mills in the same area.[54] The first to be provided for a textile mill in the West Riding was the one purchased by Marshall, Fenton and Dearlove in May 1792; at that date it was the largest supplied to Yorkshire, being able to generate 20 horsepower.[55]

For woollen manufacture Benjamin Gott was the first in the county to order a Boulton and Watt engine. He finally requested one of 40 horsepower in August 1792 and this was delivered in 1793 and immediately applied to many of the processes at Bean Ing. In September 1793 John and James Walker of Wortley ordered the second 'Sun and Planet' engine and two years later Joshua Foster bought the third for his mill at Horbury. Before the end of the decade three more firms had purchased Sun and Planet engines from the Soho Foundry. Pim Nevins and Samuel Gatliff erected a 16 horsepower engine at their mill at Larchfield, Hunslet; Nussey's bought a 20 horsepower engine for their Birstall manufactory and the

[51] See H. W. Dickinson and R. Jenkins, *James Watt and the Steam Engine* (Oxford, 1927) and Boulton and Watt MSS, Engine Books.

[52] *Leeds Intelligencer*, 27 September 1785.

[53] Boulton and Watt MSS, Engine Books.

[54] The engine at Sculcoates Oil Mill was ordered in May 1784. B. & W. MSS, Portfolio 1. The other mills were Messrs Howard and Houghton's Paper Mill, Hull where an engine was ordered in September 1786 and was later sold, in August 1802, to T. and H. Lodge of Halifax (Portfolio 16); and Messrs Thompson and Baxter's flour mill, where an engine was installed in 1788, Tann, op. cit., p. 79.

[55] Boulton and Watt MSS, Portfolio 89.

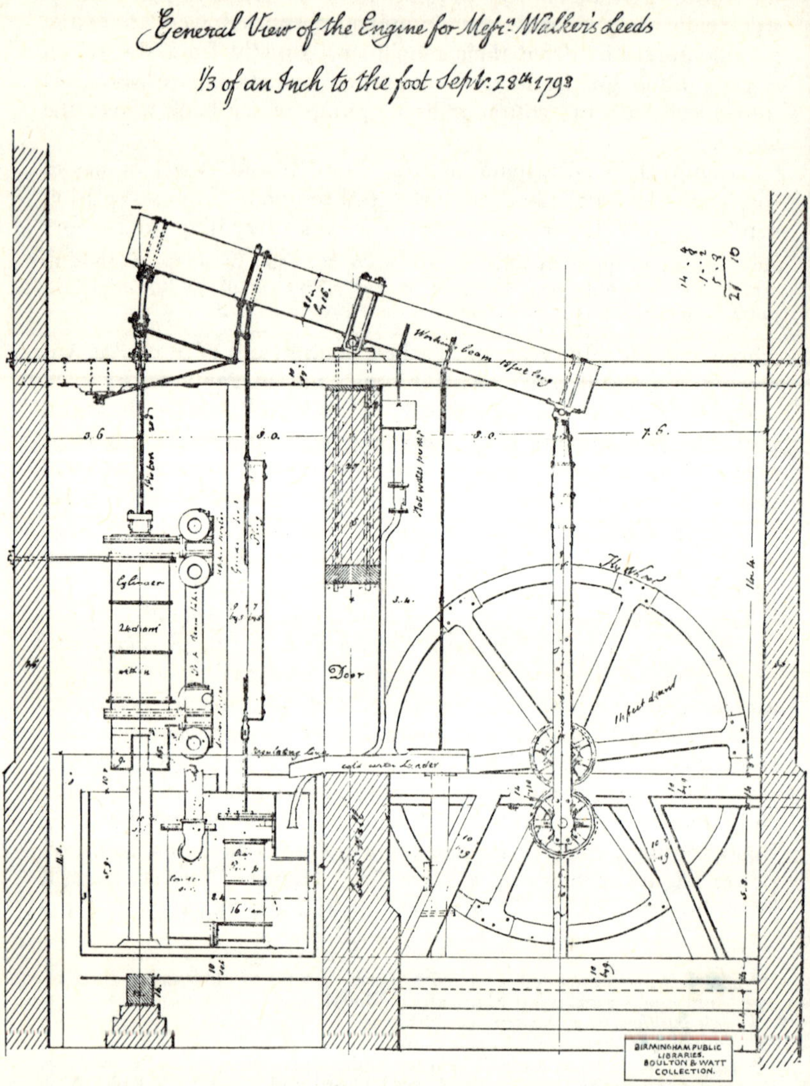

FIG. 10. John and James Walker's Boulton and Watt Sun and Planet engine, 1793

Bateson's of Wortley, Matthew and James, purchased a similar engine for their intended mill at Wortley. The foundry engine book suggests that the latter mill was to be employed for cotton but, in fact, the engine was put to use for woollen manufacture.[56]

In the worsted branch of the industry, the early use of steam power was not so prevalent in spite of it becoming relatively more important in the nineteenth century. No worsted mill has been traced using steam power before 1792, and no engines, other than the ones supplied by Boulton and Watt, appear to have been in use before the termination of Watt's patent rights in 1800. The first worsted mills were all water powered until, in August 1792, Messrs Markland, Cookson and Fawcett ordered a 30 horsepower 'Sun and Planet' engine from Birmingham. This engine, with its 28 in. diameter cylinder, 6 ft. stroke capable of lifting 100,000 lb. 10 ft. high, was set to work early in 1793 to power five large scribbling and carding engines (for coarse carpet yarn), 800 worsted spindles and 1,000 cotton spindles with carding apparatus. Its presence has been overlooked in the past by James, and subsequent writers, because the mill is normally referred to both amongst the Boulton and Watt papers and in contemporary reports as a cotton mill. However, it would seem that the production of worsted yarn was at least as important as cotton manufacture in the 1790s.[57]

The hitherto first recorded use of a steam engine in the worsted manufacture was at Halliday and Cockshott's mill at Baildon where a 12 horsepower 'Sun and Planet' engine was purchased in January 1796. John Cockshott had previously been a partner at the Low Mill at Addingham with John Cunliffe, until he moved to Gill Mill in about 1790. The mill had formerly been used for about twelve years for woollen manufacture by Halliday and Watson, using water power. When it was changed to a worsted mill the engine was put in to propel the machinery when water was scarce. It was, therefore, only really required as a secondary means of power. There appears to be no record amongst the Watt papers as to the amount of machinery it propelled but it was capable of lifting 39,600 lb. 10 ft. high with its $19\frac{1}{8}$ in. cylinder and 4 ft. stroke.[58]

[56] See Table 10 for references.

[57] Boulton and Watt MSS, Portfolio 91 and List of Leeds Engines. See Tables 10 and 13. See also Sun C.R. 8/636966/1795; 13/653223/1796; 17/666225/1797; 22/674510/1798; 24/681849/1798; 27/693428/1799; 32/701514/1800; 45/731575/1802.

[58] W. Cudworth, *Round about Bradford*, op. cit., pp. 338–9 and B. & W. MSS, Portfolio 130.

Steam power came even later to Bradford, the centre of the worsted industry. The attempt by John Buckley to apply steam to a cotton mill in 1793 met with considerable opposition. He was served with a notice that:

. . . if either you or any person in connection with you shall presume to erect and build any steam engine for the manufacture of cotton or wool in a certain field in Horton near Bradford, called or known by the name of Brick Kiln Field, we whose names are here unto described, shall, if the same be found a nuisance, seek such re-dress as the law will give.[59]

Steam did not appear in the town until seven years later when Holme Mill was built and a 15 horsepower engine installed in it. There is no record of any other steam-powered worsted mill in the vicinity before this date.[60]

After 1800 several engines were purchased by Yorkshire manufacturers from Boulton and Watt. By then, however, the firm's patent had expired and others were free to start manufacturing. Not that the patent had prevented some manufacturers from attempting to make use of Watt's ideas in the 1790s. Watt was constantly inquiring from various people about engines being manufactured elsewhere. In Leeds, Murray and Wood were advertising their new works in Water Lane in 1796, and probably commenced building engines a year later.[61] The Low Moor Iron Works were also manufacturing engines by this date although no comprehensive details survive about them.

In the autumn of 1797 John Rennie warned Matthew Boulton that Murray and Wood were becoming possible rivals and later Watt, perhaps rather worried about the competition, paid £2,500 for land next to Fenton, Murray and Wood's premises, partly it would seem, to prevent the Leeds firm expanding, and perhaps also, it has been suggested, to provide a site for Watt to open a factory to supply the growing demand for steam engines in the North of England, particularly in Yorkshire.[62]

Before the end of the century yet another Yorkshire firm was producing engines. John Sturges and Co. of Bowling were manufacturing by 1795.[63] It is, however, unlikely that a great many

[59] J. James, *The History of Bradford and its Parish, with Additions and Continuation to the Present Time* (London, 1866), p. 282.
[60] *Factories Inquiry Commission, Supplementary Reports, 1834*, Part II, C.2., Mill no. 47; J. James, *History of the Worsted Manufacture . . .*, op. cit., pp. 605–6.
[61] *Leeds Intelligencer*, 11 July 1796; T. Turner, *A History of Fenton, Murray and Wood*, unpublished M.Sc. thesis, Manchester University, 1966, Chapter II, p. 4.
[62] Turner, thesis, op. cit., Chapter II, p. 6. quoting a letter from J. Rennie to M. R. Boulton, 8 November 1797. See also Chapter III, pp. 9–10.
[63] Also Elwell at Fall Ing Foundry, Wakefield.

engines were produced that conflicted with Watt's patent rights. Both manufacturers and purchasers were well aware of the dangers of making and installing 'pirate' engines. Messrs Fisher, Nixon and Fisher of Leeds were, at one time, very worried about whether their newly installed engine conflicted with the patent. They wrote to Boulton and Watt in 1798:

Leeds, March 27th, 1798

Gentlemen,

Our engine being nearly finished we are desirous that it should be inspected by your agent, Mr. Lawson, or any other person you may appoint prior to its being put to work. For, notwithstanding the strictest attention has been paid to withhold everything which we concurred would, in its operation, interfere with your patent, we may unintentionally have erred and it will afford us a satisfaction your instructing Mr. Lawson to view the engine. For should it appear there was any actual infringement on your patent we may have the opportunity of removing it on its being pointed out to us.

Waiting your reply
We are respectfully
Gentlemen
Your obedt. servants,
Fisher, Nixon and Fisher.[64]

This letter appears to have been the result of an earlier request from the Leeds manufacturers for their engine, being constructed by Murray and Wood, to be altered to include Watt's principles. Boulton and Watt do not appear to have been in favour of this suggested arrangement by Fisher and Nixon:

. . . we can assure you with much sincerity it never was our intention to infringe upon your patent by the engine Mr. Murray is now making for us, as we meant it to be a common engine, so constructed as not to admit a single doubt of its interfering with your patent. We shall not require from it more than 17 horses but from the information we have received from Mr. Lawson regarding the considerable saving of coals that is attached to your principles, we are from this consideration inclined to offer you £400 for your permission to suffer the present engine now making for use to be converted into a patent one being as we are informed nearly your usual premium of £5 per horse as there will remain little more than two years of your patent after our engine is likely to be set to work. If you do not close with this proposal you may rest assured that to the best of our knowledge we will not do anything in this business that ought to draw upon us your censure or make us liable to a prosecution.[65]

The outcome of this correspondence is not altogether clear. There is no record, however, of Boulton and Watt having carried out any

[64] Boulton and Watt MSS, Parcel F.
[65] Ibid., Fisher, Nixon and Fisher to B. & W., 23 December, 1797.

work for Fisher and Nixon. In spite of the competition that was arising between the Birmingham and Leeds engine manufacturers, the relationship between the two was not always unfavourable. When the partners at the Soho foundry sent a letter to Leeds in 1799 requesting information about a John Parker, who had absconded from their employment and had been engaged by the Leeds firm, it appears that the latter were quite helpful in the matter.[66]

The nineteenth century heralded the more widespread manufacture of steam engines and many improvements on the basic model produced by Watt. Whereas the steam engines in use in the 1790s were mainly to be found in the eastern half of the region the use of steam power gradually spread throughout the textile area. There is insufficient information to compare the changes in the relative importance of steam and water in both the woollen and worsted branches of the industry in the first three decades of the nineteenth century. One is able, however, to discern in general terms, the speed of the introduction of steam power. In the woollen branch of the industry the use of steam developed alongside the growth in the use of water power. Much depended on the location of the mill premises. On the stronger streams and rivers a steam engine was often not necessary but with the growth in the size of mills, their changing location away from valley bottoms and perhaps the improved distribution of the supply of coal in many areas, steam began to become the rule rather than the exception. Thus in the Dewsbury, Batley and Birstall areas where running water was scarce, the number of engines increased rapidly. Also in towns such as Leeds, Halifax, and Huddersfield where space on river banks was at a premium or water power unreliable the engine also became more dominant. In the rural areas to the south of Huddersfield and Wakefield and on the western fringes of the county, water power still held its own.

In the worsted branch the growth in the importance of steam power was even more rapid, once it got under way. The mill premises for the manufacture of worsted required greater power than the small streams around Bradford could provide. Thus the majority of the worsted mills constructed from 1800 to 1830 were built with steam power in mind.

By the 1820s the number of manufacturers of steam engines

[66] Boulton and Watt MSS, Letter Book. May 1799 to March 1800, p. 112. B. & W. to Fenton, Murray and Wood, 27 September 1799.

within the county had risen sharply and engines were also being supplied from as far afield as Lancashire and the Midlands. A directory for 1822 listed at least eight steam engine manufacturers,[67] and by this date an important engineering industry had developed to serve the needs of the textile manufacturers.

The application of steam power to the various processes in woollen and worsted manufacture occurred very much alongside the application of water power to the same processes. Thus some mills were scribbling and carding or spinning wool by steam power in the 1790s. Steam power was immediately applied to work Crompton's mule when it was introduced into the industry and most of the first woollen and worsted weaving mills were using steam power according to the 1835 survey of power looms used in mills.[68] Not until 1835, however, can one make more than a guess at the relative importance of steam and water power. For the Factory Inspector's Returns, I. R. Rickards who dealt with the Yorkshire area, worked out the number of steam engines and their horsepower, parish by parish, and tabulated the results. His figures are probably an overestimate of the actual amount of power being used because in some of the mills a certain amount of power was often directed to purposes other than textile production, and, moreover, sometimes the full amount of power the engine was capable of producing was not required. In the earlier 1833 Inquiry some account was taken of this. Thus at Horton Mill, Bradford used by John Aked for worsted spinning, the latter Inquiry recorded that 'part lately used for grinding of corn'.[69] At Addison and Roper's Prospect Mill, Bowling, part of the power was let off to turn throws in a mechanics' shop.[70] William Edmondson at Idle, although having a 28 horsepower engine in his scribbling, carding, slubbing and fulling mill in 1833, was only using 12 horsepower to power his machinery.[71] The rest of the power does not appear to have been used.

The results of Rickard's survey are shown in Table 12. In the woollen branch of the industry he recorded 308 steam engines with a total horsepower of 6,218. These figures when compared with the number and power of wheels in operation illustrate that by the

[67] Edward Baines, *History, Directory and Gazetteer of the County of York*, Leeds, 1822, Vol. 1.
[68] *Number of Power Looms in Factories*, 1835.
[69] *Factories Inquiry Commission, Supplementary Reports, 1834*, Section II, C.2. Mills nos. 117 and 34.
[70] Ibid., Mill no. 32.
[71] Ibid., Mill no. 141.

early 1830s steam power was relatively far more important than water power. Although there were sixty more engines than wheels the power generated by the engines was over twice as much as that produced by water. The average power of the steam engines was just in excess of 20 horsepower whereas the figure for water-wheels was only 11 horsepower. The size of the engines in operation is also shown. Over half the engines were under 20 horsepower and only 21 were producing more than 40 horsepower. Two hundred and fifteen out of the 241 water-wheels were, however· under 20 horsepower.

TABLE 12

STEAM POWER IN YORKSHIRE WOOLLEN AND WORSTED MILLS IN 1835

Woollen Mills

Engine hp.	Total Engine hp.	No. of Engines
50+	280	4
49–40	683	17
39–30	1527	48
29–20	1815	80
19–10	1677	125
Under 10	236	34
TOTALS	6218 hp.	308

Worsted Mills

Engine hp.	Total Engine hp.	No. of Engines
50+	420	7
49–40	485	12
39–30	716	23
29–20	707	33
19–10	462	50
Under 10	216	34
TOTALS	3186 hp.	159

Source: *Factory Returns 1835*

In almost all areas steam was relatively more important than water by this time. In Leeds, the parish with the largest number of woollen mills, there were only nine water-wheels as against 81 steam engines. The water-wheels can be traced mainly to the mills on the

Aire at and above Kirkstall. At Otley all six woollen mills were water powered but all these mills were very small, two of them having wheels of 12 or 13 horsepower and the other four of no more than 3 or 4 horsepower each. The only other parishes in the woollen textile producing area where water power predominated at this time were Almondbury where the greatest number of water-powered woollen mills were to be found; Mirfield where there were several wheels on the Calder; Halifax where water was still just more important that steam and Saddleworth where there were a large number of very small water-wheels.

Although the average size of the engines was only 20 horsepower, there were several in excess of 50 horsepower. Leeds could boast two of 80 and one of 60 horsepower with another eight of about 40 horsepower. There was an engine producing 60 horsepower in Huddersfield and several just under 50 in Almondbury parish, Batley and Dewsbury. The larger engines were, however, to be found more in the worsted branch of the industry.

In worsted by 1835 over two-thirds of the power was produced by steam. Rickards recorded 159 steam engines generating 3,186 horsepower compared with 102 wheels generating only 873½ horsepower. Thus the average power of the engines was just over 20 horsepower and that of the water-wheels just under 9 horsepower. He discovered seven engines of over 50 horsepower distributed in the area as follows:

Bradford	4 engines generating 260 hp.
Wakefield	1 engine generating 50 hp.
Halifax	2 engines generating 110 hp.

The size of the steam engines being used for worsted manufacture is illustrated by Table 12. Only at Otley on the Wharfe and at Keighley, Addingham, Skipton and Gargrave on the Aire was water power of most importance in worsted manufacture.

In the next two decades steam power reinforced its position. The *1838 Factory Returns* recorded 377 engines in operation in woollen mills and 226 in worsted mills compared with almost no change in the number of wheels in use from the 1835 total. During the intervening five-year period, the average power per engine had very slightly increased and the average for wheels decreased. Water power still predominated in the Saddleworth district, in Almondbury parish, in Mirfield and Otley and some of the villages in the Upper Aire and Wharfe valleys but elsewhere the importance of steam power had grown. Twelve years later although water power was still important in the woollen manufacture, it was providing only just over a quarter of the total power used whereas in worsted only 12 per cent of the power came from the rivers.[72] Thus during the first half of the nineteenth century, steam power rapidly took the place of water power as the prime mover for woollen and worsted textile machinery. Probably by the mid-1820s steam engines outnumbered water-wheels but even so water was still performing an important role twenty-five years and more later. In the woollen and worsted industries steam power permitted the building of larger plant and the increase in the number of mills, and hence the overall development of the industry. It brought, however, difficulties for many manufacturers, not least of which was the problem of obtaining the greater capital require both for constructing the larger plant and for purchasing the more reliable, but initially expensive, form of power.

The Capabilities of Power

The amount of power available to a mill directly affected the quantity of machinery that could be put to work. Before installing an engine the manufacturer had to choose between a relatively cheap small one with limited capabilities and a more expensive larger engine which could power more machinery. Often the first enquiry an intending purchaser would make to the steam engine manufacturer would be about the number of spindles or other machinery an engine of a certain size would power. Substantial errors were still made however. There were instances of mill owners installing engines too weak for their needs and even more instances of engines being used with capabilities far in excess of the needs, or even projected needs, of the mill. The Children's Employment Commission Factory Survey listed many mills where power was substantially under utilized.

Some evidence is available about the capability of the power of steam engines in the wool textile industry at this period. Much information is to be found amongst the correspondence of Boulton and Watt. Lawson, one of the firm's mechanics, who was frequently in Leeds and became a close friend of Benjamin Gott, wrote to Soho in 1797 mentioning that Murray of Murray and Wood's had told him that an engine of 20 horsepower could turn 1,500 spindles and one 8 horsepower larger 2,300 spindles.[73] Messrs Marshall and Co. had

[72] *Factory Returns*, 1850.

[73] Boulton and Watt MSS, Box 26. Letter from Lawson to B. & W.

two engines of 20 horsepower and 28 horsepower supplied by Boulton and Watt in 1792 and 1794 respectively so, perhaps, the calculations were based on these. In fact in the list of Leeds engines, already referred to, Messrs Marshall and Co.'s two engines are recorded. The 20 horsepower one is listed as turning 1,500 flax spindles and the 28 horsepower engine 2,300 flax spindles. It also mentioned that they were spinning 12 tons of flax per week.[74] The same list, besides giving details for Marshall's and Gott's engines, also gives information about the other engines supplied to local manufacturers.

Table 13

LIST OF LEEDS ENGINES (SUPPLIED BY BOULTON AND WATT) WITH DETAILS OF THEIR WORK

1. Messrs Wormald, Fountain and Gott — 40 Horse Power, December 1793

12 Fulling stocks
38 Scribbling and Carding machines
4 Willeys
2 Rasping machines
1 Chipping machine
1 pair of edge stones
2 Indigo mills
2 Friezing engines
2 Brushing machines
2 Pumps for supplying fulling mill and dyehouse with hot and cold water.

Burns 2¼ tons of coal in 13 hours.

2. Messrs Markland and Co. — 30 Horse Power, 1793

5 large scribbling and carding engines (for coarse carpet yarn)
2 large scribbling and carding engines (for fine wool for worsted)
800 worsted spindles
1000 cotton spindles — with carding apparatus.

3. Messrs Marshall and Co. — 20 Horse Power, 28 Horse Power

20 Horse Power engine powered 1,500 flax spindles
28 Horse Power engine powered 2,300 flax spindles

12 tons of flax per week spun.

[74] See Table 13.

4.	Messrs J. & J. Walker 31 Scribbling and Carding engines 2 Willeys 2 small Willeys called puckers 4 Stocks	20 Horse Power May 1794
5.	Messrs Bateson's Scribblers, Carders and Stocks.	20 Horse Power April 1797
6.	Messrs Gowland and Co. Scribblers, Carders and one Willey and 1,100 cotton spindles with preparation	20 Horse Power
7.	Messrs Blagborough and Holroyd 2,000 Cotton spindles	20 Horse Power April 1797
8.	Messrs Nevins and Gatliff Scribblers and Carders 1 Willey and 2 Pickers 6 Stocks (2 pushers and 4 fallers)	16 Horse Power March 1797
9.	Messrs Beverley, Cross and Co. 1,800 cotton spindles (at the time it was burnt down.)	22 Horse Power August 1793
10.	Messrs Nusseys . . . Birstall Stocks, scribblers, carders and one willey	20 Horse Power May 1797
11.	Messrs Fosters . . . Horbury Scribblers, carders, willey and 6 stocks.	20 Horse Power February 1797

Source: B. & W. MSS, List of Leeds Engines.

In 1796 a specification for Benjamin Gott's 40 horsepower engine gave a rather different account of its capabilities. This suggests, perhaps, that the engine was somewhat less efficient than three years previously. It also indicates that six of the 40 horsepower were needed to turn the main gearing.[75]

[75] See Table 14.

TABLE 14

WORMALD AND GOTT'S 40 HORSE ENGINE 21 JULY 96

Geer without Machinery	.. 6	(Horses)	.. 6 Horses
Geer & Rasp	5	Horses	..11 Do
Do (&) Wood Stones	4	Do	..15 Do
Do & 2 Pushing Stocks	3	Do	..18 Do
Do & 9 falling Stocks	7	Do	..25 Do
29 Scribbling & Cardg Engines & 3 Willeys	14½		..39 D
Indigo Mill, Winch, & Nappg & brusg engines	½	Horse	..40 Horses

Source: Gott MSS, Paper no. 63 reproduced in Crump, p. 219.

Amongst the Boulton and Watt papers are other estimates and information. Watt wrote to Major John Cartwright in November 1788 to inform him that 1,000 spindles could be driven by from 8 to 10 horsepower. Three years later he wrote to Peter Ewart who had a cotton business in Lancashire:

For machine twist we reckon eight horse power can drive about 700 spindles and preparers, but for fine twist they can do more than double that number but much must decide upon the machinery, some being much heavier to drive than others.[76]

Whether these figures for cotton manufacture were comparable in the woollen trade is partly answered by Boulton and Watt themselves. In a later letter to Cartwright they state:

The powers necessary for 1,000 spindles we gave you were for cotton spinning, the wool spinning we know nothing about, but should suppose it will be much the same provided the weights which hold the drawing rollers together be not much heavier, nor the carding harder but these points you probably know.[77]

Other miscellaneous information can be found about how much machinery different size engines would turn. At Nottingham in 1792 a large new seven storey block erected by Dennison and Cates contained '3,024 spindles powered by a 30 horsepower engine, and giving employment to about 300'.[78] The 20 horsepower engine at Gomersall Mill was required to work two drawing frames with reels, warping mills and 50 power looms in 1830.[79] A cotton mill at

[76] Quoted by R. L. Hills, *Power in the Industrial Revolution* (Manchester, 1970), p. 203. B. & W. to P. Ewart, 21 February 1791.
[77] Ibid., p. 219. B. & W. to J. Cartwright, 19 December 1788.
[78] S. D. Chapman 'The Transition to the Factory System in the Midlands Cotton Spinning Industry', *E.H.R.*, XVIII, 1965, 536–7.
[79] *Leeds Mercury*, 2 October 1830.

Keighley in 1807, powered by a 14 horsepower steam engine, contained 12 water twist spinning frames of 64 spindles each, two throstles of 96 spindles, 13 carding engines, drawing and roving frames.[80] And in the same year a worsted mill in Bradford, powered by a 15 horsepower engine, contained 18 spinning frames with a total of 1,044 spindles, two twisting frames with 60 spindles each and some other machinery.[81]

These various miscellaneous figures suggest that larger engines could power relatively more machinery and that engines, gearing and machinery became more efficient over time, wasting less power and thus permitting a greater load. One can roughly generalize and say that 1 horsepower was probably required to work 100 spindles. Therefore the 3,762½ horsepower being employed for worsted manufacture in 1835 was capable of turning approximately 376,250 spindles. However, as about 3,000 power looms were also operating at this date, the total number of spindles would have been rather less than this figure.[82]

In the woollen trade where more processes were mechanized in mills by this date one cannot so easily assign the 8,000 horsepower being employed to turn different machines for different processes. Power was required to turn stocks, scribbling and carding engines, willeys, spinning machines and looms as well as other machinery for various processes and all this machinery varied in size and, therefore, in the amount of power it required.

[80] Ibid., 4 April 1807.
[81] Ibid., 19 September 1807.
[82] *Number of Power Looms in Factories*, 1835.

4

MILLWRIGHTS' AND CLOCKMAKERS' WORK

The Transmission of Power

One of the major problems that faced the early mill builder was the construction of the machinery of transmission from the source of power to the various machines. Any system of power transmission using axles, pullies and gears would, in any case, somewhat reduce the amount of power available to turn the machinery but an inefficient and clumsily built system could mean a considerable reduction in the amount of power getting through to the machines. Thus the construction of this transmission machinery, normally termed at the time as 'millwright's work', was a major consideration in the planning of a mill building, and in the investment in fixed capital.

The millwright had, for generations, been an important local craftsman. Fairbairn, in the mid-nineteenth century, described him thus:

> The millwright of former days was to a great extent the sole representative of mechanical art and was looked upon as the authority in all the applications of wind and water, under whatever conditions they were to be used, as a motive power for the purposes of manufacture. He was the engineer of the district in which he lived, a kind of jack of all trades who could, with equal facility work at the lathe, the anvil or the carpenter's bench. In country districts, far removed from towns, he had to exercise all these professions, and he thus gained the character of an ingenious, roving, rollicking blade, able to turn his hand to anything, and like other wandering tribes in days of old, went about the country from mill to mill, with the old song of 'kettles to mend' re-applied to the more important fractures of machinery.
>
> Thus the millwright of the last century was an itinerant engineer and mechanic of high reputation. He could handle the axe, the hammer, and the plane with equal skill and precision; he could turn, bore or forge with the ease and despatch of one brought up to these trades and he could set out and cut in the furrows of a millstone with an accuracy equal or superior to that of the miller himself.[1]

Thus even before the coming of textile mills the services of the millwright were sought after wherever he went. Fairbairn goes on to tell of some of his skills:

[1] W. Fairbairn, *Treatise* . . ., op. cit., first edition, Part 1, Preface.

Generally he was a fair arithmetician, knew something of geometry, levelling and mensuration, and in some cases possessed a very competent knowledge of practical mathematics. He could calculate the velocities, strength and power of machines, could draw in plan and section and could construct buildings, conducts or water courses, in all forms and under all the conditions required in his professional practice; he could build bridges, cut canals, and perform a variety of work now done by civil engineers. Such was the character and condition of the men who designed and carried out most of the mechanical work of this country, up to the middle and end of the last century.[2]

In spite of their skills and attainments, however, many millwrights found it hard to cope with the new machinery and means of power of the late eighteenth and early nineteenth century. Many of the complaints received by Boulton and Watt from customers concerned the transmission machinery rather than the engine itself. Moreover, the introduction of the steam engines created the need for more specialized skilled labour, for fitters, machine makers, and mechanical engineers. However, it was the millwrights who were first concerned with the introduction of water and steam power to textile machinery and indeed some of the early steam engine builders commenced their careers and learned their new skills as millwrights. Most of the staff of Boulton and Watt's Soho foundry started their careers as ordinary, if one could call them 'ordinary', millwrights.

With the development of textile mills and improvements in the steam engine more and more thought was given to the transmission machinery in mills. Various books were written on the subject before the end of the eighteenth century and improvements were continually made. In 1795 John Banks wrote *A Treatise on Mills* divided into the following four parts:

First Part.	On Circular Motion.
Second Part.	On the maximum of moving bodies, machines, engines, etc.
Third Part.	On the velocity of affluent water.
Fourth Part.	Experiments on circular motion, waterwheels, etc.

And a few years later, in 1803, he wrote a second work entitled *On the Power of Machines, Etc.*[3] Both these works are detailed considerations of power and its transmission. He was concerned in the first work mainly with water-wheels and he saw as his purpose:

It will not be expected that I should attempt to instruct the mechanic how to form his cogs, divide the wheels, proportion their diameters, bevels, etc., as numbers of men can be found who can both plan and execute these parts

[2] Ibid.

[3] John Banks, *A Treatise on Mills* (London, 1795), Title Page; John Banks, *On the Power of Machines* (Kendal, 1803).

well. The chief end in view is how to make the most of a given stream; and what the experiments recommend has long since been put into practice, with acknowledged advantage.[4]

He does deal, however, with the problems of friction and distance and irregular power. In his second work he examines certain mills and engines in relation to his earlier findings and considers, in particular, various types of water-wheels. He also compares the strength of wood and iron.

His works were widely read. The list of original subscribers included many well-known West Riding mill owners, engineers, and other textile manufacturers. One finds amongst them, for example, the names:

Samuel Barlow of Low Moor
George Birkbeck of Settle,
Thomas Bradley of Halifax,
Brighouse Library,
John Cockshott of Baildon,
Thomas Edmundson of Dolphineholme,
William Hirst, engineer at Gomersal,
John Marshall of Leeds,
Robert Owen of Manchester,
John Rennie,
John Raistrick of Low Moor Furnace,
Edward Smalley, engineer at Wibsey Low Moor

and many others engaged in similar trades.

In the eighteenth century the transmission machinery was very inefficient, heavy and ponderous, but in the first few decades of the nineteenth century improvements were carried out and Fairbairn was able to look back in 1851 at and '. . . follow out consecutively nearly the whole of the discoveries, improvements and changes that have since taken place in mechanical science'.[5]

There were two systems of transmission in operation in Fairbairn's time. The first was an arrangement of 'wrapping connectors' or pulleys and leather straps which was most frequently found in America and in some parts of Southern England and London. In the textile areas of Lancashire and Yorkshire, however, the normal means of transmission was through a system of gearing and light shafts, a method that Fairbairn called 'rolling contact'. He considered the latter to be much more efficient:

[4] Banks, *Treatise* . . . , op. cit., preface, p. xiii.
[5] Fairbairn, *Treatise* . . . , op. cit., Part II, Preface, p. vii.

I have been convinced by long experience that there is less loss of power through the friction of the journals, in the case of geared wheel work than when straps are employed for the transmission of motive power . . . In some of the American cotton factories, however, there is an immense drum on the first motion, with belts or straps from two to three feet wide, transmitting the power to various lines of shafting, and these in turn, through other pulleys and straps, giving motion to the machinery. From this description it will be seen that the whole of the mill is driven by straps alone without the intervention of gearing.

The advantages of straps are the smooth and noiseless motion. The disadvantages are increased friction on the journals of the shafts, cumbrous appearance, the expense of their renewal and the necessity for frequent repairs. They are inapplicable to cases where the motion must be transmitted in constant ratio, because as the straps wear slack, they tend to slip over the pulleys and thus lose time . . .[6]

Thus Fairbairn was very much against a system of belts and pulleys, possibly partly because of his work on improving the gear system and his training as a millwright. No information is available as to how frequently belts or straps were used in Yorkshire wool textile mills. The insurance inventories suggest that the normal means of transmission in the industry was through gearing and shafts, but there might well have been small mills, with only a few pieces of machinery, connecting this machinery to the engine or wheel through straps.

The arrangement of the transmission machinery was often a complicated business. With perhaps the engine in a separate building the shafts often had to reach from one building to another and extend both vertically and horizontally for some distance. Fairbairn provided a number of illustrations showing the normal type of arrangement. Figure 11 shows a vertical section of a four storey mill building, part of Saltaire Mills at Shipley, in the early 1850s. A horizontal shaft from the engine connected to a vertical shaft by a flywheel B, which in turn connected with machinery in the four storeys and the attic, horizontal shafts extending along the first, second and fourth floor to connect to the machinery by guide pulleys, straps and belts. The strength of the shafts depended upon the amount of machinery connected to them. Fairbairn pointed out:

It will not be necessary to give the dimensions of the shafts in each room, as these details and calculations must be left to the judgement of the millwright, and the nature of the work they have to perform. Suffice it to observe that the vertical shaft A is 10 inches in diameter through the first

[6] Ibid., pp. 103–5.

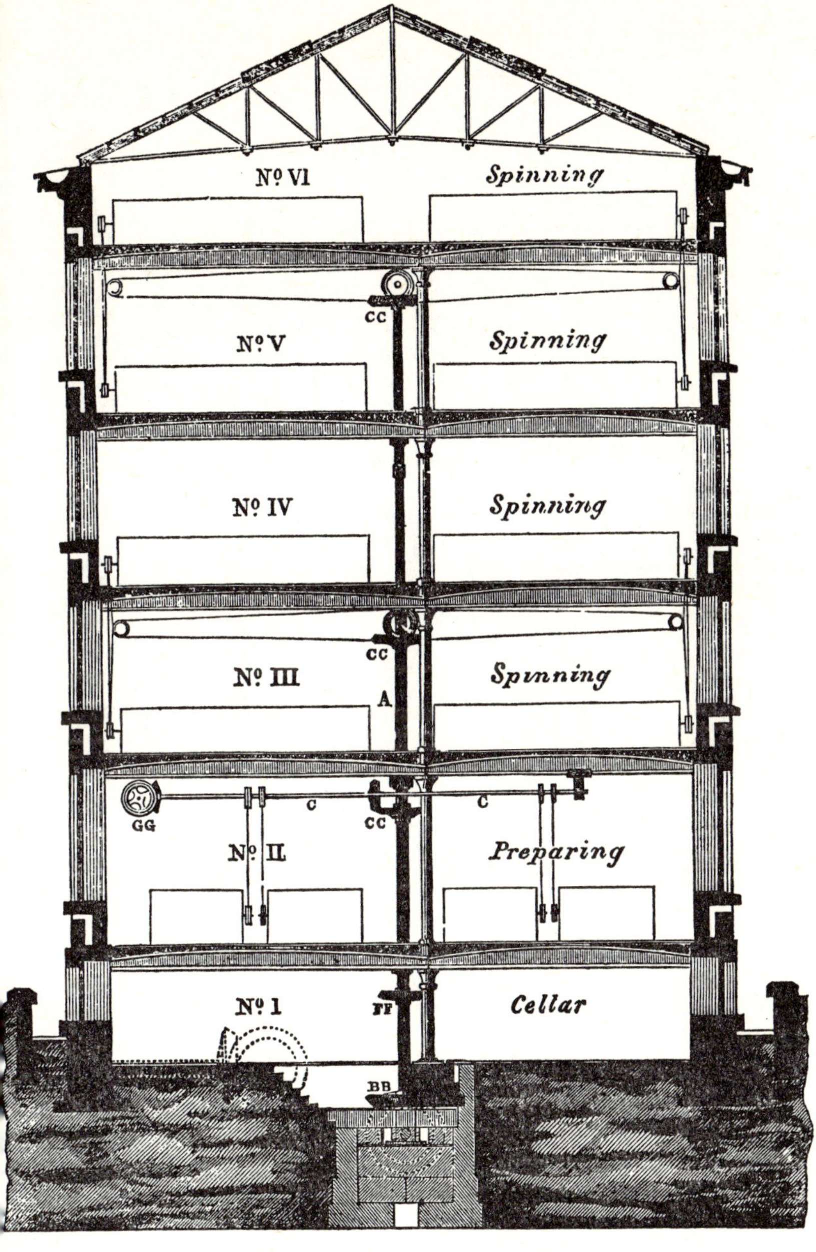

FIG. 11. Cross-section of Saltaire Mills, near Shipley
Source: W. Fairbairn, *Treatise on Mills and Millwork* (3rd edition, London, 1871, Pl. II, p. 103)

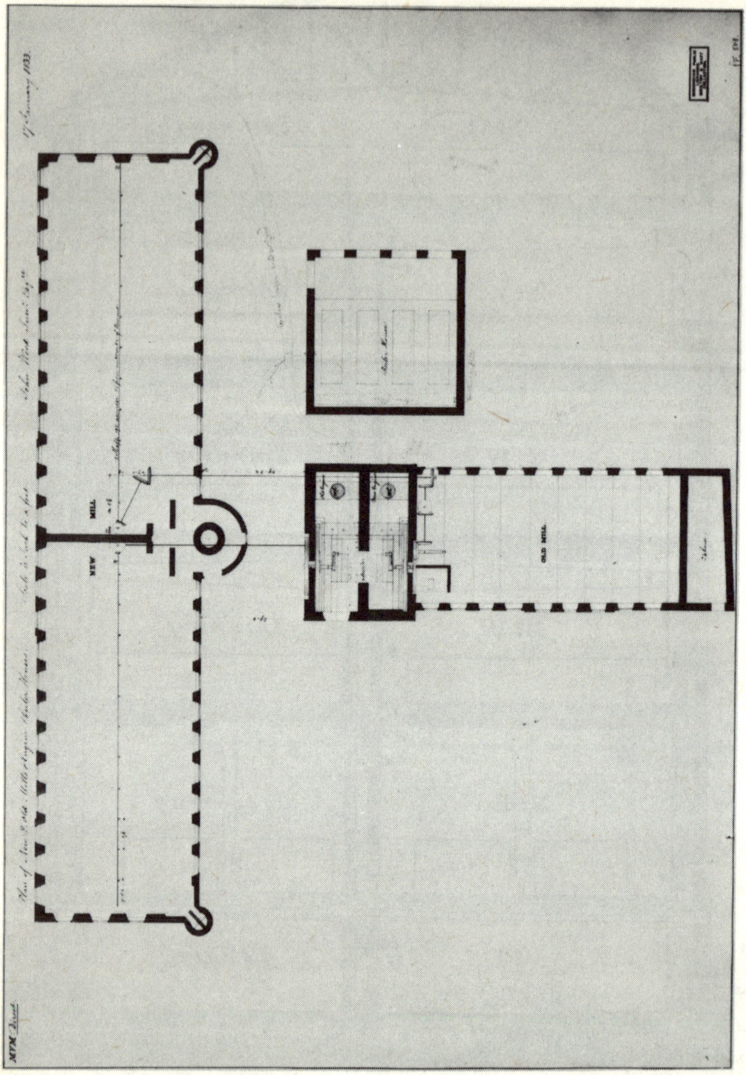
NEW MILL
OLD MILL

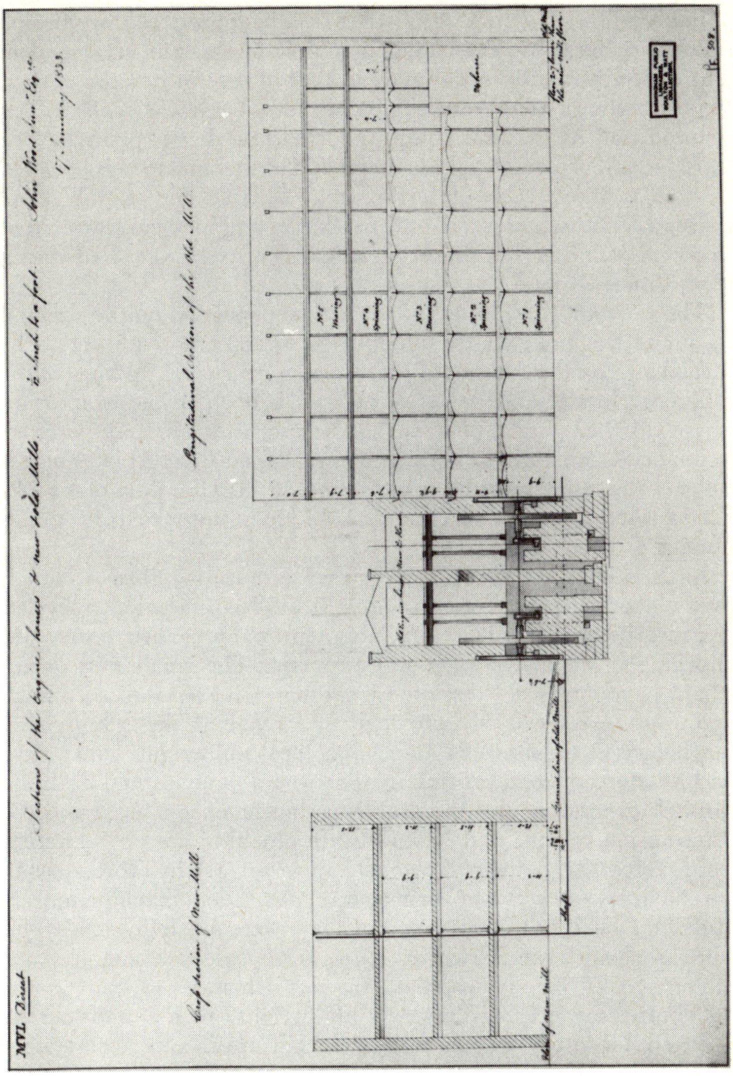

FIG. 12. Plan and cross-sections of John Wood's Mill at Bradford, constructed by Wm Fairbairn
Source: B. & W. MSS, Portfolio 508

two rooms, 8½ inches through the third room and 6½ inches to the top; the velocity being 94 revolutions per minute.[7]

Salt's mill was not built until 1851 by which time the transmission machinery had undergone much improvement, but arrangement and design was still very similar to that of several decades earlier. Figure 12 shows John Wood's mill at Bradford as it was in 1833 when Boulton and Watt were commissioned to work out plans for the introduction of a gas supply to the mill. The machinery was powered by two engines, each of 80 horsepower, and one engine of 28 horsepower, and power from the two largest engines was transmitted to the new mill across almost 30 ft. of open space, the shafts being placed underground.[8]

The amount of millwrights' work thus depended on the size and layout of the mill, on the amount of machinery requiring to be turned and on the amount of power being generated. In view of the difference in size and layout of mills, it is not possible to measure physically the quantity of millwright's work, although its importance in financial terms will be considered in Chapter Five. At present it is sufficient to stress that the construction of this vital part of a mill's fixed capital formed a very important item of investment for a mill builder.

Little is known about the early Yorkshire millwrights. Although they played such an important role in mill development they left few records of themselves, and, although many of their names are known, few details of their work remain. The small mill owner would have employed the same local man who serviced corn mills and who had previously provided and repaired the transmission machinery in fulling mills. Often this local millwright would have had little or no technical training but would have learned his trade through experience and the problems that he encountered and the transmission systems that he built were probably not very different from each other. Some mill owners appear to have had the expertise and facilities to carry out their own repairs. Local machine makers also often acted as millwrights. But there were few millwrights who could cope with the intricacies of the large scale new factories and the services of these few were in constant demand.

Perhaps the major Yorkshire millwright at the end of the eighteenth century was John Sutcliffe of Halifax, a theoretician as well as a practical engineer and mechanic. He was the millwright

[7] Ibid., p. 105.
[8] Boulton and Watt MSS, Portfolio 508.

consulted by three of the earliest Leeds factory builders, Gott, Markland, Cookson and Fawcett, and John Marshall and was responsible for much of the millwright's work at the first two establishments and appears to have supervised the construction of Benjamin Gott's first mill building at Bean Ing in 1792.[9] Sutcliffe, with other local millwrights, acted as a fire insurance assessor after the major fire at the building in August 1799.[10] Althout he appears to have been recognized as the best practical local millwright by Gott and others his advice about engine purchase was not taken by Gott, nor by Markland, Cookson and Fawcett, and there were disputes about his high charges with John Rennie being asked to arbitrate on two occasions, one of which concerned the work at Gott's mill and the other the construction of the Leeds Waterworks.[11]

Another Yorkshire millwright who appears to have had considerable business, particularly with smaller mills was John Jubb. Originally an agricultural machine maker and millwright (he was advertising Thrashing Machines in 1794) he expanded his business in the 1790s when he advertised for three journeyman millwrights and the same number of joiners 'who have been accustomed to work at scribbling and carding machines'.[12] Although described as a millwright he also supplied machinery to local mills, acted with Sutcliffe and others as a fire loss assessor and early in the nineteenth century was a partner in a woollen mill.[13] He installed a steam engine in Cocking Steps Mill, Netherton in 1801.[14]

As late as the 1820s, millwrights were probably still in short supply in the county. The local directory in 1822 listed less than a dozen firms in the main textile manufacturing area.[15] Both Jubb and Sutcliffe had cease working by that time. The Leeds machine makers and engine builders Fenton, Murray and Wood were possibly the major local millwrighting concern. They also advertised themselves

[9] Tann, op. cit., p. 99; Crump, op. cit., p. 208.

[10] Gott MSS, no. 64. Particulars of the loss by fire at Bean Ing near Leeds on Sunday 11 August 1799 the property of Messrs Wormalds and Gott — Insured in the Sun, and Royal Exchange Offices in the same proportions.

[11] Crump, op. cit., pp. 208, 217. In a letter dated 31 March 1793, Rennie wrote to Gott, 'You payed Me amply for My opinion inspecting Sutcliff's drawings . . .', and on the second occasion, in July 1795, Gott wrote to James Lawson asking him to consult with Rennie about whether Sutcliffe's charges to the Commissioners of the Leeds Water Works were justified.

[12] *Leeds Intelligencer*, 2 June 1794.

[13] *Leeds Intelligencer*, 1 March 1802; Gott MSS, no. 64; Sun C.R. 143/1007963/1823.

[14] Crump and Ghorbal, op. cit., p. 76.

[15] E. Baines, *A Directory of the County of York*, 1822.

as constructors of fireproof mills and gas lighting apparatus. By the 1830s however, the number of millwrighting concerns had increased and a number of firms were well established.

The Production Machinery

The largest capital cost for the manufaturer was normally the machinery for the mill. Often, having built a mill, manufacturers were not able to meet the cost of equipping it, because of the considerable outlay involved, but, in many cases, machinery was only gradually purchased, part of the mill remaining empty for some time. Such was possibly the case at Batley Subscription Mill, an early Company mill, where the 'clockmaker's work' was insured for £1,800 in 1802, £2,500 in 1805, and £3,700 a year later, without any extensions to the buildings having been constructed.[16] At Markland, Cookson and Fawcett's cotton and worsted spinning mill at the Bank in Leeds machinery appears to have been introduced only gradually also. Valued at £2,500 in January 1795, the machinery insurance was increased to £3,500 in March 1796; £3,600 in January 1798 to £4,000 in 1799 by which time the mill was probably fully stocked with machinery as the valuation slightly decreases in later insurance policies, possibly because of depreciation.[17]

Investment in production machinery is, undoubtedly, the most difficult item to assess when considering fixed capital investment. Within the period from 1780 to the mid-1830s, numerous technical innovations were carried out, new machines brought into use or earlier machines increased in size. One cannot easily account for all the changes and the times they came about in different mills. Some manufacturers were eager to introduce new and better machinery as soon as it came on to the market. Others would wait until they had to replace worn out machines before purchasing the new types. One has, moreover, to attempt to take into account the fairly rapid depreciation about which company accounts and insurance policies give little information.

At this stage the main technical improvements in the processes of production of both woollen and worsted cloth will be traced and an attempt made in the next chapter to estimate the value of a mill's machinery at different dates. It is, of course, necessary at this point

[16] Sun C.R. 48/736105/1802; 68/782272/1805.

[17] Sun C.R. 8/636966/1795; 13/653223/1796; 22/674510/1798; 24/681849/1798; 27/693428/1799.

to examine the woollen and worsted branches separately, because, in spite of the similarities in their buildings, sources of power and transmission machinery, their differing techniques of production required different machinery.

The production processes might be divided into four main sections:

The preparatory processes
Spinning
Weaving
The finishing processes

but within each of these main categories there were many subsidiary processes and each of these will be considered in turn. Perhaps the fullest account of the processes involved in the manufacture of woollen cloth is provided by Edward Baines, whose knowledge of the textile districts of Yorkshire and Lancashire was probably unrivalled in his day.

Baines describes the following processes being carried on at Gott's mill 'which has long ranked with the first woollen factories of any county':

1. Sorting the wool — no less than ten different qualities being found in a single fleece.
2. Scouring it with ley and hot water to remove the grease and dirt.
3. Washing it with clean cold water.
4. Drying it, first in an extractor — a rapidly revolving machine full of holes, and next, by spreading it and exposing it to the heat of steam.
5. Dyeing, when the cloth is to be wool dyed.
6. Willying, by revolving cylinders armed with teeth, to open the matted locks and free them from dust.
7. Teasing, with a teaser or devil, still further to open and clean.
8. Sprinkling plentifully with olive oil, to facilitate the working of the wool.
9. Moting, with the moting machine, to take off the motes or burs, i.e. seeds of plants or grasses which adhere to the fleece.
10. Scribbling, in a scribbling machine, consisting of a series of cylinders clothed with cards or wire brushes working upon each other, the effect of which is still further to disentangle the wool and draw out the fibres.
11. Plucking, in a plucking machine, more effectually to mix up the different qualities which may remain in the wool.
12. Carding, in a carding machine, resembling the scribbler, but more perfectly opening the wool, spreading it of a regular thickness and weight, reducing it to a light filmy substance, and then bringing it out in cardings or slivers about three feet in length.
13. Slubbing, at a frame called the billey, generally containing 60 spindles, where the cardings are joined to make a continuous yarn, drawn out, slightly twisted, and wound on bobbins.
14. Spinning on the mule, which contains from 300 to 1,000 spindles per part.
15. Reeling the yarn intended for the warp.

16. Warping it, and putting it on the beam for the loom.
17. Sizing the warp with animal gelatine, to facilitate the weaving.
18. Weaving at the power loom or hand loom.
19. Scouring the cloth with fullers earth to remove the oil and size.
20. Dyeing, when piece-dyed.
21. Burling to pick out irregular threads, hairs or dirt.
22. Milling or fulling, with soap and warm water either in the fulling stocks or in the improved milling machine, where it is squeezed between rollers.
23. Scouring, to remove the soap.
24. Drying and stretching on tenters.
25. Raising the nap of the cloth by brushing it strongly in the gig with teazles fixed upon cylinders.
26. Cutting or shearing off the nap in two-cutting machines, one cutting lengthwise of the piece and the other across.
27. Boiling the cloth, to give it a permanent face.
28. Brushing in a brushing machine.
29. Pressing in hydraulic presses, sometimes with heat.
30. Cutting the nap a second time.
31. Burling and drawing, to remove defects, and marking with the manufacturer's name.
32. Pressing a second time.
33. Steaming to take away the liability to spot.
34. Folding or cutting for the warehouse.[18]

By Baines's time much more care was going into cloth production and a higher quality product, compared with earlier in the century, was being manufactured. Some of the processes mentioned in the above list would not have been carried out at an earlier date, just as some of the materials used, such as olive oil, were fairly recent innovations for the period.

The first task of the cloth manufacturer was to sort the wool. The wool from different parts of the fleece is of different texture, not just long and short wools used respectively for worsted and woollen manufacture, but of many different grades or qualities, finenesses, softness and strengths. Dyer in *The Fleece* described sorting:

> In the same fleece diversity of wool,
> Grows intermingled, and excites the care
> Of curious skill to sort the several kinds . . .
> Nimbly with habitual speed,
> They sever lock from lock, and long and short,
> And soft and rigid, pile in several heaps.[19]

The wool was first classed by the farmer according to the breed of sheep and the quality of the wool. Then the wool would be more

[18] Baines, op. cit., pp. 631–3.
[19] Dyer, *The Fleece*, quoted by Lipson, op. cit., p. 129.

carefully sorted by woolstaplers, or sometimes the clothiers themselves, into over 10 or 12 qualities or 'counts'. Even under the factory system, this was always a hand operation. Sometimes the sorting was carried out on the premises but other times the wool was purchased, already sorted.

The next operation was to scour the wool to remove the various impurities. Often up to a third of the weight of the wool would consist of grease, burs and other objects entangled in the fibres. The natural grease found in the wool fibre is composed of two different materials. One, the suint, is soluble in water; the other, the yolk, needs soap or an alkaline solution. The dissolving and removal of grease improved the condition of the wool for dyeing and improved the texture for manufacture. Various methods were used for scouring. The suint was removed by simple washing often before the sheep were sheared, hence the description 'washed wool'. An agent was necessary to remove the yolk. In the first half of the nineteenth century the most common agent was animal or human urine but other alkaline solutions were used and occasionally soap, although the latter was more frequently employed in the worsted branch of the industry.

Scouring was also a hand operation although some of the larger mills by the 1830s had separate buildings for scouring the wool where the solvent could be heated in large baths or vats and the wool immersed. However, at that time most of the wool was probably still scoured in the open on the banks of streams. There is no mention of a scouring house at Bean Ing until 1826 although Clay and Earnshaw of Rastrick had a scouring room at their mill by 1812.[20]

After scouring the wool was sometimes dyed, although this process was often left until the cloth had been woven. Some mills carried out their own dyeing, others sent their wool or cloth to dyehouses such as Sayners's Dyehouse on the Aire at Hunslet where cloth was being dyed by the end of the eighteenth century. Dyeing facilities do not appear to have depended on the size of the mill. Joseph Rogerson of Bellisle Mill, Bramley, had dyepans. He recorded in his diary on 27 January 1808 that: 'All Dyepans in use, pretty well off for work this week', and there are several entries in his diary at later dates.[21] Benjamin Gott must have done much of his

[20] Sun C.R. 156/1040865/1826; Clay and Earnshaw MSS, Stock Account, 1812. Typescript copy at the Brotherton Library, Leeds.

[21] Crump, op. cit., 'The Diary of Joseph Rogerson', pp. 79, 85, 87, 93.

own dyeing. He had built a dyehouse adjacent to his engine house by April 1794 and three years later he had a 'New Mill for grinding dyeing wares'.[22]

Dyeing was normally carried out in a separate building. By the 1820s some mills were probably also dyeing wool or cloth for manufacturers without facilities. Perhaps this was the case with Benjamin Musgrave, a cloth manufacturer at Wellington Bridge near Leeds, who had considerable dyeing facilities. The insurance on his mill records a Pattern Dyehouse, a Black dyehouse, a Wet house and dyepans. In 1831 he built a blue dyehouse and a few years later a second.[23]

Over the fifty-year period dyeing methods improved considerably. Fires to heat the pans were being replaced by steam in the 1820s and 1830s. New colours and means of producing colours were introduced, but overall there was no great technical advance in the sort of equipment being used.[24]

The wool was then willeyed and teazed, both of which operations opened it up, loosened the matted fibres and removed dust and other extraneous particles. The willey, sometimes also known as a woolley or willow, was a very simple machine, powered by water or steam and introduced in the earliest of the scribbling mills. It consisted of a circular drum, pierced with teeth revolving against similar drums or rollers, all enclosed in a large box. The wool, that was fed in, was loosened and parted by the teeth. Teazing was a similar operation to loosen the matted wool still further in preparation for scribbling and carding.

There were some changes in the type of machinery used for willeying and teazing in the period from 1780 to 1830. Before the development of the scribbling mill the operation was carried out with rods with which the wool was beaten but when water and steam were applied to textile manufacture the willey took over. One of the earliest descriptions of the willey is given in Rees's *Cyclopaedia*:

The wool mill used in Yorkshire consists of a cylindrical drum, about three feet long and two feet and a half in diameter, which is made to revolve nearly 300 times per minute. Its circumference is furnished with teeth or spikes, and immediately about it five small rollers are placed, which are

[22] Sun C.R. 14/627124/1794; 19/667674/1797.

[23] Sun C.R. 170/1083057/1828; 184/1114596/1830; 185/1118959/1831; 193/1131689/1831; 200/1165321/1833.

[24] For this study it has not been thought necessary to discuss dyeing in detail. Accounts may be obtained from Abraham Rees, *The Cyclopaedia*, op. cit., Vol. XII, and from C. Singer et al., *History of Technology* (1946), Vol. IV, pp. 248–50. See also C. Partridge, *A Treatise on Dyeing* (new edition, Edington, 1973).

also furnished with similar teeth. The teeth of the rollers and those of the drum intersect each other when they all turn round and the teeth of the five small rollers also intersect each other. The cylinders and rollers are enclosed in a box or case, which is closed on all sides, except a door in front.[25]

Early in the nineteenth century various modifications were made to this simple machine. Some had air blown through them to remove dust and in the 1820s a larger machine was introduced, known as the shakewilley, devil or plucker, which although working on much the same lines as the teazer or willey, was stronger and could cope with more wool.[26]

The willey was introduced as early as the scribbling machine. An advertisement for the sale of one appeared in 1779.[27] The machine was an essential part of the scribbling miller's equipment. Mills normally had several of the machines as they were quite small, could only cope with small quantities of wool at a time and the wool often had to be put through more than once. It is impossible to estimate the number in operation in the textile area at any period, as the machine did vary in size. Thus when Hebble Mill, near Halifax, was put up for sale in 1804 only 'One large woolley or Teazer' was included amongst the machinery although there were seven scribbling engines and five carding engines.[28] But at Thwaite Gate Mill at Hunslet a few years later 'A valuable new Teazer and Three Willeys' were included with only two scribbling engines.[29] Gott had a number of willeys. In 1794, John Jubb, the Leeds Millwright, made 'two machines or Things called Willies' at £31.10*s*. each for the Bean Ing Factory and Samuel Fortune of Halifax also supplied one in the same year.[30] In his notebook on Mill Practice, Gott described his willeys: 'The Diameter of the Willow from Tooth end to Tooth end is 28 inches, makes 300 revolutions per minute.'[31]

From the various mill inventories that are available from newspaper advertisements, insurance records and company books, one can reasonably show that one willey was normally sufficient to supply two or three scribbling machines and sometimes more.

[25] Rees, op. cit., Vol. XXXVIII.
[26] W. Smith, *The History and Antiquities of Morley* (1876), p. 221.
[27] *Leeds Mercury*, 26 January 1779.
[28] *Leeds Intelligencer*, 13 August 1804.
[29] *Leeds Mercury*, 7 December 1811.
[30] Crump, op. cit., pp. 24, 215. There are a number of letters amongst the Gott papers concerning orders for willeys.
[31] Crump, op. cit., p. 289.

By Baines's time there were one or two other refinements to ensure that the wool, by the time it was ready for the scribbling process, was completely clean and contained no impurities, but the next main process in woollen cloth manufacture was scribbling, the second process to be mechanically powered and the one which heralded the widespread introduction of mills and steam and water power.

The purpose of scribbling and carding was to completely disentangle the woollen fibres and arrange them in slivers or cardings of similar thickness and weight. The scribbling machine worked the wool into some sort of order and the carding engine finally produced even slivers. Carding and scribbling engines were very similar in design and for this reason are often listed together in insurance policies and mill inventories: the difference between the two machines lay in the coarseness of the teeth that separated the wool and in the form that the wool emerged from the machines. The scribbling or carding machine consisted of a large cylinder known as the 'main cylinder' or 'swift' covered with protruding wire teeth and a series of several smaller cylinders or rollers known as 'workers', 'strippers' and 'doffers', or sometimes 'urchins', all with similar wire teeth and arranged in such a way that the teeth of the smaller rollers almost touched each other and the teeth of the 'swift' when they were all revolving. The machine was continually fed with wool which passed over the swift and the rollers several times before being removed by the 'doffer'.

Until the 1770s in the woollen industry carding and scribbling was carried out entirely by hand with the aid of hand-cards but a great deal of energy in this period was being put into inventing a successful machine. Around the middle of the century a number of patents were taken out for the roller process. As early as 1738 Lewis Paul invented a system of cylinder cards which he patented in December 1748. These cards were:

> Covered parallelly to the axis with fillets of leather thus mounted, having intervening stripes free from points. A concave card of the same curvature as the cylinder was applied to its under surface. Hence, on turning the cylinder by the handle at its end, the two bristling surfaces worked against each other and performed the carding operation. When the filaments were thought to be sufficiently carded, the stationary concave part was let down and the cylinder was then stripped of its wool by means of a comb made of a bar of wood bearing a row of needles.[32]

[32] A. Ure, *The Cotton Manufacture of Great Britain* (1836), p. 245.

The cards used in Paul's machine were still similar to hand cards but in May 1748 Daniel Bourne of Leominster patented a machine with four parallel rollers and metal teeth which was to be the forerunner of the machinery in use in textile mills at the end of the century.

In the 1760s James Hargreaves appears to have re-invented an apparatus similar to the forgotten Lewis Paul machine and then, with financial assistance from Peel, the Lancashire cotton manufacturer, a cylindrical carding engine which although similar to later successful machines proved to be very inefficient itself.

At about the same period, Arkwright was also experimenting with carding engines, as were no doubt many other manufacturers in the textile areas. It was probably Arkwright, however, who was the first to produce a useful and efficient carding engine using a crank and comb motion for doffing the carding and thus allowing a continual process. Other refinements on his engine included an improved feeding arrangement through what was called a feed lap roller and a method for evenly distributing fibres on the cylinders. Although in the next few decades there were minor adjustments and improvements to the design of the engine, carding machinery was still basically the same throughout the period. The engine varied in size, some had long cylinders, others short, but they all used the same principle.

Many of the nineteenth-century topographical writers on areas in the textile district of the West Riding of Yorkshire suggest dates when the first scribbling engine was introduced into the area they were describing. They are, on the whole, rather untrustworthy. There can be no doubt that scribbling or carding engines of one type or another were being experimented with in the West Riding from the middle of the eighteenth century. These early machines would have been hand powered and small enough for the clothiers to keep at home. For water or steam power to be used, the machines had to be installed in special buildings and thus the introduction and adaptation of scribbling and carding to water and steam power relates very closely to the development of the scribbling mill.

Scribbling and carding engines were rapidly introduced throughout the area from the late 1770s, much to the dismay of the hand carders. The latter in 1786 sent a: 'Humble Address and Petition of Thousands who labour in the Cloth Manufacturing' to 'The Merchants, Clothiers and all such as wish well to the Staple Manufactory of this Nation'. In their petition they complained that:

The number of Scribbling Machines extending about 17 miles south west of Leeds, exceed all belief being no less than 170! and as each machine will do as much work in 12 hours as 10 men can in that time do by hand (speaking within bounds) and they working night and day, one machine would do as much work in one day as would otherwise employ 20 men.[33]

and they went on to say that there were probably almost as many scribbling machines again elsewhere in the textile district. There is no means of knowing how this figure of over 300 scribbling engines was arrived at or how accurate it was. Perhaps they were over-exaggerating to help their case and no doubt many of these machines were hand or horse powered in private homes, but, even so, there is ample evidence that there were many in use in mills by this date.

Various evidence suggests that around 1800 the typical mill housed six to eight scribbling and carding engines and the larger factories several times that number.[34] This suggests that by the end of the eighteenth century perhaps 2,000 such engines powered by water or steam were at work in woollen mills. Although this is no more than a very rough estimate it does point out the rapidity with which the machines were introduced.[35] Unfortunately, a similar estimate for a later period is not possible, nor would it mean very much if it were possible, because of the greater variety in the size of machines later in the nineteenth century. Much carding was still, however, also being carried out by hand in the first decades of the nineteenth century.

Once the wool had been scribbled and carded the strips of wool were removed from the last doffer of the carding machine for slubbing, when the slivers or strips were pieced together and slightly twisted and drawn out ready for spinning. Slubbing was a simplified form of spinning, which had earlier been carried out on a spinning wheel but with the introduction of the 'jenny' was transferred to the new machine. The slubbing billey probably originated at about the same time as the jenny and, like the latter, was normally hand operated. However, although jenny spinning was usually carried out in the clothiers own homes, slubbing was frequently one of the processes of the scribbling mills. The insurance policies of the period often described premises as 'scribbling, carding and slubbing' mills.[36] The slubbing billies varied in size, some having

[33] *Leeds Mercury*, 13 June 1786.
[34] This rough figure is based on information for a few mills as shown in Table 15.
[35] An entry in Gott's mill notebook states '7 scribblers if properly managed will supply 8 carders'. Crump, op. cit., p. 22.
[36] Slubbing is sometimes referred to as 'slugging' in contemporary literature.

TABLE 15

EXAMPLES OF THE NUMBER OF SCRIBBLING AND CARDING MACHINES IN EARLY WEST RIDING WOOLLEN MILLS

Date	*Mill*	*Details of Machines*	*Source*
1793	Mill in Hunslet	6 Scribbling Machines 1 Carding Machine	*L.I.* 28/10/1793
1794	Nether Mills, Leeds	5 Scribbling Machines	*L.I.* 13/1/1794
1794	Castle Mill Gomersal	8 engines for scribbling and carding wool	*L.I.* 4/8/1794
1789	Armley Mills	7 Scribbling Engines	Sun O.S. 364/562208/22/10/1789
1796	Bean Ing, Leeds	29 Scribbling and Carding Engines	Gott MSS; Crump op. cit., p. 219.
1799	Mill Bridge Mill, Liversedge	2 Double 30 inch Carders 1 Double 60 inch Carder 3 Double Scribbling Engines	*L.I.* 14/1/1799
1799	Mill at Farnley	6 Scribbling and Carding Machines	*L.I.* 4/3/1799
1801	Mill at Holbeck	3 Scribblers 3 Carders	*L.I.* 23/3/1801
1802	Mill Bridge, Birstall	2 Scribbling Engines 5 Carding Engines	*L.I.* 1/3/1802
1804	Hebble Mill, Halifax	7 Scribbling Engines 5 Carding Engines	*L.I.* 13/8/1804
1809	Dudfleet Mill, Horbury	5 Scribbling Machines 4 Carding Machines	Misc. Text. MSS, Cusworth Hall
1790s	Messrs J. & J. Walker, Wortley	31 Scribbling and Carding Engines	B. & W. MSS, List of Leeds Engines

fifty spindles or more and operated by several workers, children called 'piecers' or 'pieceners' feeding them with cardings.

Although Rees mentioned:

> an improved slubbing machine has been introduced, which is put in motion by the mill, and the carriage is made to draw out by the power of the machine. The spinner has only to push the carriage in and turn the handle in order to wind up the slubbings.[37]

and the sale details for Hebble Mill in 1804 included: 'Three water billies, one of 120, one of 88 and one of 80 spindles.'[38] The machines

[37] Rees, op. cit., Vol. XXXIII, quoted by Crump, op. cit., p. 22.
[38] *Leeds Intelligencer*, 13 August 1804.

were still mainly powered by hand until the 1820s. Rogerson and Lord's scribbling mill at Bramley had hand powered billies.[39]

Most mills appear to have had more than one of the machines. There were two at Mill Bridge Mill at Liversedge, six at a new mill at Farnley, and three at Sturge's Mill at Holbeck.[40] In 1829 six were being worked at Dungeon Mill between Lockwood and Meltham and two months later seven were recorded at Messrs Brancher Brown and Co.'s mill at Mill Garth in Leeds.[41] Numerous other sale notices in the local newspapers indicate the widespread use of the slubbing billey.

The slubbings, as the wool was called once it had passed through the billey, were then ready for spinning. A great deal has been written about the invention and innovation of spinning machinery during the eighteenth century.[42] It is sufficient here to confine the discussion to use of spinning machines in wool textile mills and factories. Some mention has already been made of the application of steam and water power to the water-frame and the mule. The spinning jenny, however, was also sometimes worked in the mills even though it was hand operated.

The spinning jenny was the product of experiments by James Hargreaves in the 1760s. The jenny was able to spin several threads at once. Hargreaves claimed in the specifications for his patent that the jenny was able to spin, draw and twist sixteen threads, or more, operated by only one person. However, like the slubbing billey, the jenny was essentially a hand-powered machine normally worked in the clothiers own homes. It was probably introduced into Yorkshire before the 1780s and continued to be the main means of spinning wool in the woollen branch of the industry to at least the 1830s.

Although it was only manually operated, the spinning jenny was introduced into some mills. Jennies were being worked in the Spinners' Rooms at Bean Ing in the 1790s; in fact as soon as the mill was built.[43] As late as 1833 Eneas Walker of Holmfirth had 'one 80 spindle jenny and working wheel' valued at nine pounds in his small mill.[44] There were jennies working at Bradley Mill at about the

[39] Crump, op. cit., 'The Diary of Joseph Rogerson', p. 92.
[40] *Leeds Intelligencer*, 14 January 1799; 4 March 1799; 23 March 1801.
[41] *Leeds Mercury*, 26 December 1829; 6 February 1830.
[42] The literature on the development of spinning machinery is immense. Recent contributions have included R. L. Hills, *Power in the Industrial Revolution*, op. cit., and H. Catling, *The Spinning Mule* (Newton Abbott, 1970).
[43] Crump, op. cit., p. 212.
[44] Sun C.R. 197/1155328/1833.

same time and likewise at John Burnley's Mill at Heckmondwike and Starkey's at Longroyde Bridge, Huddersfield.[45] Many other instances can be cited.

Mechanical power was introduced to spinning by means of Richard Arkwright's water-frame also invented in the 1760s:

> Arkwright's machine was a wooden frame at the top of which were four bobbins, placed horizontally across it, containing rovings. A roving from each bobbin passed through two pairs of rollers divided into four sections corresponding to the bobbins. The second pair of rollers moved more quickly than the first and so elongated the roving, which then passed down the arm of a flyer attached to a spindle at the bottom of the machine and was wound on the bobbin carried by the spindle. The speed of the bobbin was retarded in relation to that of the spindle by a brake in the shape of a piece of worsted twisted round its base.[46]

Although first intended to be powered by a horse, the frame was quickly adapted for water and steam power and became known as the water-frame. Various modifications were made to it in the following decades. The early use of the frame appears to have been confined to producing yarn for hosiery, warp for cotton goods and yarns for worsted production, but there were still many problems. In the early years it proved difficult to maintain a constant quality of the yarn, and in any case the quality was not good. James recorded that '. . . for a long time (it) continued to be exceedingly rough and hairy, so much so as to render it very difficult to weave'.[47] However, the machine-spun yarn produced was strong and very suitable for use with the flying shuttle. So the frame came into use in the worsted branch of the industry in Yorkshire by the late 1780s.

Whether, in fact, water-frames or throstles were used for woollen products is rather uncertain. There is evidence of early water woollen spinning mills before the end of the eighteenth century and if they were not water-frames that were being used in these mills, then what spinning machinery was operating? Thus Sands Mill at Heaton Bank, Dewsbury, was described in its insurance policy as: 'A water woollen spinning, slugging and scribbling mill . . .'[48] and a similar policy for Wrigley's Mill at Dobcross refers to their '. . . water millhouse for scribbling, carding and spinning wool . . .'[49] while Joseph and Joshua Whitfield had a wool spinning mill at Idle powered by a steam engine.[50]

[45] Sun C.R. 194/1135635/1832; 206/1171385/1834; 214/1197383/1835.
[46] Singer, op. cit., Vol. IV, 277–8.
[47] James, op. cit., p. 355.
[48] Sun C.R. 12/648171/1795.
[49] Sun C.R. 12/648180/1795.
[50] Sun C.R. 68/782281/1805.

Other instances can be cited but even so their number is not great and the information that the insurance policies give does not make absolutely clear whether spinning machinery was mechanically powered or not, even though, as in the case of Sands Mill, it sometimes strongly indicates powered woollen spinning.[51]

Thus in the woollen branch of the industry spinning remained very much a hand operation until the introduction of the 'mule', invented by Samuel Crompton. Crompton set to work in the 1770s to invent a machine to spin fine threads for both warp and weft:

> He combined the rollers of the water-frame with the moveable carriage of the jenny by placing the spindles on the carriage and the rollers where the spindles had stood in the jenny. The spinner drew back the carriage at the same rate as the roller gave out the sliver, until about five-sixths of the whole distance had been traversed. Then the rollers were stopped and made to act like the clasp of the jenny, while the carriage continued to recede at a much slower rate and the spindles continued to twist. At the end of the stretch the spindles were turned a few times in the opposite direction to disengage the yarn. The carriage was then pushed in again with the spindles turning slowly in the original direction to wind on the yarn with the help of the faller as in the jenny.[52]

This new machine reduced the strain on the threads but when it was first made known in 1779 it was in a very imperfect state. In the following decades a number of refinements were made to its methods of construction and its action. The various parts of the original machine were not mechanically connected and the whole spinning operation therefore required the most careful attention of the spinner and, even so it was not easy to produce a thread of even stretch and fineness.

The original mules were hand operated but by 1790 the machine had been adapted to be powered by water, possibly first at the mills of Mr Kelly at New Lanark but then soon after by manufacturers in Lancashire. The date of the introduction of the mule to Yorkshire is uncertain. James records talking to John Hutton, an overlooker at Paper Hall, Bradford in the 1790s, who stated that he remembered spinning machines being used at Paper Hall at Bradford by Mr James Garnett in the 1790s. James discussed what the machines were:

> There has been some dispute whether these machines were jennies or mules but the evidence of a person who assisted in turning them is conclusive. He states that they were called mules, and is corroborated by another person who often saw them at work.[53]

[51] Sun C.R. 12/648171/1795.
[52] Singer, op. cit., pp. 279–80.
[53] James, op. cit., p. 329.

There are suggestions that early attempts were made to use water power for the mule spinning of wool. A Leeds clothier placed an advertisement in a local paper in 1800:

> To mule spinners. Wanted one or two mule spinners in the country. Anyone who can bring a good character for honesty and sobriety being master of the business may apply to Robt. Cookson of Holbeck near Leeds.
>
> Good wages will be given and constant employment, the mules go by water and are 288 spindles each.
>
> N.B. If a family the more acceptable.[54]

Robert Cookson gave evidence to the 1806 Inquiry in the report to which he was described as a master clothier, although no mention is made of a mill belonging to him. He was said to manufacture fine goods, second sorts, between superfine and coarse, with three looms in his house. He employed one or two outweavers. Amongst the total of 11 or 12 employees there were two spinners; possibly the ones he advertised for.[55] Whether, however, they were spinning wool with water-powered mules is a matter of considerable conjecture. There was, at the period, a John Cookson spinning cotton and worsted, but whether the two were connected is again uncertain.

William Hirst claimed to be the first to introduce mules into the woollen manufacture in 1816

> . . . I was the first who introduced spinning mules into the woollen manufacture; and I afterwards got a patent for double rod spinning mules to do double the quantity of work in the same time.[56]

Benjamin Gott, however, was employing mule spinners by 1813; probably hand spinners for the fine work although there is some doubt as to whether they spun wool or cotton warp.[57] The insurance policies taken out by Gott in 1826 and 1827 on all the Bean Ing property, machinery and stock list only spinning frames, not referring at all to mules, and they also show that only part of the spinning machinery was mechanically powered in 1827. An 1816 policy mentions only hand spinning.[58]

The returns of Crompton's Spindle Inquiry of 1811 list about 45 cotton mills in the West Riding using his mule, with a comment: '. . . the extent of the mules in the woollen trade is not mentioned though extensive.'[59] However, in view of Crompton's aims with the

[54] *Leeds Mercury*, 31 May 1800.

[55] Crump, op. cit., p. 27 quoting *Report . . . On the Woollen Manufacture of England*, 1806.

[56] W. Hirst, *A History of the Woollen Trade* (Leeds, 1844), p. 39.

[57] Crump, op. cit., p. 25.

[58] Sun C.R. 158/1055368/1827; 156/1040865/1826; 114/916916/1816.

[59] Crompton Family MSS, B.P.L. Account of Spinning Spindles taken in 1811.

inquiry one cannot be sure how true this statement was and, if the mules did exist extensively in the woollen trade, whether they were powered by water or steam.[60]

The widespread introduction of the mule did not take place until Roberts made it 'self acting' in the late 1820s and it was probably another decade before it superseded the jenny as the main means of spinning woollen yarn. Insurance inventories do show that the mules were being used in a number of mills by the early 1830s. Joseph Arundel of Rothwell had installed some in his mill by 1831.[61] There were mules as well as jennies at Bradley Mills, near Huddersfield, in the following year.[62] Mules were introduced to Rods Mill, Morley between 1825 and 1828, to Starkey's Mill at Longroyde Bridge, Huddersfield, by 1831 and to Brooke's Mill at Well House, Huddersfield, by 1830.[63] They were also being used at Crosley Mill by 1831 and by Brown and Andrews of Millgarth, Leeds in the same year.[64] Halliley and Stanley of Low Close Mill, Sheepscar had installed them by 1828.[65] One contemporary report stated that it was:

> not until the 1830s that the mule began to compete seriously with the jenny in the woollen industry; by 1840 the self acting mule had come into rapid use . . .[66]

It should be stressed that the mule that came into use in the woollen branch of the industry was substantially different from that in use in worsted manufacture. The worsted mule was a direct derivation from Crompton's cotton mule and combined a degree of roller drafting with the spindle driving. There was no roller drafting on the woollen mule and, thus, some confusion has been caused by the use of the name 'mule' for the machine. The woollen mule was more akin to a jenny and was presumably called a mule because the part containing the spindles was made the moving part. There were a variety of different woollen spinning 'mules' known under a number of names, for example 'Jacks'.

Once spun, the yarn was prepared for weaving. This again was a domestic operation until well into the nineteenth century, although

[60] In his survey Crompton provided no examples of mules in use in woollen mills.
[61] Sun C.R. 188/1127361/1831.
[62] Sun C.R. 194/1135635/1832.
[63] Sun C.R. 152/1036030/1825; 170/1083064/1828; 190/1131936/1831; 180/1104439/1830.
[64] Sun C.R. 190/1134663/1831; 188/1127922/1831.
[65] Sun C.R. 166/1068920/1827; 170/1081634/1828.
[66] PP. 1842 (31), XXII.

power was first successfully applied to a loom in the 1780s by Cartwright, who set up a factory in Doncaster with twenty cotton looms. This early machine was very imperfect in its functioning and and in the following years Cartwright carried out a number of improvements.[67] In 1791 he built a cotton mill at Manchester for the Grimshaw brothers and installed twenty-four looms powered by a steam engine; this mill was soon burnt down. But for the next two decades various improvements had still to be made. Baines estimated that by 1820 there were 14,150 power looms working in England and Scotland in all textile production. Nine years later the number had quadrupled and it doubled again in the following five years.[68]

Thus it was in the 1820s the beginnings of rapid growth of steam and water-powered weaving commenced. In Yorkshire there is no definite knowledge as to who was the first to start operating power looms in the woollen and worsted business. The 1835 Survey of Power Looms in Factories lists forty-eight mills that were operating them by that date. All but half a dozen of these were worsted mills. The list is reproduced in Table 16 and shows 175 woollen looms, 2,953 worsted looms and 533 used for more than one purpose.[69] Of those recorded in woollen factories one cannot ascertain with ease when they were first introduced. A mill in the East Riding, at Wansford near Driffield, not included in the list had power looms in November 1828. But the insurance policy does not make it very clear whether they were being used for woollen or worsted work, the mill appearing to engage in both.[70] Joseph Arundel at Rothwell, who is again not on the list, had power looms and mules in what was definitely a woollen mill in 1831.[71] Joshua Lockwood of Huddersfield, another woollen manufacturer, insured power looms in the spring of 1833 and even he, a large and well-known manufacturer, was not recorded in the survey.[72] Clearly the power loom survey of 1835 was far from complete. Of those that were recorded John Walker and Sons, who manufactured woollen cloth at Millshaw Mills, did not have power looms in 1831.[73]

[67] Hills, op. cit., pp. 213–17.
[68] Ibid., p. 219; Baines, *History of the Cotton Manufacture*, op. cit., pp. 235–7.
[69] *The Report of Power Looms in Factories*, published in 1836 but relating to 1835 was clearly far from complete. There are many more instances known of woollen and worsted mills using power looms by this time. See below.
[70] Sun C.R. 169/1083390/1828.
[71] Sun C.R. 188/1127361/1831.
[72] Sun C.R. 200/1155688/1833.
[73] Sun C.R. 188/1126142/1831.

TABLE 16

POWER LOOMS USED IN FACTORIES IN YORKSHIRE — 1835

Firm	*Parish*	*Wool Looms*	*Worsted Looms*
Edward John	Halifax	58*	
Edward John	Halifax	132*	
Crossley & Sons	Halifax		157†
Isles Michael	Halifax		2
Buckley Bros.	Halifax		150†
Ashworth & Co.	Halifax	36*	
Rawson H. W.	Halifax	59	
Akeroyd James	Halifax		357
Buck and Kershaw	Halifax		237
Milnes & Dewhirst	Bradford		40
Rhodes & Field	Bradford		55
Billingsley & Tankard	Bradford		14
Wade James	Bradford		74
Field T. B.	Bradford		40
Stowell & Co.	Bradford		50
Akeroyd R.	Bradford		48
Akeroyd C.	Bradford		6
Horsfall & Co.	Bradford		378
Waud C.	Bradford		30
Coultas G.	Bradford		8
Cousen & Co.	Bradford		16
Kershaw Isaac	Bradford		25
Leach Robt.	Bradford		20
Anderton & Co.	Bradford		33
Turner & Mitchell	Bradford		70
Haley John	Leeds		61
Hargreaves & Sons	Leeds		36
Anderton Wm.	Bingley		32
Waud & Co.	Bradford		86
Berwick E.	Bradford		4
Murgatroyd & Co.	Bradford		18
Gott B. & Sons	Leeds	68	
Calvert & Clapham	Keighley		58
Booth & Sons	Leeds		37
Dickinson & Co.	Leeds		302
Lund Wm.	Keighley		43
Varley John	Leeds		28
Molding Miss	Bingley		12
York & Sheepshanks	Leeds	30	

TABLE 16 (continued)

Firm	*Parish*	*Wool Looms*	*Worsted Looms*
Sugden Wm.	Keighley		47
Butterfield Bros.	Keighley		60
Birbeck & Co.	Linton		80
Clough John	Keighley		28
Smith J. & B.	Gargrave		8
Stansfield & Co.	Leeds		479
Haggas & Son	Keighley		29
Walker John & Sons	Leeds	18	
Clough Robt.	Keighley		2

TOTALS:

Wool Looms	175	The survey was clearly incomplete
Worsted Looms	2,953	* Wool and worsted
Looms used for weaving both wool and worsted	226	† Worsted and cotton

Source: *Returns of Power Looms in Factories in the United Kingdom*, 1836 (24), XLV.

In the woollen branch of the industry it is very unlikely that there were many mills weaving by steam or water power before 1830. This view is borne out by various contemporary comments. As late as 1841 the *Encyclopaedia Britannica* stated that: 'The hand loom is chiefly employed at present' and in evidence for a parliamentary report in 1834, William Brook stated that there were only a few experimental power looms in Leeds.[74]

The next process in woollen manufacture requiring machinery was milling or fulling. The early development of the fulling mill has already been discussed.[75] Many of the early scribbling and carding mills were converted from earlier fulling mills. Fulling stocks were also erected in newly built mills either powered by water or by steam. Not all mills, of course, fulled their own cloth but many did have machinery for fulling. Starkeys at Longroyde Bridge, Huddersfield, had fourteen stocks at work in the 1830s, and Gott was fulling most of his own cloth throughout the period.[76] The Bean Ing notebook gives an excellent description of the stocks and the process.[77]

[74] Quoted by Bischoff, op. cit., Vol. II, p. 396; *Report from the Select Committee on Hand Loom Weavers' Petitions*, PP. 1834 (556), x, p. 31.
[75] See above, Chapter 1.
[76] Sun C.R. 244/1268084/1838.
[77] See Crump, op. cit., pp. 299–300.

By the second or third decade of the nineteenth century very few separate fulling mills remained. For the estimates of total fixed capital, the early fulling mill has been excluded but the fulling machinery in mills also carrying out other processes has been included in the valuations and calculations.

The Bean Ing notebook also describes the next process in woollen manufacture as follows:

> When best Superfine Cloth is taken from the Mill it is first dryed on the Tenters, when dry it is taken off and well wet out and taken immediately to the Raising Board and given five throughs with old Teazels, using the worst first, the sixth time use new ones (and if the piece be very stout and a mixture it will require one thro' with flatter cards) — in this state it is thrown on a Horse to sipe (about 10 minutes) if thin cloth it ought to be dryed before it is taken to the Shear Board where it is cut once over without raising the wool, (this operation is called Cropping), it is then well wet out again and raised four times through with old Teazels on the Raising Board, it is then Struck twice thro' with flatter cards at the Perch which stands in a Trough of Water, roll it up for Tenter and strike it down with Cards and brush it, it is always stretched one yard to the score and if stamped 58 inch broad stretch it to 61, when dry take it to the Shear Board and cut it three times over with the best finishing Shears and once on the back side.
>
> A piece should never lay in press above 24 hours without being turned, when turned it should lay three days longer.[78]

The dressing and finishing processes varied according to the cloth being produced, and some power driven machinery was used. The early gig mill and the shearing frame were the root of much unrest amongst clothiers in the early nineteenth century. Attempts had been made to introduce the gig mill at a very early date. A Proclamation in 1633 showed that although their use was forbidden they were being operated.[79] There is an excellent picture and description of a gig mill in Rees's *Cyclopaedia*.[80] It shows a revolving cylinder with teazels in holders along its surface brushing against the cloth as the cylinder was turned from the gearing of the engine or wheel, really a very simple mechanism. Gig mills appear to have been used in early mills in the Huddersfield area. The Atkinsons of Bradley Mills and Doodlebank Mills were using them in the 1780s and 1790s.[81]

[78] Crump, op. cit., p. 301; Gott MSS, no. 91. Bean Ing Notebook.
[79] Crump, op. cit., p. 40.
[80] Rees, op. cit., Vol. XXXVIII, Woollen Manufacture.
[81] Crump, op. cit., p. 46 and Sun C.R. 1/620468/1793; 14/651954/1796; 17/666615/1797.

William Brooke of Honley had Raising and Cropping Shops there by the 1790s but his gigs do not appear to have been insured although cropping machines and shears were in 1807.[82] It appears that an attempt was made in Leeds in 1799 to introduce the gig mill but the mill was pulled down and totally destroyed.[83] Other instances may be cited of gig mills. The *Leeds Mercury* carried an advertisement for the sale of a 'Teazing machine . . . to go by water' in 1779.[84] Another 'Teazing Machine' was insured at Cookes Mill, Thongsbridge, in 1802 but the violent resistance of many of the workers perhaps prevented a more widespread use of the machines until at least the 1820s.[85] Gott was dressing cloth by machinery in 1827 although a previous insurance policy suggests he might have introduced his first gigs some years earlier.[86] Hirst, who was at one time a cropper at Bean Ing, describes going to see gig mills working at Oatlands Mill in 1813 and first using gig mills himself in 1816.[87] According to Lipson, there were only five gig mills working in Yorkshire in 1806 and seventy-two in 1817 but no clue is given as to the source of his information.[88] The introduction of the mills was, however, becoming much more widespread by the end of the 1820s but even after 1850 some cloth was still being raised by hand.[89]

Mechanical shearing was introduced before 1800 following the invention of shearing machines by Delaroche of Amiens in 1784, and J. Harmer of Sheffield three years later. The first shearing machines were very rudimentary. Several shears were open and shut together by a crank moved by a steam engine or water-wheel, the cloth being drawn over rollers. Shearing frames were being used at Honley in 1803 and elsewhere around Huddersfield within a few years, including Bradley Mills as John North's evidence to the 1806 Inquiry shows.[90] But, as with the gig mill, there was a great deal of opposition to their use. One of William Thompson's mills at Rawdon was broken into and had its shears destroyed in 1812 and a few nights

[82] Sun C.R. 72/797912/1807.
[83] *Leeds Mercury*, 25 October 1799 quoted by Crump, op. cit., p. 46.
[84] *Leeds Mercury*, 26 January 1779.
[85] Sun C.R. 52/741101/1802.
[86] Sun C.R. 136/1040865/1826; 114/916916/1816.
[87] Hirst, op. cit., p. 16.
[88] Lipson, op. cit., p. 191.
[89] Singer, op. cit., p. 304.
[90] Crump and Ghorbal, op. cit., pp. 84, 100; *Report on the State of the Woollen Manufacture in England*, 1806.

later machinery for shearing cloth was destroyed at another Leeds mill.[91]

One report suggested that the number of mechanically powered shearing frames rose from 100 in 1806 to 1,462 in 1817 but the foundation for these figures is again uncertain.[92] It was probably not until after J. Lewis of Brimscombe, near Stroud, improved the rotary machine in 1815 that mechanical shearing became more widespread although hand shearing did not entirely disappear until the middle of the nineteenth century. Gott had shearing frames in 1826 and Hirst claimed to have been the first to use the Lewis Cutter in Leeds, having, so he says, improved it by using eight cutters in it instead of the one intended by Lewis.[93]

Other machinery was also used in the finishing of some cloth. Some fancy cloths known as friezes had their nap twisted into knots. Although originally a hand operation, power had been introduced to it in some mills by the end of the eighteenth century. Gott had two friezing mills powered by his 40 hp engine by the end of the 1790s. He also called his friezing mills 'napping engines'.[94] There is evidence of friezing mills being used several years earlier. Richard Atkinson had one at Aspley, Huddersfield, in 1793 and in 1801 a mill at Heaton Bank, Dewsbury, was known as the 'Old Friezing Mill'.[95] Several others were recorded near Halifax in 1758.[96]

[91] Crump, op. cit., p. 47; 'Amongst the mischief committed by, or attributed to, the "Luddites" of 1812, was the burning of the "gig mill", at Oatlands, near Leeds, and Hawksworth corn mills, near Otley, and the destruction of the machinery in the mills or dressing shops of Joseph Hirst of Huddersfield; William Hinchliffe of Leymoor; John Garner of Honley; Clement Dyson of Dungeon; Mr. Roberts of Crosland; Frances Vickerman of Taylor-Hill; William Thompson and Brothers of Rawden; Mr. Smith of Snowgatehead, near Holmfirth; Joseph Brook of Horn Court; James Brook of Reins; and Joseph Foster of Horbury. About £500 worth of cloth was torn and cut into shreds in the finishing shops of Messrs. Dickenson, Carr and Shann, in Water-Lane, Leeds, and besides the destruction of their machinery, many of the above-named manufactures had their houses plundered and their furniture and windows broken to pieces', J. Mayhall, *The Annals of Yorkshire from the earliest period to the present time*, Vol. 1. 236.

[92] Lipson, op. cit., p. 191.

[93] Sun C.R. 156/1040865/1826; Hirst, op. cit., p. 39. The rotary cutter was invented by S. G. Dorr in the United States in the early 1790s. Various modifications were made to it both in American and England in the following two decades. Lewis and a John Collier of Paris made the biggest improvements in 1818. For a detailed account of the development of the rotary cutter see Mann, op. cit., pp. 303–7.

[94] Boulton and Watt MSS, List of Leeds Engines. See Table 13.

[95] Sun C.R. 1/620468/1793; 40/717933/1801.

[96] Watson, *History of Halifax*, op. cit.

Power was also introduced to the pressing process. Hirst again claims to have been the first to use hydraulic presses:

When I began my factory at School Close in 1816, Messrs. Fenton, Murray and Co. told me that if I would use the hydraulic presses they would let me have them at almost any price, as they wanted to get them into the hands of some party who could bring them into operation, so as to give them a fair chance.[97]

It seems surprising that it was not until 1816 that they were first used. The Gott papers show that a Bramah 'hydro-mechanical press capable of overcoming the weight of 400 tons with the power of three cwt. . . .' was purchased for Park Mills in 1799, but it does not appear to have worked well as is shown by correspondence between Gott and Joseph Bramah.[98] Hirst also records that there was some opposition from workmen to their introduction and no mention is made of the presses in the Bean Ing insurance policies.[99]

In spite of Hirst's claims about the superiority of the cloth he produced, his mill being 'the wonder of the world' and that others quickly installed the presses after they saw him using them, the fairly comprehensive insurance policies for mills in the Leeds area do not show a widespread use of the presses before the end of the 1820s.[100]

In the worsted trade many processes differed from those described by Baines for woollen manufacture. After sorting, the long wool that was normally used for worsted cloth was washed by hand and then combed by hand, with heated metal combs, in order to straighten the fibres and remove the short ones or 'noyles'. Combing continued to be a hand operation throughout the period in spite of many attempts to invent a satisfactory combing machine. In 1790 Cartwright took out a patent on a machine which attempted to imitate the hand process but little more was heard of it. Not until 1827 was a more successful attempt made. In that year Platt and Collier patented a machine with circular combs but even this was not widely adopted and nothing more acceptable to the manufacturers was introduced until the early 1840s.[101] Amongst the many insurance

[97] Hirst, op. cit., pp. 20–1.
[98] Crump, op. cit., pp. 222–6.
[99] Hirst, op. cit., p. 8.
[100] 'but at that time (1816) and for many years after I could have sold ten times the quantity of cloth I manufactured.' Hirst, op. cit., p. 39. Even by 1830 many large manufacturers, carrying out the finishing processes, had not installed hydraulic presses.
[101] James, op. cit., pp. 565–6; see also pp. 249–50 for an excellent description of the combing process.

inventories no mention is made of combing machinery although a policy in 1796 referred to a mill at Clifford near Tadcaster as a '. . . water mill used for combing and spinning wool . . .'. This must, however, have been hand combing.[102]

Most of the policies of the 1830s for worsted mills had a note to the effect that no processes preparatory to spinning were carried on in the mill.[103] A directory for 1837, however, listed four wool combers in Bradford using patent machinery, and occasional earlier references can be found to particular mills using power driven combing machinery.[104] In 1825 the *Leeds Mercury* had an account that

> . . . a number of master manufacturers have introduced machines into their mills for combing wools, which are increasing daily, thus superseding labour . . . in a short time three quarters of all the wool passing through Bradford will probably be combed by them.[105]

However, there is little evidence to suggest these manufacturers were many in number in the 1820s.

Occasionally carding machinery appears to have been used for preparing wool for worsted spinning, prior to the wool being combed. About 1820 a William Lister: '. . . commenced the working of a carding machine at Idle. A patent for it was obtained, but, owing to the adverse claims of other parties, never became beneficial.'[106] However, there is no evidence to suggest that there was more than the isolated use of carding machinery in the worsted preparatory processes until the second half of the nineteenth century.

The application of power to worsted spinning came at least three decades before its use in woollen spinning. Arkwright's water-frame, which owed a great deal to the work of Lewis Paul on roller drafting in the 1740s, was first used for cotton spinning at Nottingham and at Cromford. In the West Riding it was being used for worsted spinning by the late 1780s. James records that first attempts to spin worsted by water power in the area were just over the Yorkshire boundary at Dolphineholme near Lancaster. There in 1784 Thomas Edmondson, a Mr Addison and a Mr Satterthwaite built a mill to be powered by horses and water, '. . . Intending to carry out in worsted that which had been accomplished in cotton by the aid of machinery

[102] Sun C.R. 13/653221/1796.

[103] The hand combing of wool required a stove for heating the teeth of the comb and the wool and this was a recognized fire risk.

[104] Wm. White, *Directory of the West Riding of Yorkshire*, 1837, p. 464.

[105] *Leeds Mercury*, 29 October 1825 cited by Sigsworth, op. cit., pp. 7–8 who also has a few other references to combing machinery being used in the 1830s.

[106] James, op. cit., p. 574n.

. . .'.[107] The attempt was short lived, however; the mill closing in 1791 because of quarrelling between the three partners and many technical difficulties. Four years later it was re-opened by Thomas Hinde who replaced the old four and six spindle water-frames with larger and improved substitutes.[108] The first recorded spinning of worsted by water power in the county was at Low Mill, Addingham, in 1787 using water harnessed from the River Wharfe. Within a few years others had commenced with perhaps more than a dozen at work by the end of the century. All the worsted mills recorded in Appendix One were spinning mills and would have been employing the frame throughout the period.

Likewise power-loom weaving came earlier to worsted manufacture than to woollen. James recorded how a Mr James Warbrick attempted to use a power loom at a Shipley mill in 1822 but it was destroyed by local hand-loom weavers.[109] Two years later, however, the Horsfalls of Bradford were weaving by steam-powered looms and others soon followed their example, including Messrs Stansfield and Briggs of Burley Mill and Messrs Marshalls of Bradford.[110] Their first use, however, for worsted weaving in the county may have been at Halifax where, according to Edward Baines, James Akeroyd was using them in his mill in Old Lane by 1822. Baines also reported that Akeroyd was using a Jacquard weaving engine in March 1827.[111]

The incomplete 1835 Survey of Power Looms recorded 44 worsted mills with 2,953 worsted looms and another 226 looms being used for both wool and worsted weaving. The number of looms in a mill varied from 2 to 479 although the majority had between 25 and 70.[112]

In worsted production the finishing processes differed somewhat from those of woollen cloth manufacture, the most notable variation being that worsted cloth was not fulled. However, the difference in the machinery employed was not considerable.

Thus when calculating investment in machinery for woollen and worsted mills between 1780 and the mid-1830s there are not a large number of different types of apparatus that have to be included.

[107] Ibid., p. 327.
[108] Ibid; see also P. P. Hall, 'Dolphineholme . . .', loc. cit.
[109] James, op. cit., p. 414.
[110] Ibid., p. 415. Stansfield and Briggs first insured their power loom in January 1829. Sun C.R. 172/1085746/1829. No mention of a power loom is made in their policy Sun C.R. 166/1071452/1828.
[111] Baines, op. cit., p. 407.
[112] See Table 16.

Besides the various small utensils and hand tools, the main machinery in the mills of the period consisted of willeys, scribbling and carding engines, slubbing billeys, water spinning frames or throstles in worsted production, mules, power looms, fulling stocks, gigs, friezing engines and shearing frames. As well as these, however, many mills housed hand-powered machines such as spinning jennies and hand looms. By 1835 a number of other types of machine were coming into use but only on a very small scale.

There are formidable obstacles to suggesting the number of different machines in use at mills at different dates. There are very few contemporary estimates and those that were made are of doubtful reliability. Even fewer details are available about how machines varied in size and about the amount of power they required. One cannot assume a constant ratio between the numbers of different machines in mills as this ratio would have varied according to the processes being carried out, the type of cloth being produced, the amount of 'out work' being done and the innovating enthusiasm of the manufacturers. For the calculations of the value of fixed capital in the next chapter machinery is therefore considered as a whole and little attempt is made to determine the amount of investment in different machinery.

Heating and Lighting

At the commencement of the nineteenth century heating and lighting in mills were particularly primitive. If any heating was provided at all it was in the form of open fireplaces or, occasionally, stoves both of which created a risk of fire. Lighting was more often than not provided by candles left to flicker quite openly or placed in lanterns. Open or enclosed oil lamps were also sometimes used.

Open fires, candles and lamps continued to offer the sole means of heating and lighting in many mills until well into the nineteenth century. Lower Town Mill in Haworth was still using 'common fireplaces' and candles in 1833, as were the Kings Mill and Ramsden Mill at Huddersfield.[113] A cotton mill at Grindleton had no 'artificial heat' and was lit by 'candles in lanterns' in 1831.[114]

The first improvements in heating began to occur in the last decade of the eighteenth century when steam and warm air heating

[113] Sun C.R. 198/1158297/1833; 196/1158038/1833; 190/1134664/1831.
[114] Sun C.R. 187/1120127/1831.

systems replaced open fires and stoves in a few mills. William Strutt developed a warm air apparatus for heating his Belper Mills. Air was drawn over a fire and then directed through ducts to the various rooms of the mill. This system acted as the prototype for others. The drawing and ducting arrangements were improved and the system was widely introduced into large and small buildings. Charles Bage constructed a warm air circulating system for the Shrewsbury Flax Mill. Strutt's system was installed in three mill buildings at New Lanark.[115]

In the West Riding warm air systems were being used in some mills by the second decade of the nineteenth century. For example Thomas Atkinson had installed one at his water-powered cotton mill at Colne Bridge in 1818.[116] But warm air systems were never nearly as popular as steam heating.

Steam for factory heating was first successfully used around 1800. A Mr Snodgrass heated a cotton mill on Speyside by steam in 1799.[117] Phillips and Lee followed with their Salford Mill in 1802 and within a few years Boulton and Watt were installing similar systems in many premises.[118] The steam generated in the steam engine boiler, or in a separate boiler for the purpose, was channelled through pipes around the mill thus providing not only a more efficient system of uniformly heating the rooms in the mill but also reducing the danger of conflagration. Although warm air heating was more sensible for water-powered mills as it saved the expense of boiler installation, steam heating was clearly much more popular in the West Riding, even in water-powered mills. Many mills installed steam in the second decade of the nineteenth century and by the 1820s it had become the most frequent method of heating mills. Insurance records suggest that by 1830 over 80 per cent of Yorkshire woollen and worsted mills were heated by steam. But, whereas some water-powered mills had steam boilers, not all steam-powered mills had installed steam heating. Arundel's mill at Rothwell which had an engine at an early date was still using stoves for heating in 1831, as were Ripley and Ogle in Leeds in 1834 and Butterbowl Mill at Farnley in 1828.[119] The hot air or steam pipes of the heating system were rarely valued separately for insurance purposes nor have any

[115] Tann, op. cit., p. 109.
[116] Sun C.R. 123/943611/1818.
[117] Tann, op. cit., p. 111.
[118] Ibid., p. 113.
[119] Sun C.R. 188/1127361/1831; 210/1177577/1834; 168/1077836l/1828.

accounts of the installation of steam heating come to light. However, in insurance valuations they were normally included either as part of the mill building or as part of the machinery as shown by these clauses from two policies:

On Millwrights work including all the standing and going gear and steam pipes in a scribbling, carding and slubbing mill, brick and slated, situate at Howden Clough aforesaid in the sole tenure of Messrs. J. J. and G. Ellis, Wool scribblers . . .
On their wool scribbling and fulling mill and engine house (including steam pipes) adjoining situated aforesaid (Guiseley) . . .[120]

Thus, although it will not be possible to estimate separately capital investment in heating systems, the actual cost of the systems will be included as part of the value overall of the mill building or the machinery.

The main change in the means of lighting mill premises which required a capital outlay was the introduction of gas. First used in a Yorkshire cotton mill in 1805, a few weeks before gas lighting was installed in Messrs Phillips and Lee's cotton mill at Salford, the new system was only slowly introduced to woollen and worsted mills in Yorkshire.[121] Gott, who was in close contact with developments in Boulton and Watt's factory, was possibly the first woollen manufacturer to install a gas system. In April 1806 he was investigating the possibility of using gas at Bean Ing and was invited by Lee to meet Murdoch at the Salford Mill to inspect the installations. As it turned out he first used gas, however, at his Armley and Burley Mills possibly to gain experience for the larger installation required at Bean Ing. Gas was first lit, it would appear, at the two smaller mills in 1808 and at Bean Ing two years later.[122] At about the same time, Couplands, who were cotton spinners at Hunslet, were also installing a gas system as were Marshalls for their flax mill.[123]

[120] Sun C.R. 180/1110555/1830; 179/1106151/1830.
[121] The Soho foundry was first lit by gas in March 1802 and Phillips and Lee's Mill almost exactly four years later. Both these installations were carried out by William Murdoch. But Samuel Clegg who was employed by Boulton and Watt left the firm in 1805 and immediately set to work installing gas in a number of small factories including Henry Lodge's cotton mill at Sowerby Bridge. It was claimed by Clegg's son that Lodge's mill was lit by gas as early as 1805 but there is some doubt as to the actual time. 'Mr. Clegg, a pupil of Boulton and Watt, was, in 1805, lighting the cotton mill of Mr. Henry Lodge of Sowerby Bridge'. Samuel Clegg Jnr, *The Manufacture of Coal Gas*, (3rd Edition, 1859).
[122] Crump, op. cit., pp. 258–9; Boulton and Watt MSS, Portfolio 813.
[123] Boulton and Watt MSS, Portfolios 814 and 811.

In 1811 even Joseph Rogerson was giving some thought to gas lighting for his scribbling mill:

> Gas lights are beginning to be pretty common; there is a public house lit with it in Leeds, Publican's name is Fitzgerald; we talk of our place being lighted the next winter with it . . .[124]

and in September, two years later he was visiting Armley mills 'looking at their Gas House' and Mr Thackray's mill 'to see how they are preparing their gas house'.[125] There is however, no mention of gas lighting in Belle Isle Mill in 1825 when a new insurance policy was taken out so presumably the idea was abandoned.

Burley Cotton Mill at Otley had gas lighting by February 1812; Garnett installed a system at Barkerend, Bradford in 1819 and Atkinson's cotton mill at Colne Bridge was lit by gas in 1818.[126] It was, however, the late 1820s and early 1830s before gas lighting was becoming more general. If the mills in the insurance registers can be taken as an unbiased sample, 40 per cent of the West Riding wool textile mills had gas lighting by the early 1830s.

The building of gas plant and the installation of pipes required a considerable outlay. Some manufacturers were fortunate in that they could obtain gas from the public supply, as for example was the case at Carr Mills, Woodhouse Carr near Leeds and at Hirst, Bramley and Co.'s mill at School Close, Leeds, but most had to construct their own gas house and gasometer.[127] The installation of gas at Burley Mill appears to have cost at least £650.[128] However, it is not often possible to calculate the value of gas installations. The gas pipes, like the steam pipes, were normally included in insurance as part of the mill building or of the machinery. The insurance for Park Mills at Bean Ing included gas pipes as part of the main mill building but the gas house was insured separately.[129]

For the purpose of this study, the value of gas plant has been included as a part of the mill buildings and machinery. It has not been possible to obtain separate figures. One might, however,ask how many mills were producing their own gas by the 1830s and how many were being provided for by the public supply? As the latter

124 Crump, op. cit., p. 110. 'The Diary of Joseph Rogerson', 3 January 1811.
125 Ibid., p. 156. Mr Thackray's Mill was Gibralter Mill, Pudsey.
126 Sun C.R. 100/868473/1812; 123/943611/1818; 119/935354/1817; 130/959963/1819.
127 Sun C.R. 237/1248001/1837 and see the Cash Account Notebook of the Leeds Gas Light Company, entry for 14 August 1821. C.L.A.D.
128 Crump, op. cit., p. 259.
129 Sun C.R. 158/1055369/1827.

improved and gas companies became larger and more efficient, it would seem many of the urban mills would have been able to obtain their needs from it, thus possibly reducing capital outlay in gas manufacturing plants. This is, however, an area on which little light can be thrown at present.

5

THE VALUATION OF FIXED CAPITAL STOCK

Measurement Problems

In the previous chapters some consideration has been given to the various items of investment that must be included in a valuation of the fixed capital of the West Riding wool textile industry. The different types of buildings have been examined; the various machinery, power sources and heating and lighting installations have been discussed. Figures for the growth in the number of mills in both woollen and worsted manufacture have been calculated with, what is believed to be, a reasonable degree of accuracy. The relative importance of steam and water power has been considered Thus some idea of the changeover from a system of domestically organized manufacture to one of factory production has been provided.

The description of the changes, often necessarily in very vague detail, can give no more than a rough impression of the growth of the industry between 1780 and the mid-1830s. The task now to be considered is the quantifying of all the changes into financial terms. The calculation of the value of fixed capital assets in the industry year by year and thus also the annual net fixed capital formation is likely to provide a much more worthwhile picture of the development of the industry than any descriptive comment.

In the past historians and economists have encountered many problems in estimating capital formation from, what one might term, a 'micro' approach. Such estimates that have been made for industries have been, more often than not, based on changes of inputs of raw materials or on the output of finished products through capital: input and capital: output ratios. Very few contemporary statistics of capital formation exist. A passage from Phyllis Deane and W. A. Cole's work on British economic growth sums up the situation:

> Aggregate statistics of consumer expenditure or of capital formation are rarely needed for ordinary administration. Those who require them face the labour of building up their own aggregates from a mass of incomplete and small data and barely relevant indicators. Naturally enough this is a task which becomes more formidable as we go back in time both because the

raw material must be quarried from less and less accessible sources and because the prospects of obtaining reasonably reliable results are less and less encouraging.[1]

Such rough contemporary estimates that do exist can rarely be trusted. There is often no clue as to how they were arrived at, nor as to how accurate they were. Various estimates, differing quite considerably, were made for the cotton industry which show that even at the time there was little or no idea of the value of fixed capital in that particular section of industry which was at the forefront of British economic growth.[2] For the wool textile industry no contemporary estimates of significance exist.

The problem of defining what is meant by fixed capital is complex. Even in modern accounting practice the difficulty arises, and of course, the problems are greater when considering past investment. One modern definition, based on the stipulation of the 1947. Company Act and the Consolidating Act of 1948, draws the following distinction.

> . . . Current Assets — those which are held for realisation, that is for the transformation into cash in the ordinary course of business, together with those representing a temporary investment of surplus funds. Current assets form the starting point of any assessment of a company's potential liquidity over the ensuing year. Fixed assets, on the other hand . . . are held with the definite purpose of earning revenue by their use . . . not for sale in the ordinary course of business. Fixed assets endure a physical shape, their contribution taking the form of a flow of service lasting beyond the compass of a single financial year.[3]

In general this definition draws a satisfactory distinction but confusion may still arise, for example, when certain machinery components need regular replacement or when certain materials necessary for the efficient functioning of more identifiable fixed capital are used up and lose their 'physical shape'. The problem was discussed at length at a Conference on the 'Sources and Methods for the Study of Capital Formation in Britain, 1750–1850', at Sheffield University in January 1969.[4] The only conclusion that one could draw from these discussions was that no adequate definition was

[1] P. Deane and W. A. Cole, *British Economic Growth, 1688–1950* (second edition, Cambridge, 1966), p. 259.

[2] See M. Blaug, 'The Productivity of Capital in the Lancashire Cotton Industry during the Nineteenth Century', *E.H.R.*, XIII, 1961; S. Pollard, 'Fixed Capital in the Industrial Revolution in Britain', *J.E.H.*, XXIV, 3, 1964.

[3] H. B. Rose, *The Economic Background to Investment* (1960), p. 182.

[4] See J. P. P. Higgins and S. Pollard, eds, *Aspects of Capital Investment in Great Britain, 1750–1850; A Preliminary Survey* (London, 1971).

possible that could make the distinction between fixed and current assets for all industries and all sectors of the economy. It was apparent that if one were to discuss the fixed capital of a particular industry, the discussion would have to be prefaced by a statement of exactly what was being included. Although this would still leave room for debate about whether particular items of capital should or should not have been included, it would make clear the terms of reference that had been taken.

For the wool textile industry, most of the fixed capital is easily identifiable. This study has included as fixed assets all buildings on mill premises being used for one or more of the production processes and for administration, the source and transmission system of the power for driving the machinery, the machinery itself including those requiring regular replacement, all utensils on mill premises required for and used in the processes of production, and all external works on or connected with the mill site including the means of access to the mill and the various works associated with the provision of water to a mill. The heating and lighting apparatus have also been included. A problem does arise concerning which buildings should be included as being part of a mill's fixed capital. The question as to whether, for example, workers' cottages owned by the manufacturer or other buildings provided for the well-being of the workers, such as schools and chapels, should be considered as part of the fixed capital of the industry is discussed below.

Any omissions from this definition are only likely to be of minor importance and thus have a marginal effect on the aggregate figures of fixed capital value and formation. One might debate, for example, whether the horse and cart with which the manufacturer collected his raw materials or transported his finished product should be included. And there are no doubt other items which perhaps should or should not be considered. However, the importance of these is probably minimal.

Until quite recently economic historians have had to rely on the accounts and balance sheets of individual companies to obtain figures about capital. The difficulties involved in interpreting many of these accounts are well known. More recently the recognition of the potential value of various types of records of the fire insurance companies operating in the eighteenth and nineteenth centuries has provided new source material. The information and valuations contained in fire insurance policy registers are of immense importance but there are clearly difficulties in assessing their meaning and accuracy, particularly the reliability of the insurance values as a reflection of true capital value. Opinions do vary as to what extent the information can be used without corroboration from other sources and research is at present being carried out in this area. Appendix III considers the question in more detail. There does seem to be a realistic case for the careful use of insurance data in estimating fixed capital values in the West Riding wool textile industry. It is often possible to discern when all the buildings of a textile concern were not insured and occasionally one does note obvious cases of under insurance. Normally however, insured values of similar sized premises do relate quite well and also seem to correspond to known sizes of premises.

The insurance valuations, however, only include that capital which might have been subject to a fire risk. There were other forms of fixed capital investment necessary for the construction and adequate functioning of a mill. The heaviest items that one might expect under this heading would be the expenses in preparing the mill site prior to building, the building of dams, reservoirs, cuts and weirs for the provision of water power and the construction of a means of access to the mill, including, in some cases, the building of quite lengthy roads. One might expect a huge variation between one mill and another for capital expenses such as these. A manufacturer building an urban steam-powered mill would have had, more often than not, little to lay out in this direction whereas one building a large isolated, water-powered mill might have had to invest considerable sums.

The cost of land for the construction of a mill has been excluded from the calculations below. However, in some cases this would have involved a very large outlay for a prospective manufacturer. The price of the land would have depended on the facilities and position of the site. Thus, in general, land close to town centres would have cost considerably more than isolated plots. And sites in an ideal position for the harnessing of water power would have cost more than those on a weak and unreliable stream or at sites where power was not available. There are some examples of the price manufacturers or mill builders had to pay for land. Gott valued his land at Bean Ing in January 1803 at £5,950. As he owned about thirty acres this was almost £200 per acre. In 1820 when he had about fifty acres the estate land was valued at over £7,500.[5] Marshall paid £600 for slightly more than one acre of land for the site of his first mill in 1790 and three years later had an outlay of £2,300 for between four

[5] Gott MSS, Accounts of Co-Partnership.

and five acres for land for his second mill and other buildings.[6] In the same area, the Leeds solicitors, Nicholas and Upton, purchased (on behalf of Boulton and Watt) two and a half acres of land adjacent to Fenton, Murray and Wood's premises for £1,000 an acre in the later 1790s. This was presumably in order to attempt to prevent Fenton, Murray and Wood from expanding their premises, although Watt might have had some intention at one point of opening a factory in Leeds to supply the expanding market in Yorkshire for steam engines.[7]

At later dates there are miscellaneous examples of land prices. One account which shows the relative importance of the cost of land is that for the building of J. Hartley and Son's mill at Morley in 1836. The cost of the land, it is uncertain how much, was £675 and the cost of the conveyance £21 12*s* 8*d*. The total cost of buying the site, erecting the mill and other buildings and purchasing the steam engine was just under £8,000 so the cost of land was almost 10 per cent of building costs.[8]

There is insufficient data at present to carry this examination any further. Presumably the price fluctuated not just from one site to the next but also according to business conditions. The advertisements in the Leeds newspapers for the same land for sale week after week on some occasions suggest that at times land was difficult to sell. Although the amount of money invested in land by woollen and worsted manufacturers cannot at present be calculated, it should be borne in mind, especially when discussing the amount of money necessary to start a manufacturing concern, that the cost of suitable land could be a high initial expense.

There are examples of very high expenditure on site and service preparation. Dr S. D. Chapman has recorded that Arkwright's Bakewell Mill required a new road to it that cost £1,000.[9] Brookhouse Mill at Halifax, built by the Akroyd's, required 'an ingenious system of goits and aqueducts' to carry the water to the wheel which must have been an expensive operation.[10] For some other mills in the Halifax area and elsewhere in the west of the County, where the streams were smaller and faster flowing, it was found necessary to construct dams and reservoirs to regulate the supply of water to the mills. In some cases, owners of mills on the same stream would share

[6] Rimmer, op. cit., pp. 33, 45.
[7] Turner, thesis, op. cit., Chapter III, pp. 9–10.
[8] J. Hartley and Sons, Morley. Small account book. Acc. 1368. C.L.A.D.
[9] Cited at Sheffield Conference, 1969.
[10] T. W. Hanson, *The Story of Old Halifax* (1920), p. 240.

TABLE 17

J. HARTLEY & SONS, MORLEY, ACCOUNT OF BUILDING THE OLD MILL, 1834–1837

	£	s.	d.
Cost of Land	675	0	0
Cost of Conveying Land	21	12	8
Cost of Making Dam 1834	26	15	4½
Total work of dam up to and including 1837	4	1	0½
Stocks, etc.	1,272	2	11
Stones	182	15	1½
Scouring Pan	9	13	6
Pearson and Spurs Machine	16	0	0
Masons Work for five cottages	26	14	9
Iron for Mill and five cottages	48	0	0
Fire Bricks	31	0	0
Flags	114	1	7¾
Slates and Flags	283	0	9
Joiners Work	262	4	8
Wood or Timber	960	0	8
Plastering	19	3	8
Pipes, etc.	29	16	3
Road Making	8	9	0
Stone, Lime, Sand and Leading	351	14	10
Architect — Mark Holmes	75	4	1
Dry Walling	3	10	6
Masons Work	780	14	5
Steam Engine (total work and material)	1,800	15	3½
Glazeing	198	2	0
Bricklayers Works	162	14	6½
Bricks	343	18	8
Locks, Handles and Nails	29	8	9
Foundation Digging	35	10	3
Drift and Well Sinking	55	1	0
Sand	7	9	7
Dyehouse	97	0	5
Mill Spouting	30	6	10
Boiler House	1	16	8
Digging Reservoir, etc.	23	0	2
Painting on a/c.	10	0	0

Source: J. Hartley and Sons, Morley, Small Account Book. Accession 1368. C.L.A.D.

the cost of building a reservoir to control water supply. At the head of the Holt Stream at Slaithwaite, a large reservoir was built on Lingarth's Moor to provide a regular volume of water to four mills.[11]

In certain cases the lengths of goits which carried water to mills to provide a sufficient fall were quite considerable. At Rowley Mill at Honley the cut was between 200 and 300 yds long, and at such places as Sands Mill and Dewsbury Mills, Dewsbury, Calverley Mills, and at the Kirkstall Mills, considerable work had to be carried out to supply the wheels with an adequate fall of water. The problem was particularly great at Ossett Mills where a 'goit' 814 yds long and 14 yds wide fed from above a shallow weir had to be constructed and later enlarged.[12]

Capital works such as these varied quite considerably from one mill to the next. For the majority of mills one would expect them to have been fairly small. The urban steam-powered mill seldom required a great deal of site preparation. Even many of the smaller water-powered rural mills were lucky enough to be positioned where only a small amount of site work was required. Some mills, however, particularly the larger rural mills in inaccessible positions, required a larger outlay.

To take the expenditure on these items into consideration presents formidable problems, and in view of the almost total lack of information on costs and the amount of work, only very rough estimates may be suggested. Detailed information has only been traced for one mill, for J. Hartley and Sons' Old Mill at Morley, the accounts for which are shown in Table 17. This mill was a fairly large water and steam-powered concern built between 1834 and 1836. Out of total costs of almost £8,000, which included the land and the construction of five cottages, the building of the dam and reservoir cost only £50 and other site preparation work including the making of a road and the digging of foundation cost about £100 more. Thus here the total cost of preparatory work amounted to only two per cent of total costs.

[11] Dartmouth Estate, *Terrier*, 1805, pp. 49–50. Another example of mill owners sharing the cost of building a reservoir was in the Warley township of Halifax parish where, in 1827, the proprietors of Spring Mill, Holebottom Mill, Lumb Mill, Wainstalls Mill, Lower Wainstalls Mill, Jowler Mill, Dean Mill, Peel House Mill, Luddenden Mill and Luddenden Foot Mill all contributed £30 to £45 each for enlarging the Cold Edge Dams. See W. Onslow Garnett, *Wainstall Mills, The History of I. and I. Calvert Ltd. 1821–1951* (Halifax, 1951), p. 12.

[12] J. Goodchild, 'The Ossett Mill Company', *Textile History*, Vol. 1, no. 1, pp. 50–4.

One might expect some relationship between the cost of site preparation, excluding water courses, dams and reservoirs, and the size of the mill. The costs of clearing and levelling the site, digging a well, in many cases, and excavating foundations would seem likely to have related quite closely to the size of the plant being constructed. There appears to be no means of calculating this relationship. One can only assume it to be linear and assign it the value of five per cent of total capital costs. This estimate of five per cent is little more than an arbitrary figure. It will be allowed for in the calculations as an attempt to reduce some of the possible discrepancy in capital investment calculated from insurance values.

The cost of professional advice might possibly be allowed for in a similar fashion. Architects and engineers fees should be included as a part of building costs and building values. In the case of Hartley's Mill at Morley, the architect's fee amounted to £75 4*s* 1*d* out of a total cost for mill, houses and other buildings of about £4,000; that is just under two per cent.[13] It seems unlikely, however, that many of the builders of small mills employed an architect. The simple, almost stereotyped, buildings did not require professional design. There is no mention, for example, of an architect being employed for the construction of Lumb Mill, New Delph, in the accounts for that mill.[14] In view of the lack of knowledge of how frequently an architect was consulted and the very small proportion his fee would be of total cost, his charges and any other professional fees that might have been sometimes payable have been disregarded.

The costs of water supply are more difficult to determine. They varied so considerably that they are not likely to have correlated with the size or cost of the mill. They are likely to have been far greater for water-powered mills, although a water supply was also necessary for steam-powered mills. The exceptional works at Brookhouse, Halifax, and at Ossett Mills, Calverley Mills, and the Kirkstall Mills, have been sited. In the absence of company records the only possible way of considering the importance of this type of works is to consider each mill and its site in turn and to try and estimate from maps, plans and site survey the extent to which investment in these sorts of schemes were required.

For the urban mills, it is evident that large and costly water provision schemes requiring long cuts, weirs and reservoirs were not common. Water-powered mills were, in any case, less frequent in

[13] Hartley's account book, loc. cit., see Table 17.
[14] Lumb MSS, Upper Mill, Saddleworth.

the towns. In the rural areas it appears that only the relatively large mills required extensive work. The small mill was sited, more often than not, where water power could be easily obtained without extra expense above the actual cost of the mill. Thus the small mills in the parishes of Halifax, Saddleworth, Almondbury, and Huddersfield where water power predominated were situated on the fast flowing becks where power was easily harnessed. The larger water-powered mill, however, required the most investment. Where an originally small mill was expanded to a size that required greater power than could be provided on the site, work had to be undertaken to provide more water by damming the stream and controlling its flow, by building a reservoir or by bringing more water through an artificial channel. For the development of the larger, water-powered mills, sites were less easily obtained. A large reliable stream of water was required with a sufficient fall to turn a large wheel. To obtain this fall, a weir or dam was necessary, often some way upstream from the mill, and a cut needed to channel the water to the mill wheel. Although several mills were sometimes served by the same cut, the damming of the river would exclude the building of another mill for some distance above because water backing up behind a dam could, and did on occasions, effect the operation of the wheel of the other mill. One example of this difficulty was at Healey Mill, Ossett. The height of the weir from which water was supplied to Healey Mills had to be limited to ensure that the water did not back up to and affect the wheel at Sands Mill, Dewsbury.[15]

Examination of plans and a survey of mill sites suggests that there were very few mills where major works for the construction of goits, weirs and reservoirs had been required. One can certainly indicate a number of mills along each of the main rivers and streams where considerable work was carried out but these mills form a very small minority of the overall total. There appears, at present, to be no way of estimating the investment in this type of fixed capital. In view of the few mills involved, no account has, therefore, been made, in the aggregate figures, for the value of this fixed capital. When considered in overall terms, it is unlikely that this omission would make a significant difference to the totals.

No example of an expensive road making project similar to that recorded at Arkwright's Bakewell Mill has been discovered in the West Riding. Certainly, particularly with the rural mills, some means of access often had to be constructed. This would normally

[15] Goodchild, 'Ossett Mill Company', loc. cit., p. 51.

have taken the form of a rough track rather than an expensively engineered road. This item is, therefore, also considered as negligible in the calculation of the overall figures.

One other, perhaps more significant, form of capital investment by manufacturers has also had to be excluded through lack of sufficient data. This includes housing built by manufacturers for themselves or for their workers, other construction, not directly concerned with the production processes but provided for the benefit and well being of the workers such as schools and chapels and also warehousing for storage of raw materials or finished products, where such warehouses did not form an integral part of the mill premises. The omission of this fixed capital may have a more serious effect on the accuracy of the aggregate figures. However, because it was not directly concerned with the production processes one might reasonably suggest that it may be excluded even though, in certain cases, the provision of housing was essential, particularly in remote areas, for the provision of labour for the mill.

One mill where a considerable amount of housing had to be provided was West House Flax Mills at Fewston. In 1831 the owners, Robinson, Chippendale, Netherwood and Carr insured the following residential property as well as their mills:

On the partners house at West House near Otley — private	£200
On the Upper and Lower Apprentice Houses in equal proportions	£500
On a range of cottages near the Corn Mill in the tenure of the workpeople in equal proportion	£800
On two cottages on Hastiby Hill near in the tenure of workpeople in equal proportion	£200
On four thatched cottages on said hill in equal proportion	£400

This amounted to a total investment of over £2,000 on dwelling places for the workpeople; necessary presumably because of the shortage of labour in that remote area.[16]

Likewise John Haigh and Brothers of New Bank Mills, The Mount, Halifax, had seventeen cottages near their mill in the 1830s for workpeople.[17] And many examples of other mill owners with similar property can be cited. However, there appears to be no way of ascertaining how many houses or cottages were owned by each manufacturer so they have been totally excluded from the valuations.

[16] Sun C.R. 185/1120597/1831.
[17] Sun C.R. 228/1223615/1836.

Warehousing creates a greater problem. Some manufacturers, in particular those with large rural mills, owned warehouses in the nearest town, which they could use as a depot for their raw material and finished cloth. These have, also, had to be excluded from the calculations through lack of information. Probably they were often only rented. In some cases they were shared by several manufacturers. But at present there is little information as to their number and value. Warehousing on mill premises has, however, been included, partly because it is included in the insurance policies and partly because it often cannot be separated from buildings or rooms used for production. Thus the cellar or attic of a mill, or even in some cases, one or more storeys, was often used for storage. Where a building was actually referred to as a warehouse in the insurance policy it was often also the case that it was being used for some other purpose, particularly hand processes.

Other items of fixed capital, such as schools and chapels, not directly concerned with production have all be excluded from the calculations as well. It is open to question whether such buildings as these should be considered as part of the fixed capital of the industry. In any case, however, insufficient information is available at present for their inclusion.

The basis of the following calculations are, therefore, insurance valuations of mill premises, machinery and power units including all buildings forming an integral part of a mill site but excluding dwelling property and other buildings not concerned directly with woollen and worsted production. A five per cent additional allowance has also been included to compensate for that fixed investment on or associated with the mill site such as site preparation, courtyards, periphery walls and professional fees, which were not included in the insurance risk. No allowance has been made for exceptional fixed capital formation associated with the provision of water power and transport access to mills partly because of the difficulties involved in calculating such items and partly because of the exceptional nature of this work and its confinement to only a few mills. Minor roadmaking and water supply works will have been, it is hoped, accounted for in the five per cent addition made to insurable fixed capital values.

Fixed Capital Values and Formation in the West Riding Wool Textile Industry 1780–1835

In Chapter 1 an analysis of the numerical growth of mills in the Yorkshire woollen and worsted industry was presented. It was pointed out, however, that the rate of growth of the number of mills in the industry would not necessarily correspond to the rate of growth of the fixed capital of the industry. There was clearly a tendency for mills to become larger and mill premises more complex between the 1780s and the mid-1830s. Any attempt, therefore, to estimate the value of fixed capital must take into account the size of the plant.

To this end calculations can be made to establish the average size of a mill in value terms for the years 1800, 1810, 1820, and 1835. The averages can be obtained from insurance valuations, initially on the assumption that the mills covered by the insurance records may be used as an unbiased sample of all the mills in operation. To obtain a sufficient number of mills for the sample for each date, insurance policies dating not only for the year in question but also for the previous five years and the following three years have to be included. This may be justified by the fact that policies were normally issued for periods of seven years and thus, unless a later policy cancelled the earlier one, it may be reasonably assumed that the earlier policy was still running. Policies dated two or three years after the year for which the average was being calculated may also be included on the assumption that there was unlikely to have been any really significant change in the average value during the period. In certain cases a policy dated more than five years earlier than the date for which the average is being calculated is included, if there is a similar policy showing similar values for some later date. Where more than one policy is available for a particular mill, the one dated nearest to the year in question is included in the calculations.

The size of the sample that is available and the results of the calculations of the average value of fixed capital of mills for each of the four years is given in Table 18. A detailed analysis of the calculations is available in Appendix IV.

TABLE 18

AVERAGE VALUE OF FIXED CAPITAL OF MILLS

Date	*No. of Mills working*	*No. of Mills in sample*	*Size of Sample (percentages)*	*Average Value of Insured Fixed Capital of Mills*	*Average Value Adjusted Upwards by 5%*
				£	£
1800	243	153	63	1,578	1,657
1810	276	64	23	2,390	2,510
1820	326	36	11	4,100	4,305
1835	610	67	11	5,527	5,803

On the basis of the adjusted averages an estimate of the total value of fixed capital assets of the industry for the four years can be calculated, as shown in Table 19. Two figures are given for the year 1835. The first is based on the 577 mills that have been actually traced in that year and the second on the 610 mills recorded by the factory inspectors.

TABLE 19

ESTIMATES OF THE TOTAL VALUE OF FIXED CAPITAL OF MILLS IN THE WEST RIDING WOOL TEXTILE INDUSTRY IN 1800, 1810, 1820 and 1835

Date	*No. of Mills Working*	*Average Value of Mills*	*Total Value of Fixed Capital*
		£	£
1800	243	1,657	402,651
1810	276	2,510	692,760
1820	326	4,305	1,403,430
1835	577	5,803	3,348,331
	610	5,803	3,539,830

In these calculations a major assumption has been made concerning the accuracy or unbiasedness of the sample of mills obtained from the insurance data. Because the mills used for a sample were obtained independently of random selection from the total number of mills in operation, it must be considered more carefully whether the mills used as a sample were representative. For the years 1800 and 1810 the number of mills used as the sample would appear to be more than adequate to rule out the likelihood of their being unrepresentative. For the years 1820 and 1835, however, where the sample sizes were 11 per cent, there is a greater possibility of bias. Indeed it may be suggested that there is a good reason why a bias is likely for these two dates. The valuation data used was for mills insured with a large national insurance company at a time when a number of small provincial companies were being formed and were successfully competing with the older established offices. These local companies usually had a small risk limit, and although they would have been able to accept the total insurance risk of the smaller mills, they were often unwilling to take the full risk of larger concerns.[18] Owners and occupiers of larger mills were often unable to insure all their risk with the local company and therefore had to look to the larger national companies such as the Sun and Royal Exchange Fire Offices for insurance cover. For this reason, the business of the Sun Fire Office might be expected to have contained a more than proportionate share of larger premises and thus the average figures of fixed capital value calculated for 1820 and 1835 might be over optimistic.

There appears to be one possible means of examining and testing the significance of this bias and, perhaps, of correcting it. By comparing the average power and number of workers for all the mills in the industry in the West Riding with the averages for the mills used as a sample for 1835 some idea of the likely inaccuracies involved can be obtained.

In 1835 the average power in use for woollen and worsted mills was 19 horsepower and the average number of workers was sixty-seven. Of the sixty-seven mills used as the sample for 1835, information on power and number of employees is available for only twenty-three. However, the average horsepower for these twenty-three mills was 31 and the average number of workers 109, thus suggesting that the mills in the sample were considerably larger than those in the industry as a whole. However, these higher averages are based on only one third of the mills used as the sample. It is possible to calculate the averages for a greater number of mills. Mills for which both power and number of workers are known and for which partial insurance was issued can also be included in the calculations bringing the number to fifty. The extra twenty-seven mills appear in the Sun Fire Office registers but because not all their property is mentioned they cannot be included in the calculations to obtain the average value of mill fixed capital. However, there is no reason why they cannot be used for the general test as to whether mills insured with the Sun Fire Office were representative of all mills in the industry. For these fifty mills the average power was 30 horsepower and the average number of workers 106.5. This reinforces the previous finding that a more than proportionate

[18] All London and provincial fire offices had risk limits. The main London offices did not apply them rigidly. The limits for the small companies, sometimes as low as £2,000 on any one item, were lower than for the London offices and fewer exceptions were made to them. The insurance proposer might try to divide the risk between two or more offices but, particularly in the earlier period, the main London offices appear to have restricted the offices they would jointly insure with.

number of larger mills were insured by the Sun Fire Office. Indeed it would seem that the mills insured with the Sun had an average of 58 per cent more workers and were using 58 per cent more power than the average mill in the industry in the West Riding.

The correction of this bias does present problems. One possible way might be simply on the basis of the amount of power and number of workers, on the assumption of a constant linear relationship between each and fixed capital value. Unfortunately, however, insufficient information is available to check this assumption with any degree of confidence. Details of power and number of workers and the value of fixed capital are only available for the twenty-three mills which are known to be unrepresentative. But a very good correlation exists between the numbers employed in mills and the amount of power. Calculations based on the information given in the 1834 Report of the Children's Employment Commissioners give a correlation coefficient of r equal to 0.96 for worsted mills and r equal to 0.9 for woollen mills. A similar calculation for the twenty-three mills mentioned above gives a combined correlation coefficient of r equal to 0.67.

Thus although an orderly relationship of workers to power may be postulated for the industry as a whole, the available data does not allow a similar calculation for capital value to power or to workers. However, it is reasonable to argue the probability of a fixed relationship, particularly given the correlation between power and workers. The relationship between power and workers is not surprising. There were variations in processes being carried out from one mill to the next; some mills did employ workers for hand processes but in general the number of workers in a mill would have related closely to the amount of machinery being used, and the amount of machinery would clearly normally have related to the amount of power employed. It is moreover reasonable to suggest a fairly constant ratio between the amount of machinery, and thus number of workers and amount of power, and the size of the buildings housing it. The functional nature of mill buildings and the minimal investment in unnecessary embellishments have already been pointed out.[19] Capital: power and capital: labour ratios were used as early as 1834 to estimate the fixed capital stock of the cotton industry.[20]

If a fixed linear relationship between power and fixed capital stock and between labour and fixed capital stock is assumed then

[19] See Chapter Two.
[20] See Blaug, loc. cit., pp. 372–4.

the bias to larger mills in the sample can be eliminated by reducing the fixed capital stock values for 1835 by 37 per cent. This assumes that the fifty mills insured by the Sun for which power and employment data is available are representative of all mills insured by the Sun, which would seem likely as the fifty mills form more than half of the total.

The bias for 1820 is more difficult to eliminate. A similar exercise cannot be carried out for that year because of almost a total lack of information on power and employment. However, the factors which created the unrepresentativeness of the mills insured in the Sun Fire Office in 1835 also existed in 1820. By that year the Sun had lost a considerable proportion of its previous business to provincial fire offices, all of which were imposing limits on risks. It would therefore seem realistic to reduce the 1820 estimate of fixed capital stock by a similar amount of 37 per cent (see Table 20).

TABLE 20

ADJUSTED ESTIMATES OF FIXED CAPITAL IN THE WEST RIDING WOOL TEXTILE INDUSTRY: 1800, 1810, 1820 and 1835

Date	*No. of Mills*	*Average Value Adjusted* + 5%	*Total Value of Fixed Capital in the Industry*
		£	£
1800	243	1,657	402,651
1810	276	2,510	692,760
1820	326	2,870	935,620
1835	577	3,656	2,109,512
1835	610	3,656	2,230,160

Using these total fixed capital estimates for the four years an annual series of total fixed capital values and a series of net annual fixed capital formation can be calculated. It is first necessary to adjust the average value of fixed capital for each year. This is only possible on a rather arbitrary basis by interpolating between the four dates. For the period before 1800 it is necessary to assign an estimated average figure for each year. There can be no doubt that mills were increasing in size and value during this period but probably not by as much as they did after the turn of the century. It is, therefore, assumed that the average value of fixed capital of the mills in the period 1780 to 1790 was £1,000 and that the average value increased by the rate of £65 per annum to £1,650 in 1800.

As the early 1790s saw the beginning of the building of the larger mills, such as Gott's at Bean Ing, so one would expect the average value of fixed capital to have started increasing more noticeably in this period. From 1800 to 1810 it was assumed that the average value increased by the rate of £85 per annum and from 1810 to 1820 by £40 per annum. From 1820 to 1835 a rate of increase of £50 per annum was assumed. Such rough estimates as these might tend to either underestimate or overestimate trends and totals in particular periods, but, it is hoped, not to a considerable extent.

Table 21 shows the annual average value of fixed capital multiplied by the number of mills for each year and thus gives an annual series of aggregate fixed capital values and an annual series of net fixed capital formation.

TABLE 21

FIXED CAPITAL: FORMATION IN THE WEST RIDING WOOL TEXTILE INDUSTRY 1780–1835

Date	*Average Value of fixed Capital per mill*	*No. of Mills*	*Total Value of Fixed Capital*	*Fixed Capital Formation per annum*
1780	1,000	5	5,000	—
1781	1,000	6	6,000	1,000
1782	1,000	9	9,000	3,000
1783	1,000	12	12,000	3,000
1784	1,000	13	13,000	1,000
1785	1,000	19	19.000	6,000
1786	1,000	27	27,000	8,000
1787	1,000	32	32,000	5,000
1788	1,000	37	37,000	5,000
1789	1,000	38	38,000	1,000
1790	1,000	50	50,000	12,000
1791	1,065	57	60,705	10,705
1792	1,130	80	90,400	29,695
1793	1,195	90	107,550	17,150
1794	1,260	105	132,300	24,750
1795	1,325	126	166,950	34,650
1796	1,390	143	198,770	31,820
1797	1,455	184	267,720	68,950
1798	1,520	195	296,400	28,680
1799	1,585	213	337,605	41,205
1800	1,650	243	400,950	63,345
1801	1,735	268	464,980	64,030
1802	1,820	268	487,760	22,780
1803	1,905	273	520,065	32,305
1804	1,990	267	531,330	11,265

TABLE 21 continued

Date	Average Value of fixed Capital per mill	No. of Mills	Total Value of Fixed Capital	Fixed Capital Formation per annum
1805	2,075	268	556,100	24,770
1806	2,160	268	578,880	22,780
1807	2,245	264	592,680	13,800
1808	2,330	257	598,810	6,130
1809	2,415	260	627,900	29,090
1810	2,500	258	645,000	17,100
1811	2,540	258	655,320	10,320
1812	2,580	265	683,700	28,380
1813	2,620	269	704,780	21,080
1814	2,660	268	712,880	8,100
1815	2,700	278	750,600	37,720
1816	2,740	293	802,820	52,220
1817	2,780	298	828,440	25,620
1818	2,820	305	860,100	31,660
1819	2,860	317	906,620	46,520
1820	2,900	327	948,300	41,680
1821	2,950	340	1,003,000	54,700
1822	3,000	372	1,116,000	113,000
1823	3,050	382	1,165,100	49,100
1824	3,100	391	1,212,100	47,000
1825	3,150	404	1,272,600	60,500
1826	3,200	425	1,360,000	87,400
1827	3,250	433	1,407,250	47,250
1828	3,300	442	1,458,600	51,350
1829	3,350	461	1,544,350	85,750
1830	3,400	493	1,676,200	131,850
1831	3,450	501	1,728,450	52,250
1832	3,500	510	1,785,000	56,550
1833	3,550	528	1,874,400	89,400
1834	3,600	533	1,918,800	44,400
1835	3,650	577	2,106,050	187,250
1835	3,650	610	2,226,500	307,700

The series of annual fixed capital values and formation are clearly more reliable as indicators of trends than as exact measurements. Whereas it may be argued that the figures for fixed capital stock are realistic subject to the accuracy of the assumptions made, the figures for fixed capital formation are clearly much more subject to error. Their reliability is dependent on the trustworthiness of the information on which they are based, particularly on the figures for the number of mills in use year by year. For most mills there is definite information on when they came into or went out of use. For some mills however, the dates of the first and last references to the mill have had to be used with the consequence that the series is somewhat affected by the availability of better sources for particular periods. Thus for example, the high number of mills shown to have started working in 1822, and therefore the high level of capital formation calculated for that year is possibly an over optimistic estimate brought about by the fact that the Directory of the West Riding published in that year was rather more detailed and comprehensive than any one that had previously been produced.[21] Likewise mills first recorded through the factory returns in 1835 substantially increase the capital formation figure for that year.

Moreover, the list of the number of mills starting work annually cannot supply information on their various sizes. It might well be possible that for a year when, say, only two mills were recorded as entering the industry, the total fixed capital invested in those two mills could have been far greater than that invested in many more mills starting work in the following year. Thus the entry into the industry of a particularly large factory in one year, such as Gott's at Bean Ing in 1792, would not be reflected in the annual series of fixed capital formation, although the value of its fixed capital would be accounted for in the average and total figures for each of the four years for which calculations were made. Thus in the series there is an averaging out over time of very large separate investments in particular years. Likewise the building of very small mills may be similarly concealed.

In the series of figures of mills entering and in use in the industry, it was suggested that for several years at the end of the first decade of the nineteenth century more mills might have ceased working than commenced. However, in view of the assumption of the annual increase in average value of fixed capital of mills, positive capital formation is shown for these years. One might argue that although there was no increase in the number of mills at work investment would still have been taking place at previously established premises.

Investment in Power Plant

In the previous sections calculations were made for fixed capital investment *in toto*. The sources used in the calculations do permit, to some extent, the breakdown of these figures into their component parts. The fixed capital investment may be divided into the four categories of power, gearing and machinery, buildings, and ancillary

[21] E. Baines, *A Directory of the County of York*, 1822.

investment. Some mention has already been made of each of these areas and the changes they underwent during the period. It is now possible to consider them in financial terms.

For the provision of power for his mill the manufacturer was faced with two main possibilities. His decision was much influenced by the location of his mill but, even so, there were also financial considerations, based on capital and running costs. Short run capital costs of installation had to be examined alongside depreciation and operating expenses.

The amount of power available in mills varied very considerably from the 3 horsepower generated at Thomas Hinchcliffe's mill at Thirsting near Honley to the 194 horsepower produced by three wheels and two engines at John Brooke and Sons mill at South Crosland.[22] Likewise the sum a manufacturer might have had to invest in power plant could have ranged from a few pounds to several thousand.

There are few figures available for the cost of building water-wheels. In the majority of cases they would appear to have been constructed on the spot by a local millwright. The building account for the new mill at Lumb Mill, Delph, in 1832–5 included the following items for the construction of the water-wheel:[23]

3 February, 1835 To E. and J. Taylor — Castings for waterwheel and shafting	£50 0 0
5 February, 1835 Iron for waterwheel, shafting, etc.	£23 5 5
7 February, 1835 Work making wheel	£24 0 0
16 February, 1835 Casting for wheel	£12 9 0
19 February, 1835 Timber for wheel and stocks	£42 0 0

These items suggest that the cost of building the wheel was certainly no more than £150 and probably no more than £100. It is uncertain how large this wheel was. There was also a steam engine in the mill purchased from Zebulum Stirk of Leeds which,

[22] *Factories Inquiry Commission, Supplementary Reports,* Part II, C.2. Mills nos. 73 and 102.

[23] MSS Account Book of James Lee, Delph, in the custody of the Librarian, Upper Mill Library, Saddleworth.

with its gearing, cost £1,057 11*s* 10*d* for purchase and installation in May 1833. An entry for 10 July 1835 records a figure of £32 for connecting the steam engine with the water-wheel, so it may well be that the mill was mainly water-powered and the steam engine was only used to augment the water power when necessary. Although the size of the wheel is not known, one can compare its cost with that of the mill building and machinery. The mill itself appears to have been finished by the end of 1834 at a cost of about £4,000. Another building 'a willow house', was constructed in 1837–9 at a cost of £414 13*s* 5*d*. The investment in machinery for the mill amounted to £4,069 7*s* 9*d* from 1833 to 1845 with an extra £95 2*s* 6*d* for the installation of gas in 1838–9. Thus the total fixed capital of the mill by the early 1840s was in the region of £10,000, of which 10 per cent was for a steam engine and not much more than 1 per cent for the water-wheel. It is interesting to note that there are no items in the Account Book for the cost of bringing water to the wheel. Presumably use was made of the leats for the old mill. An examination of the site also shows that a good stream ran alongside so the expenses here were probably minimal. William Fairbairn, however, suggested that the difference between the cost of providing water and steam power, taking into account maintenance and running costs, was not so considerable. He made some calculations on the relative costs of providing water and steam power to the large and well-known Catrine Mills in Scotland, where there were two water-wheels, each 50 ft. in diameter and 12 ft. wide providing between them 200 horsepower from a 48 ft. fall of water. The water was brought to the wheels from above a weir through a system of conduits and tunnels over some considerable distance. The cost was estimated as follows:

	£
Water privileges and land	4,000
Cost of Weir	1,000
Head race, tunnel and canal	3,000
Archways, systems and sluices	1,000
Wheelhouse and foundations	1,500
Tail race	1,500
Waterwheels and erection	4,500
Contingencies	1,500
TOTAL	£18,000

The cost of power, independant of millwork equivalent to an annual rental for interest of capital, repairs and wear and tear at seven per cent amounting to £1,260. This may be contrasted with steam power in a district where coal can be purchased at 7s. per ton and we have:

	£
Cost of engine of 100 nominal horse power	4,000
Engine house and foundations	1,500
Contingencies	500
TOTAL	£6,000

This at 10 per cent for interest, capital repairs and renewals will be equivalent to:

An Annual Rental of	£600
Add consumption of coal at 4 lbs. per indicated horse power per hour, engineers wages etc.	£900
TOTAL	£1,500

Fairbairn concludes that taking into account the difficulties created by floods and droughts to water '. . . it will be seen that it frequently happens that steam power might have been purchased and maintained as at economical a rate', and that:

> . . . on the whole there appears (in the present improved state of the steam engine and the price of coal) to be no advantage in this country in water power as applied to manufactures and it is only at out districts, and where the mere wants of the inhabitants have been supplied, that water mills can be used with profit . . .[24]

Fairbairn, however, based his calculations on a mill of exceptional size with exceptional engineering construction, for which there was certainly no parallel in Yorkshire by the mid-1830s. Indeed, the average power generated by wheels in Yorkshire wool textiles would appear from the statistics of the factory inspectors to have been 10 horsepower. Very few wheels produced more than 20 horsepower in 1835 and there was certainly no wheel producing more than 60 horsepower.

The wheel at Lumb Mill, New Delph, is likely to have been far more typical of the water-wheel in the Yorkshire mill than the ones at Catrine Mills. Indeed, taking into account that the fixed capital

[24] Fairbairn, *Treatise . . .*, op. cit., Part I, pp. 91–3. The, often high, costs of water rights have not been included in the calculations.

at Lumb Mill was twice the average at least for other mills in the County in 1835, it is probably that the wheel at Lumb Mill was even larger than average. If this were so, then the initial cost of installing water-wheels in mills appears to have been very low in relation to the total fixed capital investment.

The cost of purchasing and installing steam engines was certainly much higher, and in view of the number of steam engines being used even before 1800 the value of capital invested in them must have been quite considerable. Various information is available about the costs of steam engines. Reasonably accurate data can be obtained about the price of engines purchased from Boulton and Watt's Soho Foundry. Table 22 shows the prices for engines of different horsepower charged by Boulton and Watt in the late 1790s and early 1800s.[25] The figures in this Table show that the cost per horsepower for a Sun and Planet engine was between £50 and £60 for a small engine and between £40 and £50 for a larger one. For a beam engine the charges were about £10 per horsepower lower except for the very small engines for which between £60 and £66 per horsepower was charged.

TABLE 22

AVERAGE PRICE OF BOULTON AND WATT ENGINES 1795–1802

Sun and Planet Engines, 1795–1800		*Beam Engines, 1800–1802*	
Power	Average Price	Power	Average Price
	£		£
8	500	3	200
10	530	4	250
12	600	6	295
16	760	8	350
20	840	10	410
24	1,080	12	445
30	1,325	14	490
32	1,307*	16	550
36	1,348*	20	620
45	2,175*	30	930
		40	1,060
		50	1,290

* Prices of individual engines.

Source: Boulton and Watt MSS, Engine Books.

[25] Average prices 1795–1800 and 1800–2 based on the prices as shown in the firm's Engine Books for Sun and Planet and Crank Engines, but excluding prices for engines with peculiar specifications, for example copper boilers.

By 1800 approximately £6,500 had been paid by Yorkshire woollen and worsted manufacturers for Boulton and Watt engines as is shown by Table 23. However, it is known that the patented Boulton and Watt Sun and Planet engines were more expensive than most of the engines at work in Yorkshire mills before 1800. Murray and Wood built one of 30 horsepower for Marshall's Water Lane Flax Mill in 1799 at a cost of £750.[26] Benjamin Hallas appears to have paid about £720; 'On Acct. of Engain' for his Pildacre Mill at Ossett in 1798. This engine may have been one of 38 horsepower built by Elwell at Fall Ing Foundry near Wakefield.[27] The normal engine in the Yorkshire woollen mill was certainly much smaller than these and perhaps seldom generated more than 10 horsepower. The insurance details for engines working in mills before 1800 give an average value for them of around £200, excluding the Boulton and Watt engines. Assuming a constant ratio between power and cost this would suggest an average power of 8 to 10 horsepower per engine. Working on the basis of this average value and the prices of the Boulton and Watt engines supplied to Yorkshire mills, it would seem that by 1800 engines costing about £22,000 had been purchased for those mills recorded as having been steam-powered in whole or in part;[28] and thus about five and a half per cent of total fixed capital in 1800 might have been in the form of steam engines.

Table 23

PRICES PAID BY YORKSHIRE MANUFACTURERS FOR BOULTON AND WATT ENGINES, 1790–1800

Firm	*Power of Engine*	*Price*
Wormald, Fountain and Gott	40 hp	1,500*
John and James Walker	20 hp	840*
Joshua Foster	20 hp	812
Halliday and Cockshott	12 hp	507
Nevins and Gatliff	16 hp	720
Nussey and Co.	20 hp	840*
Markland, Cookson and Fawcett	30 hp	1,250*

* Estimated price based on charges by Boulton and Watt for similar engines at about the same period.

Source: See Table 10 for references.

26 Rimmer, op. cit., p. 46.

27 J. Goodchild, 'Pildacre Mill: An Early West Riding Factory', *Textile History*, Vol. 1, no. 3, 1970, p. 341.

28 See Table II.

However, how far the insurance valuations take into account the rapid depreciation on steam engines is uncertain. The total amount of money actually spent on engines may have been more than £22,000 but the actual value of engines in use in 1800 less than that figure. Very rapid depreciation was allowed for on some engines, presumably particularly when difficulties were encountered in making an engine function satisfactorily. For those mills using steam power the engine often formed 20 per cent or more of fixed capital value. At Stonebridge Mills, Farnley, in 1805, the steam engine was insured for £600 and the rest of the fixed capital for £2,900.[29] At Markland, Cookson and Fawcett's mill at the Bank, Leeds, the engine was insured for £1,500 and the other fixed capital for £7,350 in 1795. By 1800 the value of this engine had been reduced to £1,000 although by that date the other fixed capital was insured for £8,400.[30]

For later dates, other estimates of the cost of steam engines are available. One report in 1814 gives surprisingly high prices for them although the writer admits that he had had great difficulty in obtaining figures:

> I have received many different answers when trying to discover the cost of steam power in England. The following estimate is the result of my enquiries. The cost of steam appears to vary between £300 and £400 per horse power. I think that £300 is the lowest quotation that one can hope to get. But if the steam engine is one over one horse power the cost is reduced. After the first horse power there is a reduction of half of one per cent for every subsequent unit of power. Thus if the basic charge were £300, a steam engine of 10 horse power would not cost £3,000 (i.e. £300 × 10) but only £2,850 i.e. £300 (minus 10 × ½ × 3) × 10.[31]

One, however, must suspect that Mr May was misinformed. Only a few years before Boulton and Watt were able to supply and install a 14 horsepower beam engine at Rotherham for £714 13*s* 10*d*[32] and Fenton, Murray and Wood appear to have been charging about the same. Table 24 shows the price of Fenton, Murray and Wood steam engines in 1813 and 1830. There appears to have been a very slight reduction in prices between the two years, perhaps no more than 5 per cent. Trevor Turner makes the point that the Leeds engines were probably slightly cheaper than those from Soho because of the lower piecework rates at Leeds.[33]

29 Sun C.R. 63/881333/1805.
30 Sun C.R. 8/636966/1795; 32/701514/1800.
31 W. O. Henderson, *Industrial Britain Under the Regency*, Chapter IV, 'Report on a Journey to England by Factory Commissioner J. G. May in 1814', p. 159.
32 Boulton and Watt MSS, Portfolio no. 361.
33 Turner, thesis, op. cit., Chapter 3, p. 36.

TABLE 24

FENTON, MURRAY AND WOOD ENGINE PRICES,

1813 and 1820

Engine size *hp*	*Approximate Price* *1813*	*Approximate Price* *1830*
	£	£
4	360	320
8	480	440
12	640	600
16	800	760
20	900	860
24	1,020	980
28	1,140	1,100
32	1,220	—
36	1,260	—

Source: T. Turner, *A History of Fenton, Murray and Wood*, unpublished M.Sc. thesis, U.M.I.S.T., 1966, Figure 3. 24.

According to this table, Fenton, Murray and Wood's prices in 1830 appear to have averaged about £60 per horsepower for an engine under 10 horsepower, £48 for one of 10–20 horsepower, £40 for one of 20–30 horsepower, and £36 or less per horsepower for one of 30 horsepower. If one relates these prices to the engines recording as having been operating in woollen and worsted mills in 1835 one might arrive at a reasonable estimate of the amount of capital that had been invested to provide steam power at that date. Table 25 shows the calculations according to the size of engines and suggests that about £375,000 had been spent to provide the industry with the 442 engines that were recorded in 1835. This figure amounts to 17 per cent of total fixed capital of the West Riding at this date, but since the calculations are at cost price and take no account of allowances for depreciation the proportion was certainly somewhat lower. About 10 per cent of the engines were traceable in the insurance valuations and the average value of an engine according to those figures was somewhat over £400 suggesting a total value for them in 1835 of about £200,000 or about 9 per cent of total fixed capital value of all mills and around 20 per cent for steam-powered mills. The normal depreciation assigned to steam engines in contemporary accounts is uncertain. In cotton mills there appears to have been a standard charge of about seven and a half per cent per annum for depreciation of machinery.[34] If the rate were similar for steam engines this could account quite easily for the difference between the estimated original cost and current value in 1835. However, the figures show quite definitely the significance of the value of steam power as a proportion of total fixed capital values. The installation of steam power was a major outlay for a manufacturer and accounted for an important part of all his investment in fixed capital.

TABLE 25

ESTIMATES OF CAPITAL OUTLAY ON STEAM ENGINES AT WORK IN YORKSHIRE WOOL TEXTILE MILLS IN 1835

Power of Engine	*No. of Engines*	*Total Power hp*	*Approx. Cost per hp £*	*Total Cost £*
Under 10	64	428	60	25,680
10–19	153	2,105	48	101,040
20–29	114	2,505	40	100,200
Over 30	111	4,152	36	149,472
TOTALS	442	9,190	—	376,392

Investment in Machinery, Buildings and Other Fixed Capital

The major item of capital expense for a manufacturer was the equipping of the mill with its gearing and machinery. The value of insurance risks for the early 1830s suggests that at this period the fixed capital values of buildings, millwright's work and clockmaker's work were in the ratio 5:2:9, or total fixed capital was made up in the following proportions:

Investment in:	*Percentage*
Power Plant	9
Buildings	27
Millwright's work	10
Clockmaker's work	49
Site preparation	5

Thus the value of all the machinery together amounted to over twice as much as the investment in buildings and to almost 60 per

[34] Blaug, loc. cit., p. 361.

cent of total fixed capital investment. For 1835 the total fixed capital of the industry in the West Riding might be divided as follows:

Power plant	£200,000
Mill buildings	£601,000
Millwright's work	£223,000
Clockmaker's work	£1,091,000
Site preparation	£111,000
TOTAL	£2,226,000

The value of the millwright's work appears to have related very closely to the value of the main mill building in the ratio 1:2:7. This ratio does not appear to have differed significantly between water-powered and steam-powered mills. A well functioning power transmission system in the mill was particularly important and it would seem that manufacturers would have been unwilling to install too inferior a system. Thus they were faced with an unavoidable capital outlay. Gott, for example, valued the millwright's work at his various buildings at Park Mills, Leeds at £2,200 in 1821 which was about 11 per cent of his total fixed capital.[35]

The value of production machinery in 1835 was over £1 million. It does not seem possible to divide this figure between different types of machinery. Although there is a good deal of information on costs of different machines, estimates of the amount of different machinery in use are impossible to calculate with any likely degree of accuracy with the exception of power looms. The survey of power looms in factories in 1835, although by no means complete, does provide an indication of the numbers in use by that year. Three thousand six hundred and sixty-one were recorded at work in West Riding woollen and worsted mills including 157 in a worsted and cotton mill.[36] Information is available for the price of looms at this period. In January 1836 Messrs Starkey and Buckley of Longroyde Bridge, Huddersfield installed 72 pairs of power looms in their mill and insured them for £1,500 or about £10 10*s* 0*d* each.[37] In 1839 James Lee of Lumb Mill, Saddleworth bought two pairs of power looms for £42 10*s* 0*d*, or £10 12*s* 6*d* each.[38] Assuming these were of an average size then over £40,000 had been spent by manufacturers on power looms by 1835. Scattered information is available

[35] Sun C.R. 133/975082/1821.
[36] See Table 16.
[37] Sun C.R. 214/1197383/1835; 225/1216353/1836.
[38] MSS Account Book of James Lee, loc. cit.

TABLE 26

VALUE OF MACHINERY AT STARKEY AND BUCKLEY'S MILL AT HUDDERSFIELD, 1835–6

Machinery	£
8 Gigs	200
6 Brushing Mills	300
4 Jones' Patent Traversing Machines	200
96 pair of power looms with healds and stays	2,100
A bobbin sinking machine	30
2 spinning mules with the weft and warps in process of healding and staying with the beams	420
16 pair of narrow looms	320
1 pair of mules	264
3 drying frames	90
Dressing machinery and spinning mules	1,800
9 hydraulic presses and press papers	900
14 Fulling stocks, 3 washing machines, willow and goods in process	1,500
18 scribbling and carding engines, 4 power billies and wool in process	3,570
14 spinning mules and wool in process	1,050
Going gears and 12 gigs and goods in process	1,080
7 brushing mills, shearboards, shears and goods to process	1,500
8 Lewis and 3 Miles cutting machines, shearboards, shears and goods in process	810
8 carding and scribbling engines, 1 power and 1 hand billey and wool in process	1,350
4 Lewis Cutting Machines, 4 spinning mules, wool and cloth in process	810
4 warping mills, spinning jennies and warps in process	360
TOTAL	£18,654

Machinery insured in the Sun, Globe and Atlas Fire Offices.

Source: Sun C.R. 214/1197383/1835; 225/1216353/1836.

for the prices of other machinery but often there is no way of estimating the size of the various machines.

However, a detailed list of machinery at one particularly large mill, Starkey's at Huddersfield, which carried out all the processes of woollen cloth manufacture, will serve to illustrate the amount and diversity of machinery that some mills contained and the investment required. The machinery was powered by three engines each of 28 horsepower and the mill employed 521 workers in 1834.[39] The various machinery and its insured value is listed in Table 26. All the production machinery in this mill was valued at over £18,000 whereas the buildings were only insured for about one third of that sum.

The investment in mill buildings, although often less than half of that in machinery, was still the second most important item of capital expenditure facing both large and small manufacturers Whereas the very small mills would have cost no more than a few hundred pounds to build the large six or seven storey buildings being constructed by the 1830s might have cost several thousand pounds. There is not sufficient information on enough mills at different periods of time to generalize about the construction costs of different types of buildings. A mill constructed in 1835 at Mearclough Bottom near Halifax, with five storeys and a floor area of 2,500 sq. yds, was insured immediately after it was finished for £3,500 or 28 shillings per sq. yd.[40] Except for iron framed fireproof mills, this appears to have been slightly above average cost at this period. Starkey's buildings were insured for between 20 shillings and 26 shillings per sq. yd. and the smaller stone worsted mills at Gargrave and Sutton for 20 shillings or 22 shillings per sq. yd.[41] One cannot compare very satisfactorily the cost of using different materials for construction but the different degrees of fire proofing had the most substantial effect on cost and the mill builder had to consider the extra total cost against the reduction he could obtain in his fire insurance premium and the less likely occurrence of a mill fire disrupting his business.

The average value of mill buildings in the late eighteenth century was between £300 and £500 with the notable exception of some of the larger factories such as Gott's Park Mills where buildings were valued at over £8,000 by 1800.[42] By the early 1830s, however, the average value was more in the region of £1,000 which suggests that the typical mill building was still very small even at this date.

[39] *Factories Inquiry Commission, Supplementary Reports*, Part II, C.2, Mill no. 134.
[40] Mearclough Bottom Mill, Insurance Proposal and Plan, Halifax Archives Department.
[41] Proposal Book of Thos. Brown, Royal Exchange Assurance Company Agent, Skipton, loc. cit.
[42] Sun C.R. 31/699424/1800.

An extra cost to a manufacturer was the installation of gas lighting which was becoming much more common in mills by the late 1820s and early 1830s. The information on the cost of installing gas lighting is rather piecemeal. At Lumb Mill, Saddleworth it cost £95 2*s* 6*d* in 1838–9 which amounted to only about two and a half per cent of the original cost of constructing the mill buildings.[43] The cost would have depended on whether the mill could be connected to the public supply or whether gas making apparatus and a gasometer had to be constructed. At Burley Mill, near Leeds, where the latter was the case the lighting apparatus cost at least £650 in 1808.[44] Except in the very few cases where construction costs were recorded and have survived, there appears to be no way of estimating the separate relative importance of the value of fixed capital investment in gas installations. In the insurance valuations the apparatus was often included as part of the buildings or machinery and cannot, therefore, be considered individually.

The other major item of fixed capital cost facing manufacturers has already been considered in some detail. It is less easily identifiable than the buildings and machinery and even more difficult to account for. It consisted basically of the preparation of the mill site and the expenses involved in mill construction apart from the actual cost of erecting the building itself. Details of individual costs of this type of investment are scarce because of the lack of details of building costs. An account was given for Hartley's Mill at Morley which showed site preparation costs and professional fees amounting to about £230 on top of building costs for the mill and five cottages of somewhat over £3,500.[45] Another building account is available for the construction of a drying house at a Wakefield mill in 1799–1800. It shows that besides the £450 paid for the materials and labour for the erection of the building, there was an outlay of another £37 in cartage, loading and tips as well as £32 for the building of a considerable amount of walling.[46]

A certain amount of this type of expenditure was essential to a manufacturer but some of it might have been less necessary. Moreover one might expect cartage and loading costs and, perhaps, tips to be included in insured values. In view of the lack of information on this type of expenditure one can do no more than estimate an average cost for it in relation to fixed capital cost.

[43] Lumb MSS, loc. cit.
[44] Crump, op. cit., p. 259 n.
[45] See Table 17.
[46] Account in Peterhouse MSS, Cusworth Hall.

Investment in Woollen and Worsted Mills

In the calculations of fixed capital formation, both the woollen and worsted branches of the West Riding wool textile industry have been considered together. In so far as the main input for both was raw wool and the finished product of both was cloth, one might justifiably consider the two together as one industry. However, in other ways the two branches were very different. Worsted production, as a factory based industry, had a slower start than the manufacture of woollen cloth in mills; the processes of production were not the same and although the type of premises and some of the machinery for worsted manufacture were very much akin to those used in woollen cloth production the worsted mill tended to employ more workers than did its woollen counterpart. Whereas the average power and number of workers in a woollen mill in 1835 were 19 and 58 respectively, in worsted mills the equivalent figures were 19 and 82.[47]

If one assumes that the fixed capital for both types of mill throughout the period was in a direct ratio to the amount of power being used, then the average fixed capital for both types of mill was fairly similar. It is, therefore, possible to divide the total fixed capital of the wool textile industry at different dates between the two branches. This has been done in Table 27, where it is shown that in 1835 out of a total fixed capital of £2,226,500 in the industry as a whole, about two-thirds or £1,481,900 was accounted for by woollen manufacture and one third or £744,600 by the worsted branch of the industry. Although water-wheels tended to be smaller and fewer in number in the worsted branch the proportion of steam engines to the number of mills was very similar for both branches. However, particularly in the earlier years, worsted spinning mills were in general rather larger than those engaged in woollen manufacture. If one considers individually the thirty-eight worsted mills working in 1810 they do seem to have been bigger than the average woollen mill, Perhaps, therefore, the figures in Table 27 tend to underestimate the value of fixed capital in worsted manufacture. In the insurance valuations there is relatively far more information on woollen mills than on worsted mills and it is not possible to make separate calculations for the worsted branch of the industry.

[47] *Factory Returns*, 1835.

TABLE 27

FIXED CAPITAL IN THE WOOLLEN AND WORSTED BRANCHES OF THE YORKSHIRE WOOL TEXTILE INDUSTRY, 1780–1835

Date	*Average Value of Fixed Capital Per Mill*	*No. of Woollen Mills*	*Total Fixed Capital*	*Annual Fixed Capital Formation*	*No. of Worsted Mills*	*Total Fixed Capital*	*Annual Fixed Capital Formation*
	£		£	£		£	£
1780	1,000	5	5,000				
1781	1,000	6	6,000	1,000			
1782	1,000	9	9,000	3,000			
1783	1,000	12	12,000	3,000			
1784	1,000	13	13,000	1,000			
1785	1,000	19	19,000	6,000			
1786	1,000	27	27,000	8,000			
1787	1,000	31	31,000	4,000	1	1,000	
1788	1,000	36	36,000	5,000	1	1,000	
1789	1,000	36	36,000	—	2	2,000	1,000
1790	1,000	46	46,000	10,000	4	4,000	2,000
1791	1,065	51	54,315	8,315	6	6,390	2,390
1792	1,130	71	80,230	25,915	9	10,170	3,780
1793	1,195	78	93,210	12,980	12	14,340	4,170
1794	1,260	92	115,920	22,710	13	16,380	2,040
1795	1,325	111	147,075	31,155	15	19,875	3,495
1796	1,390	126	175,140	28,065	17	23,630	3,755
1797	1,455	167	242,985	67,845	17	24,735	1,105
1798	1,520	178	270,560	27,575	17	25,840	1,105
1799	1,585	195	309,075	38,515	18	28,530	2,690
1800	1,650	221	364,650	55,575	22	36,300	7,770
1801	1,735	243	421,605	56,955	25	43,375	7,075
1802	1,820	244	444,080	22,475	24	43,680	305
1803	1,905	249	474,345	30,265	26	49,530	5,850
1804	1,990	240	477,600	3,255	27	53,730	4,200
1805	2,075	234	485,500	7,900	27	56,025	2,295
1806	2,160	239	516,240	30,740	29	62,640	6,615
1807	2,245	238	534,310	18,070	30	67,350	4,710
1808	2,330	232	540,560	6,250	32	74,560	7,210
1809	2,415	225	543,375	2,815	32	77,280	2,720
1810	2,500	222	555,000	11,625	38	95,000	17,720
1811	2,540	218	553,720	1,280	40	101,600	6,600
1812	2,580	219	565,020	11,300	46	118,680	17,080
1813	2,620	220	576,400	11,380	49	128,380	9,700
1814	2,660	218	579,880	3,480	50	133,000	4,620
1815	2,700	224	604,800	24,920	54	145,800	12,800
1816	2,740	236	646,640	41,840	57	156,180	10,380
1817	2,780	237	658,860	12,220	61	169,580	13,400
1818	2,820	237	668,340	9,480	68	191,760	22,180
1819	2,860	243	690,120	21,780	74	210,160	18,400

TABLE 27 continued

Date	*Average Value of Fixed Capital Per Mill*	*No. of Woollen Mills*	*Total Fixed Capital*	*Annual Fixed Capital Formation*	*No. of Worsted Mills*	*Total Fixed Capital*	*Annual Fixed Capital Formation*
	£		£	£		£	£
1820	2,900	244	707,600	17,480	83	240,700	30,540
1821	2,950	250	737,500	36,900	90	265,500	24,800
1822	3,000	268	804,000	29,900	104	312,000	46,500
1823	3,050	275	838,750	34,750	107	326,350	14,350
1824	3,100	279	864,900	26,150	112	347,200	20,850
1825	3,150	293	922,950	58,050	111	349,650	2,450
1826	3,200	307	982,400	59,450	118	377,600	27,950
1827	3,250	310	1,007,500	25,100	123	399,750	22,150
1828	3,300	318	1,049,400	41,900	124	409,200	9,450
1829	3,350	329	1,102,150	52,750	132	442,200	33,000
1830	3,400	350	1,190,000	87,850	143	486,200	44,000
1831	3,450	354	1,221,300	31,300	147	507,150	20,950
1832	3,500	357	1,249,500	28,200	153	535,500	28,350
1833	3,550	368	1,306,400	56,900	160	568,000	32,500
1834	3,600	372	1,339,200	32,800	161	579,600	11,600
1835	3,650	399	1,456,350	117,150	178	649,700	70,100
1835	3,650	406	1,481,900	142,700	204	744,600	165,000

The estimates of fixed capital were made for the wool textile industry in the West Riding of Yorkshire. On the basis of the figures for Yorkshire, however, one can make an estimate for the industry throughout the country for 1835. The Factory Returns for that year covered all of England, Ireland, Scotland, and Wales. They were probably fairly complete, although the Inspector for the West Country and Wales, T. J. Howell, apologized that a few small mills were missing from his returns because the owners could not read or write or could only speak Welsh. Except for Lancashire and Yorkshire woollen and worsted mills cannot be distinguished in the returns.[48]

The inspectors traced and recorded 1,333 woollen and worsted mills employing almost 71,000 workers, an average of fifty-three workers per mill. The mills outside Yorkshire appear, in general, to have been slightly smaller than those in the county. Figures for power were only recorded for 736 of the mills but they suggest an average of 18 horsepower per mill. An analysis of the returns is given in Table 28.

[48] See Jenkins, 'The Validity of the Factory Returns, 1833–50', loc. cit.

TABLE 28

WOOLLEN AND WORSTED MILLS IN GREAT BRITAIN AND NORTHERN IRELAND — 1835

County	*Wool Textile Mills*	*Total power hp*	*Total Workers*
Eastern England; South East, South and South West of England; London; parts of the Midlands	106		4,100
Cheshire	15	116	195
Cumberland	15		251
Derbyshire (part)	4	25	34
Durham	5		322
Gloucestershire	118		7,937
Herefordshire	2		19
Lancashire	99*	1,318	4,575
	8†	205	1,076
Northumberland	3		39
Oxfordshire	9		313
Shropshire	3		100
Somerset (Part)	28		1,545
Staffordshire (Part?)	1		30
Warwickshire	5		196
Westmorland	14		422
Wiltshire (Part)	59		3,080
Worcestershire	6		134
Yorkshire	406*	7,949	23,636
	204†	3,762½	16,740
ENGLAND TOTALS:	1,110		64,780
Brecon	7		31
Cardigan	2		15
Carmarthen	6		25
Glamorgan	11		118
Merioneth	7		44
Monmouth	3		20
Montgomery	52		550
Radnor	1		5
Anglesea and North Wales	8		—
WALES TOTALS:	97		808

TABLE 28 continued

County	Wool Textile Mills	Total power hp	Total Workers
Ireland	36		1,641
Scotland	90		3,505
UNITED KINGDOM TOTALS:	1,333		70,734

* woollen mills † worsted mills

TOTALS: 1,333 mills

70,734 workers in 1,325 mills
Average 53 workers per mill
therefore approx. 71,158 workers in 1,333 mills.

13,375 hp in 736 mills
Average 18 hp per mill
therefore approx. 23,998 hp in 1,333 mills.

Source: *P.P.* 1836 (138), XLV, *Factory Returns* 1835.

Assuming the constant capital: power ratio, if the value of the fixed capital in the industry in Yorkshire was £2,230,000 for a horsepower of 11,711 then the fixed capital for the whole industry with its estimated total power of almost 24,000 horsepower would have been about £4,600,000 in 1835. A similar calculation based on the assumption of a constant capital: labour ratio gives an estimate for total fixed capital value of slightly under £4 million. However, the former figure is likely to be more accurate as the capital: power ratio is probably more realistic than the capital: labour ratio.[49]

There are no other estimates for the wool textile industry with which one can compare these figures. A comparison with other industries is, moreover, not very realistic. There are various estimates of the value of the fixed capital of the cotton industry in the early nineteenth century, but cotton mills differed quite considerably from the normal wool textile mill. In general they were larger and had more fixed capital relative to power and number of employees.

[49] See p. 153; the capital: power ratio may be a more realistic guide because the employment figures probably include a proportion of hand workers.

The Trends in Fixed Capital Investment

Even though it does not seem possible to test the absolute figures for the value of fixed capital by comparing them with other estimates one can attempt to relate the trends in fixed capital formation with other indicators of the performance of the industry and of the economy as a whole. Moreover, the often widely fluctuating trends need explaining.

A problem is posed by the time lag between the decision to undertake investment and its completion. Thus it would be possible for fixed capital investment to have been recorded in a period of bad business conditions even though the investment decision was taken in a good business climate. This time lag factor must be borne in mind when relating investment performance with other indicators. To try to reduce this problem and to identify the trends in investment three-year moving averages of fixed capital formation are shown in Fig. 13. These also help to reduce discrepancies caused by the problems of the sources used.

For the woollen branch of the industry investment in fixed capital is shown as fluctuating in the 1780s. In view of the few mills coming into operation in the very early years of the new system one cannot read too much into this. From 1788, however, fixed capital formation rose rapidly until 1796 and then fluctuated to a peak in 1800. In the following decade the previous levels of investment could not be maintained and capital formation dropped substantially to a very low level around 1810. From 1812 a steady rise in annual investment in fixed capital was evident until 1816 when depression returned for three years. From 1819 until 1829, however, fixed capital formation rose substantially with only slight setbacks in 1823 and 1826–8. From 1829 to 1832, the level of investment dropped somewhat but still remained above the level for the previous decade. From 1833 a rise is again shown although this may be partly the result of the sources used for that period.

In the worsted branch of the industry in the county trends were somewhat different. The level of capital formation remained low and fairly constant until 1808. The industry did not experience the woollen sectors rise in investment in the 1790s nor its depression in investment in the 1800s. From 1808 a slow rise in the capital formation level occurred but lasted for only three years. From 1811 to 1815 there was a slight setback but from then until 1821 came the main boom in fixed capital formation in the industry. The level fell again in the early 1820s but the trend was resumed from 1824 to 1830.

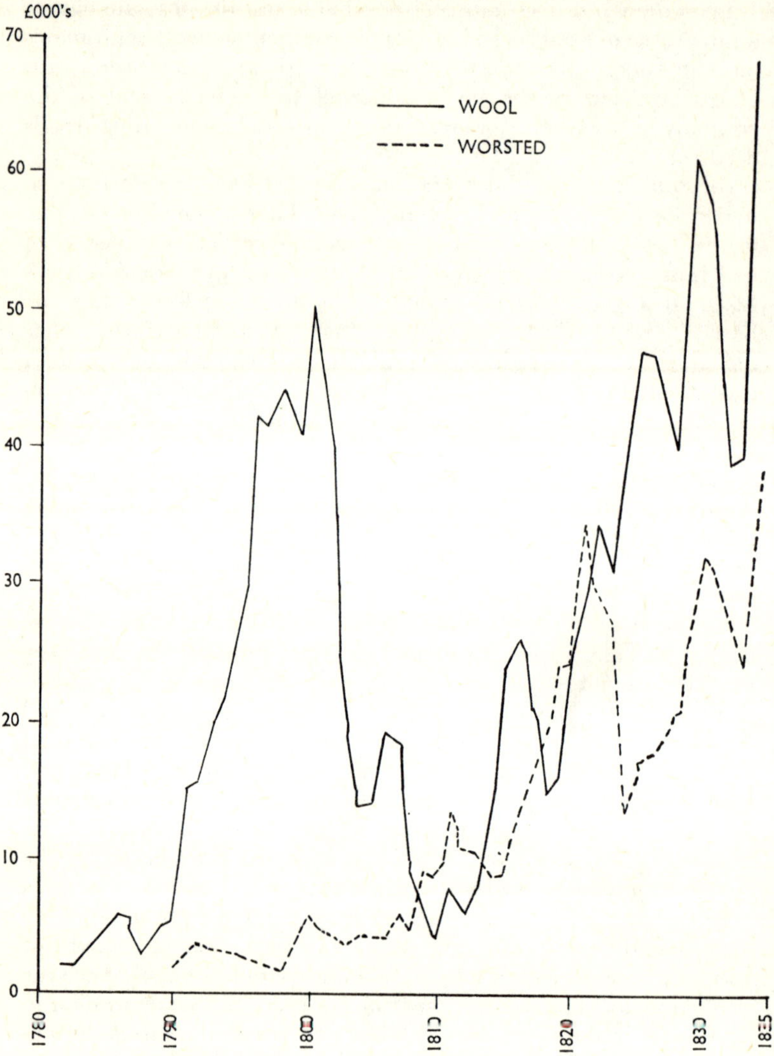

FIG. 13. Three year moving average of fixed capital formation in the Yorkshire wool textile industry, 1780–1835

For the woollen branch of the industry from 1780 to 1820, another indicator of its performance in the West Riding of Yorkshire is available. The returns of broad and narrow cloth milled are shown in Fig. 14.[50] The graph illustrates that the amount of cloth milled often fluctuated considerably from year to year, but in most periods the trends are very similar to those of the formation of fixed capital. From 1788 to 1795 a rapid rise is apparent although a slight setback is shown in 1792–4. From 1795 to 1798 there is a similar period of slight decrease in the amount of cloth milled which appears to be reflected in investment levels with a time lag of one year. In the decade from 1800 the previous twenty years rise in the amount of cloth milled is halted and output fluctuates wildly, reflecting the difficulties in the industry in this period which are also illustrated by fixed capital formation levels. There is unfortunately no similar indicator available for the output of the worsted branch of the industry. The performance of both sectors can however be considered in the light of other changes in the economy and contemporary comment about the state of trade.

R. G. Wilson in his study of the Leeds woollen merchants considered that after the three bad years of business from 1779 to 1781 the peace between Britain and America started the upward movement to prosperity and between 1782 and 1792 the production of the Yorkshire woollen industry almost doubled.[51] This increase appears to be partly explained by a general rise in the national output of woollen cloth and partly, and of more importance, by a considerable rise in Yorkshire's share of the total. Phyllis Deane estimated that:

> . . . Yorkshire's share of the total seems to have risen from about one third of total English output in 1772 to about 60 per cent by the end of the century.[52]

As the development of the woollen mill was at a very early stage at this period, this increase in Yorkshire's output is not altogether reflected in the growth of the number of woollen mills. However, this sudden increase in the prosperity of the Yorkshire industry no doubt provided the impetus for the building of woollen mills and the innovation of new techniques.

In the early 1790s the prosperity of the industry is shown in the level of investment. Exports to the United States were at a high

[50] See the discussion in Chapter 1 about the returns of broad and narrow cloth milled.
[51] Wilson, op. cit., pp. 49–51.
[52] Deane, op. cit., p. 215.

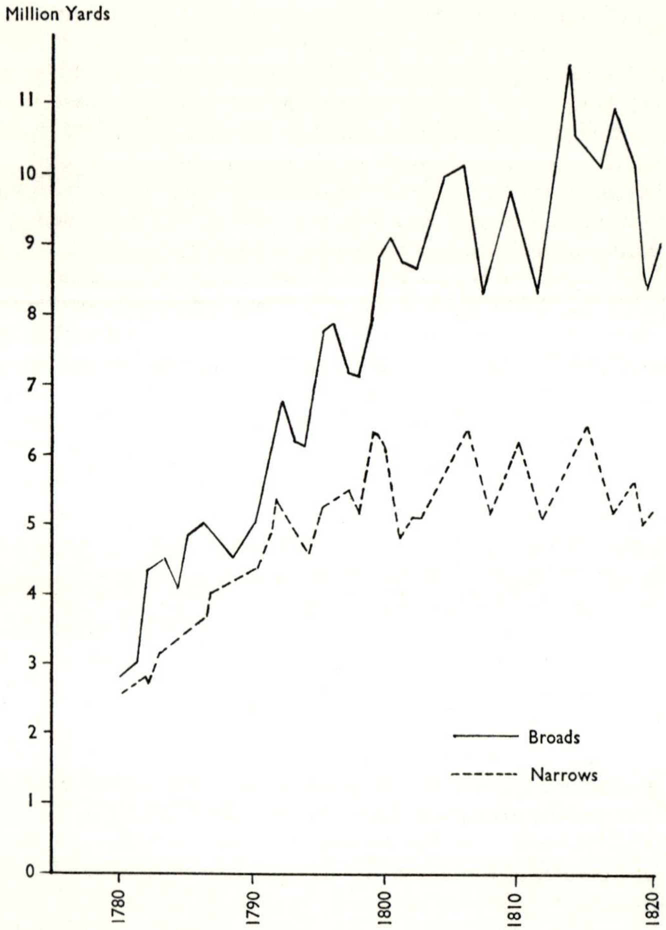

FIG. 14. Broad and narrow cloth milled in Yorkshire, 1780–1820

level and still exceeded those of the cotton industry in importance. The economic difficulties of 1792–3 with the drop in exports to the United States and France are reflected in the amount of cloth milled but not in capital formation.[53] Perhaps the crisis period was too short to have a serious effect at a time when many in the West Riding were urgently constructing mills and introducing new machinery. From 1794 trade recovered, the amount of cloth milled increased and investment in fixed capital continued at an even higher rate.[54]

The first decade of the nineteenth century was one of very fluctuating performance for the industry. The figures of investment for both the woollen and worsted branches reflect the downswing in the business cycle through the middle of the decade in so far as the increase in the rate of fixed capital formation ceases after 1800.[55] The outbreak of war in 1803 and the consequent stagnant trade position created difficulties and much worry for the woollen manufacturers. These problems and the opposition of the workers to the introduction of new machinery led to the Parliamentary Inquiry of 1806. In the second half of the decade, the industry hardly fared any better and the level of investment in the woollen branch was reduced considerably. The problems were caused, it would seem, by the massive reduction in exports to the United States, which was only partly alleviated by the opening of new markets. Many woollen manufacturers found themselves in difficulties. Joseph Rogerson complained in his diary about the state of trade in 1808:

> 28 December 1808 . . . No work for the cloth mill . . . work has been so scarce this year that Bramley townspeople took a cut to Dig of Mrs. Charnock, Monkton Moor, for the poor people to go to work at but part staid at home and pin'd before they would go . . .[56]

The position remained poor until 1812.[57] This bad period is well illustrated by the estimates of fixed capital formation for the woollen industry. Indeed, it would seem that more mills ceased working around this time than entered the industry. The reason why investment should have found such a low level is perhaps explained by the length of the depression. Downturns in the previous twenty-five years had quite short; hardly long enough, in fact, to have a

[53] See Figure 14 and Table 27.
[54] See Gayer, Rostow and Schwartz, *The Growth and Fluctuation of the British Economy, 1790–1850* (1953), Vol. 1, pp. 7–57.
[55] See Table 27.
[56] Crump, op. cit., 'Diary of Joseph Rogerson', p. 91.
[57] Gayer, Rostow and Schwartz, op. cit., pp. 102, 125.

serious effect on investment before recovery took place. The long troubled period after 1800, however, sapped the resources and enthusiasm of the manufacturers and their confidence sank to a very low level. In the worsted branch of the industry, this period of depression did not prevent a net increase in investment. Some of this is explained by the conversion of cotton mills in the Keighley area to worsted production,[58] but new mills were also built in Keighley, Halifax, and Bradford parishes.

From 1812 a slow recovery is apparent from the amount of cloth milled. Exports improved and, in spite of difficulties with the Luddites, output increased. The improvement continued until 1814–15 and is well reflected by the estimates of fixed capital formation which rise from only £11,000 in 1812 to £41,000 in 1816 for the woollen industry.

In 1816, however, depression returned. It was '. . . universally a bad year with heavy unemployment, bankruptcies, and riots'.[59] William Lupton, the Leeds merchant, complained: 'The state of trade is worse than ever I saw it.'[60] The downturn affected investment in the industry in the following two or three years in the case of the woollen branch but had little impact on the worsted sector. Recovery in the level of investment only becomes really marked from about 1820.

Gayer, Rostow and Schwartz identify a boom from 1817 to 1818 followed by a slump in 1819 and a mild recovery in 1820–1 in industrial performance.[61] The boom does not appear to be shown by the estimates of fixed capital formation. It is possible that this is because of the time lag between the decision to invest and the completion of the new investment. Most likely also the difficult times from 1806–12, the short lived recovery and the renewed slump in 1816 made manufacturers reluctant to undertake new investment until they were sure a definite and prolonged economic improvement was under way.

The mild recovery of 1820–1 was sustained and increased through the first half of the 1820s. Industrial performance, for the economy as a whole, improved, exports showed a steady increase, with a slight setback only in 1823. One nineteenth-century commentator stated:

[58] For example East Greengate Mill and Brow End Mill. See also Chapter 1.
[59] Gayer, Rostow and Schwartz, op. cit., p. 125.
[60] Wilson, op. cit., p. 113.
[61] Gayer, Rostow and Schwartz, op. cit., p. 151.

'the trade and manufactures had never before been in a more regular, sound and satisfactory state.'[62]

The statistics for the amount of woollen cloth milled cease in 1821. The estimates of fixed capital formation show, however, that as the improvement in the economy continued so manufacturers became more willing to undertake new fixed capital investment. In the woollen trade, the net annual level rose from £17,000 in 1820 to £58,000 in 1825. In the worsted branch of the industry the investment performance was considerably different. The level rose continually from 1815 to 1821 but declined to a relatively stable but low position in the middle of the decade. The reasons for this are not altogether clear. The burst of activity from 1815 to 1822 when the number of mills working doubled perhaps made some investors afraid that the capacity of the industry was outstretching the increase in demand for its product. James suggests that by 1819 there were signs of depression 'as a consequence of the speculation and excited prosperity of the former years'. He also points to a slight falling off of the worsted trade to the United States.[63] On the other hand, he states that the worsted trade in the early 1820s was 'in a very thriving vigorous condition' and that, 'The stuff markets, altogether, during the years 1820–1–2–3–4 continued steady, and the demand progressive'.[64]

In the woollen branch of the industry by 1825 boom conditions were being experienced. Wool imports and exports reached a new peak and the period saw considerable speculation with new investment. Prices were at a high level and 'the woollen trade as a whole was reported increasingly prosperous . . .'. In the last few months of 1825, however, a 'universal depression of manufactures' set in. Raw wool imports dropped from 44 million pounds in 1825 to 16 million pounds in 1826, exports declined with the collapse of the South American market and tariff increases in the United States and there appears to have been a general decline in confidence.[65]

After the problems of 1826, however, trade improved once more and maintained a high level for the rest of the decade. The period was one of falling prices and rising output and 'there was a strong

[62] Quoted by Gayer, Rostow and Schwartz, op. cit., p. 196.
[63] James, op. cit., p. 385.
[64] Ibid., p. 400.
[65] Gayer, Rostow and Schwartz, op. cit., pp. 182, 198–9; Wilson, op. cit., pp. 114, 118.

cost-reducing incentive to take advantage of new technical possibilities'.[66] The high level of activity in the wool textile industry, as shown by the level of the imports of raw wool and the export of cloth, was sustained right through to the mid-1830s. Confidence was high and the industry prospering.

The estimates of fixed capital formation reflect the good trading position until 1830. In the worsted branch the annual level of net fixed capital formation rose from £22,000 in 1827 to £44,000 in 1830. In the woollen industry, the problems of 1826 appear to be shown in the investment performance of the following year but from then until 1830 the level of annual fixed capital formation rose from £25,000 to £87,000. In both branches of the wool textile industry, however, the increase in investment in fixed capital appears to have ceased in 1830, declined until 1832–3 and then increased again with an even greater force.[67] This decrease does not stand out in the wool imports and export figures but may perhaps have been a result of the lack of confidence in the money market and general difficulties in raising finance. Shannon's index of brick duty collected for Leeds shows an apparent decline in the level of building in Leeds in these years.[68]

Thus the calculated estimates of net fixed capital formation correspond on the whole very closely to other indicators of the performance of the industry, allowing for a time lag of about one year between the investment decision and its completion. Investment appears to have followed quite closely, as one would expect, the state of the trade and the estimates reinforce the established view of the performance of the industry during the period from 1780 to 1835.

Changes in the Price Level and the Cost of Mill Construction

The calculations of fixed capital values and formation have been made on a current price basis. It seems probable that insurance values took into account price changes at least in the long run if not in the very short run. In section two of this Chapter the average value of a mill's fixed capital was estimated. It appears that in 1800 the average fixed capital was about £1,650 and in 1835 £3,650. One cannot, however, conclude from this that the size of the fixed

[66] Gayer, Rostow and Schwartz, op. cit., pp. 213, 222.
[67] Ibid., pp. 221, 226.
[68] H. A. Shannon, 'Bricks — A Trade Index', *Economica*, August 1934, p. 306.

capital of the mills increased more than twofold without considering the price changes of the period.

The question of price changes during the Industrial Revolution has undergone much debate and one is faced with considerable difficulties when attempting to calculate the changes in the cost of building mills or of purchasing machinery. The present concensus of opinion appears to be that prices were undergoing an upward trend in the closing decades of the eighteenth century and until the end of the Napoleonic Wars. However the movements of individual prices were variable and divergent and an attempt to measure specific changes through a general price index is a dubious procedure. Most of the attempts to calculate price indices have been for food and manufactured goods. Little consideration has been given to the changes in the prices of construction materials or to construction costs.

However from the end of the war in 1815 there is substantial evidence that prices started to fall and continued to do so throughout the rest of the period. This is borne out by much contemporary comment. The Select Committee on Manufactures, Commerce and Shipping in 1833 questioned mill owners and manufacturers about costs of mill construction and the changing value of their fixed capital. John Brooke of Armitage Bridge, Huddersfield was asked: 'what would be the present value of 50,000l. sunk in a mill ten years ago?' and he replied 'I think it would not be built and stocked with machinery for much less now excepting where patent machinery is used; but I cannot speak positively to this'.[69] It is incidentally interesting to note that in reply to a later question about the extent of domestic manufacture in Yorkshire, Brooke said 'I think it has rather increased'.[70]

John Marshall of Leeds was also questioned by the Committee. Some of his replies are worth quoting in full in view of the insight they give to changing price conditions.

> Do you think the fall of prices which has been 50 per cent since the peace, has been attended with very considerable losses?
> There was a very great loss in the year 1816; the fall of price was very rapid then . . .
> What should you think would be the present value of 50,000 l. sunk during the war in a mill and machinery?

[69] *Report from the Select Committee on Manufactures, Commerce and Shipping*, 1833, p. 117.
[70] Ibid., p. 118, para. 1896.

With respect to the buildings I think you may now build at a less cost, by the difference of the value of the currency.

Do you think a mill which cost 50,000 l. during the war, kept up in repair and full operation would now sell for more than 20,000 l.?
I should not value a mill at 20,000 l. that cost me 50,000 l.

Do you think it would bring more than 20,000 l. if forced to a sale?
It depends upon many circumstances; I should think it could not be built now for less than 35,000 l. or between that and 40,000 l. . . .

What should you consider would be an average return for capital employed in mills.
The same as in every other trade after deducting the loss upon the depreciation of machinery and of the mill generally.[71]

Thus Marshall suggested that the cost of mill construction dropped by about 25 per cent between the beginning of the second decade of the century and 1833. His view was borne out by the evidence of another manufacturer, George Snull, a cotton spinner at Manchester, who built a mill in 1827 which, with its machinery, cost more than £20,000. He was asked by the Committee: 'What would this mill and machinery cost you if you had it to build and fill with machinery just now?' And he replied: 'I am not prepared to say but I think it would cost considerably less; there is a reduction in building materials.' He was then pushed to make an estimate: 'Do you think it would cost £15,000?' and he appears to have agreed with this figure: '£15,000 to £20,000 — I should say; it might cost less by a fourth; it is a fireproof mill and has a deal of iron in it'. He was later questioned about the cost of machinery: 'Do you think you could obtain the machinery at any considerable reduction now from what you paid for it?' And he answered simply 'Yes'.[72]

Such scanty evidence and comments such as these are not sufficient to even attempt to estimate an index of net fixed capital formation on a constant price basis. From the available information, however, it would seem that prices were rising, perhaps quite gently, from the 1780s to the middle of the second decade of the nineteenth century. For this period it was estimated that the average value of the fixed capital of a mill rose from £1,000 to £2,700. However, in view of the price increases, one cannot conclude that the average physical amount of fixed capital rose 2.7 times. On the other hand, it was estimated that the average value of the fixed capital rose from £2,700 to £3,650 between 1815 and 1833. In view

[71] Ibid., paras. 2431, 2436–8, 2445.
[72] Ibid., p. 549, paras. 9047–68.

of the comments of Marshall and Snull, however, perhaps the increase in the physical amount of fixed capital was as much as one third more than this.

The Depreciation of Capital

The calculation of depreciation allowances poses as many problems, if not more, as the working out of the extent and the effect of price changes. It is by no means clear to what extent insurance valuations took into account an allowance for depreciation. If, as has been suggested, the valuations reflect replacement cost then they would be affected by price changes but not by depreciation from initial cost. However, there does appear to be evidence that some insurance valuations did make allowances for depreciation of capital. On examining series of policies over many years for a number of mills it does appear that some items of capital were regularly written down in value to an extent that could not be accounted for by price changes for replacement capital. It would seem that the depreciating usefulness of some capital was reflected in insured values and that some attempt was made to take it into account when losses were being adjusted. Thus actual new fixed capital formation would have been somewhat greater than the annual estimates of net fixed capital formation suggest but, on the other hand, the estimates do not reflect the depreciation of capital values.

Manufacturers at the time often had little notion as to by how much they should depreciate their capital year by year. William Graham, a Glasgow cotton spinner, stated in 1833 'We never calculate profit without deducting two and a half per cent for wear and tear of our works'. He was later asked: 'Do not the machinery and mills undergo a deterioration in value annually?' and he replied 'They certainly do, in consequence of the improvement in machinery; but if they are kept in good order, I believe they are not depreciated in real value'. He was then pressed 'Is there not a great deal of wear and tear?' and he answered 'It is always kept up in a well regulated work'.[73]

Other estimates of depreciation allowances in the cotton industry appear greater than this two and a half per cent. Blaug found that:

> Depreciation quotas seem to have varied little over the period under consideration (1834–1886). Detailed cost statements for individual mills in

[73] Ibid., p. 329, paras. 5548, 5553–4.

the 1830s and in the 1880s show a standard charge of 7.5 per cent for replacement of machinery and 2.5 per cent for maintenance of buildings and steam engines.[74]

No comparable cost statements have come to light for the wool textile industry in Yorkshire but one might expect fairly similar allowances for depreciation in view of the resemblances in the fixed capital of the two industries. However Blaug's estimates begin in the 1830s by which time construction methods had improved and machinery was more durable. It seems most unlikely that the depreciation on the value of early steam engines was as little as two and a half per cent. The earlier engines had notoriously short lives. Likewise the weaknesses of the early powered machinery, often built with inferior materials by inexperienced local machine makers, raise the question whether a depreciation allowance of seven and a half per cent was sufficient.

Kenneth Pankhurst, in his study of investment in the industry in the later nineteenth century found that '. . . assets were usually written down at widely different rates on the "diminishing balance" principle or according to arbitrary decisions taken each year . . .'.[75] This view appears to be borne out by Professor S. Pollard's study 'Capital Accounting in the Industrial Revolution'. He points out that many firms made no allowance for depreciation in their annual accounts but occasionally revalued their property.[76] The example of Pleasley Mills is cited. There, no writing down of the value of the buildings took place until six years after they had been built. It was sixteen years before the value of the machinery was written down in the accounts.[77] Moreover, capital was not just devalued for wear and tear and physical deterioration. Factors such as technical obsolescence, repair and replacement requirements and tax allowances helped determine the rate of depreciation.

Pollard cited a number of accounts and estimates of annual rates of depreciation for firms in a number of industries. Although he has no examples for woollen mills he has several for cotton mills. Greg in 1832 allowed an annual rate of depreciation of five per cent on his cotton mill buildings and steam engines and ten per cent on his machinery. In the same year another cotton mill owner was allowing

[74] Blaug, op. cit., p. 361.

[75] K. Pankhurst, 'Investment in the West Riding Wool Textile Industry in the Nineteenth Century', *Y.B.E.S.R.*, 7, 1955, p. 97.

[76] S. Pollard, 'Capital Accounting in the Industrial Revolution', *Y.B.E.S.R.*, 15, 1963, pp. 75–91.

[77] Ibid., citing S. Pigott, *Hollins: A Study of Industry, 1784–1949* (1949), p. 38.

five per cent on his steam engines and machinery. Other examples of depreciation of six per cent and ten per cent on steam engines and from ten per cent to $33\frac{1}{2}$ per cent on machinery are given.[78] John Marshall, the Leeds flax spinner, varied the rate of depreciation on his machinery. In 1827 when he commenced a 'systematic writing down of machinery' he made an allowance of seven and a half per cent per annum.[79]

The insurance policies can really give no guide to the extent of depreciation allowances in the industry. One cannot separate changes in values due to price change from those accounted for by depreciation. Moreover one can never be sure whether or not new capital had been installed between the issue of one policy and the next. Thus the problem of adjusting the estimates of net fixed capital formation to establish the rate of new investment cannot be resolved. If, however, one calculates on the basis of an annual depreciation of between two and a half per cent on buildings, between five per cent and ten per cent on steam engines and between seven and a half per cent and fifteen per cent on machinery, then the annual figures of net fixed capital formation must be adjusted upwards by between 6.25 per cent and 12.5 per cent assuming the value of steam plant, buildings and machinery was roughly in the ratio one: three: six.[80]

Circulating Capital

This study has concentrated on the fixed capital of the Yorkshire wool textile industry. Mention has only been made in passing to the value of stocks and to the other circulating capital requirements of manufacturers. There has, however, been much debate about the relative importance of fixed and circulating capital at the time and there is evidence to suggest that operating or circulating capital amounted to a far greater sum than fixed capital and that the former created more difficult problems for manufacturers trying to raise capital.[81]

The calculation of circulating capital requirements poses several problems, one of which is the diversity of the different needs. One method used to calculate it is by applying an 'average turnover rate to the flow of annual outlays' on wages and raw materials. This is

[78] Pollard, 'Capital Accounting . . . , loc. cit., p. 90.
[79] Rimmer, op. cit., pp. 196–7.
[80] See p. 165.
[81] See Crouzet op. cit., pp. 34–9 for a résumé of the debate.

what Blaug attempted to do for the Lancashire cotton industry but he points out that it is difficult to verify estimates of the turnover rates.[82] He works on the basis of a turnover on capital two or three times a year but the reliability of this figure is by no means certain. Moreover, for the wool textile industry the calculation would seem to be impossible at present. Not only are there no estimates of the rate of turnover but even information on the flow of outlays on wages, materials and other expenses is practically non-existent.

There are, however, various observations that may be made. It seems probable that there was no fixed correlation between the two types of capital over time. Under the domestic system of manufacture fixed capital requirements were minimal. The development of the early scribbling mill increased fixed capital requirements and stock but, with much of the industry remaining on a domestic basis, circulating capital dominated in the industry as a whole. For individual scribbling mill concerns, perhaps mainly working on a commission basis, fixed capital possibly formed a major part of all capital needs.

With the gradual movement of most processes of manufacture into the factory system so fixed capital requirements increased but there seems no way to estimate the ratio between fixed and circulating capital in the West Riding wool textile industry at different periods between 1780 and the 1830s. The absence of company accounts has already been noted. And it is questionable whether the few firms for which some accounts are available can be taken as representative. The co-partnership accounts of the Gott's of Leeds have been cited to illustrate the importance of circulating capital but they include the firm's operations as a major merchanting concern.[83] From them it can be seen that the Gott's often valued their stock of raw materials, goods in process and finished products at almost £100,000. Thus in 1819, for example, stocks in hand at Leeds were valued at over £80,000, and at Burley and Armley Mills at over £15,000 out of total capital, including land, of £156,000.[84] The Starkey's of Longroyde Bridge, Huddersfield, who were also described as merchants as well as manufacturers insured their stocks for well over £10,000 in the 1830s and there are many

[82] Blaug, loc. cit., p. 361.

[83] S. Pollard, 'Fixed Capital in the Industrial Revolution in Britain', *J.E.H.*, XXIV, no. 3, 1964, p. 304.

[84] Gott MSS, Accounts of Co-partnership. B.L.

other examples of merchant manufacturers insuring stock for similar or even greater sums.[85]

It is possible to make certain rough estimates of manufacturer's holdings of raw materials and stocks of finished goods from insurance policies. Stocks were almost always included in textile mill policies but it is not clear that the conclusions reached about the reliability of the insured values of fixed capital also apply to stocks. In some instances stocks were insured on a rather different basis from other property. General or floating policies, subject to the 'average clause', were at times issued and there is no way of distinguishing from policies whether the insurance on stock is the value of the stock held at a particular time or whether it is some average or maximum value. Moreover policies frequently do not include stock held in warehouses apart from the mill premises.

However a rough calculation for forty-two mills, the insurance policies of which include stock in the late 1820s and early 1830s, gives an average holding of only £1,800 for stocks of raw materials, goods in process and finished products. As these are almost the same mills for which it was suggested that their fixed capital was unrepresentatively large, it may well be that the average holdings of stock by a manufacturing concern in the industry was substantially lower than £1,800. This still leaves unanswered what proportion of circulating capital was accounted for by stocks.

There are some general views available of the relative importance of fixed and circulating capital in various areas of the textile industries. Blaug's calculations for the Lancashire cotton industry suggest that in 1834 the ratio of fixed to working capital was 2:1.[86] For the same industry, J. R. McCullock estimated that in 1834, for the country as a whole, the capital stock was divided:[87]

	£M.
Capital to purchase raw materials	4
Capital to pay wages	10
Capital vested in equipment, building and stock	20

and Blaug estimated, using a capital:labour ratio based on Greg and Company's important cotton textile concern, that the cotton industry's capital in 1834 was made up of:[88]

[85] Sun C.R. 244/1268084/1838.
[86] Blaug, loc. cit., p. 374.
[87] J. R. McCullock, *Commercial Dictionary* (1843), p. 443 cited by Blaug, loc. cit., p. 371.
[88] Blaug, loc. cit., p. 372.

	£M.
Fixed capital in spinning and weaving	14.8
Circulating capital	7·4
Fixed capital in bleaching, dyeing, printing, hosiery and lace-making	5·4
Circulating Capital	6.4

Pollard has agreed that perhaps in the cotton industry between 1780 and 1830 fixed capital amounted to a little over half of the capital invested, although Edwards has suggested that it was not until after 1815 that fixed capital overtook circulating capital in importance.[89] However Pollard's view is that the cotton industry was exceptional and that in the wool textile industry fixed capital was of less importance.[90] Hartwell is of similar opinion for the period up to 1830.[91] However it may well be that, for the relatively small but integrated manufacturing firm that was playing no part in merchanting, fixed capital costs had become more important than variable costs by the late 1820s. Variable costs also undoubtedly fluctuated. Speculation in stocks and variations in the amount of credit available and in the length of repayment periods altered investment in circulating capital at different times. These fluctuations make even more difficult the calculation of investment in circulating capital.

[89] M. M. Edwards, *The Growth of the British Cotton Trade 1780–1815* (Manchester, 1967), p. 214.
[90] Pollard, loc. cit., pp. 305–7.
[91] Hartwell, thesis, op. cit., p. 11.

6

SOURCES OF FIXED CAPITAL FINANCE

The sources used for estimating the value of the fixed capital of the West Riding wool textile industry give many indications as to from where the finance for the investment came. This subject merits, and indeed requires, a separate study but in view of the past controversy and the recently changing views concerning who provided finance some of the evidence that has been brought to light is set down and some suggestions are made for how the problems of ascertaining the sources of capital may be resolved.[1]

One cannot realistically discuss from where the money came without some assessment of the sums involved. The calculations in the previous chapter suggest typical capital costs and illustrate that the expense of the initial fixed capital for a manufacturer setting up in business could range from a few hundred to many thousands of pounds. That manufacturers were at times faced with problems of raising finance there can be no doubt. The trouble that the firm of Boulton and Watt had in persuading their customers to pay for their engines illustrates the point. At times the engine manufacturers had to plead for payment and almost all the Yorkshire textile manufacturers who purchased one of their engines were slow in settling their accounts. Thus in May 1797 the firm had to write to Joshua Foster at Horbury demanding payment and suggesting that interest should be charged. At the end of 1798 the account was still outstanding and interest was being paid.[2] At about the same period, they were demanding payment from Messrs Blagborough and Holroyd, the Batesons of Wortley, John Wood of Bradford, and Nevins and Gatliffe of Hunslet.[3] To Halliday and Cockshott at Baildon they wrote '. . . we shall be particularly obliged to you to be punctual in the payments, as we have some engagements which

[1] Miss P. Hudson, University of York, is engaged in a study of the sources of finance for the Yorkshire textile industries in the eighteenth and nineteenth centuries.

[2] Boulton and Watt MSS, Office Letter Book, August 1796 – July 1797, 20 May 1797; Office Letter Book, July 1798 – May 1799, 30 November 1798.

[3] B. & W. MSS, Office Letter Book, August 1796 – July 1797. Entries for 20 May 1797; 15 June 1797; 21 April 1797; 6 April 1797. Office Letter Book, July 1797 – July 1798. Entry for 1 November 1797.

require it'. Two months later the bill was still outstanding.[4] John and James Walker were purchasing their engine on an instalment arrangement of £100 per annum. Even they, however, appear to have had difficulties in raising this amount. Boulton and Watt had to write to them on many occasions demanding payment. In January 1797 legal action was threatened. A stronger demand was sent in May and payment was finally made at the end of that month. This might well have been for the 1796 instalment for in November 1797 and February 1798, Boulton and Watt were having to send out further strong demands.[5]

Normally, however, it must be assumed that a firm did not undertake investment without being sure where the finance was to come from. This finance should be considered in two stages as different sources may have been involved. Firstly, the sources of finance for an entirely new manufacturer setting up plant and machinery for the first time needs to be investigated. Secondly the sources for a manufacturer installing new fixed capital in an already established business must be examined. The sources were possibly often the same but perhaps a greater variety of methods of finance was available to an established firm.

Most of the debate has concerned initial sources of finance of capital. The view that 'financing was the business of the British merchant and of those on whose help he relied for accommodation'[6] and that '. . . the merchant controlled the capital needed for production throughout its course'[7] has met with considerable criticism from R. G. Wilson in his close examination of the activities of the Leeds woollen merchants. Wilson concluded that relatively few merchants became large-scale manufacturers because they were not prepared to take the trouble nor to make the investment necessary. He found that merchants invested their money elsewhere, often in Government and, later, in railway stocks, with the proviso that merchants played an important role in the finishing branch of the industry.[8]

[4] B. & W. MSS, Office Letter Book, August 1796 – July 1797. Entries for 29 April 1797; 29 June 1797.

[5] B. & W. MSS, Office Letter Books, Entries for 17 October 1795; 28 July 1796; 12 August 1796; 18 January 1797; 18 May 1797; 23 May 1797; 6 August 1797; 1 November 1797; 16 February 1798.

[6] J. H. Clapham, *An Economic History of Modern Britain, The Early Railway Age 1820–1850* (1950 edition), p. 254.

[7] Mantoux, op. cit., p. 127.

[8] Wilson, op. cit., pp. 136–59.

Little support has been given to the idea that the banks played a significant role in providing the initial fixed capital, although one more recently published view is that 'bankers were also involved in long term lending more than the books on banking have suggested' and that many firms did depend on bank capital for at least a part of their fixed capital requirements.[9] The banks were of much more importance in providing short term loans although more and more instances of long term lending by bankers to industry have been coming to light.[10]

The present consensus of opinion seems to be that the major proportion of the financing of initial fixed capital came from the private pockets of the entrepreneur, his relatives and friends and through the mortgaging of property and estates and the liquidating of other assets. And, although credit was of most importance in the provision of circulating capital, it also played some part in financing the investment in fixed capital in that manufacturers could on occasion wait for some returns from new fixed capital investment before paying for it.[11]

Moreover, it is not realistic to totally separate the discussion of the financing of fixed and circulating capital. The ease with which finance could be obtained from one source for financing circulating capital would affect the amount of money available from other sources for investment in fixed capital as some sources of finance could be used for both types.

For the West Riding of Yorkshire studies of individual firms do already provide some information about the provenance of fixed capital finance. It seems likely that the sources used in the worsted branch of the industry differed somewhat from those available to the newly establishing woollen manufacturer. This is explained by the differences in the organization of the domestic system in the two branches. The underlying factor was basically one of scale. Domestic worsted manufacture was far better organized and controlled by fewer entrepreneurs than domestic woollen production. The situation is best summed up by Heaton's often quoted statement that there were '. . . in the woollen industry a large number of small men, in the worsted a small number of big men'.[12] Thus in the worsted branch of industry there were men who already controlled large

[9] P. Mathias, *The First Industrial Nation* (1969), pp. 151, 176.
[10] F. Crouzet, *Capital Formation in the Industrial Revolution* (1972), pp. 46–8.
[11] Mathias, op. cit., pp. 150–1.
[12] Heaton, op. cit., p. 298.

businesses and had sufficient financial resources themselves. If they were unable to provide all the initial capital from their own pockets, their already established reputation as businessmen made prospective lenders, including perhaps the banks, more willing to consider their needs. One cannot always trace the background of the early worsted mill builders but many can be shown to have been important figures in the domestic worsted trade before the beginnings of the factory system. One such person was John Foster, son of a farmer and colliery owner, who in the 1820s set himself up as an entrepreneur with a warehouse at Queensbury distributing yarn to hand-loom weavers over a wide area, as well as continuing an interest in coal mining and running a shop. It is not known from where Foster obtained the initial finance to set himself up in the worsted trade. Such was his success, however, that by the early 1830s he was thinking of moving into factory production and in 1834 started to rent Cannon Mill at Great Horton, the equipping of the premises costing him the best part of £1,000. However, he had set his sights at greater targets and in 1835 commenced work building his own mill at Queensbury. In 1837 when the first mill premises had been completed, almost £10,000 had been invested in the new mill and its machinery. The balance sheet of the firm in that year gives some clue as to where this money came from if one compares it with that of three years previously. It appears to show that Foster managed to provide much of the money himself but was also able to obtain loans from the Bradford Banking Company and a number of other persons. Joseph Smith, a Bradford merchant, lent him £2,000 in 1836 at a five per cent rate of interest. Smaller sums were made available by Robert Foster and Joseph Foster, who were probably relatives, by Abraham Briggs, possibly a relative of Foster's wife whose maiden name was Briggs, and by a variety of other people including two women. In 1837 he owed £2,576 to the bank and £3,477 for other loans, besides trade debts.[13]

Whether Foster's background was fairly typical for worsted mill owners at the period is not altogether certain. Not all mills were owned; some were rented. The history of some other worsted factory manufacturers is known. Thomas Edmondson, who with a Mr Addison and Mr Satterthwaite, set up Dolphin Holme Mill, the earliest of the worsted factories, was an ironmonger by trade.

[13] For a much more comprehensive analysis of Foster's progress and financial dealings, see Sigsworth, op. cit., Chapters IV and V from where this account is taken.

Edmondson built the mill at Mytholmroyd eight years later.[14] John Rand who constructed the first worsted mill in Horton township was a member of the Worsted Committee in 1800 and, therefore, presumably of some importance in the domestic manufacture and other members of the Committee were later established as manufacturers in mills.[15] Other of the Bradford factory worsted producers rented their mills from persons with little or no connexion with the trade but who saw the possibilities of a good return from investing in the industry. Thus Samuel Cannon, a farmer, built Cannon Mill, Great Horton; James Marshall, a Bradford ironmonger, and partner in the Bierley Ironworks, built Marshall's Mill and let it to his sons; and two other mills in Great Horton, Cliffe Mill, and Beckside Mill, were built by Joseph Beanland, a corn miller and colliery owner. Another corn miller built Cross Lane Mill.[16]

In the Keighley area all but a few of the worsted mills were originally built for cotton manufacture. It would seem that the fixed capital for their conversion and re-equipping was provided from money gained from the cotton trade.[17] Likewise much of the fixed capital used for worsted manufacture in Halifax parish was first used for the cotton trade. Thus the mills in the Wainstalls area were originally cotton mills.[18] At Haworth in 1833 Lower Town Mill was mortgaged to F. Thompson of Lincolns Inn, London. One cannot, however, be sure whether he put up the money for building the mill and was holding the deeds or whether he had agreed to become mortgagee, perhaps to provide circulating capital for James Feather and Co., the mill's occupants, who were worsted spinners.[19] Thomas Dyson of Mearclough Bottom Mill near Halifax had a corn mill previous to building his worsted mill in 1835. At least part of the money for the building was, however, provided by a William Bateman of Manchester as the mill was mortgaged to him as soon as it had been built.[20] A worsted mill at Addingham in 1808 belonged to John Goodman and Samuel Elam, who were woollen and worsted merchants at Leeds.[21] Carr Mills at Woodhouse Carr, Leeds, were possibly financed by Abraham Rhodes, their occupier, as Rhodes

[14] James, op. cit., pp. 327–8.
[15] Ibid., p. 361.
[16] Sigsworth, op. cit., pp. 177–8.
[17] See Hodgson, op. cit.
[18] W. Onslow Garnett, op. cit.
[19] Sun C.R. 198/1158297/1833.
[20] Insurance proposals for Mearclough Bottom Mill, H.A.D.
[21] Sun C.R. 77/813030/1808; E. Baines, *Directory* . . . , op. cit.

was a merchant and organizer of domestic manufacturers in the area long before his mill was built.[22]

These few examples for the worsted industry in the West Riding do not provide sufficient information on which to base any generalizations about the sources of finance for the fixed capital of the industry. Only half the problem is solved when the background of the builder of a particular mill is traced. His background does not necessarily indicate from where the capital for the mill was obtained. One can, however, divide the mill builders into two categories. The first would include entrepreneurs already connected with the worsted industry, perhaps as merchants or organizers of domestic manufacture. The second would consist of persons with connexions with other trades particularly agriculture and the cotton industry but including tradespeople, colliery owners and perhaps even investors from the professions. A few mill builders, like John Foster for example, had many interests.

It is probably realistic to assume that, if persons such as these were contemplating setting themselves up as manufacturers in mills or investing in a mill building for letting, they had financial resources of their own. If these were not sufficient then, almost certainly, they would call for assistance to their relatives and friends, to their previous business connexions which might include merchants and, particularly if they already had a good reputation in business, to bankers. Perhaps John Foster was fairly typical.

The position in the woollen branch of the industry was far more complex. The system of domestic manufacture had few 'big men' in command. A whole multitude of small clothiers made up the industry and such was the scale of their business that one must question whether they were often able to earn for themselves more than was sufficient to provide for their livelihood. Yet it appears that it was, more often than not, the clothiers who became the factory manufacturers. For the villages of the woollen producing area, the insurance policies, local directories and property deeds suggest many of the manufacturers were originally small domestic clothiers. The reasons for their ability to move into often quite large mills are not too difficult to find. One can show that probably for at least half the mills at any period before the mid 1830s the occupant of the mill was not the owner. The buildings, and perhaps even much of the machinery, was often rented. Thus the clothier would have had to find only a very small proportion of the value of

22 See Wilson, op. cit., and Sun C.R. 104/880856/1813.

the fixed capital that he was using. The rent for the rest came from his circulating capital on a month to month or year to year basis.

Who then built the mills? Many were obviously provided by the landowners of the county. Consider Lord Dartmouth, one of the largest landowners in the textile area with seven and a half thousand acres in the 1820s. He had many mills on his lands at Slaithwaite, Honley, Kirkburton, and Morley. Some were very old fulling and corn mills, many were new however, and his records show that he provided all or much of the money for building them. Some of the entries in his *Terriers* illustrate the point:

Waterside Mill, Slaithwaite (a cotton mill)

... But the spirit of erecting cotton mills being high at the time Varley, Eastwood and Co. proposed to take the bare stone walls as they were at the old rent of £60 per annum provided Lord Dartmouth advanced £600 at eight per cent and gave £200 worth of timber ...

Slaithwaite Mill (scribbling and corn)

... These mills were chiefly erected with Lord Dartmouth's money as his Lordship gave £1,000 besides the scribbling mill ...

Shaw Carr Wood Mill (scribbling)

... the late Lord advanced £250.

Upper Clough House Mill and Lower or Haywood Mill (scribbling)

... Lord Dartmouth advancing £100.

Fenay Mill (fulling and scribbling)

... Lord Dartmouth, leaving land out, spent upwards of £1,300 on it.

Honley Mill (corn and scribbling)

... Lord Dartmouth gave £400 towards the new building of it.

Crank Mill, Morley (Scribbling and fulling)

... Lord Dartmouth gave £1,250 towards the building of it ...[23]

It is not possible to calculate how much money Lord Dartmouth provided for mill building and repairs but the sum must have reached many thousands of pounds. In 1805 there were twenty-three textile mills on his estates and, with only a few exceptions, Lord Dartmouth appears to have provided much of the money for building them.

[23] Dartmouth Estate, *Terrier*, 1805, pp. 45–8, 128, 145. *Morley Terrier*, 1828, p. 15.

Dartmouth was, however, just one of many large landowners in the County. Sir Thomas Pilkington at Wakefield had three mills there and at Horbury in 1798 which he let to tenants.[24] Sir James Graham of Lincolns Inn, London, who owned a considerable estate at Kirkstall, appears to have been responsible for the building of the mills there.[25] A George Hathorne of Finsbury Square, London, built Brackendale Mill and Joshua Crompton, Esq., of Esholt Hall, Lord of the Manor and the principal landowner in Esholt with several hundred acres, appears to have constructed a number of local mills.[26] Many other instances can be sited. Sir John Ramsden of Huddersfield, the Stanhopes of Horsforth Hall and the Earl of Scarbrough were amongst the landowners who owned mills.[27]

This does not, of course, answer the question about where the money came from. Perhaps, however, one can realistically assume that the landowners looked upon investment in textile mills as a means of improving their estates. It seems likely that building wool textile mills was for many a popular way of investing the returns from their estates and perhaps their other interests such as collieries and timber.

There was, however, another group that owned mills and let them to manufacturers. Wilson's conclusion that few merchants joined the manufacturers in large-scale factory production has already been indicated. There are, however, many instances of merchants owning mills and letting them to manufacturers rather than becoming merchant manufacturers themselves. Samuel Elam of Leeds, whose worsted mill has already been mentioned, also owned Sands Mill at Dewsbury in 1800 along with Benjamin Jowett, another Leeds merchant, and Jeremiah Glover of Stanley.[28] John Plowes, a Leeds merchant, owned a mill at Marsden in 1794 until he went bankrupt.[29] Lepton Dobson, another Leeds woollen merchant, let a mill at Idle.[30] David and John Cooper, merchants at Leeds, owned a wool, cotton and silk mill at Saddleworth.[31] Another

[24] Sun C.R. 22/676712/1798.
[25] Sun C.R. 29/696462/1799.
[26] Sun C.R. 32/703319/1800; 115/916650/1816; 32/701517/1800; 32/701518/1802; 32/701519/1800; 100/868472/1812; 20/667335/1797 and others.
[27] Many other smaller landowners' had close connexions with mills, mainly in the woollen manufacturing rather than the worsted area.
[28] Sun C.R. 35/711401/1800.
[29] Sun C.R. 5/631846/1794.
[30] Sun C.R. 68/782281/1805.
[31] Sun C.R. 254/1303327/1839.

Leeds merchant, George Baron, was the mortgagee of Whiteley's Mill at Addle Bottom in 1802.[32] Many other examples could be cited but these are sufficient to show that a number of mills had been built or were owned by merchants and were let by them.

This is not to say that a large proportion of merchants invested their money in mills. R. G. Wilson has carefully considered the view that it was often the merchant who started manufacturing in the factory system and concluded that, with a few very notable exceptions, merchants rarely set up as manufacturers. Such evidence as can be gained from the insurance records of mills tends to bear out his findings. There is the problem, however, of distinguishing between the established merchant who set himself up as a manufacturer and the manufacturer who merchanted his own and, perhaps, other persons goods. In the early decades of the nineteenth century many of those firms that described themselves as merchants and manufacturers had developed an interest in merchanting through their manufacturing connexions rather than vice versa. Parson's *Leeds Directory* of 1826 lists over a dozen 'manufacturers and merchants' in the town of Leeds alone and many more in the surrounding villages.[33] Most of these can be traced as having started as small manufacturing concerns. No doubt the profits gained by them from the merchanting side of their businesses went towards providing fixed and circulating capital for the manufacturing part of their business. Thus if little money came originally from the merchants perhaps more came later from merchanting.

Merchants from other trades also entered the wool textile business. Corn and seed merchants, stone merchants, and linen merchants on occasions developed wool manufacturing interests. For example William Spicer, a Wakefield corn merchant, owned the King's Mills at Huddersfield in the 1820s and let them for scribbling as well as corn milling.[34]

Other finance appears to have come from many quarters. John Jubb, the Leeds millwright had an interest in a number of mills at various times. Together with Robert Wood, a millwright of Hunslet, he provided money for a mill at Stanningley. Perhaps on occasions his links with mills developed through the millowner being unable to meet the bill for his work and taking him into partnership. Sometimes Jubb is described as the mortgagee of a mill.[35] Often

[32] Sun C.R. 45/733143/1802.
[33] Parson, Directory . . . 1826, op. cit.
[34] Sun C.R. 143/1007963/1823.
[35] Sun C.R. 24/679080/1798.

the trade or identity of other mortgagees cannot be traced but amongst those that can be recognized are Robert Stead, a local woolstapler, who was mortgagee for part of a Batley mill and Matthew and Thomas Walker of Bingley, worsted manufacturers, who were mortgagees for a small woollen spinning mill in Bradford.[36] The Company of the Proprietors of the Bradford Navigation owned Frizing Hall Mill at Bradford at the beginning of the nineteenth century.[37]

With all these and other examples, one cannot necessarily distinguish when the merchants and other persons built the mill on their own initiative for letting as an investment or took the mill on mortgage for security for loans perhaps for circulating capital, or for outstanding bills. However, there can be no doubt that many individuals with no intention of manufacturing themselves were willing to provide the fixed capital for the clothiers to rent. In 1833 in evidence to the Select Committee on Manufacturers, Commerce and Shipping, Henry Hughes stated:

> I saw several (mills being built) on the Huddersfield Road as you go out (of Huddersfield) towards Manchester; they are now erecting them or just finishing; there are two or three very large mills, and the man that built the largest of them, I was told, built it for the purpose of letting it to the manufacturers to make cloth, on hire.[38]

If it were not the merchants who set up as manufacturers in their own mills then who were the owner occupiers? Many were clothiers who organized themselves into companies. Joint stock or company mills were being developed from at least the 1790s in the area around Leeds and along and to the south of the Calder Valley. A Factory Inspector in 1843 described how the system operated:

> In the formation of a Company mill a number of clothiers, for they must be clothiers to be partners, of small capital meet together and determine to become a company of so many partners, from 10 to 50, in shares generally of £25 each, each person taking as many shares as his capital will enable him . . . With this subscribed capital deeds of partnership are drawn, land is bought, a mill erected and machinery put up.[39]

In some instances clothiers were able to raise all the finance between them to build and equip their mill. On other occasions they had to

[36] Sun C.R. 102/882485/1813; Registers of Deeds, Vol. FE, Entries 151, 214 (1808), W.Y.C.R.O.
[37] Sun C.R. 37/713369/1801.
[38] *Select Committee on Manufactures, Commerce and Shipping*, op. cit., para. 1318.
[39] Lipson, op. cit., pp. 178–9 quoting from the local Factory Inspector's report of 1843.

seek help from elsewhere. And in some instances they formed a company to rent and equip a mill, rather than to construct a new one themselves. It is not clear that partnerships were totally reserved for clothiers. There do appear to be examples of others owning shares in company mills, possibly perhaps by inheritance. But joint stock or company mills never formed a large proportion of mills in the woollen branch of the industry.

Deeds of partnership of a few of the groups of clothiers survived and give an excellent insight to the arrangements. One example is for the Clover Greaves Mill Company at Calverley in July 1834:

> The Deed of Partnership purposes to be an Indenture in two parts made between William Kellett Sen., William Brown, William Gray, William Walton, John Pratt Jun., James Holgate and Samuel Hartley all of Calverley, Cloth Makers and William Lawson and William Parkinson, both of Bramley, Cloth Makers, of the First Part . . . and the whole of the partners of the Second Part; it states that they have agreed to raise £2,700 on 108 shares of £25 each towards erecting a Mill, Buildings etc. and that the 108 shares have been raised in the following proportion.[40]

The many partners held between one and eight shares each so not one of them had to find more than £200.

Once a partnership had been formed the partners or shareholders would get together and in a democratic fashion, according to their holdings, take the necessary decisions about building and equipping a mill. Thus the Gill Royds Mill Company at Morley would meet at the Fleece Inn regularly. Persons who did not attend were fined. All decisions were taken at these meetings. For example:

> At a meeting held at Fleece Inn on the 12th Feby. 1835 it was agreed to advertise the mill building as follows —
>
> To Masons, Joiners, Bricklayers, Glaziers and Builders in general. To be let by estimate on Friday 20th inst. at 10 o'clock in the morning all the workmanship etc. belonging to the above branches of a Fulling and Scribbling Mill intended to be erected for the Gill Royds Company, Morley. Specifications and Plans may be seen at the Fleece Inn, Morley. The Company don't bind themseves to the lowest estimate and no allowance for estimates.[41]

The number of partners at this mill is not known but records for other mills show that whereas on occasions just two or three clothiers would get together at other times there would be very many more. Not all clothiers had to combine with others to build joint stock or company mills. Some were able to go ahead on their own often

[40] Quoted by Sigsworth, op. cit., p. 177 from the records of the Company at the Brotherton Library, Leeds.

[41] See the Committee Book of the Gill Royds Mill Company. C.L.A.D.

starting in a very small way in converted premises and gradually enlarging their business and fixed capital. Others were able to find a sleeping partner who would provide some or all of the initial finance.

Even though partnerships and arrangements such as these reduced the burden of finding the finance for fixed capital investment, the merchants, clothiers and others had to find the money from somewhere. A merchant, if he took the decision to start up in manufacturing, would presumably have a certain amount of money available and through his established reputation might find assistance from friends and business connexions. As Wilson ways: 'Often female relatives were requested to lend money to their nephews, for the provision of funds was a family affair.'[42] Even so merchants did not always find the problem of raising finance for fixed capital easy to solve. Benjamin Gott had to run up huge debts.[43] A lot is known about the problems of John Marshall of Leeds, who was engaged in the flax trade. Originally a draper and merchant, in 1788 he took a mill for flax spinning but could only find a part of the necessary finance himself. Before he could get started he had to obtain £2,000 from Samuel Fenton, a distant cousin, £700 from Ralph Dearlove, a Knaresborough linen merchant, and as a last resort, if necessary, lose his drapery business. His problems were even greater when he decided to build his own mill. The fixed capital of it cost £9,421. This and the £10,000 for stocks and working capital, he raised by selling the drapery business and borrowing £310 more from Dearlove; an aunt lent £100, his son was able to put up £140 and a distant relative, William Pollard, a Halifax merchant, provided £400. Neighbours and a local nonconformist merchant supplied several thousand more pounds and Beckett's Bank of Leeds provided him with an overdraft of almost £4,000 by the spring of April 1793.[44] Thus John Marshall was able to draw money from four sources to finance his new enterprise. He had some capital of his own; he was able to rely on the assistance of his relatives, friends and neighbours; he was considerably helped by merchants and a local bank also provided a large sum.

The smaller clothiers setting up in business with their own mills seldom had the reputation and connexions that the merchants could rely upon. Rarely perhaps also were their families so well off.

[42] Wilson, op. cit., p. 67.
[43] Heaton, 'Financing . . .', loc. cit., p. 10.
[44] Rimmer, op. cit., p. 26.

There is, however, one clothier who established a mill, about whose finances something is known. A small scale clothier, Benjamin Hallas, decided in 1791 to set up his own mill at Pildacre in Ossett. There is not a great deal to make one think that he was an exceptional clothier but he had managed to save, probably over some length of time, sufficient money to buy land for the mill site and a house for £1,400. To build his mill, however, he had to call upon a variety of sources. He borrowed £490 from William Thompson, a coalmaster at Hunslet. How they came to know each other is not recorded. By mortgaging part of the land to Katherine Nevile of Chevet Hall, he raised another £500. Local lawyers and solicitors appear to have been willing to help him and a hatmaker at Wakefield and his sister provide £720 for the steam engine for a mortgage as security.[45] Hallas was able to find all the necessary money from his own pocket and from his friends and acquaintances. Perhaps he was fairly typical of the clothiers who set up on their own account, but little information has come to light about the activities of others.

It is interesting to note that Hallas mortgaged part of his land to raise finance. This may well have been a method employed by many. Its extent could well be measured by a careful search through volumes of deeds in the West Riding Registry of Deeds. A first approach to them suggests that there were, in fact, many besides Hallas who used this means of raising money.

For those clothiers who formed joint stock companies, there were still financial problems even though the sums involved for each of them were smaller. The partners at Gill Royds Mill ran into difficulties. Their own money appears to have run out before the building of the mill was finished and at a meeting of them in 1836 it was resolved:

> . . . that 3 persons be appointed to wait upon the Leeds Banking Company to ascertain on what terms they will lend the said company a sum of money to compleat the mill — or wether they will do so or not.[46]

It is not known whether the bank was helpful. The clothier shareholders or subscribers to the mill probably relied on their own money and that of relatives and friends to purchase their shares. It seems unlikely that they would often have had the reputation, security and connexions to have gone much further afield in search of finance.

[45] J. Goodchild, 'Pildacre Mill . . .', loc. cit.
[46] Committee Book of the Gill Royds Mill Company, p. 11. C.L.A.D.

There was a third type of person who set up as manufacturers and should not be overlooked. There are a number of examples of people successful in other trades turning their attention to wool textile manufacture. Thus many established cotton businesses changed to woollen manufacture. Particularly in Leeds, but also elsewhere, there was a movement from flax manufacture to the woollen trade at times. Corn millers sometimes became woollen or worsted manufacturers using the same premises. Thus one must not overlook the movement of capital from other industries to wool textile manufacture. There was, of course, a movement in the opposite direction but it would seem that over the period 1780–1835 the wool textile trade received a net gain from these transfers.

These few points and examples do give some indication of the sources of finance that were being tapped for the provision of the initial fixed capital for a manufacturer setting up in business. For an established manufacturer making additions to his fixed capital stock there were other possibilities however. The mortgaging of the property could provide the extra finance. The connexions that the manufacturer had built up within the trade could also assist. It is likely that loans were more easily obtainable by someone whose name was known and respected. More important still, however, a conscientious manufacturer gradually building up his business would plough back his profits to increase his capital stock. Heaton tells of the '. . . zeal with which abstinence could be practised when necessary'. He gives the example of the Brookes of Huddersfield who ploughed back as much as 85 per cent of profit in some years when they were trying to expand their business.[47] It was often the case that a manufacturer, who had had difficulty raising the initial capital, would only partly fill his mill with machinery and gradually plough back profits to build up his stock of machinery.[48]

Nothing definite can be said about the role of the banks in providing finance for fixed capital. It is interesting to note, however, that manufacturers like Foster and Marshall did receive help from them and that even the small clothiers tried to enlist their aid, which they would not have done if the banks were totally averse to providing money for this sort of purpose. There are, moreover, a number of examples of banks actually owning mills. Messrs Beckett, Blayds and Co. of Leeds in 1836 owned the mill at Gomersall

[47] Heaton, 'Financing . . .', loc. cit., pp. 8–9.

[48] See the insurance policy registers for many apparent examples. See also *The Select Committee on Manufactures, Commerce and Shipping*, op. cit., p. 554.

occupied by William Hirst.[49] Messrs Wentworth, Chaloner and Rishworth of Wakefield, who were later to fail causing much distress, insured a small scribbling mill at Brockwell, Halifax, in 1823 and a mill at Ossett in 1818 and 1821.[50] Instances such as these of banker's connexions with the woollen trade illustrate the need for a much closer examination of their role.

The provision of circulating capital is yet another area about which not a great deal is known. Topham has thrown light on the credit structure of the industry in the nineteenth century;[51] Habakkuk considers that:

> . . . English banks concentrated on the provision of working capital because that is what industry needed; if there had been a large unsatisfied demand from industry to finance fixed capital financial institutions would, with relative ease, have adapted themselves to meet this need . . .[52]

but still many questions are left unanswered.

However, many of the sources used in this study of fixed capital formation in the West Riding wool textile industry might well provide the answers. The information that insurance policies give about ownership of premises, the vast store of unexamined papers in the West Yorkshire Registry of Deeds, now at the County Record Office, where many mortgage and partnership agreements were registered and the scattered and miscellaneous records of a few of the textile firms might well be sufficient to provide the information required on the sources of capital.

[49] Sun C.R. 225/1221719/1836.

[50] Sun C.R. 140/1000007/1823 (the risk was refused); 124/941520/1818; 133/979985/1821.

[51] A. J. Topham, 'The Credit Structure of the West Riding Wool Textile Industry in the Nineteenth Century', unpublished M.A. thesis, Leeds University, 1953.

[52] H. J. Habakkuk, *American and British Technology in the Nineteenth Century* (1962), p. 175.

Appendix I

YORKSHIRE WOOLLEN AND WORSTED MILLS

This appendix lists all the woollen and worsted mills traced working in the West Riding of Yorkshire between 1774 and 1835. It also includes a few mills, but possibly by no means all, at work elsewhere in Yorkshire. The date of establishment given is normally the year in which the mill is first known to have been used for woollen or worsted manufacture. In the case of mills that were previously fulling cloth the dates when wool scribbling was first being carried out are given. Likewise for mills that had previously been used for other purposes, for example cotton spinning, the dates of conversion to their new uses are listed. Where a mill was converted to worsted manufacture from woollen manufacture or vice versa, the fact and date of conversion is noted in the notes and references column, and allowance is made in Tables 2 and 3.

Where the name of a mill is known it is listed in column two. Occasionally mills were identified by more than one name or their names changed over the period. In these cases the name which appears to have been the most used in 1835 is recorded. Where no name is known the location of the premises is given, along with the name of the occupant in 1835.

Limitations of space allow only the briefest notes and references to be given. Normally the references provide evidence of the date of the establishment of the mill. In some instances however the date has been calculated by deduction from a number of references. In which cases the main references are given. Brief histories of most of the mills and much fuller references may be found in D. T. Jenkins, 'The West Riding Wool Textile Industry, 1780–1835: A Study of Fixed Capital Formation' D.Phil. thesis, University of York (1970), a copy of which is deposited in the J. B. Morrell Library at the University of York.

The date when mills ceased manufacturing woollens and worsteds is given, where known. Normally however evidence of cessation of business is very difficult to obtain. The following guidelines have therefore been taken for the purposes of the calculations. Where there is no available evidence of a mill continuing working after a given date this is stated and the mill is assumed to have ceased working in the year of the date of the last reference unless that reference is to an insurance policy, in which case the date of the closure of the mill is assumed to be by seven years later. The reason for this difference is that insurance policies were generally not permitted to run for more than seven years. Thus if no new policy is recorded within seven years the mills might be assumed to have closed. However it should be appreciated that there is bound to be a degree of inaccuracy in the recording of mills leaving the trade.

A wide variety of references have been used to establish this list. Additional evidence on mills listed or on mills that have been overlooked would be gratefully received.

Established by	Mill and Location	Notes and references
1774	Strawberry Bank Mill, Liversedge	Not traced after 1785. Peel, p. 230.
1778	Gill Mill, Baildon	Converted to worsted in 1790. W. Cudworth, *Rambles around Bradford* (1876), pp. 338–9.
1779	Fenay Mill, Honley	Dartmouth Estate, *Slaithwaite Terrier*, 1805, p. 128.
1780	Ing Nook Mill, Holmfirth	Crump and Ghorbal, p. 60; *Factories Inquiry Commission, First Report* (1833), p. 24.
1780	Spring End Mill, Ossett	Misc. textile MSS, Cusworth Hall.
1781	Guiseley Mills, Guiseley	Two scribbling mills in 1781. A worsted mill by 1812, possibly later reverting to woollen *Leeds Mercury*, 6 November 1781.
1782	Priestley's Mill, Sowerby	*1834 Supp. Rept.*, Mill no. 266 and Sect. C, Part 1, Mill no. 45.
1782	At Quick, Saddleworth	*1834 Supp. Rept.*, Mill no. 233.
1782	Hopton Mill, Mirfield	*1834 Supp. Rept.*, Mill no. 212.
1783	At Upper Mill (Giles & Shaw)	*1834 Supp. Rept.*, Mill no. 237; Sun C.R. 10/641138/1795.
1783	Bradley Mills, Dalton	A finishing mill later used for scribbling. Burnt and rebuilt in 1808. *1834 Supp. Rept.*, Mill no. 77; R.E. 30/149783/1795.
1783	Dewsbury Mills, Dewsbury	J. F. Glover, *thesis*, pp. 342–97.
1784	Longbottom Mill, Warley	R.E. 26/136664/1793.
1785	Millshaw Mills, Beeston	Sun O.S. 344/530101/1787; Sun C.R. 13/653405/1796; *1834 Supp. Rept.*, Mill no. 22.
1785	Dungeon Mill, South Crosland	*1834 Supp. Rept.*, Mill no. 75.
1785	Hollings Mill, Warley	R.E. 11/95667/1785.
1785	Stubbins Mill, Heckmondwike	*1834 Supp. Rept.*, Mill no. 101.
1785	Upper Clough House Mill, Slaithwaite	Out of use by 1828. Crump and Ghorbal, p. 80; Dartmouth Estate, *Slaithwaite Terrier*, 1805, pp. 26, 48.
1785	Hunsworth Mill, Gomersal	J. Parker, *Illustrated Rambles from Hipperholme to Tong* (Bradford, 1904), p. 279; Sun C.R. 19/675205/1797.

Established by	Mill and Location	Notes and references
1786	Callis Mill, Stansfield	R.E. 12/98928/1786; H. Armitage, 'The Rawdon Family', *H.A.S.*, March 1967, p. 42.
1786	At Esholt (Copley, Watkinson & Watson)	R.E. 12/97041/1786. Not traced later.
1786	Croft Mill, Dewsbury	R.E. 12/98926/1786.
1786	Healey Mill, Ossett	J. Goodchild, 'The Ossett Mill Co.', *Textile History*, 1 (1968), pp. 46–61.
1786	At Westgate Moor, Wakefield	Sun O.S. 339/521498/1786.
1786	Holmfirth Mill, Holmfirth	*Factories Inquiry Commission, First Report* (1833), p. 24; *1834 Supp. Rept.*, Mills nos. 293 and 295.
1786	Little John Mill, Brighouse	Used for wire drawing by 1828. Crump and Ghorbal, p. 72; R. Mitchell, *Brighouse, Portrait of a Town* (Brighouse, 1953), p. 46.
1786	At Underbank, Stansfield C. & J. Rawden)	R.E. 12/98928/1786. Not definitely traced after 1795.
1787	Scothall Mills, Leeds	Sun O.S. 343/528873/1787; Sun C.R. 44/728169/1802. Corn only by 1822.
1787	Millhouse, Sowerby	*1834 Supp. Rept.*, Mill no. 267 and Sect. C, Part 1, Mill no. 23.
1787	Low Mill, Addingham	Worsted. James, pp. 327–8, 355.
1787	Armley Mills, Armley	Sun O.S. 347/537499/1787; *Leeds Intelligencer*, 5 February 1788.
1787	Copley's Mill, Hunslet	R.E. 13/102199/1787; Sun O.S. 364/562205/1791; Misc. textile MSS, Cusworth Hall. Not traced after 1791.
1788	Hanging Lee Mill, Ripponden	Used for cotton after 1812. J. H. Priestley: 'Mills of the Ryburn Valley', *H.A.S.*, February 1941, pp. 5–6.
1788	At Ilkley (Hawksworth & Curtis)	Cotton mill by the 1790s. Sun O.S. 351/540956/1788; 369/572774/1790.
1788	At Marsden (Schofield, Kenworthy & Co.)	*1834 Supp. Rept.*, Mill no. 206.

Established by	Mill and Location	Notes and references
1788	Lower Holt Mill (Bottoms Mill), Slaithwaite	Dartmouth Estate, *Slaithwaite Terrier*, 1805, p. 50.
1788	Low Mill, Wortley	B. and W. MSS Portfolio 105; *1834 Supp. Rept.*, Mill no. 171.
1789	Dumb Mill, Shipley	Worsted, Cudworth, *Round about Bradford*, p. 294.
1790	At Brighouse (Thos. Sheffield)	Not traced after 1797. R.E. 20/119234/1790; 32a/155200/1797; 32a/157246/1797.
1790	At Holbeck (Browne)	R.E. 20/119326/1790. Only ref.
1790	Lob Mill, Stansfield	Worsted. Also used at various times for cotton. James, pp. 327–8; R.E. 32a/158615/1797.
1790	Aldams Mill, Dewsbury	*1834 Supp. Rept.*, Sect. C, Part 1, Mill no. 18; R.E. 32a/155966/1797.
1790	Clough House Mill, Slaithwaite	Dartmouth Estate, *Terrier*, 1828, p. 163
1790	Ross Mill, Bramley	*1834 Supp. Rept.*, Mill no. 58; Crump, pp. 72, 128.
1790	Farnley's Mill, Drighlington	A woollen mill until burnt in 1793 then probably a worsted mill until again destroyed by fire in 1807. Pontefract Quarter Session Roll, April 1793; *Leeds Mercury*, 31 January 1807.
1790	Dixon Mills, Shipley	Cudworth, *Round about Bradford*, p. 183; Sun C.R. 37/713352/1801.
1790	At Whiteley Bottom, Linthwaite	*1834 Supp. Rept.*, Mill no. 195.
1790	Cocking Steps Mill, Netherton	Crump and Ghorbal, pp. 72–6; *1834 Supp. Rept.*, Mill no. 136.
1790	Woodbottom Mill, Horsforth	*1834 Supp. Rept.*, Mill no. 116; Sun C.R. 81/820293/1808.
1790	At Thirsting, Honley	*1834 Suppt. Rept.*, Mill no. 102.
1790	At Birkenshaw, Gomersal	Wool and worsted after 1820. *1834 Supp. Rept.*, Mill no. 89.
1791	Midgley Manor Mill, Midgley	H. W. Harwood, 'Midgley Manor Mill', *H.A.S.*, March 1958.
1791	Leeming Mill, Haworth	Worsted, James, p. 328.

Established by	Mill and Location	Notes and references
1791	At Smithy Place, Honley	*Factories Inquiry Commission, First Report* (1833), p. 17; *1834 Supp. Rept.*, Mill no. 111; R.E. 32a/156624/1797.
1791	Foster's Old Mill, Horbury	*1834 Supp. Rept.*, Mill no. 114; B. & W. MSS Portfolio 125; Sun C.R. 29/696278/1799.
1791	Sutton Mill, Sutton	Worsted R.E. 32a/187046/1801; *1834 Supp. Rept.*, Mill no. 275.
1791	Meltham Mills, Meltham	Changed to cotton in 1805, Crump and Ghorbal, p. 71; Dartmouth Estate, *Slaithwaite Terrier*, 1805, p. 133; Sun C.R. 30/696784/1799.
1792	Hareholme Mill, Rossendale	James, p. 328. Not traced later. Worsted.
1792	Park Mills, Leeds	Crump; B. & W. MSS Portfolios 93,491,812; Sun C.R. 4/627124/1794.
1792	At Hunslet Lane, Leeds (J. and E. Brookes)	R.E. 32a/169295/1799; Crump, pp. 5, 219.
1792	Bell Mill, Wansford, East Riding	R.E. 23/127968/1792. Only corn later.
1792	Hebblethwaite Hall Mill, Sedbergh	W. Thompson, *Sedbergh, Garsdale and Dent*, p. 192.
1792	Hand Carr Mill, Sowerby	James, p. 328. Worsted.
1792	Copley Mill, Skircoat	R.E. 23/127385/1792.
1792	Hewnden Mill, Wilsden	Wool and worsted at times. James, p. 328; *1834 Supp. Rept.*, Mill no. 292.
1792	Woodhouse Mill Huddersfield	R.E. 32a/170324/1799; R.E. 22/127585/1792.
1792	At Mytholmroyd (Edmundson)	Worsted R.E. 32a/157479/1797; *1834 Supp. Rept.*, Mill no. 282 and Sect. C, Part 1, Mill no. 25.
1792	Elliston Mill, Greetland	R.E. 25/130832/1792.
1792	Farnley Mill, Farnley Tyas	*1834 Supp. Rept.*, Mill no. 279; Dartmouth Estate, *Terrier*, 1805, p. 129.
1792	Dudfleet Mill, Horbury	*1834 Supp. Rept.*, Mill no.115; Sun C.R. 158/1055743/1827.
1792	Crank Mill, Morley	Dartmouth Estate, *Terrier*, 1805, p. 239. *1834 Supp. Rept.*, Mill no. 215.

Established by	Mill and Location	Notes and references
1792	Lords Mill, South Crosland	Dartmouth Estate, *Terrier*, 1805; p. 145. *1834 Supp. Rept.*, Mill no. 109; R.E. 32a/155020/1797.
1792	Sowerby Bridge, Mill	R.E. 23/130856/1792. Not traced later.
1792	At Heckmondwike (Carr)	R.E. 24/128123/1792. Not traced later.
1792	Woodbottom Mill, South Crosland	Dartmouth Estate, *Terrier*, 1805, p. 145.
1792	At Cleckheaton (Birkley & Waite)	Not traced later. R.E. 32a/156293/1797.
1792	Crosland Mill, South Crosland	Mainly used for cotton until 1812. *1834 Supp. Rept.*, Mill no. 74.
1792	Brookroyd Mill, Birstal	*1834 Supp. Rept.*, Mill no. 19; Sun C.R. 49/737389/1802.
1792	Scotland Mill, near Leeds	Burnt down in 1809. Rimmer, pp. 26, 33; Sun C.R. 17/666661/1797.
1792	Foster's New Mill, Horbury	Worsted after 1814. *1834 Supp. Rept.*, Mill no. 113; B. & W. MSS Portfolio 348; Sun C.R. 52/744400/1803.
1793	St Peter's Mill, Leeds	Cloth dressing mill. *Plan of an Estate in Leeds and Wortley*, 1793 (C.L.A.D.); Sun C.R. 115/18880/1816.
1793	Bank House Lower Mill, Longwood	26/132533/1793; not traced after 1801.
1793	At Hunslet (Hodgson, Rainforth & Hinchcliffe)	Burnt down 1805, *Leeds Intelligencer*, 28 October 1793; Sun C.R. 11/649650/1795.
1793	Low Mill, Rawdon	*1834 Supp. Rept.*, Mill no. 240; Sun C.R. 85/829546/1809.
1793	Browbridge Mill, Elland	R.E. 26/132530/1793.
1793	At Browbridge, Elland	R.E. 26/132530/1793; not traced after 1797. Worsted.
1793	Dean Mill, Heckmondwike	*1834 Supp. Rept.*, Mill no. 240; Sun C.R. 206/1171383/1834.
1793	Bridge Mill, Haworth	Worsted. *1834 Supp. Rept.*, Mill no. 96; J. James, *The History of Bradford and its Parish* (1866), p. 372.
1793	Holbeck Mills, Leeds	Sun. C.R. 13/651630/1796; *1834 Supp. Rept.*, Mill no. 191; R.E. 32a/157419/1797.

Established by	Mill and Location	Notes and references
1793	At Bank, Leeds (Markland, Cookson & Fawcett)	Worsted and cotton. Sun C.R. 8/636966/1795; B. & W. MSS Portfolio 91. Out of use by 1797.
1793	At Ludhill, Kirkburton	Sun C.R. 2/622582/1793; 40/719368/1801. Not traced after 1802.
1793	Aspley Mill, Huddersfield	Also known as Doodlebank Mill. Sun C.R. 1/620468/1793.
1794	At Shelley Woodhouse near Huddersfield	R.E. 32a/156417/1797. Not traced after this date.
1794	Company Mill, Stanningley	Worsted by 1822. Crump, p. 73; Cudworth, *Round about Bradford*, p. 467; *Baines' Directory*, 1822.
1794	Scarbottom Mill, Mytholmroyd	Worsted Mill. B. R. Law, 'The Calder mill owners and the Rochdale canal', *H.A.S.*, January 1954, p. 5.
1794	Smithy Holme Mill, near Halifax	Law, 'The Calder mill owners', p. 5. Not traced later.
1794	Longlees Mill, near Halifax	Law, 'The Calder mill owners', p. 5. Not traced later.
1794	Rowley Mill, Kirkburton	Dartmouth Estate, *Terrier*, 1805, p. 129. Crump and Ghorbal, p. 76.
1794	Nether Mills, Leeds	*Leeds Intelligencer*, 13 January 1794.
1794	Whinnhill Wood Mill, Marsden	Not traced after 1804. Sun C.R. 5/631846/1794; *Factory Returns*, 1804. W.Y.C.R.O.
1794	Cooper House Mill, Luddenden Foot	Cotton and wool in 1794. Worsted after 1832. *1834 Supp. Rept.*, Mill no. 290; R.E. 32a/160721/1798.
1794	Stonebreaks, Saddleworth	Not traced after 1801. Sun C.R. 3/627881/1794; R.E. 32a/182834/1801.
1794	Lower Mill, Guiseley	R.E. 27/141502/1794;' not traced later.
1794	At Horsforth (J. Kitchen)	Not traced after 1806. Sun C.R. 4/625924/1794; 78/784482/1806.

Established by	Mill and Location	Notes and references
1794	Pildacre Mill, Ossett	J. Goodchild, 'Pildacre Mill'; An Early West Riding Factory', *Textile History*, 1, 3, 1970.
1794	Frizinghall Mill, Bradford	Worsted after 1818. Cudworth, *Round about Bradford*, pp. 267–9; Sun C.R. 37/713369–70/1801.
1794	At Silcoates, Wakefield	Misc. Textile MSS, Cusworth Hall; Sun C.R. 14/656188/1796.
1795	At Masham	A worsted mill. Not traced after 1798. R.E. 32a/144424/1795.
1795	At Heckmondwike (Hartley & North)	Not traced after 1798. Sun 12/648557/1795.
1795	Arthington Mill, Otley	Sun C.R. 12/648740/1795.
1795	At Gildersome (Turton's Mill)	Not traced after 1807. Sun C.R. 12/648555/1795; 74/799151/1807.
1795	At Sheepscar, Leeds (Cadman, Glover & Darnton)	Not traced after 1797. Sun C.R. 12/648178/1795; 19/671058/1797.
1795	At Hunslet (Wilkinson)	Not traced after 1802. Sun C.R. 12/648175/1795.
1795	At Gomersall (Carr)	R.E. 30/147839/1795. Not definitely traced later.
1795	Kebroyd Mill, Soyland	R.E. 30/147840/1795. Worsted.
1795	At Mill Green, Holbeck	Not traced after 1802. Sun C.R. 12/648553/1795.
1795	Heckmondwike Mill	Sun C.R. 12/648362/1795.
1795	At Tong (Milner & Stevenson)	Sun C.R. 9/641408/1795.
1795	Wrigley's Mill, Wadclough, Dobcross	Sun C.R. 12/648180/1795.
1795	At Upper Esholt (Carlisle)	Only reference: Sun C.R. 12/648179/1795.
1795	Sands Mill, Dewsbury	Sun C.R. 12/648171/1795.
1795	New Mill, Holmfirth	Sun C.R. 10/640927/1795.
1795	At Lockwood (Bentley)	R.E. 32/154079/1796. Not traced after 1797.
1795	Marshaw Bridge Mill, Sowerby Bridge	Only reference: R.E. 31/148516/1795.
1795	Burnley's Mill, Farnley, Leeds	Not traced after 1801. Sun C.R. 9/641413/1795; R.E. 32a/187359/1801.

Established by	Mill and Location	Notes and references
1795	At Farnley, Leeds (Burnley, Morton & Garnet)	Not traced after 1801. Sun C.R. 8/636964/1795; R.E. 32a/187359/1801.
1795	At Pye Nest near Halifax (Edwards)	R.E. 29/144522/1795. Not traced after 1800.
1795	At Dewsbury (Chaster, Wilson & Rhodes)	Two scribbling mills burnt in 1805. R.E. 32/151390/1796.
1796	Chickenley Mill, near Dewsbury	R.E. 32a/154789/1796; *Leeds Intelligencer*, 10 June 1799.
1796	At Flanshaw, Wakefield (Wood & Cook)	Wood MSS, Cusworth Hall. Sun C.R. 13/653/662/1796.
1796	Honley Mill, Honley	R.E. 32/154078/1796.
1796	At Hillhouse Bank, Leeds	Only one ref. Possibly converted to flax. R.E. 32a/154784–5/1796.
1796	Thornes Lane Mill, Wakefield	Worsted after 1807. Sun C.R. 13/653663/1796.
1796	Westgate Common Mill, Alverthorpe	R.E. 32a/182983/1801; *1834 Supp. Rept.*, Mill no. 7.
1796	At Belle Isle, Wakefield	Mainly dyeing after 1806. Sun C.R. 13/654266/1796; 199/1149537/1832.
1796	Philadelphia Mill, Gildersome	Sun C.R. 14/654387/1796; 22/678184/1798.
1796	Lower Battye Mill, Holmfirth	Sun C.R. 14/654910/1796.
1796	Troughton Mill, Drighlington	Sun C.R. 13/653861/1796; *Baines' Directory*, 1822.
1796	Providence Mill, Shipley	Cudworth, *Round about Bradford*, pp. 288, 292; Sun C.R. 69/784549/1806.
1796	Black Moor Holme Mill, Slaithwaite	Cotton by 1805. Dartmouth Estate, *Terrier*, 1805; R.E. 32a/180517–18/1801.
1796	Lower Water Clough Mill, Southowram	Worsted. R.E. 32/153718/1796. Only reference.
1796	At Hell Hole Gill, Otley (Clapham)	R.E. 32/153882/1796.
1796	Jumples Mill, Ovenden	R.E. 32/153422/1796.
1796	Garnet's Mill, Hunslet	Sun C.R. 13/656410/1796. Not traced later.
1796	At Danehouse Lane, Honley	Only reference traced: Sun C.R. 13/654476/1796.
1796	Clifford Mill, Clifford	Worsted mill later used for flax. Sun C.R. 13/653221/1796; *Factory Returns*, 1835.

Established by	Mill and Location	Notes and references
1797	Cloth Dressing Mill, Holbeck	Destroyed by fire in 1797. Mayhall, *Annals of Leeds*, p. 188.
1797	At Honley (Brooke)	Not traced after 1807. Sun C.R. 22/672380/1797; 72/797912/1807. Crump and Ghorbal, pp. 93–4.
1797	At Wakefield (Nowell, Dixon & Sunderland)	Used for other purposes by 1805. Sun C.R. 17/666454/1797.
1797	At Slaithwaite (John Varley)	R.E. 32a/158005/1797.
1797	Shaw Carr Wood Mill, Slaithwaite	R.E. 32a/158005/1797. Not traced later.
1797	Upper Mill, Wortley	B. & W. MSS Portfolio 143; R.E. 32a/156821/1797.
1797	Batley Subscription Mill, Batley	R.E. 32a/157878/1797.
1797	At Scammonden	R.E. 32a/157245/1797; 32a/158617/1797. Not traced later.
1797	Rosemary Mill, Rastrick	Worsted 1797; wool 1798. R.E. 32a/155785/1797; 164665/1798.
1797	Pool Walk Mill, Pool	R.E. 32a/156093/1797; Sun C.R. 91/840818/1810.
1797	Low Coat Mill, Meltham	R.E. 32a/155108/1797.
1797	At Horbury (Pilkington's Mill)	Sun C.R. 17/666454/1797; Goodchild, 'Osset Mill Co.', p. 54.
1797	Dogley Mill, Kirkburton	Dartmouth Estate, *Terrier*, 1805, p. 171.
1797	At Linfit, Almondbury	R.E. 32a/158616/1797. Not traced later.
1797	At Heckmondwike (Dex & Keighley)	R.E. 32a/160110/1797.
1797	At Heckmondwike (Barker)	R.E. 32a/157566/1797. Not traced after 1801.
1797	At Dewsbury (Greenwood)	R.E. 32a/157462/1797. Not traced after 1800.
1797	At Gildersome (Murgatroyd)	R.E. 32a/160338/1797; Sun C.R. 22/674145/1798. Not traced later.
1797	Brigg Mill, Holmfirth	R.E. 32a/157721/1797.
1797	At Bank, Leeds (Gowland & Cooper)	R.E. 32a/157565/1797. Not traced after 1806.
1797	Smithies Mill, Birstal	*1834 Supp. Rept.*, Mill no. 90; B. & W. MSS Portfolio 91.

Established by	Mill and Location	Notes and references
1797	Bank Bottom Upper Mill, Almondbury	*1834 Supp. Rept.*, Mill no. 3; R.E. 32a/158127/1797.
1797	Bank Bottom Lower Mill, Almondbury	*1834 Supp. Rept.*, Mill no. 3; R.E. 32a/158127/1797.
1797	Putting Mill, Hoyland	Sun C.R. 19/671410/1797. Not traced after 1802.
1797	Rods Mill, Morley	Sun C.R. 19/671412/1797; *1834 Supp. Rept.*, Mill no. 216.
1797	At Upper Esholt (Rawnsley & Cooper)	Not traced after 1817. Sun C.R. 19/667233/1797.
1797	At Lower Esholt (Wood)	Not traced after 1802. Sun C.R. 17/666459/1797.
1797	At Shipley (Lupton)	*Factory Returns*, 1804. Sun C.R. 19/667233/1797.
1797	At Armley (Wainwright)	Only reference: Sun C.R. 19/669224/1797.
1797	Buck Mill, Idle	Sun C.R. 20/667335/1797; *Factory Returns*, 1804.
1797	At Liversedge (Wormald)	Sun C.R. 19/671201/1797; *Leeds Intelligencer*, 14 January 1799, 1 March 1802.
1797	At Gomersal (Carr)	At Gomersall Cloth Hall. R.E. 32a/158699/1797.
1797	Battye Mill, Thurlstone	R.E. 32a/159898/1797. Not traced later.
1797	Dean Clough Mill, Northowram	R.E. 32a/158794/1797, 181456/1801.
1797	At Huddersfield (Townard)	Not traced later. R.E. 32a/159926/1797.
1797	Lingard Wood Bottom Mill, Marsden	R.E. 32a/155107/1797.
1797	Oddy's Mill, Hunslet	R.E. 32a/157852/1797. Not traced after 1811.
1797	Low Mill, Willow Hall, Sowerby Bridge	Wool and cotton. R.E. 32a/157243/1797. Not traced later.
1797	Dean House Mill, Almondbury	R.E. 32a/156623/1797.
1797	Larchfield Mill, Hunslet	R.E. 32a/155018/1797; *1834 Supp. Rept.*, Mill no. 138; B. & W. MSS Portfolio 134.
1797	Milnesbridge, Birstal	R.E. 32a/158829/1797, possibly worsted after 1812.
1797	At Moorcroft, Kirkburton	R.E. 32a/159608/1797.
1797	Hough Mill, Bramley	R.E. 32a/157879/1797.
1798	Union Bridge Mill, Pudsey	Cudworth, *Round about Bradford*, p. 482.

Established by	Mill and Location	Notes and references
1798	Churwell Mill, Churwell	*1834 Supp. Rept.*, Mill no. 71; Sun C.R. 65/782716/1805.
1798	At Lipton, Kirkheaton (Sheard)	Sun C.R. 21/676895/1798; 125/947442/1818.
1798	At Holbeck (Glover, Lister & Roper)	Sun C.R. 23/683144/1798. Not traced after 1816.
1798	At Bramley (Strickland)	Sun C.R. 24/679080/1798. Not traced later.
1798	Low Mill, Stanningley	Sun C.R. 24/679080/1798.
1798	At Colne Bridge	R.E. 32a/162763/1798. Later used for cotton.
1798	At Elland (Rushforth)	R.E. 32a/164664/1798; *1834 Supp. Rept.*, Mill no. 79.
1798	At Dalton, Kirkheaton (Tolson & Kilner)	R.E. 32a/161748/1798.
1798	At Stanningley (Jarrat, Dawson & Hardy)	R.E. 32a/164667/1798. Only reference.
1799	At Tyrestall, Bradford (Roberts)	Only reference: *Leeds Intelligencer*, 10 June 1799.
1799	Burley Mills, Kirkstall	Worsted after 1822. Crump, pp. 269–71; Sun C.R. 29/696462/1799.
1799	Savins Mill, Kirkstall	Sun C.R. 29/696279/1799.
1799	Old Corn Mill, Slaithwaite	R.E. 32a/180515/1801; *1834 Supp. Rept.*, Mill no. 5; Dartmouth Estate, *Terrier*, 1805, p. 46.
1799	Slead Sike Mill, Brighouse	Mitchell, *Brighouse: Portrait of a Town*, p. 46.
1799	Abbey Mills, Kirkstall	Sun C.R. 29/696279/1799; Mayhall, *Annals of Leeds*, p. 194.
1799	St Anne's Mill, Kirkstall	Sun C.R. 29/696462/1799.
1799	At Hunslet (Tuton, Waring & Wilks)	R.E. 32a/166607/1799. Not traced after 1800.
1799	King's Mill, Huddersfield	R.E. 32a/171015/1799.
1799	Lilly Mill, Halifax	R.E. 32a/170666/1799.
1799	Ripponden Mill, Ripponden	R.E. 32a/170450/1799.
1799	Roger Mill, Southowram	R.E. 32a/168284/1799.
1799	Steps Mill, Honley	Dartmouth Estate, *Terrier*, 1805, p. 199.
1799	Luddenden Foot Mill, Warley	R.E. 32a/170437/1799.
1799	At Kirkheaton (Atkinson)	*1834 Supp. Rept.*, Mill no. 30.
1799	Low Mill, Horsforth	Sun C.R. 25/688430/1799.
1799	Cape Mill, Bramley	Sun C.R. 25/688430/1799.

Established by	Mill and Location	Notes and references
1799	Blackside Mill, Meltham	Possibly destroyed 1821. Sun C.R. 29/695689/1799; Mayhall, *Annals of Leeds*, p. 291.
1799	Holme Mill, Bradford	R.E. 32a/177346/1800; *1834 Supp. Rept.*, Mill no. 47.
1799	Ottiwells Mill, Marsden	*Leeds Mercury*, 25 January 1800.
1799	At Wheatley, Ovenden	Not traced after 1801. R.E. 32a/170942/1799.
1800	Bankgate Mill, Slaithwaite	*1834 Supp. Rept.*, Mill no. 261.
1800	At Linfit Lane, Kirkburton (Cocker)	*1834 Supp. Rept.*, Mill no. 160.
1800	At Haworth (Butterfield)	Worsted. *1834 Supp. Rept.*, Mill no. 121.
1800	Marshall Hall Mill, Elland	*1834 Supp. Rept.*, Mill no. 78.
1800	Peg Mill, Cleckheaton	Worsted. *1834 Supp. Rept.*, Mill no. 72.
1800	Bank End Mill, Austonley	*1834 Supp. Rept.*, Mill no. 9.
1800	Holm Bridge Mill, Holmfirth	Sun C.R. 32/701966/1800; *1834 Supp. Rept.*, Mill no. 14.
1800	Brackendale Mill, Idle	Sun C.R. 32/703313/1800.
1800	Harden Mill, Bingley	Worsted. Cudworth, *Round about Bradford*, p. 190.
1800	At Holbeck (Sykes & Kindle)	Sun C.R. 29/699004/1800. Not traced later.
1800	Holbeck Lane Mill, Holbeck	Burnt down 1811. Sun C.R. 31/699254/1800.
1800	Broom Mill, Farsley	Cudworth, *Round about Bradford*, pp. 466–8.
1800	Firth House Mill, Stainland	J. H. Priestley, 'Mills of the Blackburn Valley', *H.A.S.*, January 1963, p. 9.
1800	At Milnesbridge, Longwood (Brookes)	*1834 Supp. Rept.*, Mill no. 201.
1800	At Doncaster (Humble)	Worsted. Only reference: James, p. 355 n.
1800	Upper Holt Mill, Slaithwaite	Burnt down 1805. Dartmouth Estate, *Terrier*, 1805.
1800	Baildon Mills, Baildon	Sun C.R. 37/713351/1801.
1800	Bolder Clough Mill, Sowerby	R.E. 32a/180078/1800. Later cotton.
1800	Bowling Dyke Mill, Northowram	R.E. 32a/180078/1800.
1800	Dudley Mill, Almondbury	R.E. 32a/173948/1800.

Established by	Mill and Location	Notes and references
1800	At Heathfield, Saddleworth (Platt)	R.E. 32a/179842/1800; *Baines' Directory*, 1822.
1800	At Heckmondwike (Brooke & Popplewell)	R.E. 32a/180077/1800.
1800	At Otley (Baldwin)	Worsted by 1822. R.E. 32a/180510/1800.
1800	Oxenhope Mill	Worsted. R.E. 32a/180991/1800; *1834 Supp. Rept.*, Mill no. 97.
1800	At Skipton (Chamberlain)	Only reference located: R.E. 32a/172251/1800.
1800	At Park Lane, Leeds (Knubley & Wainwright)	Not traced later. R.E. 32a/180045/1800.
1800	At Upper Mill, Saddleworth (Buckley)	R.E. 32a/179841/1800.
1800	Upper Steps Mill, South Crosland	R.E. 32a/172250/1800. Not traced later.
1800	Waterside Mill, Slaithwaite	R.E. 32a/177347/1800. Burnt down 1802.
1800	Kilncroft Mill, Dewsbury	R.E. 32a/180124/1800.
1800	Carr Mill, Batley	R.E. 32a/180125/1800.
1801	Paper Mill, Halifax	Worsted and other uses. R.E. 32a/183169/1801. Baines, *Yorkshire, Past and Present*, p. 407.
1801	Wharf Mill, Sowerby Bridge	R.E. 32a/186031/1801. Corn by 1830.
1801	Dapper Mill, near Halifax	R.E. 32a/187375/1801. Silk later.
1801	Coley Mill, Shelf, Halifax	R.E. 32a/181455/1801.
1801	At Southowram (Vickerman & Wrigley)	Not traced later. R.E. 32a/187056/1801.
1801	Low Mill, Mirfield	*1834 Supp. Rept.*, Mill no. 211; R.E. 32a/180989/1801.
1801	Meltham Mill, Almondbury	R.E. 32a/183391/1801. Cotton by 1805.
1801	Hebble Mills, Ovenden	R.E. 32a/187375/1801.
1801	Lister Mill, Clough, Stansfield	Not traced later. Worsted and Cotton. R.E. 32a/186874/1801.
1801	Holly Grove, Saddleworth	*1834 Supp. Rept.*, Mill no. 249; R.E. 32a/186877/1801.
1801	Hall Mills, Mirfield	R.E. 32a/184280/1801.
1801	Greenfield Mill, Saddleworth	R.E. 32a/181452/1801.

Established by	Mill and Location	Notes and references
1801	Clark Green Mill, Batley	R.E. 32a/182280/1801.
1801	Castle Mill, Gomersal	R.E. 32a/182275/1801.
1801	Brearly Mill, near Halifax	Not traced as a woollen mill later. R.E. 32a/182510/1801.
1801	Boys Mill, Skircoat	R.E. 32a/181456/1801. Not traced later.
1801	Bank House Lower Mill, Longwood	R.E. 32a/188762/1801. Not traced later.
1801	Ledgards Corn Mill, Mirfield	Only reference: R.E. 42/181856/1801.
1801	Rouse Mill, Dewsbury	R.E. 42/181860/1801. Not traced later.
1801	At Holbeck (Woodcock)	Not traced after 1810. Sun C.R. 38/713813/1801.
1801	At Idle (Wilkinson)	Not traced after 1809. Sun C.R. 41/722468/1801.
1801	At Jackson Bridge (Moorhouse)	Sun C.R. 42/720951/1801.
1801	Birks Mill, Almondbury	*1834 Supp. Rept.*, Mill no. 4; Dartmouth Estate, *Terrier*, 1805, p. 128.
1801	West Brook Factory, Bradford	Worsted. *1834 Supp. Rept.*, Mill no. 51. James, pp. 605–6.
1801	Gibralter Mill, Pudsey	Crump, pp. 73, 139.
1801	Strims Mill, Saddleworth	Only reference: Sun C.R. 46/729463/1802.
1802	Howroyd Mills, Lower Whitley	Misc. Textile MSS, Cusworth Hall; Sun C.R. 54/744782/1803.
1802	Walter Clough Mill, Southowram	*1834 Supp. Rept.*, Mill no. 265.
1802	At Lower Esholt (Cooper)	Not traced later. Sun C.R. 45/731170/1802.
1802	St Helen's Mill, Bramley	Sun C.R. 46/729667/1802. *1834 Supp. Rept.*, Mill no. 185.
1802	At Cartworth, Holmfirth	Only reference: Sun C.R. 49/739705/1802.
1802	Lower Mill, Thongsbridge	Only reference: Sun C.R. 52/741101/1802.
1802	Cookes Mill, Thongsbridge	Sun C.R. 52/741101/1802.
1803	At Liversedge (Brook)	Only reference: Sun C.R. 58/755739/1803.
1803	At Leeds (Paley)	Later a cotton mill. Misc. Textile MSS, Cusworth Hall.

Established by	Mill and Location	Notes and references
1803	Thompson's Mill, Esholt	Cudworth, *Round about Bradford*, p. 425.
1803	Cowhouse Upper Fold, Cullingworth.	Worsted. Cudworth, *Round about Bradford*, p. 243.
1803	Whitley Mill, Thornhill	Misc. Textile MSS, Cusworth Hall.
1803	Low Westwood Mills, Golcar	*1834 Supp. Rept.*, Mill no. 87.
1803	At Mirfield (Wheatley)	*1834 Supp. Rept.*, Mill no. 214.
1803	Steander Mills, Leeds	Cotton after 1830. Sun C.R. 57/758053/1803.
1803	Laister Dyke Mill, Bradford	Worsted after 1809. Sun C.R. 53/748667/1803.
1803	Bottom Hall Mill, Golcar	*1834 Supp. Rept.*, Mill no. 85.
1803	Horton Lane Mill, Bradford	Worsted. *1834 Supp. Rept.*, Mill no. 118.
1804	Linton Mills, Linton	Worsted. *Factory Returns*, 1804.
1804	Hunshelf Bank, Penistone	Not traced later. Sun C.R. 60/761566/1804.
1804	Battye Old Mill, Upper Thong	Not traced later. Sun C.R. 58/758987/1804.
1804	At Addingham (Birkbeck)	Worsted. Flax by 1809. *Factory Returns*, 1804.
1804	New Mills, Bramley	*1834 Supp. Rept.*, Mill no. 56.
1805	Park Mill, Rawdon	*1834 Supp. Rept.*, Mill no. 241; Sun C.R. 88/829546/1809.
1805	At Garden Street, Wakefield (Washington)	Only reference: Sun C.R. 64/780300/1805.
1805	Upper Luddenden Mill, Luddenden	Warley Township Survey, 1805.
1805	Brookhouse Mill, near Halifax	Worsted. Baines, *Yorkshire, Past and Present*, pp. 406–10.
1805	Stonebridge Mill, Farnley	Sun C.R. 64/774805/1805; *1834 Supp. Rept.*, Mill no. 12.
1805	Liphill Bank, Austonley	Only reference: Sun C.R. 65/774105/1805.
1805	Old Corn Mill, Brighouse	Mitchell, *Brighouse — Portrait of a Town*, p. 46.
1805	At Yeadon (Slater)	Sun C.R. 68/782266/1805.
1806	At Rothwell (Beswick)	J. Batty, *History of Rothwell* (1877), pp. 167–9.
1806	At Spink Myer, Farnley Tyas	Only reference: Sun C.R. 72/797514/1806.

Established by	Mill and Location	Notes and references
1806	Providence Mill, Keighley	Worsted. *1834 Supp. Rept.*, Mill no. 157; J. Hodgson, *Textile Manufacture in Keighley*, pp. 71–2.
1806	Hepworth Mill, Holmfirth	Only reference: Sun C.R. 73/794644/1806.
1806	Old Mill, Idle	Wool and worsted. Cudworth, *Round about Bradford*, p. 372.
1806	Upper Albion Street Mill, Leeds	Cloth Dressing Mill. *1834 Supp. Rept.*, Mill no. 169.
1806	Scholes Mill, Gomersall	Sun C.R. 74/794724/1806.
1806	Leys Mill, Bradford	Only reference: Sun C.R. 72/794119/1806.
1806	At Woodhouse Lane, Leeds (Lee)	Sun C.R. 72/791818/1806. Not traced after 1810.
1806	Calverley Mill, Calverley	Sun C.R. 70/786453/1806. *1834 Supp. Rept.*, Mill no. 62.
1807	Gomersal Mills, Gomersal	Wool and worsted. *1834 Supp. Rept.*, Mill no. 88.
1807	At Slaithwaite	Possibly called Lower Clough House Mill. *1834 Supp. Rept.*, Mill no. 258.
1807	Belle Isle Mill, Bramley	Hargrave and Crump, 'The Diary of Joseph Rogerson', *T.S.*, XXXII, 1931; Sun C.R. 74/797723/1807.
1807	Bowers Mill, Barkisland	Worsted. A Muir, *The History of Bowers Mill* (Cambridge, 1969).
1807	Butterbowl Mill, Farnley	Sun C.R. 77/805627/1807.
1807	At Cartworth (Butterworth)	*1834 Supp. Rept.*, Mill no. 64.
1807	Union Street Mill, Bradford	James, pp. 605–6. Worsted.
1808	At Bankhill, Morley (Dixon)	Dartmouth Estate, *Morley Terrier*, 1828, p. 7.
1808	Ribblesden Mill, Holmfirth	*1834 Supp. Rept.*, Mill no. 69.
1808	Flanshaw Low Mill, Alverthorpe	*1834 Supp. Rept.*, Mill no. 8.
1808	Eldwick Beck Mill, Bingley	Dodd, *Bingley*, p. 88. Worsted.
1808	Westgate End Mill, Wakefield	Sun C.R. 81/822103/1808.
1808	At Farnley (Musgrave & Newton)	Only reference: Sun C.R. 82/824226/1808.
1808	Aireworth Mill, Keighley	Worsted. Hodgson, *Textile Manufacture . . . of Keighley.*

Established by	Mill and Location	Notes and references
1808	Spring Mills, Dewsbury	Sun C.R. 83/824943/1808.
1808	Lees Mill, Golcar	*1834 Supp. Rept.*, Mill no. 86.
1808	Turvin Mill, Sowerby	*1834 Supp. Rept.*, Mill no. 268.
1809	At Daw Green, Dewsbury (Wilson) 1809	Dewsbury Valuation 1803/4.
1809	Holdworth's Mill, Wakefield	Sun C.R. 88/837440/1809.
1809	Green Lane Bottom, Cartworth	*1834 Supp. Rept.*, Mill no. 67.
1809	At Horsforth (Stables)	Only reference: Sun C.R. 89/837938/1809.
1809	Cape Mill, Farsley	Crump, p. 72.
1810	Oatlands Mill, Leeds	Finishing Mill. *1834 Supp. Rept.*, Mill no. 187.
1810	East Greengate Mill, Keighley	Cotton until 1810, then worsted, Hodgson, *Textile Manufacture . . . of Keighley*, p. 225.
1810	Wood End Mill, Shipley	Worsted. Cudworth, *Round about Bradford*, p. 194.
1810	Brow End Mill, Keighley	Originally cotton; worsted after 1810. Hodgson, *Textile Manufacture . . . in Keighley*, p. 42.
1810	Birks Head Mill, Wilsden	James, p. 607. *1834 Supp. Rept.*, Mill no. 291. Worsted Mills.
1810	At Clubhouses, Keighley	*1834 Supp. Rept.*, Mill no. 155. Worsted Mill.
1810	Dam Head Mill, near Halifax	Parker, *Illustrated Rambles . . .*, p. 426. Worsted.
1810	At Otley (Ackroyd)	Cotton 1783–1810, then worsted. *1834 Supp. Rept.*, Section C, Part 1, Mill no. 42.
1811	Elmtree Mills, Bingley	Worsted. Cudworth, *Round about Bradford*, p. 190. Ceased working in 1825.
1811	At Keighley (Constantine)	Worsted. *1834 Supp. Rept.*, Mill no. 148.
1812	Rawfolds Mill, Cleckheaton	Bischoff, 1, p. 401; Crump, pp. 45, 136.
1812	Dover Mill, Cartworth	Sun C.R. 102/876273/1812.
1812	Hope Mill, Keighley	Converted to worsted in 1812. Hodgson, *Textile Manufacture . . . in Keighley*, p. 228.
1812	Micklethwaite, Bingley	Worsted. *1834 Supp. Rept.*, Mill no. 25.
1812	Mill Bridge, Liversedge	*1834 Supp. Rept.*, Mill no. 199.

Established by	Mill and Location	Notes and references
1812	At Wakefield Road, Bradford	Worsted. *1834 Supp. Rept.*, Mill no. 34.
1812	Oak View Mills, Saddleworth	*1834 Supp. Rept.*, Mill no. 238.
1812	At Steeton, Kildwick	Worsted. Sun C.R. 100/866901/1812.
1812	Prospect Mill, Bingley	Worsted and cotton. Cudworth, *Round about Bradford*, p. 190.
1812	Walk Mill, Keighley	Worsted, previously cotton. R. Holmes, *Keighley, Past and Present*, p. 107.
1813	Bank Upper Mill, Leeds	Later a flax mill. Sun C.R. 101/882786/1813.
1813	Winker Green Mills, Armley	Crump, p. 156.
1813	Sayner's Mill, Hunslet	Originally a dyehouse. *1834 Supp. Rept.*, C.I., Mill no. 37.
1813	At Morton, Bingley	Worsted. Only reference: Sun C.R. 103/882948/1813.
1813	At Canal Side, Bradford (Mason)	Worsted. James, pp. 605–6.
1813	At Popplewell, Birstal (Blackburn)	Cudworth, *Round about Bradford*, p. 95.
1813	At Batley (Hudswell)	Only reference: Sun C.R. 102/882485/1813.
1813	Stubbing House Mill, Keighley	Worsted. *1834 Supp. Rept.*, Mill no. 143.
1814	West Mills, Mirfield	*1834 Supp. Rept.*, Mill no. 213.
1815	Sunlainbottom, Lingards (Varley)	*1834 Supp. Rept.*, Mill no. 193.
1815	Rouse's Mill, Bradford	Worsted. *1834 Supp. Rept.*, Mill nos. 49 and 52.
1815	Barker End Mill, Bradford	Worsted. *1834 Supp. Rept.*, Mill no. 38; Sun C.R. 116/923903/1816.
1815	Watergate New Mill, Dewsbury	Dewsbury Township Valuation 1803/4.
1815	Linfit Mill, Kirkburton	Crump and Ghorbal, p. 76; *Leeds Mercury*, 10 May 1817.
1815	Intake Mill, Scammonden	Scammonden Enclosure Award Plan, W.Y.C.R.O.
1815	Union Mills, Ossett	Misc. Textile MSS, Cusworth Hall.
1815	Laister Dyke Mill, Bradford	Worsted mill. *1834 Supp. Rept.*, Mill. no. 48; James, p. 605.

Established by	Mill and Location	Notes and references
1815	Bull Close Lane, Halifax	Finishing Mill. *1834 Supp. Rept.*, Mill no. 91.
1815	At Chopend, Holmfirth	Only reference: Sun C.R. 111/907051/1815.
1815	Red Beck Mill, Shipley	Worsted. Parker, *Illustrated Rambles . . .*, p. XXIV.
1816	Waterloo Mill, Bramley	*1834 Supp. Rept.*, Mill. no. 57; Sun C.R. 122/939213/1818.
1816	Neville St Mill, Leeds	Hirst, *History of the Woollen Trade*, pp. 18, 39.
1816	Holme Mill, Keighley	Worsted. Hodgson, *Textile Manufacture . . . in Keighley*, p. 86.
1816	At Southgate, Bradford	Converted to worsted in 1816. James, p. 605; *1834 Supp. Rept.*, Mill no. 50.
1816	At Millgarth, Leeds (Hargreave)	*1834 Supp. Rept.*, Mill no. 174; Misc. Textile MSS, Cusworth Hall.
1816	Waterloo Mill, Hunslet	Converted from cotton. Sun C.R. 115/918879/1816.
1816	Beck Mill, Esholt	Not traced after 1817. Sun C.R. 116/914981/1816.
1816	At Huddersfield (Schofield)	*1834 Supp. Rept.*, Mill no. 132.
1816	At Chapel Hill, Huddersfield (Fisher)	*1834 Supp. Rept.*, Mills nos. 129 and 133.
1816	Union Mill, Eccleshill	*1834 Supp. Rept.*, Mill no. 43.
1816	Old Mill, Eccleshill	Cudworth, *Round about Bradford*, p. 353.
1816	Sheepscar Mill, Leeds	Sun C.R. 114/916912/1816.
1816	Old Mill, Stanningley	Cudworth, *Round about Bradford*, p. 467.
1816	Henshaw Mill, Apperley Bridge	Sun C.R. 115/918456/1816.
1816	Lower Mills, Brighouse	Crump and Ghorbal, p. 72.
1816	At South Crosland (Brooke)	*1834 Supp. Rept.*, Mill no. 73.
1816	Pricking Mill, Shipley	Wool and worsted. Cudworth, *Round about Bradford*, p. 294.
1817	Plank Mill Gomersal	Sun C.R. 119/930315/1817.
1817	Low Mill, Holmfirth	*1834 Supp. Rept.*, Mill no. 65.
1817	At Swinegate, Leeds	Sun C.R. 119/932121/1817. Worsted. Not traced after 1822.
1817	Hoyle Bottom, Wainstalls	*1834 Supp. Rept.*, Mill no. 283. Worsted after 1829.

Established by	Mill and Location	Notes and references
1817	At Water Lane, Leeds (Maud)	Sun C.R. 118/928810/1817. Not traced after 1822.
1817	Bank Top Mill, Horton	Worsted. Parker, *Illustrated Rambles* . . ., p. xxiv.
1817	Hill Top Mill, Keighley	Worsted. *1834 Supp. Rept.*, Mill no. 154.
1818	Greengate Mill, Keighley	Worsted. *1834 Supp. Rept.*, Mill no. 152.
1818	Peel House Mill, Warley	Worsted. *1834 Supp. Rept.*, Mill no. 289. H. W. Harwood, 'Peel House Mills', *H.A.S.*, December 1946, pp. 51–4.
1818	Union Street Mill, Bradford	Worsted. *1834 Supp. Rept.*, Mill no. 38.
1818	Marshall's Mill, Bradford	Worsted. James, p. 605.
1818	At Millmoor, Meltham	*1834 Supp. Rept.*, Mill no. 209.
1818	Dowley Gap Mill, Bingley	Worsted. Dodd, *Bingley*, p. 88. Cotton later.
1818	Jowler Mill, Warley	Sale Poster, H.A.D. Worsted after 1818.
1819	Dubb Mill, Bingley	Worsted. *1834 Supp. Rept.*, Mill no. 23; Cudworth, *Round about Bradford*, p. 190.
1819	Grove Mill, Headingley	Sun C.R. 128/952998/1819.
1819	Manchester Road Mill, Horton	*1834 Supp. Rept.*, Mill no. 120. Worsted.
1819	Old Bowling Lane Mill, Bradford	Worsted. James, p. 605.
1819	Prospect Mill, Bowling	Worsted. *1834 Supp. Rept.*, Mill no. 32.
1819	Well House Mill, Huddersfield	*1834 Supp. Rept.*, Mill no. 122.
1819	Crossley Mill, Hebden Bridge	*1834 Supp. Rept.*, Mill no. 280.
1819	Starkey's Mill, Huddersfield	*1834 Supp. Rept.*, Mill no. 134.
1819	Royd House Mill, Haworth	Worsted. *1834 Supp. Rept.*, Mill no. 98; James, p. 607.
1819	Pit Lane Mill, Bradford	Worsted. James, p. 605; *1834 Supp. Rept.*, Mill no. 35.
1819	Crosley Mill, Lockwood	*1834 Supp. Rept.*, Mill no. 112.
1819	Armitage Bridge Mill, Huddersfield	Crump and Ghorbal, pp. 116–20.

Established by	Mill and Location	Notes and references
1820	St John's Mill, Wakefield	Worsted. *Thorpe's Map of Wakefield*; Sun C.R. 250/1282756/1838.
1820	Fleece Mill, Keighley	Worsted. *1834 Supp. Rept.*, Mill no. 158.
1820	New Hurst Mill, Shipley	Worsted. Cudworth, *Round about Bradford*, p. 289. *1834 Supp. Rept.*, Mill no. 252.
1820	Whitley Spring Mill, Ossett	Sun C.R. 140/1000086/1823.
1820	At Low Fold, Leeds	Wool and Cotton. *1834 Supp. Rept.*, Mill no. 181.
1820	Pitfall Mills, Leeds	Burnt down 1821. Sun C.R. 131/973835/1820.
1820	At Thongsbridge, Netherthong	*1834 Supp. Rept.*, Mill no. 218.
1820	Tammy Hall, Wakefield	Worsted. Walker, *Wakefield* . . . , II, p. 400.
1820	At Sheepscar, Leeds	Cloth Dressing Mill. Sun C.R. 128/963774/1820.
1820	Holdsworth Mill, Bradford	Worsted. James, p. 605; *1834 Supp. Rept.*, Mill no. 53.
1820	Duckitt's Mill, Horton	Worsted. *1834 Supp. Rept.*, Mill nos. 34 and 117.
1820	Cliffe Mill, Great Horton	Worsted. *1834 Supp. Rept.*, Mill no. 119.
1820	At Great Horton (Ackroyd)	Worsted. James, p. 605.
1820	Eccleshill Mill, Eccleshill	Worsted. *1834 Supp. Rept.*, Mill no. 81.
1821	Carr Mill, Leeds	Earlier mill on site. Sun C.R. 134/984522/1821. Woollen and worsted after 1831.
1821	Oakes Mill, Alverthorpe	*Thorpe's Map of Wakefield*, 1820–1.
1821	Smalewell Mill, Pudsey	Cudworth, *Round about Bradford*, p. 482.
1821	Lower Town Mill, Haworth	Previously cotton. Worsted. *Baines' Directory*, 1822.
1821	Ing Mill, Dewsbury	Peel, *Spen Valley* . . . , p. 332.
1821	Upper Mill, Wainstalls	Worsted, previously cotton. *1834 Supp. Rept.*, Mill no. 285.
1821	Old Mill, Wainstalls	Worsted. Onslow Garnett, *Wainstall Mills*, pp. 6–9, 46; *1834 Supp. Rept.*, Mill no. 285.
1821	Grove Street Mill, Leeds	Cloth Dressing. *1834 Supp. Rept.*, Mill no. 186; Sun C.R. 135/986097/1821.

Established by	Mill and Location	Notes and references
1821	Low Road Mill, Hunslet	*Plan of an Estate in the Township of Hunslet 1821*, by Jonathan Taylor C.L.A.D.
1821	Aire Dale Mill, Leeds	Baines's *Plan of the Town of Leeds*. 1821. Norwich Union Minute Book no. 2 6/12/1824 and 20/12/1824.
1821	Bailey Hall Mill, Halifax	Worsted. *1834 Supp. Rept.*, Mill no. 263.
1821	Cross Lane Mill, Horton	Worsted. James, p. 605.
1821	At Canal Side, Bradford (Margerison)	Worsted. James, p. 605; *1834 Supp. Rept.*, Mill no. 46.
1821	At Canal Side, Bradford (Rouse no. 3 Mill)	Worsted weaving. *1834 Supp. Rept.*, Mill no. 496.
1821	Naylor's Mill, Wakefield	Cloth Dressing. *Thorpe's Map of Wakefield*, 1820–1.
1822	Buckton's Mill, Leeds	*Baines' Directory*, 1822.
1822	At Farnley (Lobley)	Sun C.R. 138/994249/1822. Not traced after 1828.
1822	Low Mill, Keighley	Worsted, previously cotton. Hodgson, *Textile Manufacture . . . in Keighley*, p. 212.
1822	Black Dog Mill, Leeds	Flax and wool. Flax only after 1826. *Baines' Directory*, 1822.
1822	Woodhouse Mill, Huddersfield	Mayhall, *Annals of Leeds*, p. 369.
1822	Shibden Mill, near Halifax	Worsted, *Baines' Directory*, 1822.
1822	Bowman Lane, Leeds (Giles)	Cloth dressing, *Baines' Directory*, 1822.
1822	Skinner Lane Mill, Leeds	Cloth dressing. Sun C.R. 137/992829/1822.
1822	At Meadow Lane, Leeds (Wilkinson)	Flax by 1830. *Baines' Directory*, 1822.
1822	Dow Bridge Mill, Leeds	*1834 Supp. Rept.*, Mill no. 137.
1822	At Batley (Sheard, Spedding & Co.)	*1834 Supp. Rept.*, Mill no. 21.
1822	At Clough Bottom, Longwood (Sykes)	*1834 Supp. Rept.*, Mill no. 205.
1822	Providence Mill, Bingley	Worsted, previously cotton. *1834 Supp. Rept.*, Mill no. 26.
1822	Barkisland Mills, Barkisland	*Baines' Directory*, 1822.
1822	Scarr End Mill, Dewsbury	*Baines' Directory*, 1822.
1822	At Windhill, Calverley (Jennings)	*Baines' Directory*, Worsted.

Established by	Mill and Location	Notes and references
1822	Trafalgar Mill, Leeds	Worsted 1826, flax 1828. *Baines' Directory*, 1822; Sun C.R. 157/1050668/1826.
1822	Silver Mill, Otley	Worsted. *Baines' Directory*, 1822.
1822	Gill Mill, Yeadon	*1834 Supp. Rept.*, Mill no. 296.
1822	Beck Lane Mill, Heckmondwike	*1834 Supp. Rept.*, Mill no. 99.
1822	At Horsforth (Hague)	Sun C.R. 140/992760/1822.
1822	Glazing Mill, Skipton	Worsted. *Baines' Directory*, 1822.
1822	Castle Mills, Keighley	Worsted, previously cotton. *1834 Supp. Rept.*, Mill no. 151.
1822	Grove Mill, Keighley	Worsted, previously cotton. Hodgson, *Textile Manufacture . . . in Keighley*, p. 229.
1822	High Mill, Addingham	Worsted. *1834 Supp. Rept.*, Mill no. 1.
1822	At York Street, Leeds (Britton)	*Baines' Directory*, 1822. Sun C.R. 159/1052241/1826.
1822	At Mill Garth, Leeds (Branker, Brown & Co.)	Sun C.R. 145/1009556/1823.
1822	At Cartworth (Hinchcliffe)	*1834 Supp. Rept.*, Mill no. 68.
1822	Waterside Mill, Halifax	Worsted. *Baines' Directory*, 1822.
1822	Severhills Mill, Soyland	Cotton, silk and wool. J. H. Priestley, 'The Growth of a Township — Soyland', *H.A.S.*, February 1955, p. 43.
1822	Salterlee Mill, Northowram	Worsted. *Baines' Directory*, 1822.
1822	Soyland Mill, Soyland	Worsted. *1834 Supp. Rept.*, Mill no. 271.
1822	North Bridge Mill, Halifax	Worsted. *Baines' Directory*, 1822.
1822	Lee Bridge Mill, Halifax	*Baines' Directory*, 1822.
1822	Brick Lane Mill, Manningham	Worsted. *Baines' Directory*, 1822; Cudworth, *Manningham, Heaton and Allerton*, p. 112.
1823	Albion Mill, Eccleshill	Worsted. *1834 Supp. Rept.*, Mill no. 39; Sun C.R. 140/1000006/1823.
1823	At Fulneck (Scott)	Only reference: Norwich Union Fire Office Minute Book no. 2, 16/6/1823.

Established by	Mill and Location	Notes and references
1823	At Meadow Lane, Leeds (Wilks)	*Factories Inquiry Commission, First Report*, 1833, p. 6.
1823	Union Mill, Shipley	*1834 Supp. Rept.*, Mill no. 253.
1823	Wellington Mill, Bramley	Sun C.R. 149/1022368/1824. *1834 Supp. Rept.*, Mill no. 55.
1823	Potterdale Mill, Leeds	*1834 Supp. Rept.*, Mill no. 106.
1823	Back Lane Mill, Wakefield	Worsted. *Walkers' Map of Wakefield*, 1823.
1823	Albion Mill, Pudsey	*1834 Supp. Rept.*, Mill no. 226.
1823	Harley House, Stansfield	*1834 Supp. Rept.*, Mill no. 273.
1823	Spring Mill, Linthwaite	*1834 Supp. Rept.*, Mill no. 197.
1823	High Street Mill, Bradford	Worsted. *1834 Supp. Rept.*, Mill no. 38.
1823	At Canal Side, Bradford (Lockwood & Rhodes)	Worsted. *1834 Supp. Rept.*, Mill no. 45.
1824	At Leeds (Horsfall)	Worsted. *1834 Supp. Rept.*, Mills nos. 175 and 180.
1824	At Quick (Kenworthy)	Cotton and wool. *1834 Supp. Rept.*, Mill no. 232.
1824	Camp Road Mill, Leeds	*1834 Supp. Rept.*, Mill no. 172.
1824	Brunswick Mill, Leeds	Cloth Dressing. *1834 Supp. Rept.*, Mill no. 168.
1824	Dyson Mill, Holmfirth	*1834 Supp. Rept.*, Mill no. 70.
1824	Damens Mill, Keighley	Worsted, originally cotton. *1834 Supp. Rept.*, Mill no. 159.
1824	North Wing Mill, Bradford	Worsted. James, p. 605.
1824	At Thornton Road, Bradford	Worsted. *1834 Supp. Rept.*, Mill no. 36.
1824	At Canal Side, Bradford (Rouse no. 2 Mill)	Worsted. *1834 Supp. Rept.*, Mill no. 49a.
1824	Kershaw Mill, near Halifax	Worsted. Leeds and Yorkshire Secretary's Book no. 1, 27/10/1824.
1825	At Leeds Road, Huddersfield (Swaine & Webbs)	*1834 Supp. Rept.*, Mill no. 135.
1825	Grove Mill, Halifax	Leeds and Yorkshire Secretary's Book no. 1, 14/10/1825.
1825	At Leeds (Bruce & Dorrington)	*1834 Supp. Rept.*, C.I. Mill No. 30.
1825	At Upper Headrow, Huddersfield (Lockwood)	*1834 Supp. Rept.*, Mill no. 128.
1825	Fountains Mill, Huddersfield	Cotton and wool. *1834 Supp. Rept.*, Mill no. 131.
1825	Clayhouse Mill, Elland	Leeds and Yorkshire Secretary's Book no. 1, 9/3/1825.

Established by	Mill and Location	Notes and references
1825	Larkfield Mill, Rawdon	*1834 Supp. Rept.*, Mill no. 242.
1825	New Cape Mill, Farsley	Sun C.R. 152/1036497/1825.
1825	Bagby Mill, Leeds	*1834 Supp. Rept.*, Section C, Part 1, Mill no. 29.
1825	At Cartworth (Hinchcliffe & Horncastle)	*1834 Supp. Rept.*, Mill no. 66.
1825	Cuttell Mill, Wooldale	*1834 Supp. Rept.*, Mill no. 294.
1825	At Ashgrave, Halifax	Cloth Dressing. *1834 Supp. Rept.*, Mill no. 264.
1825	Bottoms Mill, Austonley	*1834 Supp. Rept.*, Mill no. 15.
1825	At Milnesbridge, Linthwaite (Winterbottom)	*1834 Supp. Rept.*, Mill no. 198.
1825	Royds Mill, Beeston	*Parson's Directory*, 1826.
1825	At Horton, Bradford (Illingworth, Murgatroyd & Co.)	Worsted. *1834 Supp. Rept.*, Mill no. 42.
1826	Wellington Street Mill, Leeds	*Parson's Directory*, 1826.
1826	Ingrow Mills, Keighley	Worsted, previously paper. *1834 Supp. Rept.*, Mill no. 145.
1826	Little Woodhouse Mill, Leeds	Only reference: *Parson's Directory*, 1826.
1826	Willow Hall, Leeds	Only reference: *Parson's Directory*, 1826.
1826	At Idle (Edmundson)	*1834 Supp. Rept.*, Mill no. 141; Sun C.R. 159/1052251/1826.
1826	Carlinghow Mill, Batley	*1834 Supp. Rept.*, Mill no. 20.
1826	At Rushcliffe, Huddersfield (Nelson)	*1834 Supp. Rept.*, Mill no. 130.
1826	Upper Mill, Farnley	*Parson's Directory*, 1826.
1826	Union Mill, Pudsey	*1834 Supp. Rept.*, Mill no. 228.
1826	Wellington Mill, Leeds	Register of Deeds. 1c, p. 302, 1824; Sun C.R. 170/1083057/1828.
1826	Perseverance Mill, Leeds	*1834 Supp. Rept.*, Mill no. 192.
1826	Elmwood Mills, Leeds	Baines's *Plan of the Town of Leeds*, 1826.
1826	Green House, Cumberworth Half	*1834 Supp. Rept.*, Mill no. 76.
1826	Cannon Mill, Great Horton	Worsted. James, p. 605; Sigsworth, pp. 154–6.
1826	Wood's Mill, Bradford	Worsted. B. and W. MSS, Portfolio 508; *1834 Supp. Rept.*, Mill no. 54.
1826	Wainstalls Mill, Wainstalls	Worsted. *1834 Supp. Rept.*, Mill no. 285. Garnett, *Wainstall Mills*, p. 47.

Established by	Mill and Location	Notes and references
1826	Albion Street Mill, Leeds	Norwich Union Fire Office, Minute Book no. 2, 24/12/1827
1826	Bank Top Mill, Leeds	*Parson's Directory*, 1826.
1826	Hollings Mill, Bradford	Worsted. *1834 Supp. Rept.*, Mill no. 40.
1826	At Thornton, Bradford (Wright)	Worsted. *1834 Supp. Rept.*, Mill no. 278.
1827	Holbeck Moor Mill, Leeds	Sun C.R. 158/1055363/1827.
1827	Waterloo Mill, Pudsey	*1834 Supp. Rept.*, Mill no. 224.
1827	Prospect Mill, Leeds	Worsted. *1834 Supp. Rept.*, Mill no. 190.
1827	Low Close Mill, Leeds	Cloth Dressing. Sun C.R. 166/1068720/1827.
1827	Old Lane Mill, Northowram	Worsted. *1834 Supp. Rept.*, Mill no. 219.
1827	Spring Mill, Warley	Worsted, previously cotton. Onslow Garnett, *Wainstall Mills* . . . , op. cit. pp. 47–8.
1827	Denholme Mill, Luddenden Foot	*1834 Supp. Rept.*, Mill no. 290.
1827	At Almondbury (Vickerman)	*1834 Supp. Rept.*, Mill no. 6.
1827	Stockdales Mill, Horton	Worsted. *1834 Supp. Rept.*, Mill no. 140.
1827	Cowling Mill, Bradford	Worsted, originally cotton. James, p. 605.
1828	At Keighley (Deane, Illingworth & Co.)	Worsted. *1834 Supp. Rept.*, Mill no. 149.
1828	At Husteads, Quick, Saddleworth	*1834 Supp. Rept.*, Mill no. 234.
1828	Balme Mill, Hunslet	*1834 Supp. Rept.*, Mill no. 139.
1828	Hargreave's Mill, Burley Woodhead	Cudworth, *Manningham, Heaton and Allerton*, p. 116.
1828	Howden Clough Mill, Birstal	Sun C.R. 168/1077839/1828.
1828	Healey New Mill, Ossett	*Wakefield and Halifax Journal*, 18 February 1831.
1828	Upper Mill, Slaithwaite	Dartmouth Estate, *Slaithwaite Terrier*, 1828, p. 161.
1828	Lower Howley Mill, Morley	Dartmouth Estate, *Morley Terrier*, 1828, p. 49.
1828	Burton Mill, Kirkburton	Dartmouth Estate, *Honley Terrier*, 1828.
1828	Carlton Mill, Leeds	Cloth Dressing. *1834 Supp. Rept.*, Mill no. 179.
1828	At Aire Street, Leeds	Cloth Dressing. Sun C.R. 166/107146/1828.

Established by	Mill and Location	Notes and references
1828	Lumb Mill, Warley	Worsted, previously cotton. *1834 Supp. Rept.*, Mill no. 288.
1829	Antwerp Mill, Armley	*Pigot's Directory*, 1829.
1829	At Skipton (Dewhirst)	Worsted, burnt 1831. W. Harbutt Dawson, *History of Skipton* (1882), p. 281.
1829	Dalton Lees Mill, Huddersfield	*Leeds Mercury*, 26 September 1829.
1829	Union Mill, Holbeck	*Pigot's Directory*, 1829; Sun C.R. 203/1162576/1833.
1829	Andrew Mill, Saddleworth	*Pigot's Directory*, 1829.
1829	New Mill, Longwood	*1834 Supp. Rept.*, Mill no. 202.
1829	Springhead Mill, Keighley	Worsted. *1834 Supp. Rept.*, Mill no. 153.
1829	Nether Royd Mill, Huddersfield	Only reference: *Leeds Mercury*, 12 December 1829.
1829	West Mills, Clayton	*Pigot's Directory*, 1829.
1829	Berry's Mill, Sutton	Worsted. Proposal Book of Thomas Brown, Skipton Agent of the Royal Exchange Assurance Office.
1829	Greystone Mill, Adwalton	Sun C.R. 178/1100986/1829.
1829	Flush Mills, Heckmondwike	*1834 Supp. Rept.*, Mill no. 142.
1829	Hallas Mill, Wilsden	Also called Lower Bent Mill. Worsted. *Leeds Mercury*, 12 December 1829.
1829	Morton Mill, Bingley	Worsted. *Leeds Mercury*, 26 June 1830.
1829	Linthwaite Mill, Linthwaite	*Leeds Mercury*, 21 November 1829.
1829	Old Bank Mill, Halifax	Worsted. *Pigot's Directory*, 1829.
1829	Hayley Mill, Halifax	Worsted. *Pigot's Directory*, 1829.
1829	Monk Pit Mills, Leeds	*Parson and Whites' Directory*, 1830.
1829	Bradley Mills, Elland	*Pigot's Directory*, 1829; *Parson and Whites' Directory*, 1830.
1830	North Beck Mill, Keighley	Worsted. *1834 Supp. Rept.*, Mill no. 150.
1830	Lumb Foot Mill, Stanbury	Worsted, previously cotton. W. Craven, *A History of Stanbury*.

Established by	Mill and Location	Notes and references
1830	Denbigh Square, Keighley	Worsted. *1834 Supp. Rept.*, Mill no. 156.
1830	Hick Well Croft Mill, Batley	*1834 Supp. Rept.*, Mill no. 28.
1830	Gildersome Mills, Gildersome	*Parson and Whites' Directory*, 1830.
1830	New Town Mill, Huddersfield	*Leeds Mercury*, 17 April 1830; *1834 Supp. Rept.*, Mill no. 1834.
1830	Marsh Mill, Cleckheaton	*Parson and Whites' Directory*, 1830.
1830	Leventhorpe Mill, Thornton	Worsted. *1834 Supp. Rept.*, Mill no. 277.
1830	Ramsden Mill, Golcar	Sun C.R. 190/1134664/1831.
1830	Nutting Wool Spinning Factory, Milnesbridge	Sun C.R. 184/1114571/1830.
1830	Longroyde Mill, Huddersfield	*Parson and White's Directory*, 1830.
1830	Fieldgate Mill, Huddersfield	*Parson and White's Directory*, 1830.
1830	Engine Bridge Factory, Huddersfield	*Parson and Whites' Directory*, 1830.
1830	Clough House Mill, Fartown, Huddersfield	*Parson and Whites' Directory*, 1830.
1830	Albion Mill, Idle	*Parson and Whites' Directory*, 1830.
1830	Bank House Mill, Longwood, Huddersfield	*1834 Supp. Rept.*, Mill no. 200.
1830	Dock Mill, Leeds	Worsted. *1834 Supp. Rept.*, Mill no. 175; Sun C.R. 191/1134146/1831.
1830	Eller Carr Mill, Cullingworth	Worsted. Cudworth, *Round about Bradford*, pp. 243–6.
1830	Sunny Bank Mills, Farsley	*1834 Supp. Rept.*, Mill no. 63.
1830	Allenbrigg Mill, Pudsey	*1834 Supp. Rept.*, Mill no. 59.
1830	At Lady Lane, Leeds	Worsted. *1834 Supp. Rept.*, Mill no. 189.
1830	At Yeadon (Craven)	Worsted. *Parson and Whites' Directory*, 1830.
1830	Harcourt Mill, Leeds	*Leeds Mercury*, 7 August 1830; Sun C.R. 190/1129168/1831.
1830	Upper Mill, Scammonden	*Parson and White's Directory*, 1830.
1830	Park Mills, Halifax	Worsted. *1834 Supp. Rept.*, Mill no. 93.
1830	At Nether Yeadon (Lupton & Hudson)	*Parson and White's Directory*, 1830.

Established by	Mill and Location	Notes and references
1830	At Clayton West, High Hoyland	*Leeds Mercury*, 22 May 1830.
1830	Hall Mill, South Crosland	*Parson and White's Directory*, 1830.
1830	Upper End Mill, Marsden	*Leeds Mercury*, 26 June 1830.
1830	At Yeadon (Dawson)	*Parson and White's Directory*, 1830.
1830	Ousel Hole Mill, Bingley	Worsted. *Leeds Mercury*, 19 June 1830.
1830	Littletown Mill, Littletown, Birstal	*Leeds Mercury*, 12 June 1830.
1830	Grove Mill, Shelf	*Leeds Mercury*, 29 May 1830.
1830	Crag Mill, Windhill	*Leeds Mercury*, 20 March 1830.
1830	Silsbridge Mill, Bradford	Worsted. *Parson and White's Directory*, 1830.
1831	At Bramley (Lister)	Sun C.R. 190/1134691/1831.
1831	At Guiseley (Bottomley)	Sun C.R. 189/1124029/1831.
1831	Wood Mill, Laycock, Keighley	Worsted. *1834 Supp. Rept.*, Mill no. 159a.
1831	Billingsley's Mill, Bradford	Worsted. *1834 Supp. Rept.*, Mill no. 37.
1831	Shaw Mill, Skircoat	Worsted. *1834 Supp. Rept.*, Mill no. 256.
1831	Crawshaw Mill, Pudsey	*1834 Supp. Rept.*, Mill no. 227.
1831	New Mills, Wainstalls	Worsted. *1834 Supp. Rept.*, Mill no. 285.
1831	Spring Head Mills, Delph	*1834 Supp. Rept.*, Mill no. 247.
1831	Lee Mill, Halifax	Worsted. Halifax Township Valuation, 1837.
1832	Cullingworth Mill, Bingley	Worsted. Sun C.R. 194/1135637/1832.
1832	Square Mill, Halifax	Worsted. *1834 Supp. Rept.*, Mill no. 94.
1832	Birkenshaw Bottoms Mill, Birkenshaw	Worsted, previously cotton. *1834 Supp. Rept.*, Mill no. 29.
1832	Low Fold Mill, Leeds	Cloth finishing. *1834 Supp. Rept.*, Mill no. 182.
1832	Laycock's Mill, Bradford	Worsted. Wood's *Plan of Bradford*, 1832.
1832	Healey Low Mill, Ossett	Sun C.R. 195/1147580/1832.
1832	Brandy Mill, Keighley	Worsted. Hodgson, *Textile Manufacture . . . in Keighley*, p. 124.
1832	North Hall Mill, Leeds	Cloth Dressing. *White's Directory*, 1837.

Established by	Mill and Location	Notes and references
1832	Broad Carr Mill, Holywell Green	Sun C.R. 198/1152210/1833 and inscribed stone in mill ruins.
1833	Union Mill, Yeadon	Sun C.R. 199/1151791/1833.
1833	Regulator Mill, Sowerby Bridge	Worsted. *1834 Supp. Rept.*, Mill no. 287; B. & W. MSS, Portfolio 298.
1833	Cow Bridge Mill, Stansfield	Worsted. *Halifax Guardian*, 2 October 1833.
1833	Prospect Mill, Keighley	Worsted. Hodgson, *Textile Manufacture . . . in Keighley*, p. 104.
1833	Victoria Mills, Leeds	*White's Directory*, 1837.
1833	Terry's Mill, Bowling	Worsted. James, pp. 605–6; *1834 Supp. Rept.*, Mill no. 33.
1833	At Woodbottom, Jackson's Bridge	*Factories Inquiry Commission.* First Report, 1833, p. 24.
1833	At Lady Lane, Leeds (Ripley & Ogle)	Sun C.R. 210/1177577/1834.
1833	Canal Mills, Sowerby Bridge	Wool and Worsted. J. M. Priestley, 'The Growth of a Township — Soyland', *H.A.S.*, February 1955, p. 43.
1833	Junction Mill, Bradford	Worsted. James, pp. 605–6.
1833	Royal George Mills, Saddleworth	*1834 Supp. Rept.*, Mill no. 247.
1833	At Holmfirth (Walker)	Sun C.R. 197/1155328/1833.
1833	Brittania Mills, Leeds	*White's Directory*, 1837; Sun C.R. 245/1264502/1837.
1833	Anchor Mill, Dewsbury	*White's Directory*, 1837.
1833	Woodside Mill, Horsforth	P. Slater, *History of the Ancient Parish of Guiseley* (1880), p. 286.
1833	New Bank Mill, Halifax	Cotton and worsted. Sun C.R. 200/1159190/1833.
1833	Little Mill, Dewsbury	*Walker's Map of Dewsbury*, 1833.
1833	Clover Greaves Mill, Calverley	Cudworth, *Round about Bradford*, p. 467; Sun C.R. 223/120657/1835.
1834	Rawroyd Mill, Holywell Green	*Myer's Map of the Parish of Halifax*, 1834.
1834	Old House Mill, Norland	*Myer's Map of Halifax*, 1834.
1834	Priestley Mill, Pudsey	Cudworth, *Round about Bradford*, p. 482.
1834	Hope Mill, Leeds	*Plan of a Plot of Building Ground in Leeds*, C.L.A.D.
1834	North Side Mill, Horton	Worsted. Cudworth, *Rambles around Horton*, p. 35.

Established by	Mill and Location	Notes and references
1835	At Esholt (Yewdalls & Robinson)	*List of Prosecutions under the Factory Act*, pp. XLV (1836).
1835	Black Dyke Mills, Queensbury	Worsted. Sigsworth *Black Dyke Mills*.
1835	At Luddenham (Buckley)	Worsted. *Returns of Power Looms*, 1835.
1835	Mearclough Bottom Mill, Skircoat	Worsted. Insurance proposal, H.A.D.
1835	Holme Top Mill, Horton	Worsted. *Returns of Power Looms*, 1835.
1835	Baildon Mill, Northgate, Baildon	Worsted. Cudworth, *Round about Bradford*, p. 320.
1835	Field Head Mill, Horton	Worsted. Cudworth, *Rambles around Horton*, p. 35.
1835	Penny Oaks Mill, Bradford	Worsted. *Returns of Power Looms*, 1835.
1835	Britannia Mills, Bradford	Worsted. *Returns of Power Looms*, 1835.
1835	Junction Mill, Shipley	Worsted. Cudworth, *Round about Bradford*, p. 294.
1835	Portland Mill, Bradford	Worsted. *White's Directory*, 1837.
1835	Park Mills, Clayton West	*Factory Returns*, 1835; *White's Directory*, 1837.
1835	At Spring Grove, Clayton West	*White's Directory*, 1837.
1835	Farfield Mill, Sedbergh	W. Thompson, *Sedbergh, Garsdale and Dent*, p. 192.
1835	Birchworth Mill, Oxspring, Penistone	*White's Directory*, 1837.
1835	Selby Mill, Selby	Woollen and worsted. *Factory Returns*, 1835.
1835	Haverdale Mill, Dent	Worsted. M. Hartley and J. Ingleby, *The Old Hand Knitters of the Dales*, p. 34.
1835	Smith's Mill, Gargrave	Worsted. *Returns of Power Looms*, 1835.
1835	Gilroyd Mill, Morley	Gill Royd Mill Co., Committee Book, C.L.A.D.
c. 1835	At Idle (Sharp)	Sun C.R. 245/1260927/1837.
c. 1835	Swinnow Mill, Bramley	Sun C.R. 238/1257736/1837.
1835	Calversyke Mill, Keighley	Worsted. Brigg MSS, K.P.L.
1835	At Embsay (Bland)	Worsted. *Factory Returns*, 1835, *White's Directory*, 1837.
1835	At Carlton, Skipton (Parker)	*Factory Returns*, 1835; Worsted. *White's Directory*, 1837.

Established by	Mill and Location	Notes and references
1835	At Kildwick (Smith)	*Factory Returns*, 1835; Worsted. *White's Directory*, 1837.
1835	At Hartlington, Burnsall (Ambler)	Previously a cotton mill. Worsted. *Factory Returns*, 1835; *White's Directory*, 1837.
c. 1835	At Batley Carr (Boothroyd & Fogard)	*White's Directory*, 1837.
c. 1835	Purlwell Mill, Batley	*White's Directory*, 1837.
c. 1835	At Batley Carr (Wharton, Naylor & Co.)	*White's Directory*, 1837.
c. 1835	At Gildersome (Booth)	*White's Directory*, 1837.
c. 1835	At Little Gomersall (Burnley, Firth & Co.)	*White's Directory*, 1837.
c. 1835	At Yeadon (Walsh & Padgett)	*White's Directory*, 1837
c. 1835	Spinkwell Mill, Dewsbury	*White's Directory*, 1837.
1835	Lumb Mill, Delph	Lee MSS. Upper Mill Library.
c. 1835	Court Mill, Saddleworth	*White's Directory*, 1837.
c. 1835	Berry Mill, Scammonden	*White's Directory*, 1837.
c. 1835	Nield Mill, Saddleworth	*White's Directory*, 1837.
c. 1835	Warrick Hill Foot Mill, Saddleworth	*White's Directory*, 1837.
c. 1835	Gatehead Mill, Saddleworth	*White's Directory*, 1837.
c. 1835	Mitchell Mill, Saddleworth	*White's Directory*, 1837.
c. 1835	Hull Mill, Saddleworth	*White's Directory*, 1837.
c. 1835	Thornes Clough Mill, Saddleworth	*White's Directory*, 1837
c. 1835	Moorcroft Mill, Saddleworth	*White's Directory*, 1837.
c. 1835	Bakestone Mill, Saddleworth	*White's Directory*, 1837.

Appendix II

YORKSHIRE WOOLLEN AND WORSTED MILLS INCLUDED IN THE 1835 FACTORY RETURNS

R. Rickards, the Factory Inspector for the West Riding, tabulated his 'Returns of All Mills and Factories' in two ways. His first table gives a breakdown of the type and amount of power being used, parish by parish, and his second records the number, ages and sex of the workers employed, township by township. Besides a certain small degree of inaccuracy in Rickards' calculations of the aggregate figures for power and number of workers, the number of mills tabulated differs slightly in the two lists. The first gives a total of 393 woollen mills and 210 worsted mills whereas the second table records 406 woollen mills and 204 worsted mills. The difference in the two totals may be partly explained, perhaps, by Rickards' treatment of the incomplete or unoccupied mills in different ways in the two tables and by his exclusions on some occasions of mills for which he did not have full information. Moreover it is possible that there may have been some time lapse between drawing up the two tables and that he made allowance for certain changes. Also it may be the case that premises being used for both worsted and woollen manufacture are listed under different headings in the two tables.

In this Appendix the details given in the second of Rickards' two tables are used because the number of mills, township by township, are given and because the totals are slightly higher and, therefore, possibly more accurate.

The Appendix is arranged in sections. The Factory Returns of 1835 for each township are given and the mills that have been traced are listed with their names, use, occupiers and date of erection or conversion. Where it is not certain that the mill should be included a question mark is shown before its name. Where a piece of information given is uncertain a question mark follows it.

There are certain problems that arise in attempting to list mills township by township. It is not always possible to decide in which township a mill was situated particularly when its site has not definitely been traced. Moreover some townships were divided between more than one parish. The problem has arisen in the case of Halifax parish, Almondbury parish and Bradford parish, and to a lesser extent in several others. Thus it is probably better to compare the number of mills traced with the number listed by the Factory Inspector parish by parish rather than township by township. It was probably, moreover, the case that even the Factory Inspector was not always correct in his listing of the mills.

For most parishes the number of mills traced corresponds quite closely to the number in the Factory Returns. In a few parishes, however, notably Saddleworth, a number of mills recorded by the Factory Inspector have not been traced.

For a discussion of the reliability of the Factory Inspector's Returns see D. T. Jenkins, 'The Validity of the Factory Returns, 1833–50', *Textile History*, 4, 1973.

Mill	Occupants	Use	Date
Addingham		3 worsted mills	
Low Mill	J. Cockshott	worsted	1787
At Addingham	?	worsted	1808
High Mill	Bland, Ellis & Co.	worsted	1822
ALMONDBURY PARISH			
Linthwaite		4 woollen mills 1 unoccupied mill	
Whiteley Bottom	Armitage Bros	wool	c. 1790
Spring Mill	Armitage Bros	wool	1823
At Milnsbridge*	Winterbottom and others	wool	1825
Linthwaite Mill	?	wool	1829
Nutting Factory	Jo. Armitage	wool	1830
Crosland		4 woollen mills	
Dungeon Mill	J. & T. C. Wrigley	wool	c. 1785
Cocking Steps Mill	J. Wrigley & Sons	wool	c. 1790
Woodbottom Mill	G. Beaumont	wool	1792
Lords Mill	G. Beaumont	wool	1792
Crosland Mill	W. H. Stables	wool	1792
At South Crosland	J. Brooke & Sons	wool	1817
Hall Mill	Thos Beaumont	wool	1830

* Milnsbridge also partly in Golcar township.

Mill	Occupants	Use	Date
Marsden		7 woollen mills	
At Marsden	Schofield, Kenworthy & Co.	wool	1788
Bank Bottom Upper Mill	Norris, Sykes & Fisher	wool	1797
Lingard Wood Bottom Mill	D. Haigh	wool	1797
Ottiwells Mill	A. & W. Kinder (?)	wool	pre 1800
At Sunlain Bottom	John Varley	wool	1815
Upper End Mill	?	wool	1830
Farnley Tyas		1 woollen mill	
Farnley Mill	Roberts and Co.	wool	1792
Almondbury Township		33 woollen mills 7 unoccupied mills	
Fenay Wool	?	wool	1779
Steps Mill	Beaumont & Vickermann	wool	1788
At Thirsting	Thos Hinchcliffe	wool	1790
At Smithy Place	Jos. Robinson	wool	1791
Honley Mill	Thos Hinchcliffe	wool	1797
Dean House Mill	G. & N. Berry	wool	1797
Low Coat Mill	J. Eastwood	wool	1797
King's Mill	F. Vickerman	wool	1799
Old Corn Mill	Jos. Varley	wool	1800
Bank End Mill	J. Roebuck	wool	1800
Birks Mill	Nowell, Cockhill & Bennett	wool	1801
Dudley Mill	T. Allen	wool	1801
Cookes Mill	?	wool	1802
Digley Mills	G. & J. Hirst	wool	1817

Mill	Occupants	Use	Date
At Millmoor	John Eastwood	wool	1818
Crosley Mill	David Shaw	wool	1819
At Armitage Bridge	John Brooke & Sons	wool	1819
At Thongsbridge	J. Robinson	wool	1820
Bottoms Mill	J. Harpin & Co.	wool	1825
In Almondbury Parish	Jos. Vickerman	wool	1827
Burnsall Parish			
Hartlington		1 worsted mill	
At Hartlington	Jeremiah Ambler	worsted	*c.* 1835
Bingley Parish			
Bingley and Micklethwaite		7 worsted mills	
Eldwick Beck Mill	Jos. Sharp (?)	worsted	1808
Elmtree Mills	T. Jowett	worsted	1811
At Micklethwaite	J. Illingworth	worsted	1812
Prospect Mill	J. Sharp	worsted	1813
Dowley Gap Mill	M. & T. Walker	worsted	1818
Dubb Mill	Wm Anderton	worsted	1819
Providence Mill	John Sharp	worsted	1822
Horton		6 worsted mills	
Horton Mill		worsted	1829
Ousel Hole Mill	?	worsted	1830

Mill	Occupants	Use	Date
Cullingworth and Harden		2 worsted mills	
Harden Mill	Whalley, Ambler & Smith	worsted	1800
At Cowhouse Upper Fold	Moulding (?)	worsted	1803
Eller Carr Mill	John Greenwood	worsted	1830
Cullingworth Mill	G. Townend & Bros	worsted	1832
BATLEY PARISH			
Batley Township		11 woollen mills	
Batley Old Mill	Scratchard & Co.	wool	1797
Ellis's Mill	Ellis	wool	1800
Clark Green Mill	Hall & Co.	wool	*c.* 1800
At Batley	Sheard, Spedding & Co.	wool	1822
Carlinghow Mill	John Nussey	wool	1826
Hick Lane Mill	John Burnley & Sons	wool	1830
(?) At Batley Carr	Boothroyd & Fogard	wool	*c.* 1835
Purlwell Mill	Hall, Hirst & Co.	wool	pre 1835
(?) At Batley Carr	Wharton, Naylor & Co.	wool	*c.* 1835
Gildersome		3 woollen mills	
Troughton Mill	E. & J. Troughton	wool	1796
Philadelphia Mill	Wm Gelderd	wool	1800
Gildersome Mills	Jonas, Stead & Sons	wool	1830
At Gildersome	Jno. Booth & Co.	wool	*c.* 1835

Mill	Occupants	Use	Date
Churwell		1 woollen mill	
Churwell Mill	Geo. Crowther & Co.	wool	1798
Morley		2 woollen mills	
Crank Mill	Wm Dixon	wool	c. 1793
Rods Mill	Webster & Sons	wool	1797
At Bankhill	?	wool	1808
Lower Howley Mill	?	wool	pre 1828
Gilroyd Mill	Gilroyd Mill Co.	wool	c. 1835
BIRSTALL PARISH			
Cleckheaton		2 woollen mills	
Peg Mill	Wm Atkinson	worsted	1800
(?) Marsh Mill	W. & J. Heaton	wool	1830
Liversedge		7 woollen mills 1 worsted mill	
Wormald Mill	?	wool	1797
At Millbridge	Sam Cooke	worsted	1812
Rawfolds Mill	Lawford	wool	1812
Brow Top Mill	?	worsted	1829
Littletown Mill	Jos. Waller & Sons	wool	1830
At Littletown	Cockill, Brook & Co.	wool	c. 1835

Mill	Occupants	Use	Date
Birstall Township		2 woollen mills	
Brookroyd Mill	Nusseys and Clapham	wool	1792
At Birstal Smithies	R. Nussey & Co.	wool	1797
Howden Clough Mill	Jos. Oldroyd & Co.	wool	1828
Birkenshaw		2 worsted mills	
At Birkenshaw	John Ellison	worsted	1790
Birkenshaw Bottoms Mill	Thos Ackroyd	worsted	1832
Gomersall		8 woollen mills	
Castle Mill		wool	1801
Scholes Mill	Heap, Battye & Senior	wool	1806
Gomersal Mills	J. & E. Swaine	wool	1807
At Popplewell	?	wool	1813
At Gomersal	Wm Hirst & Sons	wool	1817
Greystone Mill	Wm Hudson & Sons	wool	1829
(?) At Little Gomersal	Burnley, Firth & Co.	wool	*c.* 1835
Hunsworth		2 woollen mills	
Hunsworth Mill	Joshua Taylor	wool	1785
Heckmondwike		7 woollen mills	
Stubbins Mill		wool	1785
Dean Mill	John Burnley & Co.	wool	*c.* 1793
Heckmondwike Mill	Heckmondwike Mill Co.	wool	1795
At Heckmondwike	Dex and Keighley	wool	1797

Mill	Occupants	Use	Date
At Heckmondwike	Popplewell	wool	1800
Becklane Mill	Naylor & Cockill	wool	1822
Flush Mills	Edwin Firth	wool	1829
Tong		1 woollen mill 1 worsted mill	
At Tong	Joshua Crompton	wool	1795
Low Mill	?	wool	1831
BRADFORD PARISH			
Bowling		2 worsted mills	
Prospect Mill	Addison & Roper	worsted	1819
At Dudley Mill	W. & J. Terry	worsted	1833
Bradford Township		25 worsted mills	
Holme Mill	Milnes & Dewhirst	worsted	1800
West Brook Factory	Matthew Thompson	worsted	1801
Laister Dyke Mill	Jos. Holmes	wool	1803
Union St Mill	Illingworth, Murgatroyd & Co.	worsted	1807
		worsted	1809
At Wakefield Road	Wood & Walker	worsted	1812
At Canal Side	John Mason	worsted	1813
At Canal Side	J. Wade & W. Rouse	worsted	1815
Barkerend Mills	W. & J. Garnett	worsted	1815
At Laister Dyke	Wm Pearson & Son	worsted	1815

Mill	Occupants	Use	Date
Southgate	J. & E. Smith	worsted	1816
Union St Mill	J. Garnett	worsted	1818
Anderton's Mill	Swithin Anderton	worsted	1819
Holdsworth's Mill	Chris. Waud	worsted	1820
At Canal Side	Margerison & Peckover	worsted	1821
At Canal Side	Wm Rouse	worsted	1821
At High Street	J. Garnett	worsted	1823
At Canal Side	Lockwood & Rhodes	worsted	1823
North Wing Mill	Horsfall Bros	worsted	1824
At Thornton Road	J. Anderton & Co.	worsted	1824
At Canal Side	Wm Rouse	worsted	1824
Wakefield Road	John Wood	worsted	1826
Holling's Mill	Thos Hollings	worsted	1826
Stockdale's Mill	Cousen, Leach & Co.	worsted	1827
Silsbridge Mill	Jas Warbrick	worsted	1830
Billingsley's Mill	Billingsley & D. Tankard	worsted	1831
Laycock's Mill	Jno. Pickles	worsted	1832
Junction Mill	Roberts & Lupton	worsted	1833
Northside Mill	Nathaniel Bentley	worsted	*c.* 1833
(?) Penny Oaks Mill	Isaac Kershaw	worsted	*c.* 1835
(?) Britannia Mills	C. Waud	worsted	*c.* 1835
(?) Portland Mill	Peel, Lister, Spence & Co.	worsted	*c.* 1835
Great Horton		6 worsted mills	
Bank Top Mill	F. &. J. Mitchell	worsted	1817
Duckitt's Mill	Various	worsted	1820
Cliffe Mill	Cowling & Robt Ackroyd		

Mill	Occupants	Use	Date
At Great Horton	Denton & Co.	worsted	1820
Cannon Mill	John Foster	worsted	1826
Cowling Mill	Cowling Ackroyd	worsted	1827
Little Horton		8 worsted mills	
Horton Lane Mill	John Rand	worsted	1803
Marshall's Mill	Berry & Co.	worsted	1818
At Manchester Road	Turner & Mitchell	worsted	1819
At Manchester Road	F. & J. Mitchell	worsted	1819
Cross Lane Mill	J. & W. Cousen	worsted	1821
At Horton	Illingworth, Murgatroyd	worsted	1825
Holme Top Mill	J. & S. Stowell	worsted	1835
Field Head Mill	R. S. Ackroyd	worsted	1835
Eccleshill		2 woollen mills 1 worsted mill	
Union Mill	J. Johnson & Co.	wool	1816
Old Mill	J. Johnson & Co.	wool	pre 1816
Eccleshill Mill	Scott & Hutton	worsted	1820
Albion	Thos Dalby & Co.	worsted	1823
Haworth and 'Oxness'		17 worsted mills	
(?) Leeming Mill	?	worsted	1791
Hewnden Mills	R. Nichols & Co.	worsted	1792
Bridgehouse Mill	J. &. J. Greenwood	worsted	*c.* 1792
At Haworth	Butterfield & Co.	worsted	1800

Mill	Occupants	Use	Date
Oxenhope Mill	Wm Greenwood	worsted	1800
Birkshead Mill	J. &. J. Anderton	worsted	1810
Royd House Mill	Jonas Hird	worsted	1819
Lower Town Mill	Jas Feather & Co.	worsted	*c.* 1821
Hallas Mill	?	worsted	1829
Lumb Foot Mill	Messrs Butterfield	worsted	1830
Manningham		1 worsted mill	
Frizinghall Mill	W. & J. Hargreaves	wool	1795
		worsted	1818
Bricklane Mill	Jos. Baldwin & Co.	worsted	1822
Shipley		2 woollen mills	
		4 worsted mills	
Dumb Mill	Joseph Wood	worsted	1785(?)
Dixon Mills	Edward Barwick	wool	1790
Providence Mill	Denby, Booth & Lee	wool	1796
Woodend Mill	?	worsted	1810
Red Beck Mill	E. C. Lister	worsted	1815
New Hurst Mill	Jos. Rayner	worsted	1820
Union Mill	Wilcock, Bradley & Co.	wool	1823
(?) Junction Mill	Jos. Taylor	worsted	*c.* 1835
Thornton		5 worsted mills	
At Thornton	David Wright	worsted	1826
West Mills	Townend & Wright	worsted	1829
Leventhorpe Mill	Jos. Fairbank	worsted	1830

Mill	Occupants	Use	Date
CALVERLEY PARISH			
Idle		5 woollen mills 5 worsted mills	
Buck Mill	Wm Craven	wool	1797
Brackendale Mill	Mitchell, Glover & Illingworth	wool	1800
Old Mill	Wm Hainsworth	worsted	1806
Henshaw Mill	?	wool	1816
Pricking Mill	?	worsted	1816
At Windhill	Wm Jennings	worsted	1822
At Idle	Wm Edmondson & Co.	wool	1826
Windhill Crag Mill	?	wool	1830
Albion Mill	?	wool	1830
At Idle	John Sharp	worsted	*c.* 1835
Calverley Township		3 woollen mills	
Calverley Mill	Wm Greenwood	wool	1805
Clover Greaves Mill	Kellet, Brown & Co.	wool	1833
Farsley		1 woollen mill	
Broom Mill	?	wool	*c.* 1800
Cape Mill	A. Hainsworth	wool	1810
Sunny Bank Mill	Various	wool	1830
New Cape Mill	J. &. J. Wood	wool	1825

Mill	Occupants	Use	Date
Pudsey		7 woollen mills 1 unoccupied mill	
Union Bridge Mill	Various	wool	*c.* 1798
Gibraltar Mill	Hall & Walton	wool	1802
Smalewell Mill	Hainsworth & Co.	wool	1821
Albion Mill	Beaumont, Harrison & Co.	wool	1823
Union Mill	Rider, Dean, Carr & Co.	wool	1826
Waterloo Mill	Blackburn, Cawthery & Co.	wool	1827
Allenbrigg Mill*	Webster, Harrison & Co.	wool	1830
Crawshaw Mill	Rayner, Goodsard & Co.		1831
Priestley Mill*	?		1834
Stanningley †		1 woollen mill	
Company Mill	J. Varley	worsted	*c.* 1794
Low Mill	—	wool	1798
Old Mill	—	wool	1816
DEWSBURY PARISH			
Dewsbury Township		18 woollen mills	
Dewsbury Mills	Hagues, Cook & Wormald	wool	1780
Aldams Mill	John Halliley	wool	1790
Croft Mill		wool	1793

* This mill was half in Bramley.
† See also Leeds Parish.

Mill	Occupants	Use	Date
Kilncroft Mill	?	wool	1800
Spring Mills	John Carr & Sons	wool	1808
At Daw Green	Ben Wilson	wool	1809
Watergate New Mill	Hemingway, Wilson & Auty	wool	1815
Ing Mill	Tugg & Co. (?)	wool	1821
Anchor Mills	Jos. Rushworth (?)	wool	1833
Little Mill	?	wool	1833
?	Taylor & Ibbotson	wool	1835
Spinkwell Mill	F. & J. Day	wool	c. 1830
Soothill		3 woollen mills	
Sands Mill	Robinson, Rhodes & Co.	wool	1795
Chickenley Mill	T. Harrap & Son	wool	1795
Scarr End Mill	Wilson & Co.	wool	1822
Ossett		8 woollen mills	
Spring End Mill	Wheatley, Overend & Collett	wool	1781
Healey Old Mill	Healey Mill Co.	wool	1785
Pildacre Mill	Ben Hallas	wool	1794
Union Mills	Union Mill Co.	wool	1815
Whitley Spring Mill	Whitley Spring Mill Co.	wool	1820
Healey New Mill	Healey New Mill Co.	wool	1828
Healey Low Mill	Healey Low Mill Co.	wool	1832

Mill	Occupants	Use	Date
GUISELEY PARISH			
Guiseley Township		3 woollen mills	
Guiseley Mills	?	wool	1781
At Guiseley	John Bottomley & Co.	wool	1830
At Woodside Mill	Hutchinson & Milner	wool	1833
Horsforth		2 woollen mills	
Woodbottom Mill	Grant & Thompson	wool	1790
Low Mill	Clough & Grunt	wool	1799
At Horsforth	David Hague	wool	1822
Rawdon		3 woollen mills	
Low Mill	J. R. & J. Thompson	wool	1793
Park Mill	Wm Thompson	wool	1805
Larkfield Mill	Wm Thompson	wool	1825
Yeadon		4 woollen mills 2 worsted mills	
Union Mill	J. &. J. Slater & Co.	wool	1805
Gill Mill	Sam Bentley & Co.	wool	1822
At Yeadon	Jos. Dawson	worsted	1830
At Yeadon	Graven & Co.	worsted	1830
At Nether Yeadon	Lupton & Hulson	wool	1830
At Yeadon	Walsh & Padgett	wool	*c.* 1835

Mill	Occupants	Use	Date
GARGRAVE PARISH			
Gargrave Township		1 woollen mill	
Smith's Mill	Jos. Smith	worsted	1835
HIGH HOYLAND PARISH			
High Hoyland Township		1 worsted mill	
At Cuttlehirst	Wm or Jos. Norton	wool	1830
Park Mills	Jas Waites	worsted	1835
(?) Spring Grove	Wood & Walker	worsted	*c.* 1835
HUDDERSFIELD PARISH			
Golcar		5 woollen mills	
At Milnsbridge*	T. & J. Brooke	wool	1800
Low Westwood Mills	J. J. & E. Shaw	wool	1803
Bottom Hall Mill	Shaw, Eastwood & Taylor	wool	1803
Lees Mill	Michael Shaw	wool	1808
Ramsden Mill	Ramsden Mill Co.	wool	1830
Huddersfield Township		17 woollen mills	
Woodhouse Mill	?	?	1797
Aspley Mill	R. & T. R. Atkinson	wool	1793

* Milnsbridge is half in Golcar Township and half in Linthwaite Township.

Mill	Occupants	Use	Date
At Huddersfield	J. Schofield	wool	1816
At Chapel Mill	Fisher & Stables	wool	1816
Well House Mill	Henry Brook & Sons	wool	1819
Starkey's Mill	Starkey & Buckley	wool	1819
At Leeds Road	Swaine & Webbs	wool	1825
At Upper Headrow	Jos. Cockwood	wool	1825
At Rushcliffe	Thos Nelson	wool	1826
(?) Nether Royd Mill	?	wool	1829
Newtown Mill	Norris, Sykes & Fisher	wool	1830
Longroyde Mill	Anderson, Tyne & Co. (?)	wool	1830
Fieldgate Mill	Ben Hirst	wool	1830
Engine Bridge Factory	Various	wool	pre 1830
Clough House Mill	Jas Crosland	wool	1830
Longwood		4 woollen mills	
At Clough Bottom	Jos. Sykes	wool	1822
New Mill	A. & W. Haigh	wool	pre 1829
Bank House Mill	Armitage Bros & Co.	wool	1830
Scammonden		4 woollen mills	
Intake Mill	John Walker (?)	wool	1815
Upper Mill	David Taylor (?)	wool	1830
(?) Berry Mill	Michael Hoyle	wool	*c.* 1835
Slaithwaite		5 woollen mills	
Lower Holt Mill	T. Varley	wool	1788
Clough House Mill	J. Horsfall	wool	1790

Mill	Occupants	Use	Date
Bankgate Mill	J. & J. Farrer	wool	1800
Lower Clough House Mill (?)	Mary Horsfall	wool	1807
Upper Mill	Shaw & Haigh	wool	pre 1828
HALIFAX PARISH			
Barkisland		1 worsted mill	
Bowers Mill	S. Walker	worsted	1807
Barkisland Mills	Sam Walker	worsted	1822
Ripponden Mill	R. Hoyle	wool	1799
Elland		6 woollen mills	
Elliston Mill	B. Outram	wool	1792
Brow Bridge Mill	J. Cartledge	wool	1797
At Elland	Jos. Rushforth	wool	1798
Marshall Hall Mill	W. Balmforth	wool	1800
Clayhouse Mill	Various	wool	1825
Bradley Mills	John Hirst	wool	1829
Halifax Township		4 woollen mills 14 worsted mills	
Dean Clough Mill	Crossleys	worsted	*c.* 1797
Lilly Mill	Irven & Holden	worsted	1799
Bowling Dyke Mill	James Ackroyd	worsted	1800
Paper Mill	Gledhill, Dyson & Bairstow	worsted	1801
At Bull Close Lane	Rawson & Saltmarshes	wool	1815

Mill	Occupants	Use	Date
Bailey Hall Mill	J. & J. Baldwin	worsted	1821
Waterside Mill	Thompson & Pritchard	worsted	1822
Northbridge Mill	Various	worsted	1822
Lee Bridge Mill	J. Dennison & Sons	wool	1822
Kershaw Mill	R. & G. Kershaw	worsted	1824
Grove Mill	J. Carter & Co. (?)	?	1825
At Ashgrove	Jas Noble	wool	1825
Old Lane Mill	Jas Akroyd	worsted	1827
Old Bank Mill	J. & J. Aspinall	worsted	1829
Hayley Mill	C. H. Dawson & Co.	worsted (?)	1829
Park Mills	Wm Lister	worsted	1830
Lee Mill	R. & J. Whitworth	worsted	*c.* 1831
Square Mill	Jos. Wood	worsted	1832
New Bank Mill	John Haigh & Bros	worsted	1833
*Hipperholme**		4 woollen mills 6 worsted mills	
Roger Mill	Vickerman	wool	1799
Slead Syke Mill	J. Holland	wool/worsted	*c.* 1799
Coley Mill	Stockwell	wool	1801
Walterclough Mill	T. F. Macaulay	worsted	*c.* 1802
At Northowram	Robt Crossley	wool	1808
Dam Head Mill	Thos Taylor & Co.	worsted	pre 1810
Shibden Mill	G. & J. Holdsworth	worsted	1822
Salterlee Mill	J. Mallinson (?)	worsted	1822

* Brighouse was partly in Hipperholme and partly in Rastrick.

Mill	Occupants	Use	Date
Grove Mill	?	worsted	1830
(?) Black Dyke Mills	John Foster	worsted	1835
Ovenden		4 worsted mills	
Jumples Mill	?	wool	1796
Hebble Mill	Various	wool (?)	1801
Brookhouse Mill	Ackroyds	worsted	1805
Rastrick		10 woollen mills	
Rosemary Mill	?	wool/worsted	1797
Old Corn Mill	Clay & Earnshaw	wool	1805
Brighouse Lower Mills	?	wool	1816
Rishworth		1 woollen mill	
Kebroyd Mill	John Hadwen	worsted	1795
Skircoat		1 woollen mill 2 worsted mills	
Copley Mill	Kaye & Charlesworth	wool	1792
Shaw Mill	John Holdsworth	worsted	1831
Regulator Mill	M. & S. Morley	worsted	1833
Mearclough Bottom Mill	T. E. Dyson	worsted	1835

Dote	Occupants	Use	Date
Sowerby		2 woollen mills	
Thorp Mill	J. & W. Priestley	wool	1782
Mill House	W. H. Rawson	wool	1787
Turvin Mill	Robt Whettam	wool	1808
Soyland		1 woollen mill	
Severhills Mill	Hy Binns	wool	1822
Soyland Mill	Hy Holdsworth	worsted	1822
Stansfield		2 worsted mills 1 unoccupied mill	
Callis Mill	D. & G. Ashworth	worsted	1786
Lob Mill	G. Sutcliffe	worsted	1790
At Harley House	Andrew Aspden	worsted	1786
Cowbridge Mill	J. Booth	worsted	1833
Wadsworth		1 worsted mill	
At Mytholmroyd	Walker & Edmondson	worsted	1792
At Hebden Bridge	J. Crossley & Sons	worsted	1819
Warley		5 woollen mills 12 worsted mills	
Longbottom Mill	Sam Milne	wool	1784
Hollings Mill	J. & S. Waterhouse	wool	1785
Boy Mill	Wm Currer	worsted	1787
Mill House	Rawson & Saltmarshes	wool	1787

Mill	Occupants	Use	Date
Midgley Manor Mill	?	worsted	1791
Hand Carr Mill		worsted	1792
At Sowerby Bridge	Geo. Greenup	wool	1793
Cooper House Mill	Sam & Wm Smith	worsted	1794
Scarbottom Mill	Murgatroyd	worsted	1794
Luddenden Foot Mill	Currer	wool	1799
Upper Luddenden Mill	Hy Murgatroyd	wool	1805
At Jowler	J. Priestley		1818
Peel House Mill	Richd Whitworth	worsted	1819
Upper Mill	Wm Appleyard	worsted	1821
Old Mill	J. & J. Calvert	worsted	1821
Wainstalls Mill	Wm Appleyard	worsted	1826
Spring Mill	?	worsted	1827
Denholme Mill	S. & W. Smith	worsted	1827
Lumb Mill	Thos Murgatroyd	worsted	1828
Lower Hollings Mill	Sam Wood	worsted	1829
Hoyle Bottom Mill	John Alderson	worsted	1829
New Mill	Wm Appleyard	worsted	1831
Canal Mills	John Edwards & Sons	wool/worsted	1833
At Luddenden	Wm Buckley	worsted	1835
Norland		4 woollen mills 1 worsted mill	
Firth House Mill	S. Dyson	wool	1800
Bankhouse Mill	J. Maude & Sons	wool	1830
Broad Carr Mill	Ely Wilkinson	wool	1832
Rawroyd Mill	?	wool	*c.* 1834
Old House Mill	?	wool	*c.* 1834

Mill	Occupants	Use	Date
KIRKBURTON PARISH			
Kirkburton Township, etc.		28 woollen mills	
Ing Nook Mill	?	wool	1780
Holmfirth Mill	J. & G. Gartside	wool	1786
Howley Mill	Ibberson & Co.	wool	1794
New Mill	Butterworth & Dickenson	wool	1795
Lower Battye Mill	?	wool	1796
Dogley Mill	Thos Kenyon	wool	1797
Bridge Mill	?	wool	1797
At Moorcroft	G. Moorhouse	wool	1797
At Linfit Lane	Ben Cocker	wool	1800
Holm Bridge Mill	J. Barber & Co.	wool	1800
At Jackson Bridge	M. & J. Moorhouse	wool	1801
At Cartworth	Butterworth & Co.	wool	1807
Ribblesden Mill	Moorhouse & Dickinson	wool	1808
At Green Lane Bottom	Hinchcliffe & Taylor	wool	1809
Dover Mill	Wimpenny & Woffenden	wool	1812
Linfit Mill	Ben Cocker & Co.	wool	1815
Low Mill	Messrs Farrar	wool	1817
At Cartworth	J. & G. Hinchcliffe	wool	1822
Dyson Mill	Roberts & Sandford	wool	1824
At Carnworth	Messrs Hinchcliffe & Horncastle	wool	1825
Cuttell Mill	Jos. Cuttell & Bros	wool	1825
At Green House	?	wool	1826
Burton Mill	?	wool	pre 1828
(?) At Woodbottom	Richard Brown	wool	1833
At Holmfirth	Eneas Walker	wool	1833

Mill	Occupants	Use	Date
KEIGHLEY PARISH			
Keighley Township		22 worsted mills	
At Sutton*	John Hartley	worsted	1791
Providence Mill	Jonas Sugden	worsted	1806
Aireworth Mill	Calvert & Clapham	worsted	1808
Brow End Mill	J. Brigg & Co.	worsted	1810
Acres Mill	Berry Smith	worsted	1810
East Greengate Mill	Iveson	worsted	1810
At North Beck	N. Constantine	worsted	1811
Hope Mill	John Mitchell	worsted	1812
Walk Mill	Craighs	worsted	1813
Stubbing House Mill	Calvert & Clapham	worsted	1813
Holme Mill	Thos Binns	worsted	1816
Hilltop Mill	Richard Robinson	worsted	1817
Greengate Mill	Wm Marriner	worsted	1818
Fleece Mill	Wm Sugden	worsted	1820
(?) Low Mill	J. & J. Craven (?)	worsted	1822
Castle Mill	Lund & Sugden	worsted	1822
Grove Mill	Robt Clough	worsted	1822
Damens Mill	Wm Sugden	worsted	1824
Ingrow Mills	John Clough	worsted	1826
At Keighley	Deane, Illingworth & Co.	worsted	1828
Springhead Mill	Hartley Meerall	worsted	1829
At Sutton*	James Berry	worsted	1829
North Beck Mill	Wm Lund	worsted	1829

* Sutton Township is not listed separately.

Mill	Occupants	Use	Date
At Denbigh Square	Wm Smith	worsted	1830
Wood Mill, Laycock	Thos Waterhouse	worsted	1831
Brandy Mill	Wm Robinson	worsted	1832
Prospect Mill	John Butterfield	worsted	1833
(?) Calversyke Mill	John Brigg & Co.	worsted	1835
KIRKHEATON PARISH			
Dalton		1 woollen mill	
Bradley Mills	Various	wool	1784
At Dalton	Kilner	wool	1798
Lepton		7 woollen mills	
At Lepton	Levi Sheard	wool	1798
At Kirkheaton	T. Atkinson	wool	1799
Fountain Mill	Roberts Bros	wool	1825
Dalton Lees Mill	?	wool	pre 1829
KILDWICK PARISH			
Kildwick		1 woollen mill*	
At Kildwick	Wm Smith	wool	1835

* This mill appears only in Rickard's first table.

Mill	Occupants	Use	Date
Linton Parish			
Grassington		1 worsted mill*	
Linton Mills	J. & W. Birkbeck	worsted	1804
Leeds Parish			
Leeds Township		42 woollen mills 7 worsted mills	
Park Mills	Benjamin Gott	wool	1792
St Peter's Mill	Reed & Newby	wool	1793
Nether Mills	Various	wool	pre 1794
Upper Albion St Mill	Briggs	wool	1806
Oatlands Mill	Jos. Oates	wool	1810
At Park Lane	?	wool	pre 1816
At School Close	Wm Hirst	wool	1816
Sheepscar Mill	Jno. Pearson	wool	1816
At Mill Garth	Jas Hargreaves	wool	1816
The Old Mill	?	wool	1817
Airedale Mills	John Howard	wool	1818
At Low Fold	?	wool	1820
At Sheepscar	Clapham & Dearlove	wool	1820
Carr Mills	Wm Avens & Co.	wool/worsted	1821
Grove Street Mill	Various	wool	1821
Buckton's Mill	Jos. Buckton	wool	1822

* Rickard's first table gives two worsted mills in Linton parish.

Mill	Occupants	Use	Date
At Bowman Lane	Mr Giles	wool	1822
Skinner Lane Mill	Jno. Pearson	wool	1822
At York Street	Thos Button & Sons	wool	1822
At Millgarth	Brown & Andrews	wool	1822
At Meadow Lane	Jon Wilks	wool	1823
Potterdale Mill	John Wood & Sons	wool	1823
Dean St Mill (?)	Thos George	worsted	1824
Camp Road Mill	J. P. Dickinson	wool	1824
Brunswick Mill	Binns & Sons	wool	1824
At Wellington St	Rider, Armytage & Co. (?)	wool	1826
Wellington Mill	Various	wool	1826
Perseverance Mill	York & Sheepshanks	wool	1826
Albion St Mill	Bruce, Dorrington & Walker (?)	wool	1826
Bank Top Mill	Various	wool	1826
Bagby Mill	Jas Brown	wool	1826
Elmwood Mills	?	wool	1827
Prospect Mill	W. & E. Wilkinson	worsted	1827
Low Close Mill	Halliley, Stanley & Co.	wool	1827
Carlton Mill	Holroyd & Wilson	wool	1828
At Aire Street	Thos Shann (?)	wool	1828
Monk Pit Mills	Thos Shann	wool	1829
Dock Mills	Hindes & Derham	worsted	1830
At Lady Lane	Sam. Warburton	worsted	1830
Harcourt Mill	Various	wool	1830
Perseverance Mill	Wm Kershaw & Co.	wool	1831
Low Fold Mill	R. Jackson	wool	1832
North Hall Mill	James Naylor	wool	1832
Victoria Mills	Peter Williams & Sons	wool	*c.* 1833

Mill	Occupants	Use	Date
At Lady Lane	Messrs Ripley & Ogle	wool	1833
Britannia Mills	O. Willans & Sons	wool	1833
Hope Mills	Dickinson & Barraclough	wool	1834
Headingley		4 woollen mills 1 worsted mill	
Burley Mill	T. W. Stansfield	wool/worsted	1799/1822
Savins Mill	Johnson, Hudson & Co.	wool	1799
Abbey Mills	O. Willans & Sons	wool	pre 1799
St Annes Mill	J. & E. Brook & Co.	wool	1799
Grove Mill	John Barker	wool	1819
Hunslet		5 woollen mills	
At Hunslet Lane	J. & E. Brookes	wool	1792
Larchfield Mill	Pim. Nevins	wool	1798
Sayner's Mill	Various	wool	1813
Waterloo Mill	Binns & Co.	wool	1816
Low Road Mill	Dearlove & Fenton (?)	wool	1821
Dow Bridge Mill	Da Gama & Co.	wool	1822
Balme Mill	Robt Walker (?)	wool	1828
Arridale Mill	P. Nevins	wool	1835
Holbeck		6 woollen mills	
At Holbeck	O. Willans	wool	1793
Holbeck Moor Mill	Ben Blackburn & Sons	wool	pre 1820
Union Mill	Ripley & Ogle	wool	pre 1820

Mill	Occupants	Use	Date
Beeston		2 woollen mills	
Millshaw Mills	J. Walker	wool	1785
Royds Mill	Wm Pickles	wool	*c.* 1825
Armley		4 woollen mills	
Armley Mills	Benjamin Gott	wool	1787
Winker Green Mills	W. Eyres	wool	1813
Antwerp Mill	Matthew Moss & Sons	wool	1829 (?)
Wortley		2 woollen mills	
Low Mill	T. Charlesworth	wool	1788
Upper Mill	Jas Bateson	wool	1797
Farnley		2 woollen mills	
Stonebridge Mills	Various	wool	1805
Butterbowl Mills	Swallow, Mason & Roberts	wool	1807
Upper Mill	John Rawson & Co.	wool	1826
Bramley		10 woollen mills	
Ross Mill	J. Hudson	wool	1790
Hough Mill	J. Haley	wool	1798
Cape Mill	Various	wool	1799
St Helens Mill	J. Pollard	wool	1802
New Mills	J. Haley	wool	1804
Bellisle Mill	Rogerson & Lord	wool	1807
Waterloo Mill	J. Haley	wool	1816

Mill	Occupants	Use	Date
Wellington Mill	Barker & Musgrave	wool	1823
At Hough End	John Lister	wool	*c.* 1830
(?) Swinnow Mill	Jos. Wood	wool	*c.* 1835
Stanningley		2 worsted mills*	
MIRFIELD PARISH			
Hopton Township		5 woollen mills	
Hopton Mill	Wm Stancliffe	wool	*c.* 1782
Low Mill	Nussey & Sykes	wool	1801
Hall Mills	S. Brook	wool	1801
At Ledgard Bridge	Jos. Wheatley	wool	1804
West Mills	John Tyas & Co.	wool	pre 1814
OTLEY PARISH			
Otley Township		2 woollen mills 2 worsted mills	
At Hell Hole Gill	Wm Clapham	worsted	1797
Poole Walk Mill	Sam. Burnley	wool	*c.* 1797
Otley Mill	Wm Ackroyd	worsted	1810
Silver Mill	J. Walker	worsted	1822
At Hell Hole Gill	Wm Audsley	wool	1833

* See also Calverley Parish — this township was divided between two parishes.

Mill	Occupants	Use	Date
Burley		2 worsted mills	
At Burley Woodhead	Ben Baldwin	worsted	1822
Hawksworth		3 worsted mills	
Hargreaves' Mill	Miss Hargreaves	worsted	*c.* 1828
Esholt		2 woollen mills 1 worsted mill	
Thompson's Mill		worsted	1803
(?) Beck Mill	?	wool	1816
?	Yewdalls & Robinson	wool	1835
Baildon		2 woollen mills 2 worsted mills	
Gill Mill	Denby & Sons	wool/worsted	1778/90
Baildon Mills	Craven & Brear	wool	1800
Baildon Mill	Baildon Joint Stock Co.	worsted	1835
PENISTONE PARISH			
Penistone Township		3 woollen mills 1 unoccupied mill	
Birchwood Mill	Jos. Booth	wool	*c.* 1835

Mill	Occupants	Use	Date
ROTHWELL PARISH			
Rothwell Township		1 woollen mill	
At Rothwell	James Arundel	wool	1806
SELBY PARISH			
Selby Township		1 woollen mill	
Selby Mill	J. Dobson & Son (?)	wool/worsted	1835
SKIPTON PARISH			
Skipton Township		1 worsted mill	
(?) Glazing Mill	Jas Wilson	worsted	1822
Embsay		1 worsted mill	
At Embsay	A. Bland & Co.	worsted	1835
SEDBERGH PARISH			
Sedbergh Township		1 woollen mill	
Farfield Mill	Jos. Dover	wool	1835
Dent		1 worsted mill	
Haverdale Mill	J. Knowles & Co.	worsted	1835

Mill	Occupants	Use	Date
SADDLEWORTH PARISH			
Saddleworth Parish		54 woollen mills 4 unoccupied mills	
At Quick	Mills & Co.	wool	1782
At Upper Mill	Shaw & Co.	wool	1783
(?) At Stonebreakes	G. & J. Knight	wool	1794
(?) At Dobcross	J. & S. Wrigley	wool	1795
At Heathfield	J. Platt & Son	wool	1800
At Upper Mill	J. & W. Buckley	wool	1800
Greenfield Mill	J. & J. Buckley	wool	1801
At Holly Grove	Wrigley Bros	wool	1801
Strims Mill	J. J. & N. Winterbottom	wool	1802
Oak View Mills	R. R. Whitehead & Bros	wool	1812
At Quick	Wm Kenworthy & Sons	wool	1823
At Husteads	Thos Mills	wool	1828
Andrew Mill	Winterbottom	wool	1829
Springhead Mills	Taylor & Gibson	wool	1831
Royal George Mills	Taylor & Gibson	wool	1833
Lumb Mill	James Lee	wool	1833
(?) Court Mill	G. & J. Broadbent	wool	*c.* 1835
(?) Nield Mill	Hy Fisher	wool	*c.* 1835
(?) Warrick Hill Footmill	Michael Horsfall	wool	*c.* 1835
(?) Gatehead Mill	J. Blackburn	wool	*c.* 1835
(?) Mitchell Mill	Jas Broadbent	wool	*c.* 1835
(?) Hull Mill	Jas Shaw	wool	*c.* 1835
(?) Thornes Clough Mill	Shaw & Wood	wool	*c.* 1835
(?) Moorcroft Wood Mill	J. Schofield	wool	*c.* 1835
(?) Bakestone Mill	John Bradbury	wool	*c.* 1835

Mill	Occupants	Use	Date
THORNHILL PARISH*			
Shitlington Township		1 woollen mill	
At Middletown	T. & J. Hebblethwaite	wool	*c.* 1830
Thornhill Township		1 woollen mill	
Howroyd Mill	Tolson, Bedford, Stead & Co.	wool	1802
Whitley Mill	?	wool	1803
WAKEFIELD PARISH			
Wakefield Township		5 woollen mills 5 worsted mills	
Thornes Lane Mill	J. Chambers	wool	1796
Silcoates Mill	Lumb	wool	1796
Marriott's Mill	Thos Marriott	worsted/wool	1808
Westgate End Mill	T. & J. Holdsworth	wool	1809
St John's Mill	James Teale (?)	worsted	1820
Tammy Hall	Thos Marriott	worsted	1820
Naylor's Mill	Naylor	wool	1821
Backlane Mill	Geo. Lee	worsted	1823

* There were three woollen mills recorded in Thornhill according to Rickards's first table.

Mill	Occupants	Use	Date
Alverthorpe		2 woollen mills 1 worsted mill	
Westgate Common Mill	J. Clarkson	wool	1796
Flanshaw Mill	Anne Ward	wool	1808
Oakes Mill	?	worsted	pre 1820
Park Mill	?	?	1832
Horbury		4 woollen mills 1 unoccupied mill	
Old Mill	Jos. Foster	wool/worsted	1791
Dudfleet Mill	John Race & Co.	wool	*c.* 1792
New Mill	Jos. Foster	worsted	1792

APPENDIX III

THE MEANING AND RELIABILITY OF INSURANCE VALUATIONS OF YORKSHIRE WOOL TEXTILE MILLS

The mass of information recorded in the policy registers and minute books of the eighteenth and nineteenth-century fire insurance offices has provided historians interested in capital formation with a new approach to their research and with a vast amount of data that is unavailable from other sources.[1] But the use of this data gives rise to many problems of interpretation and to suspicion about its accuracy. Part of the uncertainty arises as a result of the lack of information on the business practices of insuring against fire at the time but perhaps of more consequence is the question whether valuations for insurance purposes were true reflections of the total value of the capital stock of the insurer.[2]

By the last quarter of the eighteenth century the fire insurance business was well established in London and the provinces and was of a highly competitive nature. The offices established in the early decades of the century were meeting new competition from both London and local companies and through agents and local offices fire insurance facilities were available throughout the country. The business was however dominated by three London offices, The Sun, The Phoenix, and the Royal Exchange, which between them accounted for about two-thirds of the total value of property insured against fire in the country. The Sun Fire Office was almost as large as the Phoenix and Royal Exchange together.[3]

In 1782 the Government placed a duty on sums insured at a rate of one shilling and sixpence per £100. In due course this duty was gradually increased to three shillings per cent. From the recorded tax payments of the different companies the relative importance of

[1] The records of a number of the most important London fire insurance offices are deposited at the Guildhall Library. Records also survive for many provincial fire offices. Mr Edwin Green, of the City University has recently conducted a survey of them and is producing a catalogue.

[2] There has been some discussion about the meaning and accuracy of insurance valuations. See J. P. P. Higgins and S. Pollard, *Aspects of Capital Investment*, op. cit., pp. 89–119.

[3] See Table I.

the different offices and the amount of business they were carrying out can be calculated. It has been estimated that in 1783 property valued at £170,533,330 was insured, the total rising to £270 million in 1805, £305 million in 1810 and to over £500 million by 1831.[4]

In 1805, twenty-seven London and country fire offices were offering insurance against fire risk with another seven offices established in Scotland and Ireland. Table I shows the relative importance of the offices at that time. Only the London based offices are included as none of the sixteen country offices insured more than £4 million of property.

TABLE I

THE RELATIVE IMPORTANCE OF THE BUSINESS OF THE LONDON AND COUNTRY FIRE OFFICES, 1805

Fire Office	*Duty Paid (2/6d per £100)* £	s.	d.		*Value of Property insured with the Company (approx.)* £
Sun	92,845	3	11		74,276,170
Phoenix	59,162	3	10		47,329,760
Royal Exchange	44,095	13	3		35,276,530
Imperial	23,141	5	11		18,513,000
British	18,744	2	6		14,995,300
Globe	17,348	10	2		13,798,800
Westminster	12,277	13	3		9,822,100
Hand in Hand	12,120	11	3		9,696,450
London Assurance	6,120	3	5		4,896,000
Union	4,783	3	1		3,826,500
Albion	3,568	4	7		2,854,600
				TOTAL	£235,285,230
Country Offices	30,652	10	4½		24,522,000
				TOTAL	£259,707,230

Source: C. Walford, *The Insurance Cyclopaedia*, Vol. III (London, 1874), pp. 421–2, 484–5.

[4] C. Walford, *The Insurance Cyclopaedia* (London, 1874), pp. 421–2, 485.

Throughout the period from the 1780s to the 1840s the Sun Fire Office had the most business in Yorkshire. At the beginning of the nineteenth century it had agents at Sheffield, Doncaster, Leeds, Wakefield, York, Malton, Hull, and Skipton and sub-agents at Bradford, Pontefract, and Holmfirth. In the following years agencies were established in a number of other towns including Whitby, Halifax, and Richmond.[5] Its strongest competitor was probably the Royal Exchange. In 1800 the Sun office had current policies for over one hundred Yorkshire wool textile mills and the Royal Exchange for about eighty. The records of the latter office do not permit an analysis of its later business but the Sun maintained its predominance until the second decade of the nineteenth century when it began to meet severe competition from local offices to the extent that in the 1830s it was only insuring about 20 per cent of the woollen and worsted mills in the county.[6] Policies for mills did not necessarily cover all their property. It was quite common for the risk to be distributed between various companies either on the basis of a proportion of the value of each item insured or through different items insured in different policies. Nor did all mills insure all or part of their property. Some mill owners only covered those items which they considered most susceptible to risk; others accepted the whole risk themselves, sometimes to their cost as newspaper reports bear witness.[7]

It was not necessary for all the capital stock of a manufacturer to be insured. Insurance was taken out only on that property that could be destroyed by fire, that is on the building, gearing, machinery, utensils and stock. There was little point in insuring against fire risk such capital assets as dams, reservoirs and cuttings, perimeter walls and approach drives. For that capital which was insured, however, the accuracy and completeness of insurance valuations must be considered. Why was insurance obtained? What was a manufacturer or mill owner actually insuring for and against?

The immediate answer to these questions might be that the insurer was covering the cost of replacing or restoring his property

[5] See Sun Fire Office Policy Registers and Country Department Minute Books; also advertisements in Yorkshire newspapers, e.g. *Leeds Mercury*, 27 June 1807.

[6] About 110 Yorkshire woollen and worsted mills were wholly or partly insured by the Sun Fire Office in 1835. The Leeds and Yorkshire Fire Office was the main local competitor.

[7] Reports of mill fires in the Leeds newspapers of the late eighteenth and early nineteenth century often include details of the insurance coverage. See, for example, *Leeds Mercury*, 5 December 1829 and 9 January 1830.

should it be destroyed or damaged by fire. In other words, the insurer would have insured his property, or the property for which he was responsible, for the amount it would have cost him to restore it to the exact state that it was in immediately before the fire, thus allowing for depreciation from the original cost of the building or other capital.

On the other hand, the insurer might have been covering his capital up to the amount that he would expect to receive for it should he have wanted to dispose of it. Thus, in this case, one might expect a high valuation on buildings in times of good business conditions and prospects and a low valuation in poor business conditions; even though in the latter case, the replacement cost might have been more than the plant would have fetched if sold. Should, however, property have been insured for more than its market value there might have been much to be gained, by an unscrupulous owner, in deliberately setting fire to property and claiming the insurance money rather than selling it. Indeed later in the century it was suggested at a meeting of the Statistical Society that, if there were no fire insurance, the number of fires occurring would be reduced considerably.[8]

Although the insurance companies were well aware of this risk, it appears that they would normally allow insurance cover up to the amount that it would cost to rebuild or reinstate property to its condition previous to its being destroyed or damaged. A valuation of the property was not normally made by an insurance company when a policy was issued although, with industrial premises, quite stringent checks were made on the fire hazard in the property. This is well illustrated by the care the Sun Fire office took to ascertain what processes were being carried out in mills and what preventive measures there were to stop fire spreading. The Sun's agents and inspectors were regularly required to visit and examine proposals for insurance and failures to observe stipulations in policies on many occasions often resulted in policies being cancelled and losses not paid.[9]

Similar care is shown by the correspondence between head office and the regional agents of the Leeds and Yorkshire Fire Office in the 1820s. The directors at Leeds were continually communicating with the company's various agents telling them to be on the look-out for

[8] This comment was made during the discussion following a paper delivered by Cornelius Walford. See *Journal of the Statistical Society*, 1877, pp. 347–432.

[9] There are many examples in the Committee Minute Books of the Sun Fire Office.

what they called, 'hazards'. Some of the correspondence will illustrate this point. With reference to one policy the directors wrote to Mr J. C. Laycock, their Huddersfield agent, about a mill belonging to a Mr Sykes:

. . . If the dryhouse in question is so constructed as occasionally to heat the perforated flooring to a red heat the creels used in such a dryhouse ought certainly not to be of wood, or we may be liable to frequent returns of the same accidents and find the whole of Mr. Sykes' insurance a losing transaction. Mr. Sykes ought certainly to make some arrangement for lessening the danger in future, the necessity of which you must press upon him.[10]

A few weeks later the directors wrote to the Dewsbury agent concerning another danger of fire in mill premises:

. . . the danger from the ignition of waste in woollen mills, particularly those where fish oil is used, is very great . . . A fire-proof mill caught fire on Friday last in this town from neglected waste and, there being a communication from room to room, great loss was sustained although the building was all stone and iron.[11]

Occasionally the Head Office was unwilling to leave the responsibility of insuring hazardous or large risks to their local agent. In these cases they would send an inspector to examine the property. This was the case when Messrs Chippendale and Company applied to the Leeds and Yorkshire Office for insurance on their flax mill at West End, Fewston. The Office secretary wrote to the agent dealing with the policy, Mr S. B. Hall of Skipton:

. . . in consequence of the large amount offered, they (the directors) resolved upon having the premises viewed by our inspector of property, Mr. B. Hill, who will ride over to West House for that purpose on Friday morning next.[12]

The Office accepted the business at West House, which incidentally had previously been in the hands of the Sun Fire Office,[13] but in some cases, presumably after inspection, refused to accept

[10] Leeds and Yorkshire Fire Office, Secretary's Book, no. 1, 3 November 1824.
[11] Ibid., 1 December 1824. Letter from the Secretary to Matthew Hale, the Dewsbury Agent. (The mill referred to was probably Aire Dale Woollen Mill at Leeds, the insurance loss for which was sustained by the Norwich Union Fire Insurance Society. Norwich Union Fire Insurance Society Minute Book, no. 2. Entries for 6 December 1824 and 20 December 1824.)
[12] Ibid., 1 December 1824.
[13] See Sun C.R. 102/876274–5/1813 and 151/1030944/1824. These policies show that from 1824 insurance cover of West House Mill was arranged jointly with the Sun and Leeds and Yorkshire Offices.

the risk. Such was the case for Larchfield Mill in Hunslet in December 1824.[14]

The directors of the Leeds and Yorkshire Office were continually reviewing their mill risks and issuing fresh instructions to their agents. In June 1825 the agents were informed:

It is the intention of the Directors to go through the whole of our woollen mill risks and to require premiums which may bear some proportion to the actual risk in this kind of property; it being ascertained that the danger in all coloured woollen mills which arises from any neglect of the waste or fuel from the machines is very great indeed . . .[15]

This kind of review was a frequent exercise for all offices. The huge increase in industrial proposals and the growing complexity of industrial processes throughout the period were a continual and severe problem for the fire office directors. The London offices often found it difficult to understand industrial changes and to know how to rate them. Directors and inspectors were frequently despatched to obtain first-hand knowledge. The Sun Fire Office, along with the Phoenix and Royal Exchange offices, at times suspended accepting new mill risks whilst they reviewed their business and their rates. Some companies refused outright to accept risks on textile mills. The Secretary of the Leeds and Yorkshire Office communicated with their Bradford agent in 1824 that: '. . . the Agent for the Suffolk in this town, Mr. Robert Oldman, called two days ago and informed us his office were in the intention of declining all mill risks.'[16] In 1827 the Directors of the Norwich Union Fire Insurance Society decided to decline and discontinue all woollen mill risks, thus foregoing a considerable amount of business. Two years later there was only one woollen mill risk in the Leeds agency of the Company.[17]

That the insurance companies had reason to be concerned with mill risks is well illustrated by their losses. Between 1789 and 1796 the three main companies sustained losses of £255,000 on cotton, corn and other mill risks. Between 1815 and 1824 the Royal

[14] L. and Y. Secretary's Book, no. 1, 15 December 1824.
Gentlemen, I think it is my duty to state to you without delay that the Directors, having taken into consideration your proposed insurance deem the risk too imminent to be taken by a newly established office and beg respectfully to decline fixing any premium of insurance thereon, signed Jon. Wilks, Secretary.

[15] Ibid., 17 June 1825.

[16] Ibid., 5 November 1824.

[17] Norwich Union Fire Insurance Society Minute Book, no. 2. Entries for 24 December 1827 and 7 December 1829.

Exchange office received premiums of £6,787 on woollen mill risks and paid losses of £6,646 and between 1818 and 1825 the Sun received premiums of £5,378 and paid losses of £5,019.[18] The surpluses were hardly sufficient to meet their expenses and agent's commission.

TABLE II

LOSSES ON MILL RISKS INCURRED BY THE SUN, ROYAL EXCHANGE AND PHOENIX FIRE OFFICES, 1789–96

Company	*Losses on*			
	Cotton Mills £	*Corn Mills* £	*Other Mills* £	*TOTAL* £
Sun	76,000	33,000	15,000	124,000
Royal Exchange	19,000	25,000	14,000	58,000
Phoenix	40,000	20,000	13,000	73,000
TOTALS	£135,000	£78,000	£42,000	£255,000

Source: Sun Fire Office, Committee of Management, Vol. 15, p. 200.

Thus, there was good reason for the fire offices to keep a careful check on their mill risks. But this check did not normally extend to the value proposed. There was, however, no point in a manufacturer or mill owner over insuring his property as when a loss occurred the offices appear to have been very careful to pay out no more than the actual damage sustained. Thus for example, even if a mill were to be insured for a fixed sum and destroyed by fire, the insurance company would not automatically pay out that sum but would have their own valuers, and in case of dispute, independent valuers, calculate the loss and would pay out the actual sum involved up to the total amount insured. The actual amount to be paid was often the cause for dispute but insurance offices allowed for the independent arbitration of losses should they be unable to resolve the sum themselves. The importance of arbitration was recorded by one nineteenth-century writer as follows:

In the event of dispute, or impossibility of agreement, between the claimant and the office, the matter may probably, under the conditions of the policy, be capable of being referred to arbitration, or it may be compulsory that

[18] See Table II and Sun Fire Office, Book of Annual Accounts, 1790–1887.

it be so referred in view of ascertaining the actual sum at which the loss is to be adjusted. The arbitration clause differs in the policies of the different companies; and even in the policy of the same company at different periods of time.[19]

Companies realized that prolonged disputes which came to the notice of the public were likely to do their business much harm and were thus often more than fair in paying for losses. Note the extract from a letter to one of the Leeds and Yorkshire agents in 1824 concerning the payment of a claim:

. . . Some of the Directors, whom I have spoke to, consider that the affair is of too trifling a character to become the object of a newspaper paragraph . . .[20]

The care taken in assessing a loss is well illustrated by the calculations for the damage caused by a fire at Gott's mill at Bean Ing, Leeds in 1799. The Royal Exchange and Sun offices paid a total of £11,946 after an assessment by a few local valuers, who included the millwrights John Jubb and John Sutcliffe. An even more detailed valuation survives amongst papers appertaining to Gott's Armley Mill. It accounts for all the materials used in the mill construction, item by item.

TABLE III

PARTICULARS OF THE LOSS BY FIRE AT BEAN ING NEAR LEEDS ON SUNDAY, THE 11TH AUGUST 1799, THE PROPERTY OF MESSRS WORMALDS AND GOTT — INSURED IN THE SUN AND ROYAL EXCHANGE OFFICES IN THE SAME PROPORTIONS

Losses Ascertain on the Risks Below				*(Total) Sums Insured in the Sun and Royal Exchange Offices*	*Joint Loss to Both Offices*		
	£	s.	d.	£	£	s.	d.
On the buildings, mill, etc.	3,264	17	3½	3,000	3,000	0	0
On the millwright work and going gears	1,953	10	6	1,000	1,000	0	0
On the machinery and moveable utensils	3,899	5	6	3,000	3,000	0	0
On the engine house	223	6	3	400	223	6	3
On the engine	285	0	0	1,200	285	0	0

[19] Walford, op. cit., III, 518.
[20] L. and Y. Secretary's Book, no. 1, 29 October 1824.

TABLE III continued

Losses Ascertain on the Risks Below				(Total) Sums Insured in the Sun and Royal Exchange Offices	Joint Loss to Both Offices		
	£	s.	d.	£	£	s.	d.
On the stock in the mill	3,920	12	4½	4,000	3,920	12	4½
Weaving shops and warehouse west side of yard		—		200		—	
Stock and utensils therein	48	0	0	300	48	0	0
Woollen drying house and warehouses connecting		—		300		—	
Stock therein	29	15	0	300	29	15	0
Workshops and hot pressing house	3	14	0	200	3	14	0
Stock and utensils therein	16	11	0	2,000	16	11	0
Shops, wool warehouse, etc., east side of yard	19	11	11	200	19	11	11
Stock and utensils therein	277	18	0	2,000	277	18	0
	13,924	1	10	18,100	11,824	8	6
Cash paid for Extinguishing the Fire	89	8	0½				
Inholders notes	135	1	5				
	224	9	5½	the offices allow ⅔ of it. viz.	149	12	11
To 4 valuers viz. Jubb, Briggs, Sutcliffe and Croft 2 guineas each					8	8	0
					11,982	9	5
Deduct for error in carrying moveable utensils (viz. 222 wool sheets) to Stock					36	1	6
				TOTAL	£11,946	7	11
				Sun Fire Office	5,973	4	0
				Royal Exchange Office	5,973	3	11
					£11,946	7	11

Source: Gott MSS, Paper no. 69 reproduced in Crump, *The Leeds Woollen Industry*, p. 220.

TABLE IV

VALUATION OF DAMAGE AND LOSS SUSTAINED BY FIRE AT ARMLEY MILLS. NOVEMBER 20TH, 1805, BELONGING TO BENJAMIN GOTT, ESQ.

		£	s.	d.
250 Roods 5 yds of strong stone wall	40/–	501	8	0
511¾ yds of strong flagging	4/6	115	2	10½
6,229 feet of doorsteads, windowsteads, etc.	10	259	10	10
774 yds of slating	2/9	106	8	6
56½ yds of ridge stones	1/4	3	15	4
45 yds of chimney pipes	4/–	9	0	0
3 ranges, hearths, jambs and mantles	30/–	4	10	0
Stonework damaged in wheelraces	—	85	10	6
66 squares 46 feet of roofing	90/–	298	1	10
99 squares 75 feet naked floor	80/–	399	0	0
1,023¾ yds 1¼ ins. floor boards	4/9	243	2	9½
270 feet skylight wood, lead and glass	2/6	33	15	0
36 feet doorstead 6 × 3	8	1	4	0
10¾ yds of gutter boards	4/6	2	6	1½
97 feet of wall pipes	1/–	4	17	0
301 feet of moulded spouts	1/6	22	11	6
426 feet of strong batted doors	1/2	24	17	0
1,022 feet gutted window and glass	1/8	85	3	4
648 feet leaded windows and iron bars	10	27	0	0
4 staircases, hand rails and ceilings		24	12	0
2,182½ feet 3 inch planks and joints	1/6	163	13	9
bands, crooks, locks etc. for 12 doors	10/–	6	0	0
540 feet of studd and board ceiling	7	15	15	0
490 feet cube of lintles, band, timber and props	3½	77	11	8
46 stone of lead	6/6	14	19	0
60 sprout irons	1/–	3	0	0
2 large stone cisterns, locks and pipes	—	6	0	0
Wood partitions, fixed cupboards and guard bed in mill house		31	4	6
To painting windows, doors and spouts		16	12	6
		£2,586	13	0½
Deduct for old stones, small quantity of wood, lead and iron belonging to roof		87	15	0
		£2,498	18	0½

Source: Gott MSS, Paper 119.

Thus all this suggests that there was little reason for mill owners to over insure their property. There is, however, some evidence of a greater incidence of fires in bad business periods. Walford outlined the problems involved here:

One of the most important, yet one of the most difficult, duties incident to the conduct of the business of fire insurance is the adjustment of claims following upon losses by fire. The popular view is always in favour of 'liberality' on the part of the office. Practical experience shows that liberality is productive of abuses; in fact leads up to the creation of claims — and so changes the base of the business; for to the element of accident becomes superadded the element of design. The former is usually regarded as being in some sort within the range of average. The latter known to insurance officials as the 'moral hazard' is probably affected by fluctuations in trade — for in 'bad times' fires do seem to increase; but it is mostly arbitrary, depending perhaps mainly on the supposed chance of detection.[21]

Besides the deliberate setting fire to buildings of which no doubt there were instances, but which were always in danger of being detected, it was not difficult for manufacturers to increase the fire risk in their mill. The bad maintenance of machinery, the leaving of quantities of waste materials and a slackening of security procedure could all have heightened fire risk and perhaps caused fire, without the direct action of the manufacturer, although perhaps with the intent. Fires caused through these actions were, of course, far more difficult to trace and even more difficult to prove. A dispute between the Leeds and Yorkshire Office and a mill owner at Huddersfield arose through doubt as to the cause of the fire. The Secretary wrote concerning the fire:

I do not see a possibility of its having occurred in the manner you surmise, for wool is not an article which could be ignited so as to flame up, through a perforated iron flooring and set fire to creels placed on such a perforated floor — I conjecture then it has occurred through some malicious intent or otherwise from gross carelessness and neglect of Mr. Sykes' servant, most probably from the former . . .[22]

The incidence of fraud cannot have been too considerable in view of the efforts of the insurers. Even disregarding malicious intent, however, one might suggest there was a likelihood of more fires in periods of bad business through the inability or unwillingness of manufacturers to maintain equipment, make good depreciation and carry out repairs.

In times of falling prices it may have been possible for property to have been unintentionally over-insured. However, in view of the

[21] Walford, op. cit., III, 517.
[22] L. and Y. Secretary's Book, no. 1, 29 October 1824.

frequency with which policies were reviewed and readjusted it is unlikely that any temporary over-valuation could have been considerable.

The more difficult question concerns whether there was a tendency for property to be undervalued for insurance purposes. To what extent were the insurance values a true reflection of replacement cost? Is it possible that many manufacturers were under-insured either intentionally or unintentionally? If it were common for only part of the risk to be insured, insurance values would be of little use for estimating fixed capital values unless there was some constant proportion of undervaluation discernible.

Recent work on insurance records has led to varying conclusions about undervaluation. Dr S. D. Chapman 'surmised that insurance policies approached a conservative estimate' in the cotton industry but Dr J. Butt has found a 'systematic bias' to undervaluation in some Scottish mills.[23]

Unintentional inaccuracy in valuation was possible. When insuring his property for the first time, unless it had just been built and he knew the cost of its construction, the manufacturer might have been at a loss to decide the total risk to insure against. Perhaps in some cases he might have called in a valuer and he could also have got some advice from the insurance agent, but even so the accuracy of the decided valuation might not have been too good. However if the manufacturer wished to fully insure his property it must be assumed that he did his best to make an accurate assessment of its value and that inaccuracy in the figures would have been small.

Unintentional undervaluation might also have occurred if a manufacturer was slow in increasing the amount of his insurance as he continued his building or installation of machinery. If, for example, he was in the habit of reconsidering his insurance yearly, at the time of the annual renewal of the policy, as was often the case, any additions to his capital stock in the previous twelve months would not be accounted for. Although this causes no problems for our purposes it might well give rise to some of the contemporary statements one finds about property having been under-insured at the time of a fire. Perhaps an interesting example of this possibility is afforded by a fire at Marshall's no. 2 mill building in 1796, when the building and its contents were totally destroyed.[24] Only half the

[23] Crouzet, *Capital Formation in the Industrial Revolution*, op. cit., pp. 66–7.
[24] Rimmer, op. cit., p. 45; *Leeds Intelligencer*, 15 February 1796, 22 February 1796.

value of the property was covered by insurance about £5,000 out of a total of £10,000. The mill was very new. It only started working in September 1795 and there were no more than 1,200 spindles in operation at the end of 1795. The Leeds paper records that the mill was only partly filled with machinery.[25] In January 1795 Marshall and Benyon insured the only partly constructed building and were possibly about to reformulate their insurance at the time of the fire.[26] When the mill was rebuilt the new building and its contents were insured for £9,600 which was probably a fairly realistic figure in view of the previous loss of £10,000 and the mill having been rebuilt to the same specifications.

Unintentional undervaluation of capital could also have arisen through a failure to take into account rising prices. It is possible that mill occupiers were not always aware of the true replacement cost of their property. In times of rapidly rising prices, they may have been unaware that they had become under-insured. This factor could have given rise to inaccuracies in the insurance valuations but rising prices would be somewhat offset by the depreciation on the property and, in any case, the insurance records show that most mill owners reviewed their policies very regularly, often once a year or more. The insurance companies, moreover, normally insisted that all policies had to be reformulated every seven years. Thus although it would seem that a certain amount of undervaluation could have arisen through these causes, it is unlikely to have been very significant.

There were a number of factors that could have led to the insurance of only part of a risk. Most of the fire offices, if not all, had an upper limit for what they would insure on any one risk. This limit varied from company to company and from time to time. The Leeds and Yorkshire had a maximum limit of £5,000 on any mill or any one special risk in 1825.[27] The Globe Insurance Company had the same limit on mills and manufactories in 1803.[28] The Anchor Fire Office, The Norwich Union Society, The Newcastle upon Tyne Fire Office, and the Albion Company had various limits.[29] Even the major London offices had standard limits which could only be exceeded by the special permission of the directors.

[25] *Leeds Intelligencer*, 22 February 1796.
[26] Sun C.R. 5/636251/1795.
[27] L. and Y. Secretary's Book, no. 1, 13 August 1825.
[28] Globe Insurance Office, Committee Minutes, Vol 1, 1803, p. 35, 2 June 1803 at the Guildhall Library, City of London.
[29] Prospectuses of the offices at the Northumberland County Record Office.

The number of risks that these limits would have affected was very small and, in any case, the risks could have been divided between two or more different offices so the limit need not necessarily have restricted the amount of insurance cover available nor have led to under insurance.

Fire offices required sums insured in other offices to be declared and these sums are normally recorded in the policy registers. However there are instances of multiple insurances not being recorded either because they were not declared or, more likely, because the office clerks failed to note them. A failure to declare insurance in another office could invalidate a policy.

Premiums may at times have been a serious obstacle. Occasionally they were made very high when offices were concerned about the level of their losses. The premiums paid on mill policies varied according to the construction, safety precautions, methods of heating and lighting and use of the premises. The rates fluctuated wildly and appeared to have differed quite considerably at times between different companies. The presence of naked lights or open fires in a mill could add one shilling or two shillings per £100 to the premium as could, for example, connecting doors between two separate but attached buildings. The different processes carried out often required different rates of premium. The amount paid on a mill building appears to have varied from as little as five shillings per £100 value to thirty shillings per £100 value for different buildings at different dates through different companies. The Leeds and Yorkshire Office was charging between ten shillings and fifteen shillings per £100 in 1824 and 1825. They charged Jno. and Geo. Shaw of Halifax eleven shillings per £100 for their woollen mill in 1824, which, they said, to be more favourable than the ten shillings which had been offered by the Hope Fire Office 'in consequence of the returns'.[30] A certain amount of barter over premiums appears to have taken place, in spite of the apparent dislike of it by the insurance companies as is well illustrated by a letter from the Leeds and Yorkshire Office to their Bradford agent:

> . . . You may now inform him (Mr. J. G. Horsfall) that we are not at all anxious to have his mill even at 16 shillings and that we are above entering into that system which Mr. Swann deems so great an adept.[31]

[30] L. and Y. Secretary's Book, no. 1, 3 October 1824. Letter from Secretary to Mr Simpson Baines, Halifax agent.

[31] Ibid., 23 December 1824.

Mr Swann was presumably the agent of another office.

In 1825 the Leeds and Yorkshire charged Claytons of Settle twelve shillings for their smaller mill building and fifteen shillings for the larger, reduced the premium on Mr Gill's Mill near Bradford from eight shillings to seven shillings in view of the installation of gas, charged sixteen shillings on the machinery at Jas. Holdforth's Bank Low Mills near Leeds and charged twelve shillings on Messrs J. Carter & Co.'s Grove Woollen Mill at Halifax.[32] Gott was paying eleven shillings on the main mill at Bean Ing in the mid 1820s and as much as eighteen shillings on a warehouse and teazle drying room.[33] The total premium on his property insured with the Sun Office for £17,700 amounted to £67 10*s.* 3*d.* with duty amounting to an extra £26 11*s.* 0*d.* As there was also a total of £26,700 insured with the Royal Exchange, Imperial and Phoenix Offices, Gott was probably paying over £250 per annum in insurance premiums and duty, not a small sum. He was having to pay over £100 as early as 1797.[34] The premiums seem high especially when compared with the rate of one shilling and sixpence for an ordinary slated roof dwelling house in 1827. However the risk involved was very high and the premiums clearly reflected the risk. One half to one per cent of total value was not considerable when compared with the possibility of total loss.

The tax on insured value which rose from one shilling and sixpence per cent to three shillings per cent during the period may have affected insurance on certain types of property. The insurance companies argued very strongly that this would be the case each time the Government proposed to increase the tax. For dwelling houses the tax doubled or even trebled the cost of insurance but on industrial property with higher premium rates the proportional effect was smaller. Where the tax did have an impact it may well have been through property ceasing to be insured rather than by it being reduced in insured value. If a manufacturer went to the trouble to arrange insurance it seems possible that he would do it for an adequate amount unless there was some reason for only insuring part of the risk. But there may have been good reasons. One possibility is that the insurance was taken out to cover that amount of money owed to creditors, perhaps, to pay back those

[32] Ibid., Entries for 24 January 1825, 5 October 1825, 14 October 1825, 18 October 1825.
[33] Sun C.R. 158/1055369/1827.
[34] Sun C.R. 20/667675/1797.

persons who had lent money for the building of the mill. It is possible that in the original agreements for loans a requirement for insuring the security was laid down, just as some landlords required their tenants to insure their mills (through their tenancy agreements).[35] If this, however, were the case one would expect to find amongst the insurance policies examples of very low insurance cover; examples which would stand out as being blatant undervaluations. Moreover, a requirement to insure property to cover the money owed to creditors did not preclude the manufacturer from insuring against his own loss. Although in isolated cases mills might have been under-insured for this reason all the evidence suggests that the instances were very few and far between.[36]

There was, however, a more important reason for possible undervaluation. In present day insurance business an 'average clause' is inserted in policies. The average clause was described by Walford:

> Apportionment of contributive liability under policy subject to average will require from the insured a valuation of the entire property under the protection of the insured at the time of the loss, and gives him only such proportion of the loss as this value may bear to the insurance, specific or in the aggregate, as the clause may read: thus making him co-insurer for such excess of value as there may be beyond the insurance; and requiring him to contribute, as co-insurer, in the same proportions.[37]

Thus, under the 'average clause' the amount of the damage to be paid for would depend upon the proportion of the total value insured. That is, if, for example, a premium was paid on an insurance valuation of £2,000 but this was only half the total value of the property, then if only half the property was destroyed only £1,000 would be paid out.

The inclusion of an 'average clause' possibly dates back to the early days of insurance for mercantile policies but was only introduced at a comparatively late date for the insurance of property against fire.[38] Although on the Continent in the eighteenth century payments were made on a pro rata basis according to the relation between the value of the property and the amount insured, in Great Britain the insurance companies, instead, worked on the basis of limiting insurance to a given sum and would pay losses up to that sum. The introduction of an average clause in fire insurance

[35] See Dartmouth Estate, *Terriers*.

[36] There are many instances in the Sun Fire Office policy registers of both owners and tenants of mills having insurance policies.

[37] Walford, op. cit., III, 521.

[38] Ibid., I, 224–32.

was delayed by the difficulties created by the duties imposed on insurance, and it was not until 1828 that a move was made to allow for them. A new Stamp Act contained the following proviso:

It is hereby declared and agreed, that in the case of the property belonging to the insured in all the buildings places or limits herein described, shall at the breaking out of any fire or fires, be collectively of greater value than the sum insured then the Company shall pay and make good to the assured such a proportion only of the loss or damage as the sum insured shall bear to the whole value of the property aforesaid, at the time such fire or fires shall first happen . . .[39]

The Sun Fire Office directors regularly discussed using the 'average clause' and used it in some warehouse policies. After 1811 some of their printed policies included the clause but it does not appear to have been used for buildings and machinery until later in the century. The average clause was strange to the Norwich Union Fire Office in 1821. The following entry was made in their Minute Book:

Read a letter from Mr. Dawson dated the 18th inst. handing 30 orders for new policies, three of which to the amount of £25,000 are floating risks, proposed to be affected with the average clause.

Ordered — That the Secretary address Mr. Dawson for information generally as to the nature of these risks and the extent to which insurances of this description are affected in the town of Liverpool and what may be expected to be done with this Society and particularly what amount of insurances may possibly centre in one stack of warehouses and whether any precaution can be devised by which this amount can be kept within any definite limit . . .[40]

However, insurance companies did take certain measures to protect themselves. They insisted that all risks had to be itemized as far as possible and insured separately so that damage could be identified and paid for item by item. Even so the system still gave rise to difficulties. Manufacturers and mill owners realized that, particularly with fireproofed buildings of solid construction, the chances of a mill being completely razed to the ground were very remote even though the risk of the contents being destroyed or the interior gutted was fairly high. Rather than pay a premium on the full value of the mill and its contents they would try to insure only that amount that they considered was most likely to be destroyed in a fire. Thus, although the insurer would take into account, when calculating the premium, the chances of the property being partially

[39] 9 Geo. IV c. 14, Quoted by Walford, op. cit., I, 232–3.
[40] Norwich Union Fire Insurance Society Minute Book, no. 2, p. 27.

destroyed, the assured was also sometimes allowing for this when taking out his policy, much to the disadvantage of the insurance company.

This, therefore, might have been a valid reason for under-insurance. There is perhaps one example of it, either intentional or unintentional, in the insurance at Bean Ing in 1799. All the machinery and movable utensils of the mill were destroyed. The loss was calculated at almost £3,900 but the total insurance on the machinery and utensils amounted to only £3,000, just over three-quarters of the total value. Instead, however, of paying out only three-quarters of the loss the Sun and Royal Exchange Offices paid the full £3,000. This was probably not deliberate under-insurance but more an oversight and a failure to alter policies as new machinery was fitted in the mill but, in any case, the effect was very much the same.[41]

There is no denying that insurance companies were very much aware of the means of obtaining what amounted to cheaper insurance cover, and they did take certain steps to prevent it. Although there is no evidence that they accurately valued property for insurance they did require a detailed description and plans of industrial premises, together with details of construction, heating arrangements and so on. The underwriter could thus make some estimate of the likely value of the property and any gross under-valuation would be evident to him. An example of this occurred in the Leeds and Yorkshire Office in 1828. It appears that the Office was asked to insure a mill near Oldham but having seen the plan and particulars the secretary wrote to the local agent:

> . . . This amount, if one may judge by the size of the mill, will not be one tenth of the real value and therefore, if a fire were to happen, in the Switch and Carding room for instance, we might suffer a loss equal to the whole amount insured and be receiving only one tenth of the proper premium.[42]

There is some suggestion also from the Sun Registers that the Sun Fire Office were, likewise, very alert to the problem. Many policies are cancelled in the register with the words 'Refused' and an examination of some of these suggests that a possible reason may have been that the sum insured was not sufficient. In more than one case the insurance was accepted a few days later for a greater amount. Even so, however, there might well have been some under-valuation in spite of these precautions. It is unlikely that it would

[41] This may have been the case at Marshall's flax mill at Leeds in 1796. See above.
[42] L. and Y. Secretary's Book, no. 1, 29 August 1828.

have been considerable in proportionate terms as the greater it was the more noticeable and traceable it would have become. It, moreover, seems rather doubtful, in view of the high fire risk in mills, the probable shortage of ready money for rebuilding after a fire and the uncertainty about the course a fire would take on mill premises, that many mill owners would have been willing to accept even part of the risk of a fire.

At least one fire office, however, expected the owner of the property to accept some of the risk. The Essex and Suffolk Equitable Insurance Society in its earlier years at the beginning of the nineteenth century discouraged full insurance on the grounds that owners of property would take care to avoid fire if that property were not fully covered by insurance. In 1806 the Secretary of the Society wrote to an Agent:

> It is not usual nor fair for any person to insure buildings to the full value — two thirds or three fourths is a fair value; the same of stock, household goods etc.[43]

This attitude seems to have been exceptional and was probably the result of a small, new office being extra careful.

The only way of deciding whether, in fact, some undervaluation did take place is to compare insurance values with other valuations and costs, and also to rely on contemporary comment after fires, as to the extent to which mills were covered by insurance. The newspaper columns provide a certain amount of useful evidence. Mill fires in the Leeds area were normally reported in the *Mercury* and the *Intelligencer*. Thus in December 1829 there was a disastrous fire at Calverley Mills near Leeds that was reported in the *Leeds Mercury* as follows:

> Fire at Calverley Mills: On Wednesday night last (2/12/1829) about half past ten o'clock the flames were observed to issue from the windows in the scribbling mill in the occupation of Mr. William Greenwood of Calverley . . . fire engines called . . . found impossible to save any part of the scribbling mill which is totally destroyed . . . damage £3,000 . . . The building, water-wheels and fulling stocks are insured in the Norwich Union Office for £1,800. The machinery and stock are insured in the North British Office for £1,650. The mill which burnt down about six years ago is the property of Thomas Thornhill, Esq., who has had 3 mills burnt within the last 12 months.[44]

[43] B. Drew, *The Fire Office, being the History of the Essex and Suffolk Equitable Insurance Society Limited, 1802–52* (1952), pp. 22–3.

[44] *Leeds Mercury*, 5 December 1829.

This report suggests the damage was fully covered by the insurance. It is interesting that Greenwood may have had some trouble re-insuring his premises after the mill was rebuilt as it was with the Sun Fire Office and not the Norwich Union that he took out a policy in 1830.[45]

In January 1830 the reports of two mill fires appeared in the Leeds newspaper. At one, 'the very extensive cotton and woollen factory of Mr. James Greenwood in Wheatley', the paper recorded that although the property was insured by the Manchester Fire Office it was 'not to its full value'.[46] In the other, however, at the woollen mill of Messrs Barker and Musgrave at Bramley where the damage supposedly exceeded £4,000, the paper recorded 'we are happy to hear that insurance has been effected in the Sun and Protector Fire Offices' and the Sun records indeed show that in the previous October a risk of £3,000 was insured with each of the 'Sun' and 'Protector' offices. New policies were issued a few weeks after the fire but only for £700 suggesting that was the value of the property surviving the fire and a rebuilt and equipped mill was insured again with the Sun and Protector Offices the following August.[47]

In the first decade of the century, for 1807, a year selected at random, the *Leeds Mercury* records two mill fires. The first in September was at Titley, Tatham and Walker's Flax Mill when a fire caused by friction of machinery destroyed the mill and its contents. After this fire the paper stated: 'Fortunately the property was insured to almost the full amount of the damage sustained.'[48]

The second was at Isaac Crowther's scribbling Mill at Morley where two small boys started a small fire. Here the paper records that insurance with the Sun Fire Office covered the damage.[49]

The many other newspaper accounts suggest that as a rule fire losses on mill premises were reasonably covered by insurance. Although one does find the occasional comment that a building or

[45] Sun C.R. 184/1112327/1830. Calverley Mills was the last woollen mill risk at the Norwich Union Fire Office in the 1820s. Norwich Union Fire Insurance Minute Book, no. 2, 7 December 1829.

[46] *Leeds Mercury*, 9 January 1830.

[47] *Leeds Mercury*, 30 January 1830 and Sun C.R. 178/1100201/1829; 179/1106152/1830; 182/11122122/1830. The Sun Fire Office paid Barker and Musgrave £2,104 4*s*. 0*d*. and the Protector Office possibly paid a similar amount. See Sun Fire Office, Register of Country losses by Fire, 1820–64. Vol. 1.

[48] *Leeds Mercury*, 5 September 1807.

[49] *Leeds Mercury*, 21 November 1807.

property was uninsured or under-insured, these are the exception rather than the rule.

There are other means of checking the accuracy of insurance values. These include the comparison of valued loss with insurance value, the comparison of insurance value with original cost and also a comparison with company accounts and balance sheets.

The first can only rarely be made as very few records of this nature survive. It is, however, as has been seen, possible on two occasions with the Gott mills. At the fire at Bean Ing in 1799 the independent valuation of the loss on buildings was over £3,500 and the insurance cover on the buildings was £4,000, the loss on machinery was £6,138 and the insurance cover £5,200 excluding movable machinery and utensils. The total loss was £13,942 'of which £11,946 was covered by insurance'. Crump calculated that:

> The total insurance was £18,000 of which at least £6,000 was upon the stock so that the building and machinery were only insured for £10,000 to £12,000 though they were certainly not fully covered.

He might well have been wrong, however, in his view that the buildings were not fully covered. The total loss on the mill building corresponds quite closely to the insurance, and a policy taken out with the Sun, the year before the fire, when the main mill was insured for £3,000, shows that the 'Particulars of Loss' do not include all the buildings at Bean Ing, other buildings besides the mill being insured in fact for £1,800.[50] The machinery does appear to be undervalued, possibly because new machinery had been installed since the policy had been taken out over twelve months before, but the value of the stock in the mill, which was totally destroyed, is fairly accurately insured. Except for the machinery the property at Bean Ing appears to have been almost fully covered by insurance.[51]

After the fire at Armley Mills a few years later, an independent valuation of the damage was obtained and amounted to almost £2,500. Taking into account the value of salvaged materials this would appear to correspond fairly well with the £3,000 insured on the building, two months before the fire.[52]

Some figures are also available for a loss at Ossett Mill in 1829. In May of that year a fire destroyed most of the mill buildings. The

[50] See Crump, op. cit., pp. 179, 257 and Sun C.R. 23/679117/1798.
[51] See Table III.
[52] Sun C.R. 61/766081/1804.

loss was put at just over £4,000 and £4,046 5*s.* 10*d.* was paid out by the insurance companies.[53]

The comparison of insurance value with original cost gives rise to a number of difficulties not least of which is to decide what part of the original cost of a building it was necessary to insure. One might expect insurance, in many cases, to be slightly less than the cost of building, taking into account site preparation for example. Thus a comparison along these lines must be fairly rough. It is possible, to make some estimate in the case of Marshall's flax mill in Leeds. In 1793 the firm's list of assets valued land, fabric and plant at £7,937.[54] Discounting the price originally paid for the land in 1790, the figure of £7,337 for fabric and plant corresponded very closely to the insurance valuation of £7,380.[55] As this list of assets was drawn up very soon after the first mill was built, it presumably reflects building costs.

Detailed and accurate accounts of building costs are hard to come by and even more difficult to interpret. It is, however, possible to make a more direct and satisfactory comparison with one item, the steam engine. One can, in a number of cases, compare the price a firm paid for a steam engine from the Soho Foundry with the amount for which that engine was insured.

Joshua Foster ordered a 14 horsepower crank engine from Boulton and Watt in April 1804. This engine was delivered later the same year and the account for it was as follows:

	£	*s.*	*d.*
Cast Iron	256	7	9½
Wrought Iron	97	18	9½
Copper, Brass, etc.	69	16	8
Stores	5	15	2
Patterns and Boxes	28	2	5
Carriage		4	6
Fitting	122	15	6
Total	£581	10	0 [56]

[53] See Goodchild, 'Ossett Mill Co. . . .', op. cit., p. 55.
[54] Rimmer, op. cit., p. 39.
[55] Ibid., p. 33 and Sun C.R. 15/663500/1797.
[56] B. & W. MSS, Portfolio 348 and Engine Book, 20 June 1804.

This figure corresponds quite closely to the £500 for which the engine was insured in 1805,[57] but is not absolutely similar. A greater similarity appears with the engine supplied to Gowland, Clark and Co. at Hillhouse, Bank. The cost of this engine was £770 and an insurance policy taken out by Benjamin Gowland, a few years later, insured an engine for £800.[58] Few manufacturers who purchased engines on an instalment basis appear to have insured the engines themselves, perhaps because they were covered by Boulton and Watt in the instalment agreement. However, Markland, Cookson and Fawcett who ordered a 30 horsepower engine from Boulton and Watt in 1792 were insuring this engine two years later for £1,500. Thirty horsepower engines from the Watt foundry were costing between £1,300 and £1,500 at that time so that insurance coverage was probably fairly realistic.[59] Similarly Messrs Beverley, Cross and Billam purchased a 22 horsepower sun and planet engine for their cotton mill at Hunslet at about the same time. This they insured for about £800 which was the price that Boulton and Watt were charging for similar sized engines at the time.[60] Messrs J. & J Walker insured their 20 horsepower engine for £800 in 1797. Messrs Nevins and Gatliffe's 16 horsepower engine was insured for £500 in 1800 and Messrs M. & J. Bateson's 20 horsepower engine for the same sum in 1802, both of which were somewhat below their cost price.[61] Depreciation may account for the difference. However, most of the Boulton and Watt earlier engines in textile mills in the county were insured close to their purchase price and replacement cost.

Another possible source for testing the reliability of insurance values is company accounts and valuations of assets. However, accountant's valuations did not always cover the same items as the insurance. The accountants might have been considering the value of the firm as a going concern and not just the value of its site, fixed capital and stock. If many company accounts existed, it would be necessary to examine this further but, in fact, these sort of figures are available for so few firms that the problem does not arise. Those figures that are available are insufficient or not a great deal of use for the purposes of this study.

[57] Sun C.R. 65/773797/1805.
[58] B. & W. MSS, Portfolio 126 an Sun 73/794641/1796.
[59] See Tables 22 and 23 and Sun C.R. 8/636966/1795 and 13/653223/1796.
[60] See Table 23 and Sun C.R. 11/649649/1795.
[61] R.E. 32a/188836/1802; 172616/1800.

However, a comparison is possible to some extent for the Gott mills. The 'Accounts of Co-Partnership' of the firm were recorded for most years between 1785 and 1840. These accounts were an estimate of the value of the assets of the firm at different times. Table V shows the annual accounting figures for the value of buildings and machinery at Bean Ing, Leeds, for the first two decades of the nineteenth century.

The sudden writing down of the valuation on 1 January 1817 and the following year, still more, was due to the bad business situation following the end of the Napoleonic Wars. Thus the figures for these years cannot be expected to correspond with the insurance. For some of the other years, however, a comparison is possible.

In 1801 the buildings and machinery at Bean Ing were valued by the accountants at £23,000. Insurance taken out the same year amounted to £10,900 for buildings and £7,200 for millwrights work, clockmakers work, steam engine, boilers and pipes. Unfortunately in the insurance policy stock and utensils which were insured for £21,000 are not itemized separately, but one might reasonably suggest that the difference between the £23,000 on the one hand and the £18,100 on the other could well at least be partly covered by the utensils.[62]

Table V

VALUE OF BUILDINGS AND MACHINERY AT PARK MILLS, BEAN ING, LEEDS, 1800–20, ACCORDING TO THE ACCOUNTS OF CO-PARTNERSHIP

Date	*Value of Buildings and Machinery*
1 January 1801	23,000
1 January 1803	24,700
1 January 1804	24,700
1 January 1805	24,700
1 January 1806	24,700
1 January 1807–12	26,500
1 January 1813	25,000
1 January 1814	23,000
1 January 1817	10,000
1 January 1818	5,000

Source: Gott MSS, Paper no. 20.

62 Gott MSS, no. 20. Accounts of Co-Partnership and Sun 40/719778/1801.

Another insurance policy traced for Bean Ing was for April 1816 when the insurance on buildings and fixed machinery was very similar, not a great deal of change having taken place in the firm's buildings in the intervening years. The insurance on buildings and machinery but excluding 'utensils' amounted to just over £18,000 and the co-partnership valuation, two years previously (none being recorded for 1815 and 1816) again showed £23,000.[63]

Although these figures do not show the two valuations as being exactly the same, they do, however, point to a considerable degree of similarity. However, too much reliance on such a firm as Gott's may not be very satisfactory in view of the size and success of that firm. Few accounts for other companies have been traced and in no other case has it been possible to use them as no corresponding insurance records are available. Perhaps, however, in the future other records will come to light, not necessarily just for woollen and worsted mills, which could be used to test the validity of insurance valuations.

Some information is available as to the price woollen and worsted firms fetched when sold but these figures are, likewise, not very useful as a sale price would include land, possibly stocks and even more difficult to consider 'goodwill'. The price fetched by a going concern might be expected to bear little relation to the capital value of the plant.

It was earlier suggested that where mills were let to tenants the tenants might often have been required to insure the premises as part of the tenancy agreement.[64] This was not always the case. There are many examples of the owner insuring the mill building and the tenants, the contents and machinery.[65] In the cases where tenants were under an obligation to insure a mill, and these appear to be the majority, one might expect an insistance upon insurance for a realistic sum. The Earl of Dartmouth required that his mill tenants insured their mills and he stipulated a value. Thus John Varley had to insure Shaw Carr Wood Mill for £700 from 1806 and Edmund Shaw and Thomas Haigh of Upper Mill were responsible for an insurance of £1,500.[66] Another entry in the Estate Terrier, for Upper Clough House Mill and Clough House Mill reads: 'The two mills with the above premises were granted on a

[63] Sun C.R. 114/916916/1816.
[64] See above.
[65] For example, the mills at Kirkstall owned by Sir James Graham. See Sun C.R. 139/998918/1823; 146/1018687/1824; 159/1052240/1826; and others.
[66] Dartmouth Estate, *Slaithwaite Terrier*, 1828, p. 161.

lease containing the usual covenants and to insure for £1,000 to Richard and Sarah Horsfall for 31 years from 1 August 1806.'[67]

It appears from these Terriers that all the Dartmouth mills that were let to tenants had to be insured by the latter and insurance records suggest that Dartmouth was by no means the only mill owner to insist on this.

The meaning and reliability of insurance values will undoubtedly be the subject of much further inquiry and debate. Instances of under-insurance are evident and more will come to light. There are clearly reservations about the use of the insurance figures for estimating fixed capital values but it would seem that they do provide by far the best and most detailed information that is available. Any inaccuracy that does result from their use will be an under-estimate of the value of capital stock. However, whilst it cannot categorically be said that insurance values were a true reflection of replacement cost there is little to suggest that Yorkshire wool textile mills were substantially under-insured.

[67] Ibid., p. 163.

Appendix IV

AVERAGE FIXED CAPITAL CALCULATIONS

Mill	*Location*	*Value of Fixed Capital* £	*References*
		1800	
Stonebreakes	Saddleworth	400	Sun C.R. 3/627881/1794
Plowe's Mill	Marsden	1,000	Sun C.R. 5/631846/1794
Upper Mill	Farnley	550	Sun C.R. 11/649652/1795
Carlisle's Mill	Upper Esholt	200	Sun C.R. 12/648179/1795
Dob Cross	Saddleworth	325	Sun C.R. 12/648180/1795
Heckmondwike Mill	Heckmondwike	800	Sun C.R. 12/648362/1795
Mill Green	Holbeck	310	Sun C.R. 12/648553/1795
Clifford Mill	Clifford	600	Sun C.R. 13/653221/1796
Danehouse Lane	Honley	850	Sun C.R. 13/654476/1796
Old Mill	Dewsbury	5,800	Sun C.R. 13/656219/1796
New Mill	Dewsbury	1,700	Sun C.R. 13/656219/1796
Millshaw Mill	Beeston	680	Sun C.R. 13/653405/1796
Cooper's Mill	Esholt	650	Sun C.R. 19/667233/1797
Wood's Mill	Lower Esholt	800	Sun C.R. 19/667233/1797 Sun C.R. 19/667669/1797
Buck Mill	Idle	950	Sun C.R. 20/667335/1797
Murgatroyd's Mill	Gildersome	1,130	Sun C.R. 22/674145/1798
Strickland's Mill	Bramley	750	Sun C.R. 24/679080/1798
Blacksike	Meltham	350	Sun C.R. 29/695689/1799
Foster's Mill	Horbury	1,000	Sun C.R. 29/696278/1799
Doodlebank Mill	Huddersfield	1,300	Sun C.R. 17/666615/1797
Bates' Mill	Ludhill	530	Sun C.R. 17/666600/1797

Mill	Location	Value of Fixed Capital £	References
Kitchen's Mill	Horsforth	500	Sun C.R. 34/705778/1800
Burnley & Garnett	Farnley	450	Sun C.R. 25/686921/1799
Wainwright's	Armley	170	Sun C.R. 12/669224/1797
Milner's	Tong	470	Sun C.R. 30/698722/1800
New Mill	Holmfirth	960	Sun C.R. 19/669074/1797 Sun C.R. 20/667110/1797
Upper Mill	Saddleworth	450	Sun C.R. 20/667783/1797
Turton's	Gildersome	825	Sun C.R. 21/676893/1798
Arthington Mill	Otley	750	Sun C.R. 18/663910/1797
Troughton Mill	Drighlington	540	Sun C.R. 13/653861/1796
Rods Mill	Morley	2,450	Sun C.R. 27/695289/1799
Putting Mill	Hoyland	400	Sun C.R. 19/671410/1797
Jos. Brooke	Honley	2,300	Sun C.R. 30/696784/1799
Lipton	Kirkheaton	800	Sun C.R. 21/676895/1798
Holmebridge	Holmfirth	1,300	Sun C.R. 32/701966/1800
Philadelphia Mill	Gildersome	1,050	Sun C.R. 22/678184/1798
Stancliffes'	Hopton	1,600	Sun C.R. 44/728981/1802
Frizinghall Mill	Bradford	1,950	Sun C.R. 37/713369–70/1801
Abbey Mills	Kirkstall	3,600	Sun C.R. 34/705774/1800
Savins Mill	Kirkstall	1,450	Sun C.R. 34/705774/1800
Low Mill	Stanningley	750	Sun C.R. 24/679080/1798
Thornes Lane	Wakefield	1,400	Sun C.R. 34/708102/1800
Garnet's Mill	Hunslet	380	Sun C.R. 13/656410/1796
Glover, Lister & Roper	Holbeck	1,580	Sun C.R. 23/683144/1798
Holbeck Lane Mill	Holbeck	1,300	Sun C.R. 31/699255/1800
Highgate	Hunslet	1,200	Sun C.R. 19/671089/1797
Hodgson's	Hunslet	550	Sun C.R. 20/667111/1797
Sykes and Kindle	Holbeck	1,750	Sun C.R. 29/699004/1800

Mill	Location	Value of Fixed Capital £	References
Woodhouse Carr	Leeds	400	Sun C.R. 12/648554/1795
Scothall Mills	Leeds	1,600	Sun C.R. 24/679828/1798
Pilkington's Mill	Wakefield	1,100	Sun C.R. 22/676712/1798
Kirkgate Bridge	Wakefield	550	Sun C.R. 13/654266/1796
Silcoates Mill	Wakefield	950	Sun C.R. 14/656188/1796 Sun C.R. 66/780068/1805
Flanshaw	Wakefield	2,300	Sun C.R. 13/653662/1796
Park Mills	Leeds	15,380	Sun C.R. 31/699424/1800
Dixon Mills	Shipley	2,430	Sun C.R. 32/701520/1800 Sun C.R. 37/713352/1801
Wilkinson's	Idle	700	Sun C.R. 41/722468/1801
Strim's Mill	Saddleworth	800	Sun C.R. 46/729463/1802
Hoyle and Whiteley	Cartworth	430	Sun C.R. 49/739705/1802
Cooke's Mill	Thongs Bridge	700	Sun C.R. 52/741101/1802
Brook's Mill	Liversedge	1,000	Sun C.R. 58/755739/1803
Sutcliffe's	Ovenden	2,350	R.E. 40/182623/1801
Whinney Bank	Huddersfield	830	Sun C.R. 48/734586/1802
Lower Battye Mill	Holmfirth	700	Sun C.R. 48/734585/1802
Whiteley's	Adel	2,760	Sun C.R. 45/733143/1802
Brookroyd Mill	Birstal	1,400	Sun C.R. 49/737389/1802
Burley Mills	Leeds	7,800	Sun C.R. 34/705774–6/1800
Churwell Mill	Churwell	2,800	Sun C.R. 65/782716/1805
Whitfields	Idle	750	Sun C.R. 68/782201/1805
Woodbottom Mill	Horsforth	5,000	Sun C.R. 44/728328/1802
Old Friezing Mill	Dewsbury	950	Sun C.R. 60/761926/1804
Spring End Mill	Horbury	850	Insurance Policies, Cusworth Hall
Armley Mills	Armley	4,800	R.E. 32a/154787/1796
Chickenley Mill	Dewsbury	1,100	R.E. 32a/154789/1796

Mill	Location	Value of Fixed Capital £	References
Elliston Mill	Greetland	2,000	R.E. 32a/154846/1796
Low Coat Mill	Meltham	380	R.E. 32a/155108/1797
Sheffield's Mill	Brighouse	800	R.E. 32a/155200/1797
Longbottom Mill	Warley	1,000	R.E. 32a/155221/1797
Masham Mill	Masham	3,200	R.E. 32a/155860/1797
Low Mill	Addingham	5,580	R.E. 32a/156092/1797
Walk Mill	Pool	1,400	R.E. 32a/156093/1797
Bell Mill	Wansford	3,950	R.E. 32a/156287–8/1797
Birkley & Waite's Mill	Cleckheaton	1,300	R.E. 32a/156293/1797
Smith Place Mill	Honley	900	R.E. 32a/156624/1797
Sowerby Bridge Mill	Sowerby Bridge	7,200	R.E. 32a/156708/1797
Oddy's Mill	Hunslet	820	R.E. 32a/157852/1797
Bank Bottom Mill	Marsden	1,300	R.E. 32a/158127/1797
Woodhouse Mill	Huddersfield	2,000	R.E. 32a/158612/1797
Ingham's Mill	Langfield	2,200	R.E. 32a/158615/1797
Linfit Mill	Almondbury	1,000	R.E. 32a/158616/1797
Bottomley's Mill	Scammonden	300	R.E. 32a/158617/1797
Lower Mill	Holbeck	900	R.E. 32a/158659/1797
Old Mill	Wortley	580	R.E. 32a/158659/1797
Moorcroft Mill	Kirkburton	500	R.E. 32a/159608/1797
Battye Mill	Thurlstone	650	R.E. 32a/159898/1797
Brow Bridge Mill	Elland	1,550	R.E. 32a/159925/1797
Brow Bridge Worsted Mill	Elland	1,600	R.E. 32a/159925/1797
Bentley's Mill	Lockwood	320	R.E. 32a/160108/1797
Clapham's Mill	Otley	525	R.E. 32a/160337/1797
Cooper House Mill	Warley	525	R.E. 32a/160721/1797
Tolson's Mill	Dalton	1,430	R.E. 32a/161748–9/1798
Day's Mill	Colne Bridge	650	R.E. 32a/162763/1798

Mill	*Location*	*Value of Fixed Capital* £	*References*
Rosemary Mill	Rastrick	950	R.E. 32a/164665/1798
Rushforth's Mill	Elland	500	R.E. 32a/164664/1798
Jarrat's Mill	Stanningley	1,070	R.E. 32a/164667/1798
Roger Mill	Southowram	800	R.E. 32a/168284/1799
Wormald's Mill	Liversedge	2,600	R.E. 32a/169088/1799
Hunsworth Mill	Gomersal	1,840	R.E. 32a/169157/1799
Hough Mill	Bramley	1,750	R.E. 32a/169821/1799
Burnely's Mill	Farnley	1,360	R.E. 32a/170191/1799
Elam's Mill	Hunslet	1,300	R.E. 32a/170318/1799
Hewnden Mill	Hewnden	850	R.E. 32a/170324/1799
Farnley Mill	Farnley Tyas	1,630	R.E. 32a/170436/1799
Luddenden Foot Mill	Warley	1,700	R.E. 32a/170437/1799
Beaumont's Mill	South Crosland	4,400	R.E. 32a/171622/1799
Steps Mill	South Crosland	600	R.E. 32a/172250/1800
Upper Steps Mill	South Crosland	200	R.E. 32a/172250/1800
Sutcliffe's Mill	Wheatley	1,700	R.E. 32a/174382/1800
Waterside Mill	Slaithwaite	1,400	R.E. 32a/177347/1800
Barker's Mill	Heckmondwike	1,350	R.E. 32a/178485/1800
Buckley's Mill	Saddleworth	620	R.E. 32a/179841/1800
Pratt's Mill	Saddleworth	430	R.E. 32a/179842/1800
Brooke's Mill	Heckmondwike	600	R.E. 32a/180077/1800
Kiln Croft Mill	Dewsbury	3,200	R.E. 32a/180124/1800
Carr Mill	Batley	1,800	R.E. 32a/180125/1800
Dewsbury Mill	Dewsbury	4,000	R.E. 32a/180162/1800
Dex's Mill	Heckmondwike	949	R.E. 32a/180197/1800
Low Mill	Mirfield	1,600	R.E. 32a/180989/1801
Greenfield Mill	Saddleworth	3,800	R.E. 32a/181452/1801
Coley Mill	Shelf	375	R.E. 32a/181455/1801

Mill	*Location*	*Value of Fixed Capital* £	*References*
Hollins Mill	Warley	4,450	R.E. 32a/181456/1801
Dean Clough Mill	Northowram	1,800	R.E. 32a/181456/1801
Clark Green Mill	Batley	1,050	R.E. 32a/182280/1801
Upper Bank Bottom Mill	Marsden	1,550	R.E. 32a/182274/1801
Castle Mill	Gomersal	2,500	R.E. 32a/182275/1801
Brearley Mill	Halifax	850	R.E. 32a/182510/1801
Thorp Mill	Halifax	1,650	R.E. 32a/182832/1801
Dean House Mill	Honley	2,300	R.E. 32a/182833/1801
Knight's Mill	Saddleworth	470	R.E. 32a/182834/1801
Clarkson's Mill	Wakefield	1,370	R.E. 32a/182983/1801
Lingarth's Wood Mill	Almondbury	800	R.E. 32a/183392/1801
Aldams Mill	Dewsbury	2,700	R.E. 32a/183393/1801
Jumples Mill	Ovenden	900	R.E. 32a/183693/1801
Subscription Mill	Batley	4,125	R.E. 32a/183723/1801
Hall Mills	Mirfield	800	R.E. 32a/184280/1801
Wharf Mill	Sowerby Bridge	1,050	R.E. 32a/186031/1801
Holme Mill	Bradford	1,800	R.E. 32a/186633/1801
Croft Mill	Dewsbury	900	R.E. 32a/186876/1801
Sutton Mill	Keighley	500	R.E. 32a/187046/1801
Bowling Dyke Mill	Northowram	950	R.E. 32a/187358/1801
Lobb Mill	Langfield	2,300	R.E. 32a/187370/1801
Dapper Mill	Wheatley	800	R.E. 32a/187375/1801
Hebble Mill	Wheatley	5,800	R.E. 32a/187375/1801

Total fixed capital for 153 mills: £241,434

Average fixed capital: £1,578

Mill	Location	Value of Fixed Capital £	References
	1810		
Providence Mill	Shipley	2,450	Sun C.R. 69/784549/1806
Vincent's Mill	Idle	750	Sun C.R. 86/827037/1809
Hepworth Mill	Holmfirth	1,000	Sun C.R. 73/794644/1806
Howroyd Mill	Whitley	3,850	Sun C.R. 78/803597/1807
Musgrave & Newton	Farnley	1,150	Sun C.R. 82/824226/1808
Crank Mill	Morley	2,415	Sun C.R. 89/840120/1810
Woodbottom Mill	Horsforth	4,900	Sun C.R. 49/728328/1802 Sun C.R. 86/837250/1809
Low Mill	Rawdon	5,000	Sun C.R. 85/829546/1809 Sun C.R. 86/837248/1809
Park Mill	Rawdon	3,800	Sun C.R. 85/829546/1809 Sun C.R. 89/840105/1810
Linton Mill	Linton	4,750	Sun C.R. 85/835754/1809
Milnes & Stevenson	Tong	680	Sun C.R. 84/826416/1809
Old Friezing Mill	Dewsbury	950	Sun C.R. 86/831409/1809
Mill adjoining above	Dewsbury	650	Sun C.R. 86/831409/1809
Rods Mill	Morley	4,090	Sun C.R. 71/818230/1808
Wm Brooke's	Honley	3,150	Sun C.R. 72/797912/1807
Batley Mill	Batley	7,500	Sun C.R. 68/782272/1805
Churwell Hill	Churwell	3,100	Sun C.R. 86/827039/1809
Jackson Bridge	Wooldale	900	Sun C.R. 63/771353/1805
Philadelphia Mill	Gildersome	1,700	Sun C.R. 101/878368/1813
Lower Mills	Calverley	950	Sun C.R. 70/786453/1806
Upper Mills	Calverley	660	Sun C.R. 70/786453/1806
St Helen's Mill	Bramley	4,300	Sun C.R. 90/838406/1809
Bellisle Mill	Bramley	4,200	Sun C.R. 84/826427/1809
Hough Mill	Bramley	4,500	Sun C.R. 68/784467/1806

Mill	*Location*	*Value of Fixed Capital* £	*References*
Silcoates Mill	Wakefield	950	Sun C.R. 66/780068/1805
Low Mill	Wortley	2,400	Sun C.R. 68/784482/1806
New Mill	Wortley	1,945	Sun C.R. 68/784482/1806
Pawson and Haley	Bramley	3,560	Sun C.R. 63/771333/1806
Stonebridge Mill	Farnley	4,450	Sun C.R. 64/774805/1805
Musgrave's	Farnley	1,150	Sun C.R. 82/824226/1808
Butterbowl Mill	Farnley	4,910	Sun C.R. 77/805627/1807
Fisher & Nixon	Holbeck	2,100	Sun C.R. 89/840101/1810
Dayson & Denton	Holbeck	1,600	Sun C.R. 94/851127/1810
Roper and Glover	Holbeck	2,000	Sun C.R. 91/842305/1810
Holbeck Lane Mill	Holbeck	1,250	Sun C.R. 63/773571/1805
Steander Mills	Leeds	3,585	Sun C.R. 89/840116/1810
Scothall Mills	Leeds	3,200	Sun C.R. 87/838385/1809
Woodhouse Lane	Leeds	4,000	Sun C.R. 91/840816/1810
Hill House	Leeds	3,800	Sun C.R. 72/797915/1807
Steeton Mill	Keighley	650	Sun C.R. 100/866901/1812
Hudswell	Batley	1,235	Sun C.R. 102/882485/1813
Chopend	Holmfirth	1,100	Sun C.R. 111/907051/1815
Foster's no. 1 Mill	Horbury	2,500	Sun C.R. 77/813036/1808
Foster's no. 2 Mill	Horbury	4,500	Sun C.R. 77/813036/1808
Foster's New Mill	Horbury	1,430	Sun C.R. 77/813036/1808
Dover Mill	Cartworth	650	Sun C.R. 102/876273/1812
Troughton Mill	Drighlington	1,950	Sun C.R. 74/801765/1807
Laister Dyke Mill	Bradford	1,800	Sun C.R. 70/784204/1805
Flanshaw	Wakefield	2,300	Sun C.R. 66/780065/1805
Armley Mill	Leeds	7,400	Sun C.R. 64/778070/1805
Abbey Mills	Kirkstall	3,100	Sun C.R. 66/778284/1805
Savins Mill	Kirkstall	800	Sun C.R. 66/778284/1805

Mill	Location	Value of Fixed Capital £	References
Cocking Steps Mill	Honley	900	Crump and Ghorbal, op. cit., p. 76
Beule End Mill	Penistone	380	Sun C.R. 60/761566/1804
Kitchen's Mill	Horsforth	550	Sun C.R. 66/780730/1805
Turton's Mill	Gildersome	1,550	Sun C.R. 53/746782/1805
Battye Old Mill	Holmfirth	800	Sun C.R. 58/758987/1804
Liphill Bank	Austonley	470	Sun C.R. 65/774105/1805
Low Mill	Stanningley	3,650	Sun C.R. 83/820530/1809
Brookroyd Mill	Birstal	2,050	Sun C.R. 73/799847/1807
Buck Mill	Idle	1,850	Sun C.R. 45/731574/1803 Sun C.R. 48/734115/1803
Thorne Lane	Wakefield	1,550	Sun C.R. 74/799145/1807
Whitefield's Mill	Idle	750	Sun C.R. 68/782201/1805
Batty Mills	Mirfield	750	Sun C.R. 79/817453/1808

Total Fixed Capital for 64 mills: £152,960

Average Fixed Capital: £1,443

1820

Mill	Location	Value of Fixed Capital £	References
Crank Mill	Morley	2,765	Sun C.R. 122/939219/1818
Chopend	Holmfirth	1,100	Sun C.R. 111/907051/1815
Ossett Mill	Ossett	4,550	Sun C.R. 124/941520/1818
Stubbing House Mill	Keighley	1,600	Sun C.R. 127/955629–30/1819
Holdworth's Mill	Shipley	3,600	Sun C.R. 130/969799/1820
Rods Mill	Morley	9,200	Sun C.R. 140/1000074/1823
Barkerend	Bradford	5,900	Sun C.R. 130/939963/1819

Mill	Location	Value of Fixed Capital £	References
Carr Mills	Leeds	7,600	Sun C.R. 134/984522/1821
Lipton	Kirkheaton	1,250	Sun C.R. 125/947442/1818
Churwell Mill	Churwell	6,450	Sun C.R. 121/943871/1818
Philadelphia Mill	Gildersome	1,700	Sun C.R. 129/963493/1820
Hogg's Mill	Holbeck	8,500	Sun C.R. 130/959959/1819 Sun C.R. 129/957601/1819
Walker's Mill	Hunslet	4,600	Sun C.R. 112/914158–9/1816 Sun C.R. 114/920112/1816 Sun C.R. 115/918879/1816
Holroyd's Mill	Leeds	3,000	Sun C.R. 114/916912/1816 Sun C.R. 128/963774/1820
Scothall Mills	Leeds	4,500	Sun C.R. 114/907712/1815
St Helen's Mill	Bramley	6,200	Sun C.R. 104/880853/1813 Sun C.R. 145/1015374/1824
Waterloo Mills	Bramley	3,250	Sun C.R. 127/952494/1819
New Mill	Bramley	4,050	Sun C.R. 127/952493/1819
Bellisle Mill	Bramley	3,840*	Sun C.R. 151/1032783/1825
Westgate St	Wakefield	7,400	Sun C.R. 142/1002436–7/1823
Flanshaw Low Mill	Wakefield	3,600	Sun C.R. 144/1004029/1823
Steander	Leeds	5,400	Sun C.R. 130/971952/1820
Abbey Mills	Kirkstall	4,350	Sun C.R. 139/998919/1823
Savins Mill	Kirkstall	4,150	,,
Stonebridge Mills	Farnley	7,150	Sun C.R. 127/952489–90/1819
Butterbowl Mill	Farnley	6,560	Sun C.R. 170/1075864/1828
Steeton Mill	Steeton	650	Sun C.R. 107/890754/1814
Linton Mill	Linton	5,800	Sun C.R. 119/928522/1817

* Approximately.

Mill	Location	Value of Fixed Capital £	References
Thornton's	Eccleshill	2,150	Sun C.R. 158/1046840/1826
Hague's Mill	Horsforth	2,300	Sun C.R. 140/992760/1822
Pitfall Mills	Leeds	1,000*	Sun C.R. 131/971214/1820 Sun C.R. 131/973835/1823
King's Mill	Huddersfield	1,000	Sun C.R. 143/1007963/1823 Sun C.R. 144/1009084/1823
Park Mill	Rawdon	4,700*	Sun C.R. 89/840105/1810 Sun C.R. 118/928811/1817
Low Mill	Rawdon	4,600*	Sun C.R. 86/837248/1809 Sun C.R. 118/928812/1817
Water Lane	Leeds	800	Sun C.R. 118/928810/1817
Walker & Dickinson's Mill	Holmfirth	1,450	Sun C.R. 134/984532/1821 Sun C.R. 140/992757/1822

* Approximately.

Total Fixed Capital for 36 mills: £146,715
Average Fixed Capital: £4,100

1835

Mill	Location	Value of Fixed Capital £	References
Lobley's	Farnley	1,500	Sun C.R. 168/1075207/1828
Oldroyd's	Howden Clough	3,490	Sun C.R. 168/1077839/1828
Dudfleet Mill	Horbury	1,700	Sun C.R. 187/1118593/1831
Arundel's	Rothwell	4,240	Sun C.R. 170/1079420/1828 Sun C.R. 188/1127361/1831
Millhouse	Halifax	5,200	Sun C.R. 176/1097240/1829

Mill	*Location*	*Value of Fixed Capital* £	*References*
Bottomley's	Guiseley	4,450	Sun C.R. 230/1229046/1836
Dex, Croft & Burnley	Heckmondwike	2,250	Sun C.R. 206/1171385/1834
Walker's	Holmfirth	690	Sun C.R. 197/1155328/1833
Cloth Hall Mill	Gomersal	7,500	Sun C.R. 197/1155361–2/1833
Edmondson's	Idle	2,500	Sun C.R. 206/1171383/1834
Lockwood's	Huddersfield	8,500	Sun C.R. 200/1155689/1833
Norton's	Clayton West	500	Sun C.R. 233/1233599/1836
Asquith Clark's	Morley	7,820	Sun C.R. 233/1243925/1837
Hainsworth Johnson's	Farsley	5,050	Sun C.R. 246/1265403/1838
Hemingway, Tong and Co.	Earlsheaton	5,000	Sun C.R. 249/1280001/1838
Musgrave's	Bramley	4,100	Sun C.R. 256/1314075/1839
Claughton Garth Mill	Pudsey	5,685	Sun C.R. 254/1292765/1839
Cullingworth Mill	Bingley	8,400	Sun C.R. 194/1135637/1832
Larkfield Mill	Rawdon	4,330	Sun C.R. 206/1171372/1834
Ramsden Mill	Huddersfield	1,500	Sun C.R. 190/1134664/1831
Clover Greaves Mill	Calverley	4,900	Sun C.R. 223/1206571/1835
Greystone Mill	Adwalton	2,100	Sun C.R. 212/1189441/1834
Albion Mill	Eccleshill	5,400	Sun C.R. 157/1052076–7/1826
Healey Mill	Ossett	3,680	Sun C.R. 181/1110664/1830
New Bank Mill	Halifax	22,440	Sun C.R. 228/1223615/1836
Dewsbury Mills	Dewsbury	18,100*	Sun C.R. 165/1068075/1827
Kebroyd Mills	Halifax	1,350	Sun C.R. 198/1158295–6/1833
Old Mill	Eccleshill	2,150	Sun C.R. 158/1046840/1826
Spring Mills	Dewsbury	1,250	Sun C.R. 156/1040880/1826
Wellhouse	Huddersfield	4,570	Sun C.R. 188/1104039/1830
Healey Low Mills	Ossett	1,800	Sun C.R. 195/1147580/1832

* Approximately.

Mill	*Location*	*Value of Fixed Capital* £	*References*
Crosley Mill	Honley	9,600	Sun C.R. 190/1134663/1831
Dixon's Mill	Morley	3,300	Sun C.R. 172/1085752/1829
Rods Mill	Morley	6,300	Sun C.R. 202/1166198/1833
Starkey's Mill	Huddersfield	24,000*	Sun C.R. 214/1197383/1835
Eli Sheard's	Kirkheaton	950	Sun C.R. 192/1132179/1831
Philadelphia Mill	Gildersome	1,700	Sun C.R. 194/1137146/1832
Millshaw Mills	Beeston	5,360	Sun C.R. 188/1126142/1831
Winker Green	Armley	9,870	Sun C.R. 209/1179648/1834
Union Mill	Holbeck	7,000	Sun C.R. 203/1162576/1833
Holbeck Moor Mill	Holbeck	4,880	Sun C.R. 189/1135137/1832
Walker's	Hunslet	6,600	Sun C.R. 168/1079226/1828; Sun C.R. 195/1149733/1832
Sheepscar Low Mill	Leeds	6,280	Sun C.R. 208/1177313/1834
Wellington Bridge	Leeds	4,800	Sun C.R. 234/1237252/1836
Lady Lane	Leeds	9,150	Sun C.R. 210/1177577/1834
Carlton Cross Mills	Leeds	3,900	Sun C.R. 191/1134145/1831
Millgarth	Leeds	9,100	Sun C.R. 223/1221721/1835
St Helen's Mill	Bramley	6,900	Sun C.R. 153/1044596/1826
Wellington Mill	Bramley	4,100	Sun C.R. 193/1131694/1831
Waterloo Mill	Bramley	12,750	Sun C.R. 218/1192176/1835
Hough Mill	Bramley	1,950	Sun C.R. 190/1134691/1831
Lister & Farrars	Bramley	5,500	Sun C.R. 170/1075863/1828
Hough End Mill	Bramley	3,500	Sun C.R. 193/1134361/1831
Bellisle Mill	Bramley	1,400	Sun C.R. 252/1301396/1839
Swinnow	Bramley	2,700	Sun C.R. 238/1257736/1837
Westgate Street	Wakefield	3,100	Sun C.R. 194/1139438/1832

* Approximately.

Mill	*Location*	*Value of Fixed Capital* £	*References*
Flanshaw	Wakefield	3,950	Sun C.R. 238/1257706/1837
Westgate Common	Wakefield	1,200	Sun C.R. 222/1209282/1835
Flanshaw Low Mill	Wakefield	3,500	Sun C.R. 232/1237012/1836
Stonebridge Mill	Farnley	5,550	Sun C.R. 189/1124033/1831
Butterbowl Mill	Farnley	6,560	Sun C.R. 170/1075864–5/1828
Upper Mill	Farnley	1,800	Sun C.R. 216/1200843/1835
Abbey Mills	Kirkstall	9,300	Sun C.R. 172/1085745/1829
Savins Mill	Kirkstall	3,490	Sun C.R. 172/1085746/1829 Sun C.R. 172/1085751/1829
Park Mills	Leeds	22,450	Sun C.R. 158/1055369/1827
Armley Mills	Leeds	4,050	Sun C.R. 152/1036492/1825

Total Fixed Capital for 67 mills: £370,345
Average Fixed Capital: £5,527

BIBLIOGRAPHY

I. Manuscript Sources

At the West Riding County Record Office, Wakefield:
- Returns of Cotton and Other Mills for 1803 and 1804.
- Quarter Session Order Books and Rolls.
- Registers of Deeds.

At Birmingham City Library:
- The Boulton and Watt Collection.

At the Royal Insurance Group Office, Park Row, Leeds:
- Records of the Leeds and Yorkshire Assurance Company.

At the Royal Insurance Group Office, North John Street, Liverpool:
- Papers relating to the Liverpool and London and Globe Insurance Company and associated fire insurance companies.

At the Northumberland County Record Office:
- Papers relating to the Newcastle upon Tyne Fire Office and prospectuses of the Anchor Fire Office, The Albion Fire and Life Assurance Company and the Union Fire Office.
- Papers relating to the North British Insurance Company in the Lockhart Collection.

At the Norwich Union Insurance Group, Norwich:
- Early papers of the Norwich Union Fire Office.

At the Brotherton Library, University of Leeds:
- The Gott MSS.
- The Marriner Papers.
- The Marshall Papers.
- The Lupton MSS.
- Miscellaneous records of William Ackroyd, Otley Mills, Otley; J. T. Clay and Sons, Raistrick; Robert Clough (Keighley) Ltd, Grove Mills, Keighley; and of Messrs Kellett, Brown and Company Ltd, Clover Greaves Mill, Calverley.
- Jowitt Papers . . . a notebook entitled 'Account of Failures in and connected with the Wool and Woollen Trade, 1840'.

At Upper Mill Public Library, Saddleworth:
- MS Account Book of James Lee, Delph.

At Keighley Public Library:
- Brigg MSS

At Sheffield City Library (Department of Local History and Archives):
- Miscellaneous papers relating in the Sheffield Fire Office and prospectuses of other offices in the Bagshawe Muniments and the Fairbank Collection.

At the South Yorkshire Industrial Museum, Cusworth Hall, Doncaster:

Lumb MSS.

Wood MSS.

Flanshaw Mill MSS.

Miscellaneous textile MSS.

At Leeds City Archives Department, Sheepscar Library, Leeds:

Account book of the Leeds Gas Light Co.

Account book of John Hartley and Sons, Morley, ACC. 1368.

Mortgage agreement for Potterdale Mill, Leeds, DB 39/29.

Committee Book of the 'Gill Royds' Mill Company, Morley, and various accounts for the mill.

At Dewsbury Public Library:

A Valuation of the Messuages, Lands, Buildings, Tenements, Tythes and Hereditaments in the Township of Dewsbury, 1803–4.

A Valuation of . . . the Township of Dewsbury, 1843–4.

A Valuation of . . . the Township of Thornhill, 1803 and 1817.

At the Archives Department, Halifax Public Library:

Survey and Valuation of the Township of Warley, 1805.

Survey and Valuation of the Township of Warley, 1829.

Fairbank's Survey of Halifax, 1826.

A Valuation of . . . the Township of Halifax, 1837.

A Valuation of . . . the Township of Halifax, 1852.

Insurance proposals for Mearclough Bottom Mill, near Halifax.

At the Estate Office, Slaithwaite:

The Dartmouth Estate Terrier.

At the University of Hull Library:

Sun Fire Office Policy Books — Hull and District.

At Messrs Charlesworth, Wood and Brown, Solicitors, Skipton:

Policy Book, Account Book and Order Book of Thomas Brown, Agent for the Royal Exchange Assurance Company at Skipton.

At the Guildhall Library, City of London:

The Sun Insurance Office Archives:

Committee Minute Books.

'Old Series' Policy Registers.

'Country Department' Policy Registers.

Endorsement and Account Books.

The Globe Insurance Office Committee Minute Books.

The Hand in Hand Fire and Life Insurance Society:

General Ledgers.

Committee Minute Book.

Policy Registers.

The Royal Exchange Fire Office:

Committee Minute Books.

Fire Policy Registers (ordinary series).
Fire Policy Registers (supplementary Agents Series).

At the Yorkshire Insurance Group, York:
Early papers of the Yorkshire Insurance Company.

At the Museum and Art Gallery, Civic Centre, Bolton:
The Crompton Family Records.

At Wakefield Public Library:
Accounts of the Overseers of the Poor of Wakefield, 1790.

At the Chartered Insurance Institute, Aldermanbury, London:
The Walford MSS.

At the Essex County Record Office, Chelmsford:
Papers relating to the Essex and Suffolk Insurance Society.

At the Phoenix Assurance Company, Glasgow:
Notebooks relating to Phoenix agencies in Scotland.

II. Maps and Plans

1. *Manuscript Plans*

Aire and Calder Navigation Maps and Plans, 1774. W.Y.C.R.O.
Enclosure Map of the Manor of Meltham, 1830. W.Y.C.R.O.
Enclosure Plan of North Crosland, 1802. W.Y.C.R.O.
Tythe Map of Parts of Idle, 1813. W.Y.C.R.O.
Enclosure Map of Pudsey, 1820. W.Y.C.R.O.
Enclosure Map of Scammonden, 1815. W.Y.C.R.O.
Enclosure Maps of Wakefield, 1805. W.Y.C.R.O. and W.P.L.
Wormald's Map of the Township of Horton (and Reference Book), 1839, B.C.L.
Tythe Map of Hunslet, 1846. C.L.A.D.
Tythe Map of the Township of Wortley, 1846. C.L.A.D.
Plan of Rods Mill, Morley, 1848. C.L.A.D.
Plan of a plot of Building Ground situate in the Township of Leeds, 1833 (the land for Hope Mill). C.L.A.D.
Survey and Map of Hunslet, 1791. C.L.A.D.
Tythe Map of Beeston, 1847. C.L.A.D.
Tythe Map of Armley, 1846. C.L.A.D.
Tythe Map of Holbeck, 1846. C.L.A.D.
Tythe Map of Farnley, 1844. C.L.A.D.
Plans for proposed routes of railways in the West Riding. W.Y.C.R.O.
Insurance plan of Mearclough Bottom Worsted Mill, near Halifax. H.A.D.

MSS Plans of Park Mill and the Bean Ing Estate — various dates. B.L.

MSS Plans of the Dartmouth Mills and Estates — various dates. Estate Office, Slaithwaite.

2. *Printed Maps and Plans*

Ordnance Survey: *First series 5′ Town Plans of Leeds, Bradford, Halifax, Huddersfield, Keighley, Skipton, Dewsbury and Wakefield.* Published *c.* 1851–2. British Museum Map Room and, in some cases, the local Public Library.

Ordnance Survey: *Six inch to one mile Ordnance Survey of Yorkshire.* First Series. Surveyed 1845–54. Published 1847–57. British Museum Map Room and C.L.R.L.

Ordnance Survey: *One inch, two and a half inch, six inch and twenty-five inch to one mile maps of the West Riding of Yorkshire.* 1841 to the present day.

Map of the County of York. Surveyed in MDCCLXVII, VIII, IX and MDCCLXX. Engraved by Thomas Jeffery's, Geographer to His Majesty, 1775 Edition. British Museum Map Room.

Map of the County of York . . . surveyed by C. Greenwood, Wakefield (1815–17). Published in 1817. British Museum Map Room.

A Map of the Parish of Borough of Leeds . . . From an actual survey by John Tuke, 1781. L.C.R.L.

'A Map of 10 miles round Leeds', in *A History of Leeds* . . ., T. Wright, 1797. L.C.R.L.

Plan of the town of Leeds and its environs. Surveyed by Giles, Netlam and Francis, 1815. L.C.R.L.

A Map of near 10 miles round Leeds. Published by E. Baines, 1817. L.C.R.L.

Plans of the town of Leeds. Published by E. Baines, 1821, 1822 and 1826. L.C.R.L.

Map of the Borough of Leeds. Published by E. Baines and R. Newsome, 1834. L.C.R.L.

Plan of the town of Leeds. Published by Charles Fowler in 1845. L.C.R.L.

Map of the Parish of Halifax . . ., J. F. Myers, 1834–5. H.P.L.

Wormald's Map of the Township of Horton, 1839. B.C.L.

Wood's Plan of Bradford from an Actual Survey, 1832. B.C.L.

Plan of the Township of Dewsbury, J. Walker, 1833. D.P.L.

Rawson's Map of the Calder, 1796.

Halifax Gas and Coke Co. Plan of Halifax 1846 (?). (In the care of Geoffrey Holden, Esq., Borough Engineer and Surveyor, Halifax.)

Map of Wakefield, J. Walker, 1823. W.P.L.

Thorpe's Map of Wakefield, 1820–1. W.P.L.

Map of Wakefield, J. Walker, 1832. W.P.L.

III. Directories

The Universal British Directory, 1793 (compiled by Peter Barfoot and John Wilkes).

J. Ryley, *Leeds Directory for the Year*, 1798.

A Directory for the Town of Leeds, Binns and Brown, 1800.

E. Baines, *Directory of Leeds*, 1809, 1814, 1817.

Pigot and Dean, *A Commercial Directory of the West Riding*, 1814–15.

Pigot and Dean, *A Commercial Directory of the West Riding*, 1818 and 1820.

E. Baines, *A Directory of the County of York*, 1822.

W. Parson, *General and Commercial Directory of Leeds*, 1826.

Pigot and Co., *Commercial Directory — Yorkshire Section*, 1829.

Parson and White, *Directory of the Borough of Leeds and the Clothing District of Yorkshire . . .* , 1830.

Baines and Newsome, *General and Commercial Directory of Leeds*, 1834.

W. White, History, *Gazetteer and Directory of the West Riding*, 1837.

W. White, *Directory and Topography of the Borough of Leeds and the Whole Clothing District of the West Riding*, 1842 and 1847.

J. Ibbetson, *General and Classified Directory . . . of Bradford*, 1850.

Collinson, Burton and Co., *West Riding Worsted Directory*, 1852.

IV. Newspapers

The Leeds Intelligencer.

The Leeds Mercury.

The Northern Star.

The Wakefield and Halifax Journal.

Yorkshire Magazine, 1786–7.

V. Unpublished Theses

Trevor Turner, 'History of Fenton, Murray and Wood', Manchester University. M.Sc. Tech. thesis, 1966.

F. J. Glover, 'Dewsbury Mills: A History of Messrs Wormalds and Walker Ltd, Blanket Manufacturers, of Dewsbury. With an Economic Survey of the Yorkshire Woollen Cloth Industry in the Nineteenth Century'. Leeds University Ph.D. thesis, 1959.

R. Max Hartwell, 'The Yorkshire Woollen and Worsted Industries, 1800–1850', Oxford University (Balliol), D.Phil. thesis, 1955.

D. Roberts, 'The Development of the Textile Industry in the West Craven and the Skipton District of Yorkshire', L.S.E. M.Sc. Dissertation, 1956.

D. A. Dean, 'Economic and Social Development of Dewsbury', Sheffield University M.A. thesis, 1963.

W. D. Shepherd, 'Early Industrial Buildings, 1700–1850', R.I.B.A. thesis, 1950.

VI. Parliamentary Papers

Abstract of Answers and Returns, pursuant to Act 41 Geo. 3, for taking an Account of the Population of Great Britain in 1801:
1801 (140) VI.
1801–2 (9) (112) VI. VII.

Report from the Select Committee on the Petitions of Merchants and Manufacturers concerned in the Woollen Manufacturers in the county of York and town of Halifax:
1802–3 (71) VI.

Report from the Select Committee on the Petition of the Manufacturers of Woollen Cloth in the county of York:
1803–4 (66) IV.

Report from the Select Committee on the Petition of the Clothworkers, Shearmen, Weavers and Clothiers of the counties of York, Somerset, Gloucester, and Wilts, and other parts of the United Kingdom: 1805 (105) III.

Report from the Select Committee appointed to consider the state of the Woollen Manufacture of England:
1806 (268) (268a) III.

Report of the Minutes of Evidence taken before the Select Committee on the State of Children employed in the Manufactories of the United Kingdom:
1816 (397) III.

Report from the Select Committee to whom the Bill to regulate the Labour of Children in Mills and Factories of the United Kingdom was referred: 1831–2 (706) XV.

Report from the Select Committee appointed to inquire into the present state of Manufactures, Commerce, and Shipping in the United Kingdom: 1833 (690) VI.

Reports from Commissioners appointed to collect information in the Manufacturing Districts, relative to Employment of Children in Factories, and as to the propriety and means of curtailing the Hours of their Labour; with Minutes of Evidence and Reports of District Commissioners:
First Report 1833 (450) XX.
Second Report 1833 (519) XXI.
Supplementary Reports 1834 (167) XIX. XX.

First Report of the Commissioners for inquiring into the state of Large Towns and Populous Districts: 1844 (572) XVII.1.
Second Reports 1845 (602) (610) XVIII.

Reports by Inspectors of Factories made to the Government:
1835 (342) XL.
1836 (78) XLV.
1837 (73) XXXI.
1837–8 (119) (131) XXVIII.
1837–8 (612) XLV.
1839 (159) (201) XIX.
1851 (1304) (1396) XXIII.

Accounts and Papers

Persons employed in the Mills and Factories of the United Kingdom, distinguishing ages: 1836 (138) XLV.

Number of Power Looms used in Factories in the Manufacture of Woollen, Cotton, Silk and Linen respectively, in each county of the United Kingdom: 1836 (24) XLV.

Returns of Mills and Factories, specifying the Firms which have neglected to transmit Returns to the Inspectors when called upon at any time during the twelve months ending 30 June 1838; of the Number of Persons employed in Cotton, Woollen, Worsted, Flax and Silk Factories, of the United Kingdom, etc., and of Names of all Mills and Firms from which answers have not been obtained: 1839 (41) XLII.

Number of Factories within the District of each Inspector, the Number of Mills visited, etc.: 1839 (135) XLII.

Number of Cotton, Woollen, Worsted, Flax, and Silk Factories, subject to the Factories' Acts in each County, distinguishing each description of Factory; Amount available for each description of Factory of Steam and Water Power; Children under Thirteen years of age, Boys and Girls; distinguishing in Silk-throwing Mills, Children between Eleven and Thirteen years of age; Young Persons between Thirteen and Eighteen years of age, and of Females above Thirteen years of age; the Number of Males above Eighteen years of age, including all Managers, Clerks, Overlookers, Engineers, Mechanics, and all others employed in the Factory with a General Summary: 1850 (745) XLII.

VII. Articles

1. *Topographical*

H. W. Harwood, 'Midgley's Manor Mill', *H.A.S.*, 1958.

H. W. Harwood, 'Peel House Mills', *H.A.S.*, 1946.

H. W. Harwood, 'Wainstalls Mills', *H.A.S.*, 1953.

H. W. Harwood, 'Wainstalls — Some Industrial History', *H.A.S.*, 1953.

H. P. Kendall, 'The Mill at the Brigg', *H.A.S.*, 1923.

B. R. Law, 'The Calder Millowners and the Rochdale Canal', *H.A.S.*, January 1954.

J. H. Priestley, 'The Growth of a Township — Soyland', *H.A.S.*, February 1955.

J. H. Priestley, 'The Town of Rishworth', *H.A.S.*, March 1956.

J. H. Priestley, 'Mills of the Blackburn Valley', *H.A.S.*, 1963.

J. H. Priestley, 'Mills of the Ryburn Valley', *H.A.S.*, 1941; *H.A.S.*, 1933; *H.A.S.*, 1934.

W. G. Rimmer, 'Castle Foregate Flax Mill — Shrewsbury', *Transactions of the Shropshire Archaeological Society*, Vol. LVI, 1959.

W. G. Rimmer, 'Middleton Colliery, Near Leeds (1770–1830)', *Y.B.E.S.R.*, Vol. VII, 1955.

'The Illustrated Diary of Mr. W. H. Stott', *H.A.S.*, December 1955.

2. *Others*

T. Bannister, 'The First Iron Framed Buildings', *The Architectural Review*, CVII, 1950.

F. Beckwith, 'The Population of Leeds During the Industrial Revolution', *T.S.*, Vol. 41, Part II, 1948.

M. Blaug, 'The Productivity of Capital in the Lancashire Cotton Industry during the Nineteenth Century', *E.H.R.*, XIII, 1961.

E. M. Carus-Wilson, 'An Industrial Revolution of the 13th Century', *E.H.R.*, XI, 1941.

S. D. Chapman, 'The Transition to the Factory System in the Midlands Cotton Spinning Industry', *E.H.R.*, XVI, 1965.

S. D. Chapman, 'The Pioneers of Worsted Spinning by Power', *B.H.*, VII, 1965.

S. D. Chapman, 'The Cost of Power in the Industrial Revolution in Britain: The Case of the Textile Industry', *Midland History*, I, 2, 1971.

J. H. Clapham, 'Industrial Organization in the Woollen and Worsted Industries of Yorkshire', *E.J.*, XVI, 1906.

J. H. Clapham, 'Some Factory Statistics of 1815–16', *E.J.*, XXV, 1915.

J. H. Clapham, 'The Transferrence of the Worsted Industry from Norfolk to the West Riding', *E.J.*, XX, 1910.

P. Deane, 'The Output of the British Woollen Industry in the Eighteenth Century', *J.E.H.*, XVII (1957).

P. Deane, 'Capital Formation in Britain Before the Railway Age', *Economic Development and Cultural Change*, 1961.

G. A. Feather, 'A Pennine Worsted Community in the mid-nineteenth century', *Textile History*, III, 1972.

F. J. Glover, 'The Rise of the Heavy Woollen Trade of the West Riding of Yorkshire in the Nineteenth Century', *B.H.*, IV, 1961.

J. Goodchild, 'The Ossett Mill Company', *Textile History*, I, I, 1968.

P. P. Hall, Dolphineholme, 'A History of the Dolphineholme Worsted Mill, 1784 to 1867', *Transactions of the Fylde Historical Society*, no. 3, 1969.

J. R. Harris, 'The Employment of Steam Power in the Eighteenth Century', *History*, LII, 1967.

N. B. Harte, 'On Rees's Cyclopaedia as a source for the History of the Textile Industries in the Early Nineteenth century', *Textile History*, V, 1974.

H. Heaton, 'Benjamin Gott and the Industrial Revolution in Yorkshire', *E.H.R.*, III, 1931.

D. T. Jenkins, 'The Validity of the Factory Returns, 1833–50', *Textile History*, IV, 1973.

D. T. Jenkins, 'Early Factory Development in the West Riding of Yorkshire, 1770–1800', in N. B. Harte and K. G. Ponting (eds), *Textile History and Economic History* (Manchester, 1973).

A. E. Musson and E. Robinson, 'The Early Growth of Steam Power', *E.H.R.*, VI, 1958.

A. E. Musson and E. Robinson, 'Science and Industry in the Late Eighteenth Century', *E.H.R.*, XIII, 1960.

K. V. Pankhurst, 'Investment in the West Riding Wool Textile Industry in the Nineteenth Century', *Y.B.E.S.R.*, VII, 1955.

S. Pollard, 'Fixed Capital in the Industrial Revolution in Britain', *J.E.H.*, XXIV, 3, 1964.

S. Pollard, 'Capital Accounting in the Industrial Revolution', *Y.B.E.S.R.*, XV, 1963.

H. A. Shannon, 'Bricks: A Trade Index', *Economica* (New Series), I, 1934.

E. M. Sigsworth, 'History of the Local Trade at Morley', *Journal of the Textile Institute*, Vol. 40, no. 10, 1949.

The Journal of the Textile Institute, Vol. 18, Special Issue for the Centenary of Samuel Crompton's Death, 1927.

C. Walford, 'Fires and Fire Insurance Considered Under Their Historical, Financial, Statistical and National Aspects', *J.R.S.S.*, 1877.

C. A. W. Ward, 'A Bibliography of the History of Industry in the

West Riding of Yorkshire', *Proceedings of the Leeds Philosophical and Literary Society*, Vol. XIII, Part I, 1968.

J. T. Ward, 'West Riding Landowners and Mining in the Nineteenth Century', *Y.B.E.S.R.*, XV, 1963.

M. T. Wild, 'The Saddleworth Parish Registers', *Textile History*, I, 2, 1969.

R. G. Wilson, 'The Supremacy of the Yorkshire Cloth Industry in the Eighteenth Century', in N. B. Harte and K. G. Ponting (eds), *Textile History and Economic History* (Manchester, 1973).

VIII. Books

1. *Topographical*

J. Aikin, *A Description of the Country from Thirty to Forty Miles Round Manchester* (London, 1795).

T. Allen, *A New and Complete History of the County of York* (London, 1828–31).

W. Bagshaw, *Jubilee Handbook of Batley* (Batley, 1919).

T. Baines, *Yorkshire Past and Present: A History and a Description of the Three Ridings of the Great County of York, from the Earliest Ages to the Year 1870; with an Account of its Manufactures, Commerce and Civil and Mechanical engineering. Including an Account of the Woollen Trade of Yorkshire by Edward Baines* (London, 1871–7).

J. Batty, *History of Rothwell* (1877).

M. W. Beresford and G. R. J. Jones (ed.), *Leeds and Its Region*, British Association (Leeds, 1967).

R. Brook, *The Story of Huddersfield* (Huddersfield, 1968).

C. E. Camidge, *A History of Wakefield . . .* (London, 1866).

G. A. Cooke, *Topographical and Statistical Description of the County of York* (London, 1818).

J. Crabtree, *A Concise History of the Parish and Vicarage of Halifax in the County of York* (Halifax, 1836).

Craven, *A History of Stanbury.*

W. Cudworth, *Round About Bradford: A Series of Sketches of Forty Two Places Within Six Miles of Bradford* (Bradford, 1876).

W. Cudworth, *Manningham, Heaton and Allerton Treated Topographically* (Bradford, 1896).

W. Cudworth, *Histories of Bolton and Bowling . . .* (Bradford, 1891).

W. H. Dawson, *History of Skipton* (London, 1882).

E. E. Dodd, *Bingley: A Yorkshire Town Through Nine Centuries* (Bingley, 1958).

T. W. Hanson, *The Story of Old Halifax* (Halifax, 1920).

J. Hodgson, *Textile Manufacture and Other Industries in Keighley* (Keighley, 1879).

R. Holmes, *Keighley, Past and Present* (London, 1858).

Rev. J. Hughes, *History of Meltham.*

Jackson's Guide to Leeds (1889).

M. A. Jagger, *History of Honley.*

J. James, *The History of Topography of Bradford with Topographical Notices of Its Parish* (London, 1841).

J. James, *The History of Bradford and its Parish, with Additions and Continuation to the Present Time* (London, 1866).

J. Lawson, *Letters to the Young on Progress in Pudsey During the Last Sixty Years* (Stanningley, 1887).

T. Langdale, *Topographical Dictionary of Yorkshire* (1882).

J. Le Page, *The Story of Baildon* (1951).

W. Marshall, *The Rural Economy of Yorkshire* (London, 1796).

J. Mayhall, *Annals of Leeds and the Surrounding District* (Leeds and London, 1860).

R. Mitchell, *Brighouse: Portrait of a Town* (Brighouse, 1953).

J. Parker, *Illustrated Rambles from Hipperholme to Tong* (Bradford, 1904).

E. Parsons, *The Civil, Ecclesiastical, Literary, Commercial and Miscellaneous History of Leeds, Halifax, Huddersfield, Bradford, Wakefield, Dewsbury, Otley and the Manufacturing Districts of Yorkshire* (London and Leeds, 1834).

W. Parson and W. White, *Annals, History and Guide of Leeds and York, Together With All the Towns and Villages of the Clothing District of Yorkshire . . .* (Leeds, 1830).

F. Peel, *Spen Valley: Past and Present* (Heckmondwike, 1893).

S. Rayner, *The History and Antiquities of Pudsey* (London, 1887).

H. Schroeder, *The Annals of Yorkshire* (Leeds, 1831–2).

W. Scruton, *Pen and Pencil Pictures of Old Bradford* (Bradford, 1889).

P. Slater, *History of the Ancient Parish of Guiseley* (1880).

S. B. Smith, *Thwaite Mill, Hunslet, Near Leeds*, Typescript History at L.C.R.L. (1968).

W. Smith, *History and Antiquities of Morley . . .* (London, 1876).

W. Smith, *Morley: Ancient and Modern* (London, 1886).

W. Smith, *Rambles About Morley, with Descriptive and Historical Sketches; also An Account of the Rise and Progress of the Woollen Manufacture in This Place* (London, 1866).

H. Speight, *Chronicles and Stories of Old Bingley* (1898).

H. E. Strickland, *General View of the Agriculture of the East Riding of Yorkshire* (1812).

D. F. E. Sykes, *The History of the Colne Valley* (Slaithwaite, 1906).
Rev. W. Thompson, *Sedbergh, Garsdale and Dent* (1910).
J. Travis, *Historical and Biographical Notes of Todmorden* (1896).
G. H. Tupling, *The Economic History of Rossendale* (Manchester, 1927).
J. Horsfall Turner, *Haworth — Past and Present* (Brighouse, 1879).
J. W. Walker, *Wakefield: Its History and People* (Wakefield, 1939).
J. Watson, *The History and Antiquities of the Parish of Halifax in Yorkshire* (London, 1775).
J. Williams, *Batley Past and Present; Its Rise and Progress Since the Introduction of Shoddy* (Batley, 1880).
E. Wilson, *Our Village* (Bramley) (1860).
G. Wright, *A History of the Town and Parish of Leeds . . .* (Leeds, 1797).
The History of Batley, Birstall and Heckmondwike; with notices of Gomersal, Cleckheaton, Batley Carr and Carlinghowe (Batley, 1860).

2. *Technical*

J. Banks, *On the Power of Machines* (Kendal, 1803).
J. Banks, *A Treatise on Mills* (London, 1795).
J. Bourne, *A Treatise on the Steam Engine* (London, 1844).
S. Clegg, Jun., *A Practical Treatise on the Manufacture and Distribution of Coal Gas* (3rd edition, 1859).
T. K. Derry and T. I. Williams, *A Short History of Technology* (Oxford, 1960).
R. W. Dickinson and H. Jenkins, *James Watt and the Steam Engine* (Oxford, 1927).
W. Fairbairn, *On the Application of Cast and Wrought Iron to Building Purposes* (4th edition, London, 1870).
W. Fairbairn, *Treatise on Mills and Millwork* (3rd edition, London, 1871).
R. L. Hills, *Power in the Industrial Revolution* (Manchester, 1970).
J. R. Richards, *The Functional Tradition in Early Industrial Buildings* (London, 1958).
C. Singer (ed.), *A History of Technology* (Oxford, 1957).

3. *Others*

F. Atkinson, *Some Aspects of the Eighteenth Century Woollen and Worsted Trade in Halifax* (Halifax, 1956).
J. R. Allan, *Crombies of Grandholm and Cothal*, 1805–1960 (Aberdeen, 1960).
C. Babbage, *On the Economy of Machinery and Manufactures* (London, 1832).

E. Baines, *History of the Cotton Manufacture in Great Britain* (1835).

P. E. Bentley, *Colne Valley Cloth: From the Earliest Times to the Present Day* (Huddersfield, 1947).

J. Bischoff, *A Comprehensive History of the Woollen and Worsted Manufacture . . .* (London, 1842).

J. Burnley, *History of Wool and Wool Combing* (London, 1889).

S. D. Chapman, *The Early Factory Masters* (Newton Abbot, 1967).

J. H. Clapham, *An Economic History of Modern Britain: The Early Railway Age, 1820–1850* (2nd edition, Cambridge, 1950).

J. H. Clapham, *The Woollen and Worsted Industries* (London, 1907).

E. Collinson, *History of the Worsted Trade and Historic Sketch of Bradford* (London, 1854).

W. B. Crump, *The Leeds Woollen Industry 1780–1820* (*T.S.*, 32, 1931).

W. B. Crump and G. Ghorbal, *History of the Huddersfield Woollen Industry* (Huddersfield, 1935).

W. Cudworth, *Worstedopolis. A Sketch History of the Town and Trade of Bradford, the Metropolis of the Worsted Industry* (Bradford, 1888).

Phyllis Deane, *The First Industrial Revolution* (Cambridge, 1965).

Phyllis Deane and W. A. Cole, *British Economic Growth 1688–1959* (Cambridge, 1962).

P. G. M. Dickson, *The Sun Insurance Office, 1710–1960.*

F. M. Eden, *The State of the Poor* (London, 1797).

M. M. Edwards, *The Growth of the British Cotton Trade, 1780–1815.*

R. I. Fitton and A. P. Wadsworth, *The Strutts and the Arkwrights, 1758–1830* (1958).

H. D. Fong, *Triumph of the Factory System in England* (Tientsin, 1930).

W. Onslow Garnett, *Wainstalls Mills: The History of I. and I. Calvert Limited, 1821–1951* (Halifax, 1951).

Reuben Gaunt and Sons Ltd, *Springfield and Broom Mills: A Record of Three Centuries' Connection with the Woollen Industry* (Farsley, 1923).

A. D. Gayer, W. W. Rostow and A. J. Schwartz, *The Growth and Fluctuation of the British Economy. 1790–1850* (Oxford, 1933).

W. F. Gephart, *Principles of Insurance*, Vol. II (1917).

C. Gulvin, *The Tweedmakers: a history of the Scottish fancy woollen industry, 1600–1914* (Newton Abbot, 1973).

H. J. Habakkuk, *American and British Technology in the Nineteenth Century* (Cambridge, 1962).

M. Hartley and J. Ingleby, *The Old Hand Knitters of the Dales* (Clapham, 1951).

George Head, *A Home Tour Through the Manufacturing Districts of England, in the Summer of 1835* (London, 1836).

N. B. Harte and K. G. Ponting (eds), *Textile History and Economic History Essays in Honour of Miss Julia de Lacy Mann* (Manchester, 1973).

H. Heaton, *The Yorkshire Woollen and Worsted Industries from Earliest times up to the Industrial Revolution* (1st edition, Oxford, 1920; 2nd edition, Oxford, 1965).

H. Heaton (ed.), *The Letter Books of Joseph Holroyd and Sam Hill* (Halifax, 1914).

W. O. Henderson, *Industrial Britain Under the Regency*, Chapter IV, 'Report on a Journey to England by Factory Commissioner J. G. May in 1814'.

W. O. Henderson, *J. C. Fisher and His Diary of Industrial England, 1814–51.*

W. Hirst, *History of the Woollen Trade for the Last Sixty Years, etc.* (Leeds, 1844).

J. James, *History of the Worsted Manufacture in England, from the Earliest Times* . . . (London, 1857).

J. G. Jenkins (ed.), *The Wool Textile Industry in Great Britain* (London, 1972).

S. Jubb, *The History of the Shoddy Trade: Its Rise, Progress and Present Position* (Batley, 1860).

K. Lipson, *The History of the Woollen and Worsted Industries* (London, 1921).

J. Lord, *Capital and Steam Power* (2nd edition, London, 1966).

J. de L. Mann, *The Cloth Industry in the West of England from 1640 to 1880* (Oxford, 1971).

Paul Mantoux, *The Industrial Revolution in the Eighteenth Century: An Outline of the Beginnings of the Modern Factory System in England* (New Edition, London, 1961).

P. Mathias, *The First Industrial Nation — An Economic History of Britain, 1700–1914* (London, 1969).

J. R. McCulloch, *A Dictionary . . . of Commerce etc.* (London, 1843).

B. R. Mitchell and Phyllis Deane, *Abstract of British Historical Statistics* (Cambridge, 1962).

A. Muir, *The History of Bowers Mills* (Cambridge, 1969).

R. A. Pelham, *Fulling Mills: A Study in the Application of Water Power to the Woollen Industry* (Society for the Protection of Ancient Buildings, 1958).

S. Pollard and D. W. Crossley, *The Wealth of Britain 1085–1966* (London, 1968).

K. Ponting, *A History of the West of England Cloth Industry* (London, 1957).

K. Ponting, *The Woollen Industry of South West England* (London, 1971).
K. G. Ponting (ed.), *Baines's Account of the Woollen Manufacture of England* (Newton Abbot, 1970).
G. R. Porter, *The Progress of the Nation* (London, 1836).
L. S. Pressnell, *Country Banking in the Industrial Revolution* (1956).
Proceedings of the Second International Conference of Economic History, Aix en Provence (1962).
A. Rees, *The Cyclopaedia: or Universal Dictionary of Arts, Sciences and Literature* (1802–19).
W. G. Rimmer, *Marshalls of Leeds: Flax Spinners, 1786–1886* (Cambridge, 1960).
E. Roll, *An Early Experiment in Industrial Organisation* (London, 1930).
H. B. Rose, *The Economic Background to Investment* (London, 1960).
W. W. Rostow, *British Economy of the Nineteenth Century* (Oxford, 1948).
E. M. Sigsworth, *Black Dyke Mills: A History. With Introductory Chapters on the Development of the Worsted Industry in the Nineteenth Century* (Liverpool, 1958).
S. Smiles, *Lives of the Engineers* (London, 1861–2).
Adam Smith, *The Wealth of Nations* (London, 1776).
B. Supple, *The Royal Exchange Assurance Company*.
J. Sutcliffe, *A Treatise on Canals and Reservoirs* (1816).
J. Tann, *Gloucestershire Woollen Mills* (Newton Abbot, 1967).
J. Tann, *The Development of the Factory* (London, 1970).
D. G. Towner, *The Leeds Pottery* (London, 1963).
A. Ure, *The Philosophy of Manufactures* (London, 1835).
Victoria History of the County of York (London, 1907–25).
C. Walford, *The Insurance Cyclopaedia etc. . . .* (London, 1874).
J. Walker, *Fortunes Made in Business* (1884).
R. G. Wilson, *Gentlemen Merchants, The Merchant Community in Leeds 1700–1830* (Manchester, 1971).

INDEX

I NAMES AND PLACES

II SUBJECTS

The index does not include references to Appendices I, III and IV.

I NAMES AND PLACES

Addingham, 16, 25, 95, 133
Airedale Mill, Leeds, 61, 280
Aked, John, 93
Akroyd, James, 37, 143
Almondbury, 8, 19, 30, 43, 78, 95
Alverthorpe, 8, 40
Arkwright, Richard, 117, 121, 143
Armley, 72, 136, 137, 188
Armley Mill, 136–7, 188, 283–5, 296
Arundel, Joseph, 124–5, 135
Atkinson, Richard, 130
Atkinson, Thomas, 76, 135

Bage, Charles, 59, 135
Baildon, 19, 22, 25, 89
Baines, Edward, 111–12, 133
Baines, Simpson, 289
Bank Low Mills, Leeds, 290
Bankgate Mill, Slaithwaite, 51–3
Banks, John, 102–3
Barker and Musgrave, 295
Baron, George, 199
Bateson, John, 72
Bateson, Matthew and James, 89, 98, 191, 298
Batley, 23, 41, 92, 95
Batley Subscription Mill, 110
Bean Ing, *see* Park Mills, Leeds, and Gott, Benjamin
Beanland, Joseph, 195
Beck Mill, Great Horton, 195
Beckett, John, 75
Beeston, 22
Belleisle Mill, Bramley, 113, 137 *see also* Rogerson, Joseph
Benyon and Bage, 59
Beverley, Cross and Billam, 98, 298
Bewicke, Phillip, 59
Bingley, 18
Birstall, 87, 92
Blackmoor Holme Mill, Slaithwaite, 51–2
Blagborough and Holroyd, 98, 191
Boulton and Watt, 19, 35, 56, 81–2, 96–100, 102, 135–6, 143, 161–3, 191, 297–8
Bourne, Daniel, 117
Boynton, Bridlington, 72
Bradford, 8, 22, 25, 30–2, 33, 61, 90–2, 100
Bradley Mills, 42, 120–1, 124, 128, 129
Bramah, Joseph, 131
Bramley, 14, 73, 79
Brancher, Brown and Co., 120
Brooke, Henry, 68
Brooke, William, 127, 129
Brookehouse Mill, Halifax, 143
Brown and Andrews, 124
Buckley, John, 90
Burley Mill, near Leeds, 14, 76, 79, 133, 136, 137, 169, 188
Burley Mill, Otley, 60, 137
Burton Constable, 8
Butterbowl Mill, Farnley, 135

Calverley Mills, 78, 294
Cannon Mill, Great Horton, 194–5
Cannon, Samuel, 195
Carr Mills, Leeds, 137, 195
Carter, J. and Co., 290
Cartwright, John, 99
Castleford, 8
Catrine Mills, Scotland, 159
Chaster, Wilson and Rhodes, 85
Chippendale, Netherwood and Carr, 280
Clegg, Samuel, 136n.
Cliffe Mill, Great Horton, 195
Clifford, 132
Clough House Mill, Slaithwaite, 300
Clover Greaves Mill Company, 201
Cocking Steps Mill, Netherton, 109
Colne Bridge, 135–7

Cook, Thomas, 79
Cookson, Robert, 123
Cooper, David and John, 198
Crank Mill, Morley, 32n., 197
Cromach, George, 73
Crompton, Samuel, 75, 93, 122–4
Crowther, Isaac, 295
Cunliffe, John, 89

Dade, Rachel, 74
Dean Clough, Halifax, 61
Dearlove, Ralph, 202
Denby Dale, 42
Dent, 35
Dewsbury, 41, 66–7, 86, 92, 95, 121, 130
Dewsbury Mills, 77–8, 79, 145
Dobcross, 121
Dobson, Lepton, 198
Dogley Mill, 85
Dolphineholme Mill, 73–4, 132, 194
Doodlebank Mills, 128
Drighlington, 9
Dungeon Mill, Meltham, 120
Dyson, Thomas, 195

Edmondson, Thomas, 132
Edmondson, William, 93
Elam, Samuel, 198
Elland, 45
Ellis, J. J. and G., 136
Ellis, James, 73
Ewart, Peter, 99

Fairbairn, William, 59, 63, 79, 81, 101–2, 103, 159
Farnley, near Leeds, 14, 64, 72, 58, 120
Feather, James and Co., 195
Fenton, Murray and Wood, 90, 96, 109, 131, 143, 162–4
Fenton, Samuel, 202
Fisher, Nixon and Fisher, 91
Fortune, Samuel, 115
Foster, John, 194–6
Foster, Joshua, 87, 98, 191, 297
Frizing Hall Mill, Bradford, 200

Gargrave, 35, 95, 168
Garnett, James, 122–3, 137
Gatliffe, Samuel, 87
Gill Mill, Baildon, 89
Gill Royds Mill Company, 201–3
Glover, Jeremiah, 198
Gomersal, 14, 85–6, 99
Gomersal Mill, 99
Goodman and Elam, 195
Gott, Benjamin, 39, 50, 54, 56, 59–60, 63–4, 66, 68, 87, 97–9, 109, 113–14, 115, 118n., 123, 127, 130, 136, 142, 188, 202, 283
Gowland and Co., 98, 298
Graham, Sir James, 198, 300
Greenwood, James, 295
Greenwood, William, 294
Grimshaw, Benjamin, 73
Grindleton, 134
Grove Mill, Halifax, 290

Hague, Samuel, 73
Haigh, John and Bros, 148
Halifax, 10, 34–7, 45, 67–8, 95, 130
Hall, S. B., 280
Hallas, Benjamin, 162, 203
Halliday and Cockshott, 89, 191
Halliley and Stanley, 124
Hargreaves, James, 75, 117, 120
Harmer, J., 129
Hartley, J. and Son, 143–6, 169
Hartlington Mill, Burnsall, 51
Haworth, 25
Healey Mill, Ossett, 147
Heaton, Robert, 5
Hebble Mill, Halifax, 115, 119–20
Heckmondwike, 41, 121
Heckmondwike Mill Company, 86
High Hoyland, 35
Hinchcliffe, Thomas, 158
Hinde, Thomas, 133
Hipperholme, 45
Hirst, Bramley and Co., 137
Hirst, William, 123, 129, 130–1, 205
Holbeck, 10, 39, 86
Holme Mill, Bradford, 90
Holmfirth, 22, 120
Honley, 12, 22, 68, 86, 129, 145
Horbury, 40, 87
Horsfall, J. G., 289
Horton Mill, Bradford, 93
Huddersfield, 10, 19, 42–4, 95, 134
Hunslet, 39, 87

Idle, 93, 121
Ilkley, 25

Jowett, Benjamin, 198
Jubb, John, 109, 115, 199, 283

Keighley, 18, 22, 32, 34, 95, 100, 180
Kings Mill, Huddersfield, 134, 199
Kirkburton, 45
Kirkstall, 8, 145
Knostrop Fulling Mill, 9

Larchfield Mill, Hunslet, 87
Lawford, Peter, 86
Lawson, 91, 96
Laycock, J. C., 280
Ledgard Mill, 9n.
Lee, James, 166
Leeds, 10, 19, 22, 25, 35, 37–9, 74, 95
Leeming, 25
Lewis, J., 130
Linton, 35, 78
Lister, William, 132
Liversedge, 19, 120
Lockwood, Joshua, 125
Low Close Mill, Leeds, 124
Low Mill, Addingham, 89, 133
Lower Town Mill, Haworth, 134, 195
Lumb Mill, New Delph, 146, 158, 166, 169
Lupton, William, 180

Malton, 72
Markland, Cookson and Fawcett, 35, 89, 109, 110, 163, 298
Marshall, J. and Co., 25, 50, 60–1, 63, 87, 96–7, 109, 136, 142, 162, 183, 187, 202, 287–8, 297
Marshall, James, 195
Masham, 8, 29
May, J. G., 163
Mearclough Bottom Mill, Halifax, 168, 195
Meltham, 61
Micklethwaite, Thomas, 61
Millshaw Mills, Beeston, 125
Milnsbridge, 14
Mirfield, 95
Morley, 41–2, 124, 143–6
Murdock, William, 136n.
Musgrave, Benjamin, 114
Myers, Robert, 73
Mytholmroyd, 25, 195

Nevile, Katherine, 203
Nevins, Pim, 87, 98, 191, 298
New Bank Mills, Halifax, 148
New Lanark, 122
North, John, 129
Nottingham, 99
Nussey and Co., 98

Oatlands Mill, 129
Old Mill, Horbury Bridge, 9
Oldman, Robert, 281
Ossett, 22, 42, 145
Ossett Mill Company, 145, 196–7
Otley, 22, 30, 78, 95

Paper Hall, Bradford, 122
Papplewick, 27
Park Mills, Bean Ing, Leeds, 47, 54–6, 57–8, 59–60, 63, 64, 66, 113, 123, 131, 136, 137, 142, 155, 166, 168, 283–4, 293, 296, 299
Parker, John, 92
Paul, Lewis, 116, 132
Penistone, 42
Pildacre Mill, 162, 203
Phillips and Lee, 59, 135–6
Pilkington, Sir Thomas, 198
Platt and Collier, 131
Plowes, John, 198
Pollard, William, 202
Ponden, 5
Prospect Mill, Bowling, 93

Queensbury, 194

Ramsden Mill, Huddersfield, 134
Ramsden, Sir John, 198
Rastrick, 45, 113
Rawden, 73, 129
Rennie, John, 90, 109
Rhodes, Abraham, 60, 195
Richards, I. R., 93
Ripley and Ogle, 135
Ripon, 26, 72
Robinson, Chippendale, Netherwood and Carr, 148
Rods Mill, Morley, 124
Rogerson, Joseph, 50, 113, 120, 137, 179
Rothwell, 8, 124, 135
Rouse Mill, 9n.
Rowley Mill, Honley, 80, 145

Saddleworth, 43–5, 95
Salt, Titus, 41, 61, 108
Saltaire, 41, 61, 104–5
Sands Mill, Dewsbury, 51, 121, 145, 147, 198
Sayner's Dyehouse, 113
Scarbrough, Earl of, 198
Sculcoates, 87
Selby, 30
Settle, 5, 90
Shaw, G., 289
Shaw Carr Wood Mill, Slaithwaite, 54–5, 300
Shipley, 61, 133
Shrewsbury, 59, 74
Skipton, 30, 95
Slaithwaite, 22, 145, 197
South Crosland, 22, 158
Smithies, Israel, 74
Spence, Robert, 87

Stansfield and Briggs, 76
Starkey and Buckley, 42, 65–6, 121, 127, 166–8, 188
Stead, Robert, 200
Stirk, Zebulum, 158
Stonebridge Mill, Farnley, 163
Strawberry Bank Mill, Liversedge, 86
Strickland, Sir George, 72
Strutt, William, 56, 135
Sturges Mill, Holbeck, 120
Sutcliffe, John, 108–9, 283
Sutton, 168

Taylor, James, 74
Thirsting, Honley, 158
Thompson, William 129, 203
Thurlstone, 42
Thwaite Gate Mill, Hunslet, 115
Thwaite Fulling Mill, Hunslet, 9
Titley, Tatham and Walker, 60, 295

Upper Swift Place Mill, Ripponden, 9

Varley, John, 300

Wainstalls, Halifax, 145
Wainwright, Joseph and John, 72
Wakefield, 8, 22, 40–1
Walker, Eneas, 120
Walker, John and James, 87–8, 98, 125, 192, 298
Walker, Matthew and Thomas, 200
Wansford, Driffield, 125
Warbrick, James, 133
Warley, 67, 145
West House Mills, Fewston, 148, 280
Whettam, Robert, 76
Whitfield, Joseph and Joshua, 121
Wilsden, 25
Wood, John, 60, 106–8, 191
Wood, Robert, 199
Wormald, Fountaine and Gott, *see* Gott, Benjamin
Wortley, 87, 89
Wrigley's Mill, Dobcross, 121

Young, Arthur, 72

II SUBJECTS

Apprentice houses, 148
Architects, 146

Bankers:
- Beckett, Blayds and Co., 202, 204
- Bradford Banking Co., 194
- Wentworth, Chaloner and Rishworth, 205

Banks, 193
- Supply of capital, 192–205

Bierley ironworks, 195
Broad and narrow cloth milled returns, 3–4, 9n., 177–80

Canals:
- Aire and Calder Navigation, 38
- Bradford Navigation, 200
- Calder and Hebble Navigation, 80
- Leeds and Liverpool, 38

Capital:
- Circulating, 187–90
- Contemporary estimates, 140
- Depreciation, 160, 164, 185–7
- Fixed, 139–87
- Measurement of, 139–49
- Supply of, 191–205

Children's Employment Commission, *see* Factories Enquiry Commission

Cloth:
- broad, 3, 40, 43, 46
- fancy, 39, 43, 46
- mixed, 39, 46
- narrow, 43, 46
- worsted, 36–7

Cloth dressing, 9–10, 19, 60, 128–30
Cloth Halls, 14, 40
Cloth searchers, 7, 8n.
Clothiers, 3, 5, 113, 117, 120
Coal, 23, 47
Cold Edge Dams, 145
Company mills, 200–1
Corn mills, 18, 19, 38
Cotton:
- industry, 22, 86, 99
- mills, 18, 32, 75, 97–8
- spinning, 35, 132

Credit, 191, 193–5
Crompton's Spindle Inquiry, 123

Dartmouth Estate, 19n., 42n., 51–5, 79–80, 85, 145, 197–8, 300–1
Dyeing, 23, 111–12, 113–14

East Anglian trade, 2–4, 6
Employment, 68–70

Factories:
  definition, 11
  design, 49–60
  location, 23–5
Factories Inquiry Commission, 12, 13, 45, 68, 93, 96, 153
Factory Inspectorate, 11, 34, 93
Factory returns 1803/4, 35n.
Factory returns 1835/50, 13, 35, 44, 45, 76, 93, 95, 172
Fall Ing Foundry, 162
Fire Insurance:
  'average clause', 291–3
  disputes, 282–3
  duty, 276–7, 289–90
  fraud, 279–80, 286–7
  losses, 281–2
  premiums, 289–90
  risk limits, 288–9
  valuation of property, 226–30, 279–80, 286–301
Fire insurance offices:
  Albion Fire Office, 288
  Essex and Suffolk Equitable Fire Insurance Society, 294
  Globe Insurance Company, 288
  Hope Fire Office, 289
  Imperial Fire Office, 290
  Leeds and Yorkshire Fire Office, 61n., 278n., 279–81, 286, 289–90
  Manchester Fire Office, 295
  Newcastle-upon-Tyne Fire Office, 288
  North British Fire Office, 294
  Norwich Union Fire Office, 61n., 380, 292
  Phoenix Fire Assurance Company, 276, 281–2
  Protector Fire Office, 295
  Royal Exchange Assurance Company, 152, 276–301
  Suffolk Fire Office, 281
  Sun Fire Office, 59, 152–4, 276–301
Fire insurance policies, 9, 16, 35n., 56, 61, 64, 66, 72, 73, 86, 110, 137, 141–2, 150, 189, 276–301
Fire loss assessors, 109, 283–6
Fire proof buildings, 55, 59, 61, 110, 168, 184, 280
Flax mills, 18, 59
Fulling:
  mills, 6–9, 13, 19, 38, 75, 127
  process, 6, 13, 112, 127–8

Gas lighting, 110, 136–8, 169

Heating, 134–6
Hydraulic press, 112, 131

Iron construction, 56, 59–61

Jacquard loom, 133
Joint stock mills, 200–1

Labour, 23, 47
Land, cost of, 142–3
Leeds Gas Light Company, 137n.
Leeds Waterworks, 109
Lewis cutter, 130
Lighting, 134, 136–8
List of Leeds Engines, 97–8
Low Moor Iron Works, 90
Luddism, 130, 180

Merchants, 9–10, 188–9, 199
  investments by, 192
Mill buildings, 49–56
  size, 50
  design, 49–50, 61–8
Mill gearing and transmitting machinery, 49, 98–9, 101–10
Millwrights, 101–2
Millwrights work, 101–10
Mortgages, 199–200

Power:
  hand, 71–3
  horse, 71, 73–4, 132
  steam, 23, 42, 69–70, 81–96, 97–100, 157–65, 297–8
  water, 10, 19, 23, 43, 47, 69–70, 73, 75–81, 146, 157–65
Power loom, 125–7, 133
Power looms in factories, report of 1835, 125–7, 133, 166
Price changes, 180, 182–5

Rees's Cyclopaedia, 114–15, 119, 128
Rivers:
  Aire, 23, 38, 95
  Calder, 23, 40, 46, 78, 95
  Colne, 23, 42, 47, 66, 77
  Holme, 47
  Wharfe, 8, 78

Scribbling and carding machines, 115–18
Scribbling and carding mills, 8, 19–23, 38, 75, 85, 112–13, 127
Select Committee on Manufactures, Commerce and Shipping, 183, 200
Select Committee on the State of the Woollen Manufacture of England, 63
Silk, 32, 75
Slubbing, 75, 111, 118–19

Soap drawback, 27–30
Spinning, 75, 111, 119–24
  jenny, 75
  water-frame, 75–6, 121–2, 132–3
Steam heating, 135
Steam power, 23, 42, 69–70, 81–96, 157–65
  capabilities, 96–100
  cost, 161–4, 297–8
  list of Leeds engines, 97–8
  steam engines, 19, 73, 81–98, 186–7
Stocks of raw materials, 189–90

Warehousing, 63, 148–9
Warm air heating, 135
Water, need for, 23, 47
Water power, 10, 19, 23, 43, 47, 69–70, 73, 75–81, 146, 157–65
  capabilities, 96–100
Water rights, 159–60
Water supply disputes, 80
Water supply problems, 80–1, 160
Waterwheels, 76, 78–9, 102
Weaving sheds, 62–3
West of England trade, 2–3, 6, 43, 47
West Riding Registry of Deeds, 203
Wire drawing mills, 18
Wool textile manufacture:
  machinery, 110–34
  processes, 111–24
  value of output, 2–4
Woollen industry:
  growth, 18–19, 37–46, 175–82
Woollen mills:
  numbers, 15, 17, 173–4
  location, 20–1, 46–8
  closures, 16–18
Woolstaplers, 113
'Worsted Acts', 26
Worsted Committee, 25–30, 195
Worsted industry, 2, 19, 25–37, 132–4, 175–82
Worsted mills:
  numbers, 15, 17, 173–4
  location, 20–1, 64–8
  closures, 18